Where to S...
Wa...

Hotels, Guest Houses, Farmhouses, B&Bs, Holiday Cottages, Caravan and Camping Parks

2001 accommodation guide

Published by the Wales Tourist Board, Brunel House, 2 Fitzalan Road, Cardiff CF24 0UY
Written by Roger Thomas Freelance Services
Design by Martin Hopkins Partnership, Cardiff www.martinhopkins.co.uk
Colour reproduction by Bay Graphics
Printed by MWL Print Group
Copyright © 2001 Wales Tourist Board
ISBN 1 85013 111 2

BWRDD CROESO CYMRU
WALES TOURIST BOARD
Quality Inspected

Contents

Wales is divided into 12 Holiday Areas. Within each area, accommodation is listed under hotels, B&Bs, holiday cottages and caravan and camping parks. The resorts and towns described at the start of each Holiday Area have map references enabling you to pinpoint them on the detailed gridded maps in the back of the book. To help you find your way around there's also a town index on the inside back cover.

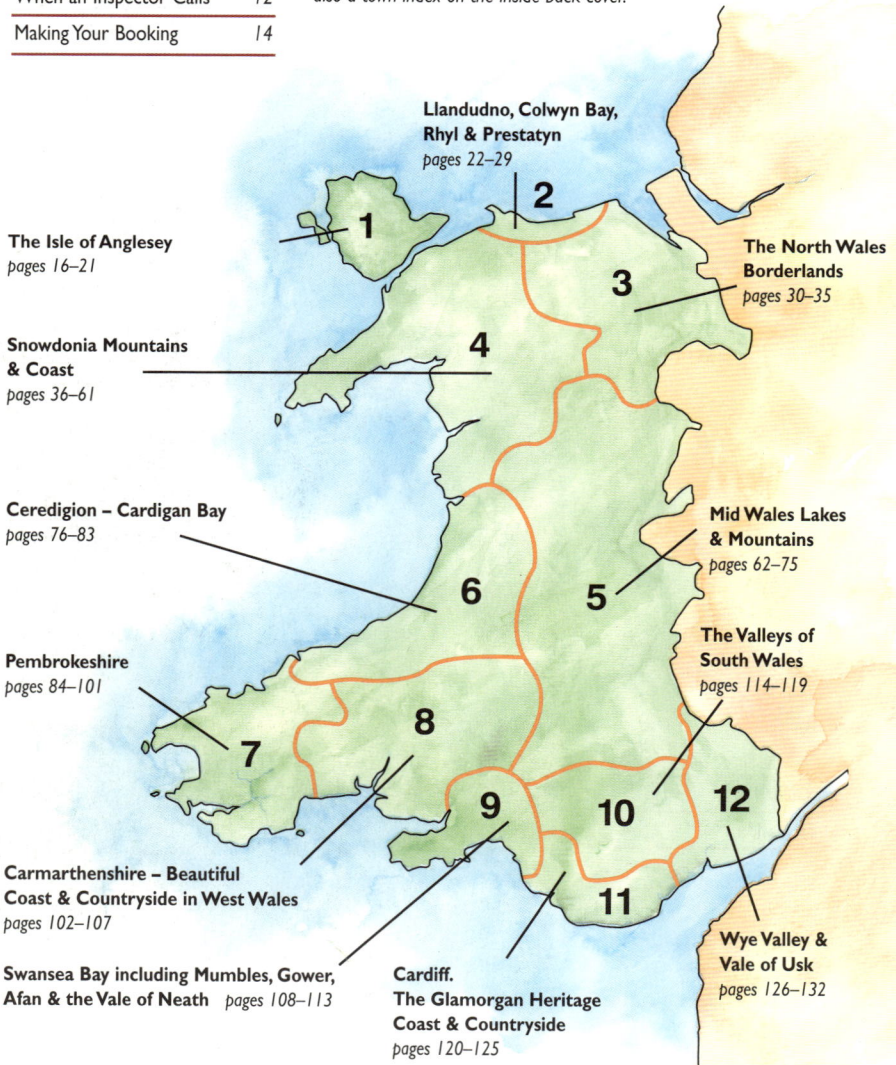

Llandudno, Colwyn Bay, Rhyl & Prestatyn
pages 22–29

1

2

3

The Isle of Anglesey
pages 16–21

The North Wales Borderlands
pages 30–35

Snowdonia Mountains & Coast
pages 36–61

4

Ceredigion – Cardigan Bay
pages 76–83

Mid Wales Lakes & Mountains
pages 62–75

6

5

The Valleys of South Wales
pages 114–119

Pembrokeshire
pages 84–101

8

7

9

10

12

Carmarthenshire – Beautiful Coast & Countryside in West Wales
pages 102–107

11

Swansea Bay including Mumbles, Gower, Afan & the Vale of Neath   pages 108–113

Cardiff. The Glamorgan Heritage Coast & Countryside
pages 120–125

Wye Valley & Vale of Usk
pages 126–132

Where to Stay
Wales

Choosing Your Accommodation

Classified Advertising Too!

In addition to the display advertising, there's more accommodation to choose from in an all-Wales classified advertising section, which is again divided into the 12 Holiday Areas.

Additional Information

Location Maps

Below: In the heart of Snowdonia

Inset: Aberaeron, Cardigan Bay

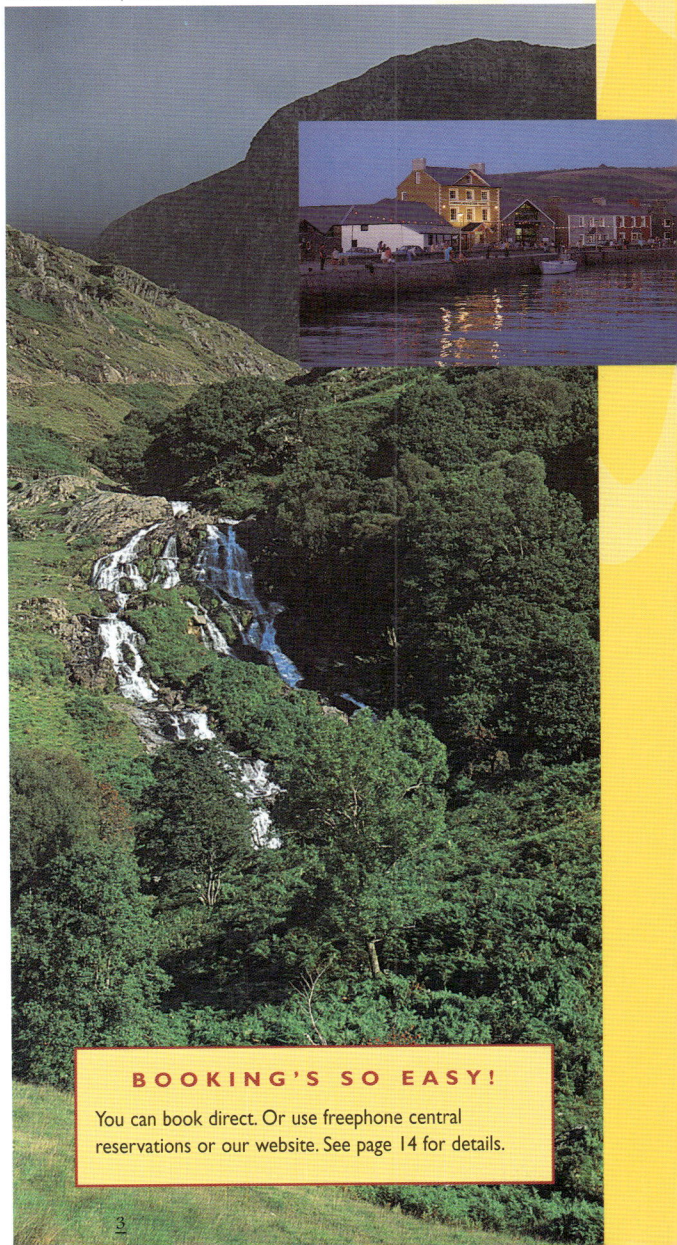

BOOKING'S SO EASY!

You can book direct. Or use freephone central reservations or our website. See page 14 for details.

Where to Stay?

That's an easy question to answer with the help of this guide. All styles and price ranges of accommodation are included – hotels, guest houses, farmhouses, B&Bs, holiday cottages, caravan and camping parks. Looking for a luxury break in a top country house hotel? Or a self-catering family holiday beside the sea? A friendly farmhouse or caravan holiday home park? You'll find these – and many other choices – in this comprehensive accommodation guide.

What's more, every property listed – no matter how big or small – is subject to the Wales Tourist Board's Quality Assurance schemes, backed up by regular inspection visits. Which means that you can make your choice in confidence, knowing that each place has been given a Star grading which reflects the quality it has to offer.

There's a wide choice of accommodation at Llandudno

Visitors to Wales come for a week or a weekend, in summer and the quieter months. Whatever your needs, this guide is the only one you'll need to book your stay. Use it to plan your holiday, short break or business visit. All parts of Wales are covered. All kinds of places to stay are listed. And all have been inspected for quality. You'd expect nothing less from the Wales Tourist Board's official 'Where to Stay' accommodation guide.

Take Your Pick

Although Wales isn't a big country, it boasts a huge variety of scenery and places to stay. Here's a snapshot guide to point you in the right direction. It's by no means definitive – for a fuller picture please see the descriptions of the individual Holiday Areas within Wales, beginning on page 16.

For Families

For sand, scenery and the attractions of a seaside resort you can't go wrong along the North Wales coast, Barmouth on Cardigan Bay, and Tenby and

Saundersfoot in Pembrokeshire. Elegant Llandudno has a genuinely restrained atmosphere which appeals to many – if you want all the fun of the fair, then take a look at neighbouring Colwyn Bay, Rhyl and Prestatyn. Along the South Wales coast, Porthcawl and Barry Island also offer a good measure of family fun.

For Quieter Times

There's so much choice along Wales's 750-mile seashore. Small resorts and fishing villages are dotted around the Isle of Anglesey and along the Llŷn Peninsula, both official 'Areas of Outstanding Natural Beauty'. Try Trearddur Bay, for example, or Nefyn, both with beautiful beaches – you won't be disappointed. Cardigan Bay is full of understated charm, with a wonderful coastline and walking – stay at places like Georgian Aberaeron, Victorian Aberystwyth or picturesque New Quay. The Pembrokeshire Coast National Park is one area where you're truly spoilt for choice. Almost anywhere along this 180-mile coastline, one of Europe's finest stretches of coastal natural beauty, will fit the bill. The Gower Peninsula,

On the beach, Llangrannog

Britain's first 'Area of Outstanding Natural Beauty', should also be on your shortlist – and don't forget sandy, atmospheric Carmarthen Bay between Pembrokeshire and Gower.

For Couples

Where to begin? Any of the smaller resorts are ideal for refreshing breaks – and most have the bonus of being close to magnificent countryside. If you want to enjoy the best of Wales's landscapes …

For Country Lovers

… It has to be the Brecon Beacons National Park or the Snowdonia National Park. They're very different places. The green, open spaces of the rolling Beacons are set against a backcloth of big skies. Snowdonia is altogether more rocky and dramatic, dominated by the highest peaks south of the Scottish Highlands

For More of the Great Outdoors

Great countryside doesn't end at the boundaries of Snowdonia and the Brecon Beacons. In fact, many visitors prefer the remote hills, farmlands, forests and lakelands of the Cambrian Mountains in Mid Wales, haunt of the rare red kite. This is undiluted 'Wild

Wales' – as are the undiscovered Berwyn Mountains and hidden Ceiriog Valley in border country between Llangollen and Welshpool.

For Weekend Breaks

Many people don't realise how easy it is to get to Wales. The leafy Wye Valley – another 'Area of Outstanding Natural Beauty' – is only a few hours' drive from the centre of London. From the North-West, you can easily escape from the city to the Clwydian Range (yes, you've guessed it: it's yet another AONB). This exhilarating range

►

Cregennen Lakes, Mid Wales

Llyn Brianne near Llandovery

Picturesque Tenby

of hills comes as a real breath of fresh air – and that's not to mention the breathtaking views from its summits into the verdant Vale of Clwyd. Similarly, the timeless, relaxing border country around Montgomery, Welshpool and Knighton is just a short hop from the Midlands.

For City Breaks

Cardiff is *the* happening city. The big news here is the transformation of the city's old waterfront into a dynamic new bay area, with shops, restaurants, arts and crafts and attractions. That's in addition to the existing city centre with its stunning neoclassical architecture, superb shopping and vibrant nightlife. Swansea has also transformed its waterfront into an award-winning Maritime Quarter. The city is an appealing mix of old and new – Wales's best fresh foods market sits incongruously amongst modern city-centre developments. And its location, along the sweeping arc of sandy Swansea Bay, couldn't be better.

For Activity Fans

It's all go. Go walking in Snowdonia or along the long-distance Pembrokeshire Coast, Offa's Dyke or Glyndŵr Way paths. Go mountain biking or pony trekking in the Brecon Beacons. Go sailing from Saundersfoot or Abersoch. Go fishing on Wales's many lakes and rivers. Go golfing at friendly 9-holers or world-class courses (Harlech, Porthcawl, St Pierre at Chepstow and Newport's new Celtic Manor, for example). And go to Llanwrtyd Wells, the little Mid Wales town with the big reputation for organising an imaginative – not to say bizarre – range of activity-based events, including a Man versus Horse marathon, mass mountain biking, and something called International Bog Snorkelling!

Cardiff's Café Quarter

Where to Stay
Wales

Precipice Walk above Dolgellau

Star Quality

*A*ll the accommodation in this book has been inspected and graded by the Wales Tourist Board, based on a visit from one of WTB's Quality Advisers. The WTB's Quality Assurance schemes are your passport to an enjoyable holiday, for they help pinpoint the type of accommodation that's just right for you.

Hotels, Guest Houses and Farmhouses

It's All in the Stars

STARS are your guide to QUALITY. They tell you what you *really* want to know about places to stay. Places which score highly will have an especially welcoming atmosphere and pleasing ambience, high levels of comfort and guest care, and attractive surroundings enhanced by thoughtful design and attention to detail. Each place will have been personally – and thoroughly – checked out by highly trained Quality Advisers and given a Star rating on a scale of one to five – so when you check in you can be confident of the quality on offer.

Star Quality

★★★★★ Exceptional quality, with the highest standard of furnishings, flawless service, meticulous guest care and exemplary provision and presentation of all aspects of the business

★★★★ Excellent quality, with a high standard of furnishings, service and guest care

★★★ Very good quality in the overall standard of furnishings, service and guest care

★★ Good quality in the overall standard of furnishings, service and guest care

★ Fair to good quality in the overall standard of furnishings, service and guest care

It's important to bear in mind that the Star Grade takes into account the *nature* of the property and *expectation* of the guests – so a farmhouse is just as entitled to Five Stars as a country hotel, as long as what it offers is of the highest quality.

Style of Accommodation

Although quality is of paramount importance, places to stay must also provide facilities and services appropriate to their style and the expectation of guests. Obviously, these will vary with the type of accommodation – you would not, for example, expect hotels and B&Bs to offer the same facilities to guests.

For grading purposes, we have therefore divided the accommodation into various categories, for example: Hotel, Bed & Breakfast, Inn, Farm, Hostel.

Please note:

◆ Farms offer Guest House or B&B accommodation on a working farm.

◆ You will see the categories 'Country Hotel' and 'Country House' in the accommodation listings. The latter offers non-hotel style accommodation.

Holiday Cottages

As with hotels and guest houses, the Wales Tourist Board uses STARS to denote QUALITY at self-catering accommodation. The grading runs from One to Five Stars, reflecting the quality of the facilities and services provided. This is a new scheme that replaces the former Dragon grading scheme. Because there have been some changes in the way grades are awarded, it is not possible to directly compare the new Star Grades with the former Dragon Grades.

★★★★★	Exceptional quality
★★★★	Excellent quality
★★★	Very good quality
★★	Good quality
★	Fair to good quality

All Three-, Four- and Five-Star accommodation will be entirely self-contained. In addition, Five-Star accommodation will have: an additional bath/shower and WC for units sleeping seven or more people; beds made up for guests on arrival; freshly laundered bath mats for each letting; washing machine either in the property or available in a shared facility; full-sized cooker; outside drying area or electric dryer; sleeping exclusively in designated bedrooms; on-site parking/reserved space.

Please note: Occasionally it may not have been possible to undertake a Holiday Cottage grading. This situation is clearly identified by 'Awaiting Grading' or a provisional Star rating (indicated by the letter P alongside the Stars) appearing within the advertisement/entry.

Caravan and Camping Parks

STARS also apply to caravan and camping parks, the grade reflecting the overall QUALITY of the park.

★★★★★	Exceptional quality
★★★★	Excellent quality
★★★	Very good quality
★★	Good quality
★	Fair to good quality

Style of Park

To help you make the right choice, each park is categorised as one of the following:

HOLIDAY PARK (for holiday caravans, but may also provide touring/camping facilities)

TOURING PARK (for touring caravans and possibly camping; no static holiday caravans)

CAMPING PARK (for tented accommodation only)

Plus combinations of the above, for example HOLIDAY, TOURING AND CAMPING PARK, HOLIDAY AND CAMPING PARK, etc.

Awards and Other Features

*H*ere we explain the various awards and additional features which apply to the accommodation in this guide.

Applicable to All Accommodation

Welcome Host

Customer care is our top priority. It's what the Wales Tourist Board's Welcome Host scheme is all about. Open to everyone from hotel staff to taxi drivers, the scheme places the emphasis on hospitality and first-class service. Welcome Host badge and certificate holders are part of a tradition of friendliness. There are three categories:

GOLD — At least 90% of staff are participants

SILVER — At least 75% of staff are participants

BRONZE — At least 50% of staff are participants

Accommodating Visitors with Disabilities

Accommodation providers can decide if they wish to be graded for access by wheelchair users.

Accessible to a wheelchair user travelling independently

Accessible to a wheelchair user travelling with assistance

Accessible to a wheelchair user able to walk a few paces and up a maximum of three steps

Please note: When booking, please check that the establishment of your choice meets your requirements.

For further details, please see 'Information for Visitors with Disabilities' in the 'Further Information/Useful Addresses' section of this guide.

Please Note

All Gradings and Awards were correct at the time of going to press. Occasionally it may not have been possible to undertake a grading. This situation is clearly identified by 'Awaiting Grading' appearing within the advertisement/entry. Inspections are on-going and improvements made by establishments may have resulted in a revision since publication. Please check when booking.

Further information on Gradings and Awards is available from the Wales Tourist Board's Trade and Consumer Relations Department, Brunel House, 2 Fitzalan Road, Cardiff CF24 0UY.
Tel (029) 2047 5281/2047 5278
Fax (029) 2047 5319
E-mail: info@tourism.wales.gov.uk
Website: www.visitwales.com

Any Problems?

At the time of the assessment, all premises met with the standard required for the Wales Tourist Board quality grade indicated in our publication. The WTB cannot be held responsible for any deficiencies in standards and quality of service which manifest themselves after the assessment has taken place. We nevertheless care about your stay in Wales, so if you are dissatisfied with the accommodation in any way please contact the owner or manager of the business at the time of your stay so that matters can be put right. If, having made your views known at the time, you have received no satisfaction please put your complaint in writing to the business immediately, and send a copy to the Wales Tourist Board's Trade and Consumer Relations Department for their information (see 'Please Note' on previous page for address).

The WTB is not in a position to provide compensation where customers have been unable to resolve any disputes with tourist businesses in Wales.

Applicable to Hotels, Guest Houses, Farmhouses and B&Bs

Walkers and Cyclists Welcome

Walking and cycling enthusiasts should look out for this sign, which includes the 'boot' and 'bike' symbols (some properties qualify for both symbols, others just the one). It's displayed by places which have undertaken to provide features which walkers and cyclists always find welcome – drying facilities for wet clothes and boots, secure lockable areas for bikes, adequate storage space for rucksacks, packed lunches and so on.

A Taste of Wales

Look out for the TW symbol in the accommodation section. It signifies membership of a scheme, A Taste of Wales–Blas ar Gymru, that promotes the use of Welsh produce and high standards of cooking and service. All establishments are inspected annually for quality.

Applicable to Guest Houses/ Farmhouses Only

Award Winners

The Guest House or Farmhouse Award is given to proprietors who have successfully completed an approved course in guest house management or farm-based tourism, together with the Welcome Host Manager Course. A high level of customer care can be expected.

Applicable to Caravan and Camping Parks

Dragon Award Winners

For excellence in **individual caravan accommodation**, ask for a caravan which has won the Wales Tourist Board Dragon Award. The caravan will be something special, with a bath or shower and toilet and many extras such as colour TV and heating.

Daffodil Award Winners

This award recognises excellence in **touring caravan parks**. All award winners must have at least Four Stars (or be working towards that grade). Expect high standards of landscaping, with each pitch clearly marked (and at least 50% with electricity), good lighting levels at night, and a separate station for waste disposal from motor homes.

Key to Symbols

🇮	Bed booking though TIC available
P2	Number of parking spaces available
🛏 9	Number of bedrooms
🛁 9	Number of en-suite bathrooms
🐕	Dogs/pets accepted by arrangement
C	Special offers for children
⍥	Evening meals available/by arrangement
✗	Café or restaurant on park
♟	Licensed club or bar
▭	TV in each unit
≋	Indoor heated swimming pool
≋	Outdoor heated swimming pool
£	Credit cards accepted
♨	Tea/coffee making facilities in bedrooms
🛒	Foodshop/mobile foodshop on park
SP	Special weekend/midweek or short break holidays available, including Christmas or New Year
✗	Totally non-smoking establishment
◡	Areas provided for smoking
❀	Garden available for guests' use
⌂	House of historical interest
⊡	Laundry service/launderette available
M	Extra charge for gas/electricity/solid fuel
▤	Bed linen for hire
▤	Bed linen provided free of charge
⍀	Showers available on park
⌖	Butane or propane gas available on park
⚡	Electric hook-ups available
♠	Advanced booking necessary in peak season
♫	Evening entertainment provided
⊟	Cot available/accepted in unit
⬒	Number of pitches on park
🚐 9	Number of caravans for hire
🚐 9	Number of touring caravan pitches
🚐 9	Number of motor caravan pitches
▲ 9	Number of tent pitches
⇥	Railway Station
🏴󠁧󠁢󠁷󠁬󠁳󠁿	Welsh language spoken
✗ (FR)	Foreign language spoken

(FR) FRENCH, (GR) GERMAN, (I) ITALIAN, (SP) SPANISH, (D) DUTCH, (PGS) PORTUGUESE, (CH) CHINESE, (YBA) YORUBA, (IN) INDIAN, (CAN) CANTONESE, (N) NORWEGIAN, (SW) SWEDISH, (GK) GREEK, (DSH) DANISH, (AR) ARABIC

Please note: The symbols, together with the descriptive wording in the accommodation listings, are based on information provided by the proprietors.

When an Inspector Calls

*W*e're often asked how we measure the quality of holiday accommodation. Teams of Quality Advisers are out and about in Wales assessing properties on an annual basis for the 'Star' grading scheme, which runs from one to five Stars. If you think it's an easy life, then read on.

With 'serviced' accommodation (hotels, guest houses, B&Bs and so on), the adviser never reveals his or her identity when booking. Even at this early stage, the property is under examination. Initial impressions are so important, and the way in which the reservation is handled forms the first stage of the grading procedure.

On arrival, first impressions are again crucial – the neatness and look of the property and so on. Then comes the welcome – or lack of it! The warmth of welcome is especially important when grading B&Bs. Typically, these will be small and family run, with limited facilities in comparison with, say, a country hotel. But everything is judged in its proper context – so a small B&B can receive a high Star rating if it offers very high quality.

In the bedroom, the quality of the furniture, décor, lighting, carpeting, beds, bedlinen, in-room amenities and personal touches are put under the microscope. There has to be a consistency of quality. A sumptuously furnished hotel with an inferior, lumpy bed won't attract a top grade.

In the evening, the public areas come under scrutiny. In hotels, the adviser firstly takes a pre-dinner drink to test the bar service. Then it's into the restaurant to assess the surroundings, menu, atmosphere and ambience, together with the staff's attitude, appearance and efficiency. Starter, main course and dessert are individually graded, and the adviser will also observe the reactions of other guests to the service and quality of the food.

After dinner, the adviser has to compile a detailed grading report with supporting comments. It's not quite over yet, for breakfast and check-out (and any other relevant elements such as leisure facilities where available) are also taken into account before the final, overall grade is given.

At the presentation of the bill, the adviser announces his or her identity. In the words of one old hand, 'It's at that stage that the proprietor faints!' And, for the poor adviser, the whole thing happens again and again – for about 200 days a year.

With self-catering properties and caravan and camping parks the principle is the same, though the procedure obviously differs.

In the caravan sector, all parks are graded while individual caravans wishing to be assessed for the Dragon Award have to be looked at.

One experienced inspector, when assessing a caravan park, makes a point of walking around the perimeter first, looking at the hidden nooks and crannies to gauge tidiness and cleanliness. In arriving at an overall judgement, a host of individual items will be examined – the reception area's efficiency, the lighting, recreational facilities, road surfaces and so on.

With caravan parks, the inspector always turns up unannounced. That's not possible when examining self-catering properties such as holiday cottages, flats and apartments. Here, special attention is paid to the kitchen and the quality of its equipment – and, of course, cleanliness is paramount.

Space is also an important factor, along with the quality of the beds, furnishings, décor, bathroom fixtures and so on. As with hotels, the inspector looks for a consistency of quality.

For all types of accommodation it's important to remember that in arriving at a considered judgement, the adviser is always guided by the nature and style of the business – which is why it's possible for a top-class farmhouse (and, as we've said, an excellent B&B) to receive a high Star rating along with a luxurious country hotel. Or for a small, immaculate caravan park with limited facilities to achieve a top grade if what it offers is of the highest quality.

Book Now!

*I*t's easier than ever to book your accommodation in Wales:

◆ Book Direct
Simply pick up the phone to book the accommodation of your choice. You'll receive personal attention and will be speaking to someone who can answer all your questions.

◆ Central Reservations
If you're undecided about where to stay, or are looking for late availability or last-minute offers, call our freephone 0800 numbers: **0800 834820** for North Wales, **0800 273747** for Mid Wales or **0800 3289597** for South and West Wales.

◆ Book Online
The Wales Tourist Board's website – **www.visitwales.com** – is your gateway to online booking.

◆ Teletext
See Teletext page **251** for all the latest offers. (Look out for the Wales Tourist Board grading on Teletext entries to make sure that the accommodation has been checked out by us.)

◆ Book through a TIC
Properties featuring the *i* symbol can be booked through a Tourist Information Centre – this service is especially handy when you're out and about in Wales.

QUALITY FIRST

You can book with confidence, for all accommodation in this guide has been thoroughly checked out by a visit from one of the Wales Tourist Board's Quality Advisers.

Prices

Hotels, Guest Houses and Farmhouses

Prices are PER PERSON, based on TWO PEOPLE sharing a double or twin room. SINGLE OCCUPANCY will usually be charged extra, and there may be supplements for private bath/shower. Nightly rates are for bed and breakfast. Weekly rates are for dinner, B&B.

Bed and Breakfast

Single rates are for ONE PERSON in a single room. Double rates are for TWO PEOPLE sharing a double or twin room. There may be supplements for private bath/shower and single occupancy of a double/twin room.

B&B Prices: The maximum you'll pay for B&B accommodation in this guide is £27.50 per person. You'll find that most rates quoted are considerably less.

Self-Catering Accommodation

(holiday cottages, other furnished properties and caravan holiday home parks)

Rates are PER UNIT PER WEEK.

Touring Caravan and Camping Parks

Rates are for TWO PEOPLE and their caravan, motor home or tent PER NIGHT.

Special Offers for Children

C Many hotels, guest houses and farmhouses have special offers for children, ranging from discounts to free accommodation if they share their parents' room (you only pay for their meals). Family holiday hotels, especially in major resorts, also cater for one-parent families.

Deposits

Most operators will ask for a deposit when a reservation is being made. Some establishments may request payment in advance of arrival.

Cancellation and Insurance

When you confirm a holiday booking, please bear in mind that you are entering a legally binding contract which entitles the proprietor to compensation if you fail to take up the accommodation or depart earlier than planned. It's always wise to arrange holiday insurance to cover you for cancellation and other unforeseen eventualities. If you have to alter your travel plans, please advise the holiday operator or proprietor immediately.

All prices quoted include VAT at the current rate (17½%). Prices and other specific holiday information in this publication were supplied to the Wales Tourist Board during July–October 2000. So do check all prices and facilities before confirming your booking.

The Isle of Anglesey

*A*nglesey's 125-mile shoreline is an 'Area of Outstanding Natural Beauty'. Here, you'll find the North Wales coast at its peaceful best — charming little resorts, pristine sandy beaches, rocky headlands and sheltered harbours, all ideal for the quieter style of seaside holiday and wonderful coastal walks. Anglesey also attracts birdwatchers and history-lovers — the island is dotted with some of Wales's finest prehistoric sites.

Amlwch harbour

Beaumaris Castle

On Your Travels ...

The handsome seatown of Beaumaris is packed with attractions — a magnificent medieval castle (the finest in North Wales according to military historians), chilling Victorian Gaol and, on a lighter note, charming Museum of Childhood. At nearby Menai Bridge there's Pili Palas, an enchanting 'butterfly palace' and tropical jungle. Further along the Menai Strait stands Plas Newydd. It's difficult to decide what's best about this National Trust property — the elegant, treasure-filled mansion itself, or its surrounding grounds and gardens on the shores of the Menai Strait.

The Anglesey Sea Zoo at Brynsiencyn is one of Wales's top attractions, and rightly so. The island's sea-life is imaginatively and intelligently presented — visitors can even walk through an undersea shipwreck without getting wet. Anglesey is also famous for its sea-birds. The best place to see them is from the RSPB's Ellin's Tower Sea-bird Centre perched on the South Stack cliffs near Holyhead. Don't worry if you don't have binoculars — TV cameras give close-up views of nesting birds.

For further information please tel (01248) 752411;
e-mail: tourism@anglesey.gov.uk

Where to Stay **Wales**

Amlwch
Map Ref Ac1

Old port on northern shores of
Anglesey – nearby copper mines
at Parys Mountain responsible for
its past prosperity. Picturesque
harbour, rugged coastal scenery,
golf course close by.

Beaumaris
Map Ref Ae3

Beautifully sited Anglesey coastal
resort with splendid 13th-century
moated castle. A handsome town
full of interest; historic buildings
along main street, Victorian Gaol,
enchanting Museum of Childhood,
fascinating old courthouse.
Yachting centre with golf course
and excellent fishing. Sixteenth-
century Penmon Priory nearby.
Ideal touring centre for
Snowdonia with superb views of
mountains across Menai Strait.

Beaumaris

Bodorgan
Map Ref Ac3 ⇌

Anglesey village conveniently
located for exploring interesting
and varied south-west corner of
the island – small resorts, huge
beaches, wildlife estuary and many
attractions all close by.

Brynsiencyn
Map Ref Ad4

Anglesey hamlet near shores of
Menai Strait, looking across to
Snowdonia. Plas Newydd stately
home, Anglesey Model Village,
Anglesey Bird World, Foel Farm
Park, Bryntirion Open Farm, and
award-winning Anglesey Sea Zoo
all nearby.

Bull Bay
Map Ref Ac1

Pretty little harbour and
sands on rugged north coast
of Anglesey. Golf course
overlooking the sea. Close
to Cemaes, another
picturesque little port, and
the old harbour town of
Amlwch. Magnificent cliff
scenery.

Plas Newydd, on the coast near Brynsiencyn

Dwyran
Map Ref Ac4

Village handy for the south coast
and Menai Strait. Magnificent
beach and dunes at Newborough
only minutes away; also many
attractions, including Anglesey Sea
Zoo, Foel Farm Park, Anglesey
Bird World and Bryntirion Open
Farm.

On the sandy west coast

Benllech's attractive beach

Benllech
Map Ref Ad2

Popular holiday village above a
sweeping bay on Anglesey's east
coast. Four miles of good sands,
swimming, sailing, walking. Nearby
cliffs are rich in fossils. Red Wharf
Bay a next-door neighbour.

South Stack, Holyhead

Pretty harbours are a feature of the island

Holyhead
Map Ref Aa2 ⇌

Stands on Holy Island, linked by causeway to Anglesey. Port for Irish ferries. Roman remains and maritime museum in town. Sea angling, sailing, cliff and hill walking. From South Stack cliffs enjoy the sight of sea-birds, coastal flora and spectacular views, and visit RSPB centre and lighthouse. Holyhead Breakwater Country Park and Penrhos Coastal Park on either side of town.

Llannerch-y-medd
Map Ref Ac2

Central Anglesey village with easy access to island's beaches. Visit Din Llugwy, ancient remains of fortified village, the working windmill at Llanddeusant and the Llyn Alaw Visitor Centre.

Lligwy
Map Ref Ad1

Close to some of Anglesey's finest coastline – Traeth Lligwy, Dulas Bay and the little resort of Moelfre. Fascinating historic sites in the neighbourhood, including Din Lligwy ancient village and Lligwy Burial Chamber.

Marian-glas
Map Ref Ad2

Village well placed for exploring the sandy bays and rocky shores of Anglesey's east coast – Red Wharf Bay, Moelfre and Benllech all very close; also Din Lligwy ancient village and Lligwy prehistoric burial chamber.

Telford's elegant Menai Suspension Bridge

Menai Bridge
Map Ref Ad3

Sited by Telford's Suspension Bridge (built 1826) over the Menai Strait. Views of Snowdonia on mainland. Tegfryn Gallery exhibits contemporary Welsh art; Pili Palas Butterfly Farm and Anglesey Column nearby.

Pentraeth
Map Ref Ad2

The expansive sands of Red Wharf Bay and the beach at Benllech are just minutes away. Also handy for visiting handsome Beaumaris with its wealth of attractions and views across the Menai Strait.

The popular little resort of Trearddur Bay

Trearddur Bay
Map Ref Aa3

Most attractive little seaside resort set amongst low cliffs on Holy Island near Holyhead. Golden sands, golf, sailing, fishing, swimming. Other beautiful coastal spots nearby, including bay of Porth Dafarch.

Hotels, Guest Houses & Farmhouses

VALLEY HOTEL ★★ HOTEL
London Rd, Valley, **HOLYHEAD** LL65 3DU
Tel: (01407) 740203 Fax: (01407) 740686
E-mail: valleyhotel@tinyworld.co.uk
Website: www.valley-hotel-anglesey.co.uk

Only four miles from ferries to Ireland. Direct phone link from terminal. Ideal for meals and superior en-suite accommodation before or after sailing, or whilst touring North Wales. Lounge bars open and food served all day. Also public bar, snooker and beer garden. Private party rooms. RAC ◆◆◆.

Months open 1-12; B&B p/p £16.50-£24.75. 2 Nights Break D, B&B p/p £45.00. Weekly D, B&B p/p by arrangement.

DRWS-Y-COED ★★★★ FARM
LLANNERCH-Y-MEDD LL71 8AD
Tel: (01248) 470473 Fax: (01248) 470473

Enjoy wonderful panoramic views of Snowdonia and excellent hospitality on a working beef, sheep and arable farm. Drws-y-Coed offers the best in comfort and excellent breakfast, so as to make your stay most enjoyable. Beautifully furnished and decorated deluxe en-suite bedrooms. Interesting, historic farmstead and walks. Games room. 25 minutes to Holyhead.

Months open 1-12; B&B p/p £22.50-£24.50.

Still Undecided?

Then call Central Reservations on freephone 0800 834820 for North Wales, 0800 273747 for Mid Wales or 0800 3289597 for South and West Wales – and you'll be plugged into a great choice of places to stay.

Bed & Breakfast
£27.50 p.p. is the most you'll pay

PENYCEFN HOUSE ★★ BED & BREAKFAST GOLD
Salem St, **AMLWCH** LL68 9DD
Tel: (01407) 832122 Fax: (01407) 832122

Months open 1-12; Single B&B per night £15.00. Double B&B per night £30.00.

BELVOIR ★★★★ BED & BREAKFAST GOLD
8 Lon Fferam, **BENLLECH BAY** LL74 8RL
Tel: (01248) 852907
Website: www.belvoirbenllech.co.uk

Detached residence, quietly situated with panoramic sea views: near beach. Two double bedrooms each with private bathroom, colour TV, free tea-making. Sumptuous breakfasts served in large conservatory overlooking garden. Sitting room, private parking, friendly, relaxed atmosphere. High standard, clean, comfortable accommodation. Recommended in 'Which! Good Bed & Breakfast Guide'. Excellent value. Colour brochure.

Months open 3-10; B&B p/p £20.00-£21.00.

PLAS CICHLE ★★★ FARM AWARD GOLD
BEAUMARIS LL58 8PS Tel: (01248) 810488
Website: www.globalvillas.com/plascichle.htm

This large period farmhouse, standing in 200 acres close to historic Beaumaris, offers accommodation in spacious, tastefully furnished rooms equipped for your comfort and enjoyment. Panoramic views of Snowdonia. Excellent breakfast menu to start your day. Adjacent to an 18 hole golf course. On walking and cycling route. Riding, fishing boat trips nearby. Brochure available.

Months open 2-11; Single B&B per night £27.50. Double B&B per night £45.00-£50.00.

TYDDYN GOBLET ★★★ FARM AWARD
Tyddyn Goblet, **BRYNSIENCYN** LL61 6TZ
Tel: (01248) 430296

Peace and quiet is assured at this character farmhouse set back 200 yards from A4080 Newborough Road. Ground floor en-suite bedrooms with colour TV, full central heating and open fire for cooler evenings. Dining room with separate tables. Lovely views from all rooms, some of Snowdonia. Convenient for many of Anglesey's attractions and Snowdonia.

Months open 1-11; B&B p/p £17.00-£18.00. 2 Nights Break B&B p/p £34.00-£36.00.

TAL-Y-FOEL ★★★★ FARM SILVER
DWYRAN LL61 6LQ
Tel: (01248) 430377 Fax: (01248) 430977
E-mail: hutchings@talyfoel.u.net.com
Website: www.tal-y-foel.co.uk

Attractive stone built house in a spectacular rural location on Menai Straits shore, landscaped gardens overlooking Snowdonia. Beautifully appointed en-suite rooms, three with whirlpool baths, many other facilities. Ideal for fishing, walking, birdwatching or relaxing. Individually designed riding breaks for all abilities at our British Horse Society Approved Riding Centre. WTB 1998 best small tourism business award.

Months open 1-12; Single B&B per night from £27.50. Double B&B per night £45.00-£50.00.

VALLEY HOTEL
★★ HOTEL

London Rd, Valley, *HOLYHEAD* LL65 3DU
Tel: (01407) 740203 Fax: (01407) 740686
E-mail: valleyhotel@tinyworld.co.uk
Website: www.valley-hotel-anglesey.co.uk

Only four miles from ferries to Ireland. Direct phone link from terminal. Ideal for meals and superior en-suite accommodation before or after sailing, or whilst touring North Wales. Lounge bars open and food served all day. Also public bar, snooker and beer garden. Private party rooms. RAC ♦♦♦.

Months open 1-12; B&B p/p £16.50-£24.75. 2 Nights Break B&B p/p £33.00-£49.50. Weekly B&B p/p by arrangement.

BWTHYN B&B
★★★★ BED & BREAKFAST GOLD

Bwthyn, Brynafon,
MENAI BRIDGE LL59 5HA
Tel: (01248) 713119 Fax: (01248) 713119

Warm, welcoming, non-smoking B&B 1 minute from the sparkling Menai Strait. 5 minutes village/Suspension bridge, 2 miles A5/A55 Expressway, 35 minutes Holyhead ferry port. 15 minutes from beautiful beaches, historic castles, Snowdonia's magnificent National Park. Two beautifully fitted en-suite doubles, CTVs, powershowers, tea-makers. Scrumptious home cooking. Special Break Over 45's - 3 nights B&B £49 p/p. D, B&B £89 p/p.

Months open 1-12; Double B&B per night £32.00-£35.00.

INGLEDENE B&B
★★ BED & BREAKFAST

Ingledene, Ravenspoint Rd,
TREARDDUR BAY LL65 2YU
Tel: (01407) 861026 Fax: (01407) 861026
E-mail: ingledene@hotmail.com

Enjoy a warm and friendly welcome in our Edwardian seaside home with magnificent views across Trearddur Bay. Spacious rooms have sea views, central heating and colour TV. Relax and watch the glorious sunsets and wake up to the sound of the waves. Ample parking with room for boats. Ferries to Ireland only 10 mins away.

Months open 1-12; Single B&B per night £25.00. Double B&B per night £36.00-£45.00.

MORANEDD GUEST HOUSE
★★ BED & BREAKFAST AWARD GOLD

Trearddur Rd, *TREARDDUR BAY* LL65 2UE
Tel: (01407) 860324 Fax: (01407) 860324

Months open 1-12; Single B&B per night £20.00.
Double B&B per night £45.00.

Holiday Cottages

TIR NA NOG COTTAGES
★★★★

Tir Na Nog, *BODORGAN* LL62 5BN
Tel: (01407) 840054 Fax: (01407) 840873
E-mail: tnnog@aol.com

Quietly situated, well equipped cottages including TV and video, washing machine, dishwasher, microwave. Nearby are beaches, fishing, walking, birdwatching, watersports and cycle routes.

Months open 1-12; 2 Nights £100.00-£150.00. 3 Nights £120.00-£170.00. 4 Nights £140.00-£220.00. Weekly/unit £120.00-£380.00.

UNITS 2 SLEEPS 5

RHIANFA HOLIDAY APARTMENTS
★★★

Rhianfa, *BULL BAY*, Amlwch LL68 9SU
Tel: (01407) 830557 Fax: (01407) 830557
E-mail: angleseyselfcatering@telco4u.net
Website: www.absolute68.com/rhianfa

Months open 3-11; 2 Nights £56.00-£110.00. 3 Nights £70.00-£185.00. 4 Nights £79.00-£199.00. Weekly/unit £89.00-£310.00.

UNITS 7 SLEEPS 2-6+

HAFAN
★★★★

MARIANGLAS LL73 8NY
Tel: (01942) 715518/ 0468 601655
Fax: (01942) 718714

Cottage, Benllech, Anglesey. Convenient beaches. Fully furnished, four poster bed, two single beds. Settee, log burning stove central heating. Fitted kitchen, bath/wc, washing machine. Ample parking three cars, boat.

Months open 1-12; Price on Application.

UNITS 1

PEN-Y-GARNEDD FARM
★★★

Nr *PENTRAETH* LL75 8YW
Tel: (01248) 450580

Months open 1-12; 2 Nights £90.00. 3 Nights £120.00. 4 Nights £150.00. Weekly/unit £250.00.

UNITS 1 SLEEPS 5+

The rugged coastline near South Stack, Holyhead

A N G L E S E Y

Cemaes, on Anglesey's north coast

TREARDDUR HOLIDAY BUNGALOWS

AWAITING GRADING

Lon Isallt, *TREARDDUR BAY* LL65 2UP
Tel: (01407) 860494 Fax: (01407) 861133
E-mail: stuartconradsmith@freenet.co.uk

Good quality self-catering bungalows near beach. Fully equipped units. Indoor heated swimming pool, tennis court, licenced club, launderette, site shop. Nearby horse riding, golf, fishing, birdwatching, Irish ferries. Please write or phone for colour brochure.

Months open 3-10; 2 Nights £50.00-£130.00. 3 Nights £60.00-£170.00.
4 Nights £60.00-£170.00. Weekly/unit £75.00-£485.00.

UNITS 50 SLEEPS 3-7

MENAI HOLIDAY COTTAGES

★★ UP TO ★★★★★

GOLD

1 Greenfield Tce, Hill St,
MENAI BRIDGE LL59 5AY
Tel: (01248) 717135 Fax: (01248) 717051
E-mail: wsc@menaiholidays.co.uk
Website: www.menaiholidays.co.uk

Guests return year after year to generously equipped peaceful houses. Choose from a converted chapel, gamekeeper's house, traditional farmhouses, seaside cottages or mountain retreats. Historic sights, fishing, beaches, birdwatching, walking all close by. Choose as carefully as we do from our detailed brochure, with the best selection on Anglesey.

Months open 1-12; 2 Nights £75.00-£920.00. 3 Nights £75.00-£920.00.
4 Nights £88.00-£1050.00. Weekly/unit £110.00-£2000.00.

UNITS 100+ SLEEPS 2-20

Caravan & Camping Parks

CLASSIFIED ADVERTISING *There's more accommodation to choose from in the classified advertising section of this book. Please see the listing at the end of the 12 Areas display adverts.*

MINFFORDD CARAVAN PARK & LUXURY HOLIDAY PROPERTIES

★★★★★ HOLIDAY PARK

SILVER

LLIGWY, Dulas LL70 9HJ
Tel: (01248) 410678 Fax: (01248) 410378
E-mail: hhughesroberts@talk21.com

Superior luxury accommodation in a beautiful coastal setting
¹/₂ mile to Lligwy beach. A small garden caravan park with top quality holiday homes. Also large four bedroomed family house in own private landscaped gardens nearby. In other separate grounds stands a delightful two bedroomed 5 star cottage again luxuriously furnished.

Months open 1-12; 3-11. 2 Nights £60.00-£100.00.
3 Nights £75.00-£125.00. 4 Nights £100.00-£150.00.
Weekly-cottage/unit £195.00-£775.00. Weekly-/unit £125.00-£450.00.

UNITS 2/ 5 SLEEPS 2-9

WALES CYMRU

TWO HOURS AND
A MILLION MILES AWAY

Llandudno, Colwyn Bay, Rhyl & Prestatyn

Llandudno's stylish promenade

*N*orth Wales's sandy coastal strip is famous for its popular mixture of big beaches, colourful attractions and family entertainment. Llandudno still retains a Victorian air while catering for the needs of today's holidaymakers. Colwyn Bay, Rhyl and Prestatyn are packed with seaside amusements. But it's not all sand and sea. On this lively coast there's also medieval Conwy with its ancient castle and town walls.

On Your Travels ...

Rhyl

If you're looking for things to do, then head for Llandudno's Great Orme. Just getting to this towering headland is an entertainment in itself – it's reached by an alpine-style Cabin Lift (one of the longest in Britain) or San Francisco-style Tramway. At the top you'll find a country park, visitor centre and prehistoric copper mines open to the public. Cruise back down to town – at least part of the way – on Ski Llandudno's artificial slope. Neighbouring Colwyn Bay's Welsh Mountain Zoo is home to wildlife from all over the world. It's a highly regarded place which plays a serious conservation role as well as entertaining its many visitors.

Rhyl's Sun Centre, with its tropical pool, and the exciting rides at Ocean Beach Amusement Park are also top North Wales attractions – and there's more family fun on offer at Prestatyn's Nova Centre. In complete contrast, this popular holiday area also boasts one of Europe's great historic towns – Conwy, with its mighty castle, medieval houses and ring of ancient, well-preserved walls.

For further information on LLANDUDNO/COLWYN Bay please tel (01492) 876413/530478; e-mail: gwen.roberts@conwy.gov.uk websites: www.llandudno-tourism.co.uk www.colwyn-bay-tourism.co.uk For RHYL/PRESTATYN please tel (01745) 344515; e-mail: rhyl.tic@denbighshire.gov.uk

Where to Stay
Wales

Colwyn Bay
Map Ref Bc4 ⇌

Bustling seaside resort with large sandy beach overlooked by wooded hills. Superb 3-mile promenade with many amusements. Good touring centre for Snowdonia. Leisure centre, Eirias Park, Dinosaur World, famous Welsh Mountain Zoo with Chimpanzee World. Harlequin Puppet Theatre and Theatr Colwyn. Golf, tennis, riding and other sports. Quieter Rhos on Sea at western end of bay. Wales in Bloom award winner 2000.

Queen's Gardens, Colwyn Bay

Conwy Castle

Conwy
Map Ref Bb4 ⇌

Historic town with mighty 13th-century castle and complete ring of medieval town walls. Dramatic estuary setting. Many ancient buildings including Aberconwy

House and Plas Mawr, a wonderfully preserved Elizabethan town house. Telford Suspension Bridge, popular fish quay, spectacular wall walks. Golf, pony trekking, Butterfly House, art gallery, aquarium, pleasure cruises. Tiny 'smallest house' on quay. Touring centre for Snowdonia.

Llandudno
Map Ref Bb3 ⇌

Premier coastal resort of North Wales. Two beaches, spacious promenade, Victorian pier, excellent shopping. Donkey rides, Punch and Judy, ski slope. Alice in Wonderland exhibition, art gallery, museum, old copper mines open to the public, splendid North Wales Theatre. Visit the Great Orme headland and ride by cabinlift or tramway. Conference centre. Daily coach excursions. Wales in Bloom award winner 2000.

Llandudno and Great Orme

Prestatyn
Map Ref Be3 ⇌

Family seaside resort on popular North Wales coast. Entertainment galore at Nova Centre including heated swimming pools and aquashute. Challenging 18-hole golf course and superb indoor bowls at the North Wales Bowls Centre, Ffrith Beach. Sailing, swimming on long, sandy coastline. Close to pastoral Vale of Clwyd and Clwydian Range. At northern end of long-distance Offa's Dyke Path.

Prestatyn's spacious beach

Hotels, Guest Houses & Farmhouses

Conwy Castle

EDELWEISS HOTEL

Off Lawson Rd, COLWYN BAY LL29 8HD
Tel: (01492) 532314 Fax: (01492) 534707
E-mail: edelweisshotel@hotmail
Website: www.hotelvenues.com/edelweiss

Impressive 19thC country house hotel. Extensive wooded grounds, footpath to beach. All rooms en-suite, hospitality tray, TV. Friendly staff, quality home cooking. Pets welcome. Ideal touring base for North Wales. Private car park. Ground floor bedrooms. 40 minutes from Irish ferry port. Group rates available.

Months open 1-12; B&B p/p £22.50-£25.00.
2 Nights Break D, B&B p/p £65.00.
Weekly D, B&B p/p £227.50.

NORFOLK HOUSE HOTEL

39 Prince's Drive, COLWYN BAY LL29 8PF
Tel: (01492) 531757 Fax: (01492) 533781
E-mail: bookings@norfolkhousehotel.fsnet.co.uk
Website: www.wow-cymru.com

Discover old-fashioned courtesy, cordial hospitality and comfort in this family-owned hotel. With a relaxed and welcoming atmosphere, excellent food and service. Pretty bedrooms, all en-suite, comfortable lounges and charming restaurant and bar. Situated close to beach, town and railway station. Pleasant gardens. Large car park. Ideal for touring North Wales.

Months open 1-12; B&B p/p £28.50-£45.00.
2 Nights Break D, B&B p/p £45.00-£55.00.
Weekly D, B&B p/p £295.00-£325.00.

LAST-MINUTE OFFERS

Looking for late availability or last-minute offers? For details of great-value breaks call Central Reservations on freephone 0800 834820 for North Wales, 0800 273747 for Mid Wales or 0800 3289597 for South and West Wales.

QUALITY HOTEL COLWYN BAY

Penmaenhead, Old Colwyn, COLWYN BAY LL29 9LD
Tel: (01492) 516555 Fax: (01492) 515565
E-mail: colwynbayhotel@cwcom.net
Website: www.choiceeurope.net

Situated high on a cliff top overlooking the sea and majestic sweep of the bay. This unique hotel offers a high standard of comfort and service throughout. Enjoy our spectacular Horizon Restaurant serving excellent cuisine complemented by panoramic views. Conference and Banqueting facilities for up to 200 people. Approved venue for Civil Ceremonies.

Months open 1-12; B&B p/p £29.75-£32.00.
Weekly D, B&B p/p £178.50-£192.00.

SYCHNANT PASS HOUSE

Sychnant Pass Rd, CONWY LL32 8BJ
Tel: (01492) 596868 Fax: (01492) 596868
E-mail: bresykes@sychnant-pass-house.co.uk
Website: www.sychnant-pass-house.co.uk

Come and enjoy our Victorian country home set in the national park less than two miles from medieval Conwy. Dine in the relaxed candlelit restaurant and unwind in big sitting rooms with big sofas and log fires. Stroll through our 2 1/2 acre garden with stream and ponds. Warm welcome assured.

Months open 1-12; B&B p/p £27.50-£45.00.
2 Nights Break D, B&B p/p £90.00-£126.00.

BELLE VUE HOTEL
HOTEL ★★★ · **SILVER**

26 North Parade, *LLANDUDNO* LL30 2LP
Tel: (01492) 879547 Fax: (01492) 870001

Comfortable, friendly, highly recommended Victorian seafront hotel. Magnificent sea and mountain views. Rooms have en-suite, television, video, radio, telephone, hairdryer, tea/coffee, bar, lift, car park. Beautiful south-facing sun terraces. Excellent home cooking. Mini breaks. AA and RAC awarded. Runner up 'Llandudno in Bloom' competition 2000.

Months open 1-12; B&B p/p £25.00-£34.00.
2 Nights Break D, B&B p/p £68.00-£114.00.
Weekly D, B&B p/p £250.00-£295.00.

THE IMPERIAL HOTEL
HOTEL ★★★ · **SILVER**

The Promenade, *LLANDUDNO* LL30 1PS
Tel: (01492) 877466 Fax: (01492) 878043
E-mail: imphotel@btinternet.com
Website: www.theimperial.co.uk

The hotel occupies a central promenade position. All modern amenities and facilities are available including a health and fitness centre with 45ft. indoor swimming pool. Elegant award winning restaurant. An ideal base for touring North Wales. We also cater for functions, weddings and conferences.

Months open 1-12; B&B p/p £47.50-£57.50. 2 Nights Break D, B&B p/p £120.00-£140.00. Weekly D, B&B p/p from £360.00.

LYNTON HOUSE HOTEL
HOTEL ★★ · **SILVER**

80 Church Walks, *LLANDUDNO* LL30 2HD
Tel: (01492) 875009/875057 Fax: (01492) 875057
E-mail: jfair75440@aol.com
Website: www.smoothhound.co.uk/hotels/lyntonho.html

Situated close to pier, promenade, shops and amenities. All rooms are individually designed and have en-suite facilities. Tea/coffee tray, television, direct dial telephone, hairdryer and toiletries. Breakfast, with a very extensive menu, is served until 10am. Recently awarded AA ♦♦♦♦. Ground floor bedroom and four posters with whirlpool bath available. Parking.

Months open 1-12; B&B p/p £24.00-£30.00.
2 Nights Break B&B p/p £44.00-£60.00.
Weekly B&B p/p £150.00-£170.00.

THE MONTCLARE HOTEL
HOTEL ★★

North Parade, *LLANDUDNO* LL30 2LP
Tel: (01492) 877061

Come and be one of the family with Ian and Tess Duffield at the 'Montclare Hotel'. Ideally situated overlooking lovely, Llandudno Bay, adjacent to main shopping street, pier and all amenities. All bedrooms have private facilities, TV, tea/coffee making, central heating, and we have a ground floor bedroom. We are renowned for our excellent food.

Months open 3-10; B&B p/p £21.50-£23.50.
2 Nights Break D, B&B p/p £60.00-£65.00.
Weekly D, B&B p/p £200.00-£210.00.

QUEENS HOTEL
HOTEL ★★

Promenade, *LLANDUDNO* LL30 2LE
Tel: (01492) 877218 Fax: (01492) 877218

Centrally situated on seafront. Family-run with excellent chef cuisine. All bedrooms en-suite with complimentary beverage tray, radio, colour TV, and are centrally heated. Entertainment programme. Themed breaks and special offers. Children welcome. Hospitality with a relaxed atmosphere and courteous service awaits you. Please telephone or write for our brochures.

Months open 1-12; B&B p/p £24.75-£34.00.
2 Nights Break D, B&B p/p £60.00-£89.00.
Weekly D, B&B p/p £224.00-£283.00.

SHERWOOD HOTEL
★★ HOTEL

**Craig y Don Parade, The Promenade,
LLANDUDNO LL30 1BG
Tel: (01492) 875313 Fax: (01492) 875313**

Enjoy a comfortable and friendly stay at our family-run seafront hotel overlooking Llandudno Bay. We offer non-smoking throughout. All bedrooms en-suite. Extensive menu, freshly cooked. Large car park. Licensed lounge bar. Close to theatre/conference centre. Eddie and Lyndsey Marshall look forward to welcoming you. Please ring for details.

Months open 3-11; B&B p/p £20.00-£23.00.
2 Nights Break D, B&B p/p £57.00-£63.00.
Weekly D, B&B p/p £187.00-£208.00.

🛏8 ➡8 C ⑩♥♨ SP ⅄✕✿🏧 P8 ℹ

Colwyn Bay

Bed & Breakfast
£27.50 p.p. is the most you'll pay

CLASSIFIED ADVERTISING *There's more accommodation to choose from in the classified advertising section of this book. Please see the listing at the end of the 12 Areas display adverts.*

CROSSROADS GUEST HOUSE
★★★ GUEST HOUSE · GOLD

**15 Coed Pella Rd, *COLWYN BAY* LL29 7AT
Tel: (01492) 530736
E-mail: wte@crossroadsguesthouse.co.uk
Website: www.crossroadsguesthouse.co.uk**

Crossroads is one of the oldest established guest houses in Colwyn Bay, homely and tasteful, central for all the wonders of North Wales. Just a short drive to visit the mountains, lakes and rivers with a stunning coastline of castles, stately homes, narrow gauge railways. Come and explore this land of myths and legends. En-suite supplement £3.00 per person per night. AA ♦♦♦.

Months open 1-12; Single B&B per night £14.50-£16.50.
Double B&B per night £29.00-£39.00.

🛏5 ➡5 C SP✿ P3 ℹ

LLYSFAEN HOUSE
★★ BED & BREAKFAST

**58 Llysfaen Rd, *COLWYN BAY* LL29 9HB
Tel: (01492) 517859
E-mail: views@compuserve.com
Website: www.marl.com/lds/llysfaenhouse.html**

For all year round holidays and short breaks. A warm welcome awaits you. Cleanliness assured. Situated above the village of Old Colwyn we have genuinely spectacular views over the Bay of Colwyn. We are a small family guesthouse the perfect base for visiting many attractions, touring Snowdonia and gateway to wild North Wales

Months open 1-12; B&B p/p £17.50.

🛏3 🛏 C ⑩♥✕ ✿ P2 ℹ

NORTHWOOD HOTEL
★★★ HOTEL · BRONZE

**47 Rhos Rd, Rhos on Sea, *COLWYN BAY*
LL28 4RS Tel: (01492) 549931
E-mail: mail@northwoodhotel.co.uk
Website: www.northwoodhotel.co.uk**

Months open 1-12; B&B p/p £23.00-£23.50. 2 Nights Break
D, B&B p/p £56.00-£60.00. Weekly D, B&B p/p £175.00-£185.00.

🛏12 ➡11 🛏 C ⑩♥⅄💷♥ SP ⅃ TW P12 ℹ

SUNNY SIDE
★★ BED & BREAKFAST

**146 Dinerth Rd, Rhos-on-Sea
COLWYN BAY LL28 4YF
Tel: (01492) 544048**

A warm welcome at our home just out of Rhos-on-Sea. Adjacent to Colwyn Bay and Llandudno. Close to beaches and golf courses. Easy drive to mountains of Snowdonia and castles. Lovely surounding country views. Good home cooked breakfast to start your day. Excellent value accommodation.

Months open 3-11; Double B&B per night £30.00.

🛏2 🛏 ⅄ ✕ ✿

THE WHITEHALL HOTEL
★★★ HOTEL · GOLD

**51 Cayley Promenade, Rhos on Sea, *COLWYN BAY*
LL28 4EP Tel: (01492) 547296 Fax: (01492) 543160
E-mail: whitehallhotel@talk21.co
Website: www.whitehall-hotel.co.uk**

Months open 1-12; Single B&B per night £24.50-£26.50.
Double B&B per night £49.00-£53.00.

🛏12 ➡12 🛏 C ⑩♥💷♥ SP ⅃✿ P5 ℹ

GLAN HEULOG GUEST HOUSE
★★★ GUEST HOUSE

**Llanrwst Rd, *CONWY* LL32 8LT
Tel: (01492) 593845
E-mail: glanheulog@no1guesthouse.freeserve.co.uk**

Fine Victorian house in an elevated position 500 yards from castle, having six bedrooms, five en-suite. All have colour TV and tea/coffee facilities. The rooms are tastefully decorated one of which has a four poster bed. Off road parking. Vegetarians catered for. A warm welcome awaits you.

Months open 1-12; Single B&B per night £17.00-£23.00.
Double B&B per night £32.00-£40.00.

🛏6 ➡5 🛏 C ⑩♥♨ SP ⅄ ✕✿ P7 ℹ

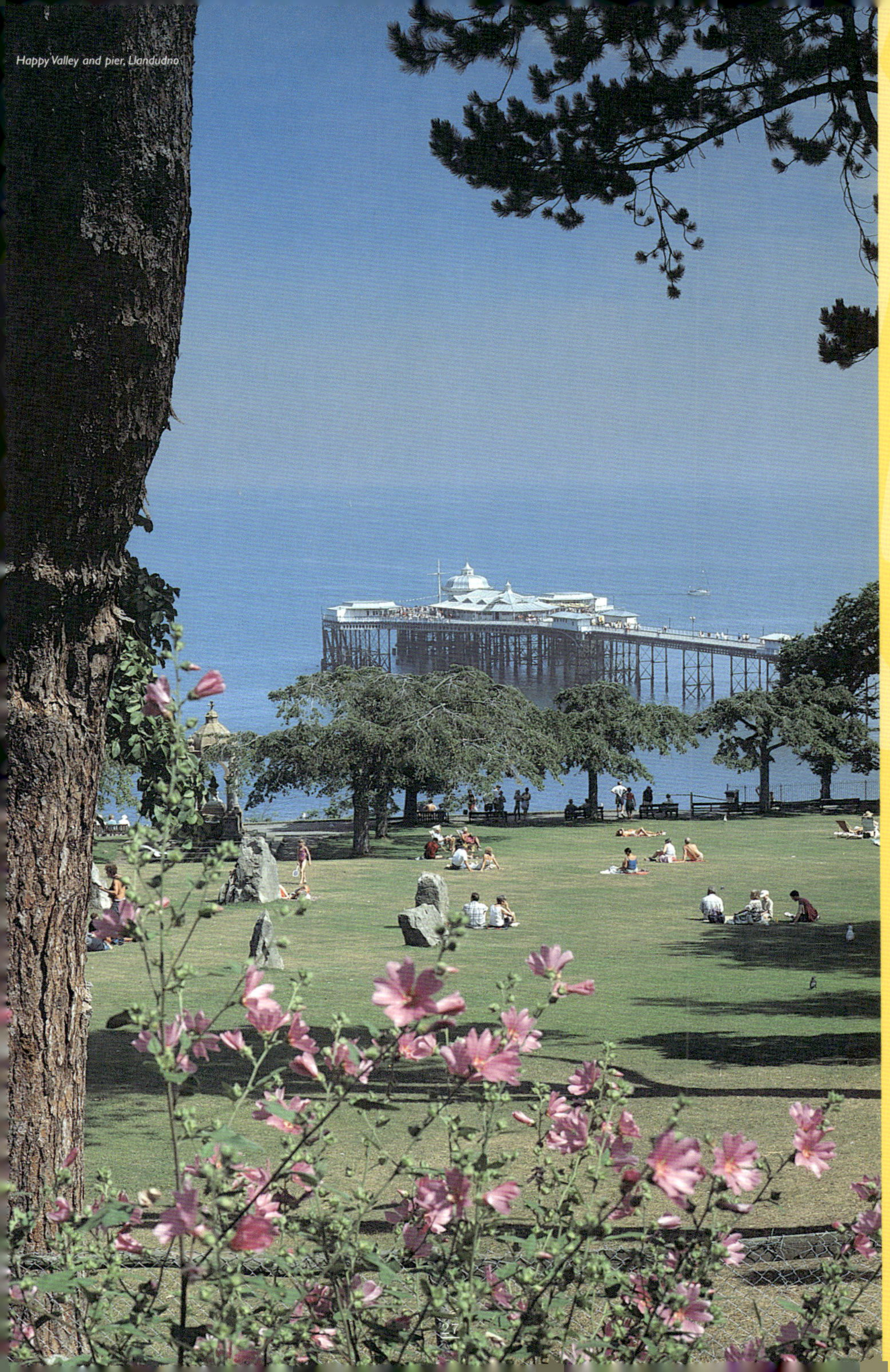

Happy Valley and pier, Llandudno

CARMEL PRIVATE HOTEL
17 Craig-y-Don Parade, Promenade,
LLANDUDNO **LL30 1BG**
Tel: (01492) 877643

Months open 1-12; B&B p/p £16.00-£19.00.
Weekly D, B&B p/p £157.50-£175.00.

HEATHERDALE
30 St Davids Rd, ***LLANDUDNO*** **LL30 2UL**
Tel: (01492) 877362 Fax: 0870-125-817
E-mail: heatherdale@btinternet.com
Website: www.heatherdale.btinternet.co.uk
Comfortable, non-smoking accommodation in a select area of Llandudno
where the local beaches and attractions are a short walk away. All rooms
en-suite with beverage tray, TV, hairdryer and clock radio. Comfortable lounge
and airy dining room. Excellent traditional choice cooking and friendly service
from your established family hosts. Short or long stays welcome.

Months open 1-12; B&B p/p £18.00-£19.00.

KINMEL HOTEL
12 Mostyn Crescent, Central Promenade,
LLANDUDNO **LL30 1AR**
Tel: (01492) 876171 Fax: (01492) 876171

Months open 2-11; Single B&B per night £23.00-£25.00.
Double B&B per night £40.00-£52.00.

LYNTON HOUSE HOTEL
80 Church Walks, ***LLANDUDNO*** **LL30 2HD**
Tel: (01492) 875009/875057 Fax: (01492) 875057
E-mail: jfair75440@aol.com
Website: www.smoothhound.co.uk/hotels/lyntonho.html
Situated close to the pier, promenade and all amenities. All rooms are
individually designed and have en-suite facilities, tea/coffee tray, television,
direct dial telephone, hairdryer and toiletries. Breakfast, with a very extensive
menu, is served until 10am. Recently awarded AA ♦♦♦♦. Four posters with
whirlpool bath available. Car park.

Months open 1-12; Single B&B per night £24.00-£25.00. Double B&B per
night £48.00-£50.00.

THE MIN-Y-DON HOTEL
North Parade, ***LLANDUDNO*** **LL30 2LP**
Tel: (01492) 876511 Fax: (01492) 878169

Min-y-Don Hotel occupies an unrivalled position on the seafront almost
opposite the pier entrance, overlooking the bay. You are assured of a warm
and friendly welcome. The decor and furnishing enhance a feeling of comfort
and a relaxing atmosphere. Our excellent cuisine with choice menu is
unrivalled. Traditional five course dinner is served in our restaurant
overlooking the bay and we will be delighted to send you our brochures.

Months open 2-12; Single B&B per night from £25.00.
Double B&B per night from £50.00.

SLIDE SETS

*Ask about our attractive range of 35mm colour slides
showing views of Wales, available at 75p per slide.*

For a complete list of subjects please contact the Photography
Library, Wales Tourist Board, Brunel House, 2 Fitzalan Road, Cardiff
CF24 0UY. Tel: (029) 2047 5215.

Llandudno is equally attractive at night

CALL IN AT A TOURIST INFORMATION CENTRE

Wales's network of TICs helps you get the best out of your holiday.

- Information on what to see and where to go ● Local events
- Brochures, maps and guides ● And a Bed Booking Service

Properties displaying the **i** *symbol can be booked through any
networked Tourist Information Centre – this service is especially handy
when you're out and about in Wales.*

THE MONTCLARE HOTEL
North Parade, ***LLANDUDNO*** **LL30 2LP**
Tel: (01492) 877061

Come and be one of the family with Ian and Tess Duffield at the 'Montclare
Hotel'. Ideally situated overlooking lovely, Llandudno Bay, adjacent to main
shopping street, pier and all amenities. All bedrooms have private facilities,
TV, tea/coffee making, central heating, and we have a ground floor bedroom.
We are renowned for our excellent food.

Months open 3-10; Single B&B per night £23.50. Double B&B per night
£43.00-£47.00.

WESTDALE HOTEL
37 Abbey Rd, ***LLANDUDNO*** **LL30 2EH**
Tel: (01492) 877996 Fax: (01492) 877996

Westdale is a comfortable hotel with a good friendly atmosphere. Situated on
the level in a quiet road facing Haulfre Gardens, within easy walking distance
of shops and beaches. Large ground and first floor bedrooms with en-suite
bathrooms. Centrally heated throughout. Choice of menu. Licensed bar. Car
park. Dinner optional. SAE for brochure.

Months open 2-10; Single B&B per night £17.50-£21.00.
Double B&B per night £35.00-£42.00.

Holiday Cottages

Caravan & Camping Parks

AUGUSTA HOLIDAY FLATS

AWAITING GRADING

7 Augusta St, *LLANDUDNO* LL30 2AE
Tel: (01492) 878330 Fax: (01492) 878330

Near sea, shops, theatre, railway, coaches, all amenities. On level ground, no front steps. Various sizes, some ground floor. Forecourt parking. Resident manageress. Colour brochure.

Months open 1-12; 2 Nights £50.00-£140.00. 3 Nights £65.00-£190.00. 4 Nights £75.00-£230.00. Weekly/unit £125.00-£420.00.

UNITS 40 SLEEPS 2-8

BALMORAL SELF-CATERING APARTMENTS

★★

6 Trinity Square, *LLANDUDNO* LL30 2RA
Tel: (01492) 544018 Fax: 020 89030763
E-mail: N.Wales@btinternet.com
Website: www.baalmoral.fsnet.co.uk

Months open 1-12; 2 Nights £75.00-£150.00. 3 Nights £90.00-£180.00. 4 Nights £100.00-£200.00. Weekly/unit £100.00-£350.00.

UNITS 14 SLEEPS 2-7

PENDYFFREN HALL

★★ HOLIDAY PARK

Glan yr Afon Rd, Penmaenmawr,
***CONWY* LL34 6UF**
Tel: (01492) 623219

Months open 3-10; Per night (Tourers/Tents) £8.00-£15.00.

🚐 25 🚐 & ▲ 75

LIDO BEACH HOLIDAY PARK

★★★★ HOLIDAY PARK

GOLD

Central Beach, Bastion Rd,
***PRESTATYN* LL19 7EU**
Tel: (01745) 855626 Fax: (01745) 887123

Close to a lovely sweep of golden sandy beach. Lido Beach provides a tranquil haven with a friendly atmosphere.
A gentle stroll from the resort of Prestatyn. David Bellamy Silver Award.

Months open 4-9; Weekly/unit (Static) £100.00-£500.00.

No. ON PARK 650 🚐 50

The beautiful Conwy Valley inland from Llandudno

The North Wales Borderlands

Green, rolling border country

*W*ales's border country is a mix of rolling green hills, lovely valleys, high moor and forest. The airy Clwydian Range, an 'Area of Outstanding Natural Beauty', guards the broad Vale of Clwyd. Llangollen's vale is much deeper, its steep-sided hills rising to dramatic mountains. There's more beautiful countryside above Denbigh, where wild moorlands are covered in heather, forest and the waters of Llyn Brenig.

On Your Travels ...

Llangollen Canal

Erddig, near Wrexham, is a National Trust house with a difference. You don't just get to see the splendid rooms 'above stairs', but also the 'below stairs' servants' quarters. All in all, it gives a complete insight into a vanished way of life on a country estate. Tucked away at the foot of the Clwydian Range near Mold there's one of the most popular of Wales's many country parks. Loggerheads Country Park is a fascinating and unusual place, combining great natural beauty with remnants of the area's industrial past.

The famous little town of Llangollen is brimming with attractions. From here, you can ride a steam railway in one direction or cruise the Llangollen Canal in the other, while the town itself contains museums, a historic house, cultural centre, castle – and even a Dr Who Experience! Further north-west, amongst the Hiraethog moorlands, is the brooding presence of Llyn Brenig, a massive man-made lake with many leisure pursuits and an excellent visitor centre.

For further information please tel (01352) 702468;
e-mail: david.p.evans@flintshire.gov.uk
website: www.tourism-flintshire.org.uk

Where to Stay
Wales

Llangollen stands on the Dee

Carrog
Map Ref Ca7

Village in delightful setting in the steep-sided Dee Valley west of Llangollen. Wonderful walking country – Berwyn Mountains to the south, Clwydian Range to the north, Snowdonia National Park to the west.

Chirk
Map Ref Ed1 ≷

Pleasant border town at gateway to lovely Vale of Ceiriog. Chirk Castle an impressive National Trust property set in splendid grounds. Also good location for exploration of Vale of Llangollen and border country.

Corwen
Map Ref Be7

Pleasant market town in Vale of Edeyrnion. Livestock market held regularly. Fishing in River Dee, swimming pool, good walks. Well-located touring centre for Snowdonia and border country.

Denbigh
Map Ref Be5

Castled town in Vale of Clwyd with much historic interest. The 13th-century hilltop fortress is built from locally quarried white limestone. Friary and museum. Pony trekking, riding, fishing, golf, tennis and bowls. Gwaynynog Country World farm-based attraction. Indoor heated swimming pool. Centrally located for enjoying the rolling hills of North-east Wales, a rich farming area full of attractive villages.

Denbigh, Vale of Clwyd

Gresford
Map Ref Cc6

Border village with notable church – superb stained glass windows and Gresford Bells, mentioned as one of the traditional 'Seven Wonders of Wales'. Close to Wrexham, Llangollen and the beautiful Clwydian Range.

Higher Wych
Map Ref Ce7

Village on the Welsh border. Good centre for exploring Llangollen, the Vale of Dee and the mountainous Berwyns and Clwydian Range. Erddig Hall (National Trust) and Clywedog Valley Heritage Park at nearby Wrexham.

Llanarmon Dyffryn Ceiriog
Map Ref Eb2

Delightful little village locked away in Berwyn Mountains, with good walking and fishing. Home of the bard Ceiriog (John Hughes) – the church has a memorial to him. Pistyll Rhaeadr, Wales's highest waterfall, nearby.

Ruthin, an architectural gem

Wrexham
Map Ref Cc6 ⇌

Busy commercial and industrial town, gateway to North Wales. St Giles's Church has graceful tower and altarpiece given by Elihu Yale of Yale University fame (his tomb is in the churchyard). Visit Erddig Hall (National Trust), an unusual country house on outskirts, and the Clywedog Valley rich in heritage and visitor attractions from the area's industrial and rural past.

Llangollen
Map Ref Ec1

Romantic town on River Dee, famous for International Musical Eisteddfod in July. Attractions include museums, pottery, weavers, ECTARC European Centre for Traditional and Regional Cultures and standard-gauge steam railway. Plas Newydd (home of 'Ladies of Llangollen' fame) nearby. Valle Crucis Abbey is 2 miles away and ruined Castell Dinas Brân overlooks the town. Golf course and wonderful walking countryside.

Northop
Map Ref Cb5

At gateway to North Wales and surrounded by historic sites – Ewloe Castle, Flint Castle and St Winefride's Well, Holywell, one of the 'Seven Wonders of Wales'. Close to superb walking in Clwydian Range. Wales in Bloom award winner 2000.

Ruabon
Map Ref Cc7 ⇌

Border town close to Llangollen. Lots to see and do locally – Llangollen Canal, Pontcysyllte Aqueduct, Wrexham's Clywedog Valley Heritage Park, National Trust's Erddig Hall and Chirk Castle, Tŷ Mawr Country Park.

Ruthin
Map Ref Ca6

Attractive and historic market town noted for its fine architecture, a mixture of medieval, Tudor and Georgian. Many captivating old buildings. Medieval banquets in Ruthin Castle. Ancient St Peter's Church has beautiful gates and carved panels. Good range of small shops; craft centre with workshops. Ideal base for exploring lovely Vale of Clwyd and Clwydian Range.

Wrexham

Hotels, Guest Houses & Farmhouses

MORETON PARK LODGE

AWAITING GRADING

Gledrid, *CHIRK*, nr Wrexham LL14 5DG
Tel: (01691) 776666 Fax: (01691) 776655
E-mail: enquiries@moretonparklodge.com
Website: www.moretonpark.com

Conveniently located just off A5. Rooms, suites (ideal for families). Freshly prepared food, fine wines, traditional ales and a warm welcome. www.moretonpark.com

Months open 1-12; 1 Night p/p £44.95-£54.95.

🛏 46 🚻 46 [C] 📺 🍽 🖥 🛁 🌊 ❄ P i

WEST ARMS HOTEL

★★★ HOTEL

LLANARMON DC, nr Llangollen, Wrexham LL20 7LD
Tel: (01691) 600665 Fax: (01691) 600622
E-mail: gowestarms@aol.com
Website: www.hotelwalesuk.com

Months open 1-12; B&B p/p £41.50-£51.50.

🛏 16 🚻 16 🐴 [C] 📺 🍽 🖥 🛁 🌊 SP ❄ 🎏 ⚄(FR) TW P i

Plas Newydd, Llangollen

GOLDEN PHEASANT HOTEL

★★★ COUNTRY HOTEL

Glyn Ceiriog, nr *LLANGOLLEN* LL20 7BB
Tel: (01691) 718281 Fax: (01691) 718479

Relaxing atmosphere, good food and friendly staff make this 18th century hotel the ideal base for exploring the unspoilt valleys of Llangollen and Snowdonia. Easy to reach - only 15 minutes from A5. Restaurant and snack room with picturesque views. Some rooms with whirlpool baths. Four-poster beds. Pets welcome.

Months open 1-12; B&B p/p £30.00-£40.00.
2 Nights Break D, B&B p/p £90.00-£110.00.
Weekly D, B&B p/p £300.00-£350.00.

🛏 19 🚻 19 🐴 [C] 🍽 🖥 🛁 🌊 SP ⚄ 🎏 ❄ TW P i

WILD PHEASANT HOTEL

★★★ HOTEL

Berwyn Rd, *LLANGOLLEN* LL20 8AD
Tel: (01978) 860629 Fax: (01978) 861837
E-mail: wild.pheasant@talk21.com
Website: www.wildpheasanthotel.co.uk

Beautifully located in acres of grounds overlooking mountains. Within short scenic riverside walk of central Llangollen. Relaxing and friendly with excellent service, cosy restaurant and bistro. Ride a horse-drawn canal boat or a steam train alongside the picturesque river. Tour the beautiful countryside and visit historic Chester and Shrewsbury. Excellent value for money. AA 3 Stars.

Months open 1-12; B&B p/p £43.00. 2 Nights Break D, B&B p/p £130.00-£150.00. Weekly D, B&B p/p £385.00-£450.00.

🛏 34 🚻 34 🐴 [C] 🍽 🖥 🛁 🌊 SP ⚄ ❄ TW P i

HIGHFIELD HALL HOTEL

AWAITING GRADING

NORTHOP CH7 6AX
Tel: (01352) 840221 Fax: (01352) 840221
Website: www.confetti.co.uk

A grand Georgian building set in acres of delightful gardens. À la carte restaurant, public bar and bistro. Chester 7 miles Liverpool 22 Manchester 40.

Months open 1-12; B&B p/p £30.00-£50.00. 2 Nights Break D, B&B p/p £95.00. Weekly D, B&B p/p £332.50.

🛏 14 🚻 14 🍽 🖥 🛁 🌊 SP 🎵 ❄ 🎏 P

Bed & Breakfast
£27.50 p.p. is the most you'll pay

PEN-Y-BONT FAWR
★★★ BED & BREAKFAST
Cynwyd, CORWEN LL21 0ET
Tel: (01490) 412663

Pen-y-Bont Fawr is on the outskirts of Cynwyd village near Corwen. Llangollen, Bala, Betws-y-Coed and Snowdonia are nearby. An ideal area for walking, cycling, fishing and horseriding, also watersports in Bala. You can be assured of the legendary welsh hospitality. Choice of twin or double bedrooms.

Months open 1-12; B&B p/p £15.00.
2 Nights Break D, B&B p/p £42.00. Weekly D, B&B p/p £147.00.

BERLLAN BACH
★★★ BED & BREAKFAST
Ffordd Las, Llandyrnog, DENBIGH LL16 4LR
Tel: (01824) 790725

Months open 1-12; B&B p/p £20.00-£25.00.

CAYO GUEST HOUSE
★★ GUEST HOUSE
74 Vale St, DENBIGH LL16 3BW
Tel: (01745) 812663

Long established centrally heated guest house. Ideal base for touring North Wales. Excellent area for walking, golf and the town has a leisure centre. Good food using local produce, special diets catered for. Well-behaved dogs and children welcome. Pick-up service for 'Offa's Dykers' from Bodfari.

Months open 1-12; Single B&B per night £18.00-£19.00. Double B&B per night £36.00-£38.00. (excludes Christmas)

ALYN LODGE
★★ LODGE
Pont-y-Capel Lane, GRESFORD, Wrexham LL12 8SA
Tel: (01978) 855811 Fax: (01978) 855729
E-mail: info@alynlodge.co.uk
Website: www.alynlodge.co.uk

Alyn Lodge: a modern comfortable country house set in its own wooded grounds on the outskirts of Gresford. Wrexham is situated in North Wales with easy access to the motorway system. Just 15 minutes from Chester, on the site of an Iron Age hill fort, it offers a peaceful and tranquil setting.

Months open 1-12; Single B&B per night from £22.50.
Double B&B per night £45.00.

MILL HOUSE
★★★ GUEST HOUSE
HIGHER WYCH, Malpas SY14 7JR
Tel: (01948) 780362 Fax: (01948) 780566
E-mail: chris.smith@videoactive.co.uk

Months open 1-11; Single B&B per night £20.00-£25.00.
Double B&B per night £40.00-£45.00.

LATE AVAILABILITY For the latest offers call our freephone Central Reservations service. North Wales – 0800 834820 Mid Wales – 0800 273747 South and West Wales – 0800 3289597

BOOK DIRECT

Just pick up the phone and talk direct to your chosen accommodation. You'll receive personal attention – and will be speaking to someone who can answer all your questions so you can make your booking there and then. Nothing could be simpler.

In looking through these pages you'll also find that much of the accommodation can also be contacted by e-mail.

GWYNFA GUEST HOUSE
★★★ GUEST HOUSE
GOLD
LLANARMON DYFFRYN CEIRIOG,
nr Llangollen LL20 7LF Tel: (01691) 600287

Months open 2-11; Single B&B per night £20.00-£22.50.
Double B&B per night £45.00.

TY ISAR PLWYF
AWAITING GRADING
Glyndyfrdwy, LLANGOLLEN LL21 9HW
Tel: (01490) 430342
E-mail: jenny.carpenter3@virgin.net

Months open 1-12; B&B p/p £16.00-£22.00.
2 Nights Break B&B p/p £30.00-£40.00.
Weekly D, B&B p/p £150.00-£195.00.

WHITEGATE
★★★ BED & BREAKFAST
Grange Rd, LLANGOLLEN LL20 8AP
Tel: (01978) 860960 Fax: (01978) 861699

Welcome to Whitegate! The perfect base for exploring this beautiful area. Whitegate is an attractive Edwardian house set in its own grounds on the edge of Llangollen, close to Plas Newydd. Bedrooms are en-suite and well supplied. Ample secure parking. Reduced terms for longer stays. Packed lunches available. French spoken.

Months open 1-12; B&B p/p £20.00-£24.00.

TIR Y FRON
★★★ BED & BREAKFAST
RUABON, Wrexham LL14 6RW
Tel: (01978) 821633 Fax: (01978) 810690
E-mail: g.manuel@micro-plus-web.net

Attractive 16ᵗʰC. house with oak beams situated on Offa's Dyke in a 2 acre garden. Open for N.G.S. Midway between Wrexham/Llangollen, 15 minutes from National Trust properties, Erddig, Chirk castle, golf courses, horseriding and picturesque Llangollen canal nearby.

Months open 1-12; Single B&B per night £20.00.
Double B&B per night £38.00-£40.00.

BETTISFIELD HALL
AWAITING GRADING
Bettisfield, Whitchurch, WREXHAM SY13 2LB
Tel: (01948) 710525 Fax: (01948) 710819
E-mail: g.springett@aol.com Website: www. hometown.aol.com/gspringett/myhomepage/business.html

Months open 1-12; Single B&B per night £26.00-£27.50.
Double B&B per night £52.00-£55.00.

Holiday Cottages

CARROG MILL COTTAGES ★★★★★

Y Felin, *CARROG* LL21 9AL
Tel: (01490) 430640 Fax: (01490) 430572
E-mail: carrogmill@lineone.net
Website: www.carrogmill.com
      www.carrogmill.co.uk

At the hub of North Wales the cottages reflect the 1900's with all the comforts of the 21st century. Relax in the tranquility of Carrog. With log fires, plus full central heating. Make this an ideal location for a holiday or breakaway any time of the year. A warm welcome awaits you with a "welcome pack" provided. View us on the web.

Months open 1-12; 2 Nights £68.00-£180.00. 3 Nights £102.00-£270.00. 4 Nights £120.00-£312.00. Weekly/unit £182.00-£504.00.

UNITS 3 SLEEPS 2-6 🐾 ⌨ SP 🖥 ✗ (GR) P8 *i*

THE COACH HOUSE ★★★★★

Maes-y-Llan Farm, Llanarmon-yn-Ial,
***RUTHIN* CH7 4QF**
Tel: (01824) 780429 Fax: (01824) 780434
E-mail: vector.partnerships@virgin.net

BRONZE

17th Century stone-built cottage in owners' courtyard. Idyllic setting. Unobstructed views of Clwydian Hills and Horseshoe Pass. Amidst hills, forest, mountains, lakes, wildlife. Private, peaceful retreat on edge of friendly quiet village, with pub, shop, post office. Ideal walking, fishing, cycling base. On Offa's Dyke.

Months open 1-12; 2 Nights £80.00-£120.00. 3 Nights £120.00-£180.00. 4 Nights £160.00-£240.00. Weekly/unit £195.00-£295.00.

UNITS 1 SLEEPS 2+2 CHILDREN (UNDER 5 YEARS) ⌨ 🖥 SP ✗ ✗ (FR) P1

PLEASE NOTE

All the accommodation in this publication has applied for grading. With Holiday Cottages it may occasionally not have been possible to undertake a grading. This situation is clearly identified by 'Awaiting Grading' or a provisional Star rating (indicated by the letter P appearing alongside the Stars) within the advertisement/entry.

CENTRAL RESERVATIONS

Your free one-stop shop for holiday accommodation. A wide choice of places to stay, last-minute offers, late availability, bargain breaks.

Call freephone 0800 834820 for North Wales, 0800 273747 for Mid Wales or 0800 3289597 for South and West Wales.

CLASSIFIED ADVERTISING *There's more accommodation to choose from in the classified advertising section of this book. Please see the listing at the end of the 12 Areas display adverts.*

Pistyll Rhaeadr, the highest waterfall in Wales

Snowdonia Mountains & Coast

Llyn Gwynant, set amongst Snowdonia's highest peaks

*T*he Snowdonia National Park takes its name from Snowdon's jagged peaks, yet this huge park extends southwards for over 800 square miles all the way to Dolgellau and beyond, and eastwards to Bala. It's a national park of contrasts, with wooded vales, moors, lakes, sandy estuaries and beaches as well as dramatic mountains. Snowdonia's coastal equivalent is the spectacular Llŷn Peninsula, an 'Area of Outstanding Natural Beauty'.

Portmeirion

On Your Travels ...

Ask anyone from Tokyo to Timbuktu to name the most famous Welsh castle, and the answer will be 'Caernarfon'. It's entirely understandable, for this massive 13th-century fortress was built to serve both as a royal palace and military stronghold. Seven hundred years on, its soaring towers and battlements remain a vivid testament to bygone times. History of another kind was made at the former 'slate capital' of Blaenau Ffestiniog. North Wales's slate industry is remembered at the Llechwedd Slate Caverns, where visitors can take an enthralling trip into vast underground chambers.

Blaenau Ffestiniog's slate was carried by narrow-gauge railway to the coast at Porthmadog. The scenic Ffestiniog Railway now transports people in place of its original cargo. If you're near Porthmadog don't miss Portmeirion. This village really is unique – southern Italy magically recreated in North Wales. Another intriguing place is the Centre for Alternative Technology, deep in the woods near Machynlleth, where waterwheels, solar panels and all manner of ingenious devices make the best possible use of the Earth's natural resources.

For further information please tel (01341) 423558 (24 hr); e-mail: tourism@gwynedd.gov.uk website: www.gwynedd.gov.uk

Where to Stay
Wales

Aberdaron, at North Wales's 'Land's End'

Llyn Tegid, Bala

Aberdaron
Map Ref Aa5

Village on wild western shores of Llŷn. Attractive beach and spectacular headland with wonderful views across to Bardsey Island. Dramatic coastal scenery all around. Porth-oer (Whistling Sands) close by.

Abersoch

Aberdyfi/Aberdovey
Map Ref Db6 ⇌

Picturesque little resort and dinghy sailor's paradise on Dovey Estuary. Watersports, thriving

yacht club, good inns looking out over the bay, 18-hole golf links. Superb views towards hills and mountains.

Abersoch
Map Ref Ac5

Popular Llŷn Peninsula resort with sandy beaches. Also a dinghy sailing and windsurfing centre. Superb coastal scenery with easy walks. Pony trekking, golf, fishing and sea trips. Llanengan's historic church nearby.

Bala
Map Ref De2

Traditional Welsh country town with tree-lined main street and interesting little shops, inns and eating places. A narrow-gauge railway runs along the southern shore of Llyn Tegid (Bala Lake). The lake is 4 miles long (the largest natural lake in Wales) and

ringed with mountains. Golf, sailing, fishing, canoeing, white-water rafting – and a natural touring centre for Snowdonia.

Bangor
Map Ref Ae3 ⇌

Compact cathedral city of character overlooking the Menai Strait; gateway to Anglesey and Snowdonia's Ogwen Valley, with

Bangor Pier

university college and a cathedral founded in the 6th century by St Deiniol. Attractions include Theatr Gwynedd, museum and art gallery housed in the Old Canonry, an exquisitely renovated Victorian pier and imposing neo-Norman Penrhyn Castle. Heated swimming pool, yachting and fishing.

The little sailing centre of Aberdyfi

Barmouth, at the mouth of the Mawddach

Barmouth
Map Ref Db4 ⇌

Superbly located resort at the mouth of lovely Mawddach Estuary. Golden sands, miles of wonderful mountain and estuary walks nearby. Promenade, funfair, harbour and pony rides on the beach. Lifeboat and shipwreck museums. Town trail to Dinas Oleu viewpoint – the first piece of land ever acquired by the National Trust (1895). Good shops and inns. Excellent parking on seafront.

Beddgelert
Map Ref Ae6

One of Snowdonia's loveliest mountain villages, home of the legend of Gelert, set amongst glorious scenery – Nant Gwynant Valley to the east and picturesque Aberglaslyn Pass to the south. Winner of numerous awards including Europe in Bloom and 2000 Wales in Bloom. Marvellous walks; Wordsworth made a famous dawn ascent of Snowdon from here. Ideal destination for that mountain break. Visit nearby Sygun Copper Mine.

Beddgelert, in the heart of Snowdonia

Betws-y-Coed
Map Ref Bb6 ⇌

Wooded village and popular mountain resort in picturesque setting where three rivers meet. Good touring centre, close to best mountain area of Snowdonia. Tumbling rivers and waterfalls emerge from a tangle of treetops. Trout fishing, craft shops, golf course, railway and motor museums, Snowdonia National Park Visitor Centre. Nature trails very popular with hikers. Swallow Falls a 'must'.

Betws-y-Coed, a popular mountain resort

Caernarfon
Map Ref Ad4

Dominated by magnificent 13th-century castle, most famous of Wales's medieval fortresses. Many museums in castle, maritime museum in town. Narrow-gauge Rheilffordd Eryri/Welsh Highland Railway runs into hills from quay. Caernarfon Air World at Dinas Dinlle, Segontium Roman Fort and Museum. Popular sailing

Caernarfon

centre, old harbour, market square, Lloyd George statue. Holiday centre at gateway of Snowdonia. Parc Glynllifon nearby.

Chwilog
Map Ref Ac7

Village near Llŷn's south coast, close to resorts of Criccieth and Pwllheli. Next-door village of Llanystumdwy has Lloyd George memorabilia. Historic house of Penarth Fawr also worth a visit.

Colwyn Bay
Map Ref Bc4 ⇌

Bustling seaside resort with large sandy beach overlooked by wooded hills. Superb 3-mile promenade with many amusements. Good touring centre for Snowdonia. Leisure centre, Eirias Park, Dinosaur World, famous Welsh Mountain Zoo with Chimpanzee World. Harlequin Puppet Theatre and Theatr Colwyn. Golf, tennis, riding and other sports. Quieter Rhos on Sea at western end of bay. Wales in Bloom award winner 2000.

Conwy
Map Ref Bb4

Historic town with mighty 13th-century castle and complete ring of medieval town walls. Dramatic estuary setting. Many ancient buildings including Aberconwy House and Plas Mawr, a wonderfully preserved Elizabethan town house. Telford Suspension Bridge, popular fish quay, spectacular wall walks. Golf, pony trekking, Butterfly House, art gallery, aquarium, pleasure cruises. Tiny 'smallest house' on quay. Touring centre for Snowdonia.

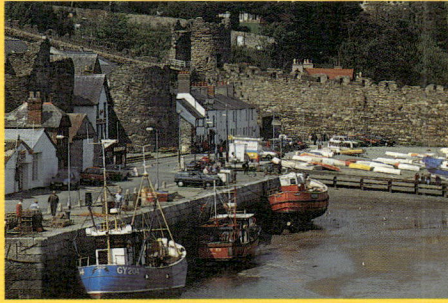

The quay, Conwy

Criccieth
Map Ref Ad7

Ideal family resort with good sand and shingle beach. Romantic ruin of Criccieth Castle, sacked by Owain Glyndŵr in 1404, is set on a prominent headland overlooking sea with panoramic views. Salmon and trout in nearby rivers and lakes. Festival of Music and the Arts in June. Village of Llanystumdwy with Lloyd George Museum nearby. Wales in Bloom award winner 2000.

Dinas Mawddwy
Map Ref Dd4

Village nestling in the mountains below steep-sided, forested slopes. Dramatic landscapes all around – drive over Bwlch y Groes, the highest road in Wales, to Bala. Well-stocked craft shop in former woollen mill.

Criccieth, on Llŷn's south coast

Dolgellau
Map Ref Dc4

Handsome stone-built market town which seems to have grown naturally out of the mountains. The heights of Cader Idris loom above the rooftops. Interesting shops, inns. Museum of the Quakers in town centre. Gold was discovered here in the 19th century. The old mines are near village of Bontddu on the beautiful Mawddach Estuary. Excellent base for touring the coast and countryside.

Spectacularly sited Harlech Castle

Dolgellau, beneath Cader Idris

Dyffryn Ardudwy
Map Ref Da3 ⇌

Pleasant village near the coast on Barmouth–Harlech road, set between sea and mountains. Prehistoric burial chamber and stone circles nearby; also scenic Shell Island and Museum and Bird Gardens.

Ffestiniog Railway

Ffestiniog
Map Ref Dc1

Stands on a high bluff looking towards the sea. Neighbour of Blaenau Ffestiniog with its slate caverns and narrow-gauge railway. Cynfal waterfalls spring from the moors above the town.

Garndolbenmaen
Map Ref Ad6

Small hillside village high above the sea, 4 miles from Criccieth. Woollen mill nearby, excellent walking country. Good base for touring Llŷn Peninsula and Snowdonia.

Harlech
Map Ref Da2 ⇌

Small, stone-built town dominated by remains of 13th-century castle – site of Owain Glyndŵr's last stand. Dramatically set on a high crag, the castle commands a magnificent panorama of rolling sand dunes, sea and mountains. Home of 18-hole Royal St David's Golf Club. Shell Island nearby. Theatre and swimming pool. Explore the chambers of Chwarel Hên Slate Caverns just south of Harlech.

Llanbedr
Map Ref Da3 ⇌

Attractive village between mountains and sea close to Shell Island and Harlech. Maes Artro Village a popular family attraction. Wild Rhinog Mountains in background are excellent for walking – visit lovely Llyn Cwm Bychan.

Llanbedrog
Map Ref Ab7

Small Llŷn resort with sheltered sands, popular with families. Wooded walks, Mynydd Tir y Cwmwd headland with spectacular views across Tremadog Bay. Plas Glyn-y-Weddw a fascinating historic house and art gallery.

Llanberis
Map Ref Ae4

Popular centre for walkers and climbers, least difficult (5 miles) walk to Snowdon summit starts here. For an easy ride up take Snowdon Mountain Railway. Many things to see and do in this lively mountain town – Llanberis Lake Railway, slate industry museum, a trip into the awesome tunnels of the Dinorwig Hydro-Electric Scheme, activity-packed Padarn Country Park, ancient Dolbadarn Castle and nearby Bryn Brâs Castle.

The clocktower, Machynlleth

Llanberis has grown up alongside its lake

Machynlleth
Map Ref Dc5 ⇌

Historic market town near beautiful Dovey Estuary. Owain Glyndŵr's Parliament House in the wide, handsome main street is now a museum and brass-rubbing centre. Superbly equipped Bro Ddyfi Leisure Centre offers wide range of activities. Celtica

centre tells the story of Celtic myth and legend. Outstanding art gallery. On Glyndŵr's Way long-distance walk. The inventive Centre for Alternative Technology is 3 miles away.

Nefyn
Map Ref Ab6

Old fishing village, now popular holiday spot, on Llŷn's north coast perched above sweeping bay with 2 miles of sand. Visit the Llŷn Historical and Maritime Museum. Picturesque Porthdinllaen next door.

Penmaenmawr
Map Ref Ba4 ⇌

Small coastal resort, now by-passed, below mighty headland which posed immense challenges to road and rail engineers. Attractive promenade. On edge of Snowdonia National Park. Medieval Conwy is next-door neighbour.

Dramatic coastal views around Nefyn

Porthmadog
Map Ref Ae7 ⇌

Bustling harbour town and shopping centre named after William Madocks, a 19th-century MP, who built the mile-long Cob embankment. Steam narrow-gauge Ffestiniog Railway runs along a scenic route to Blaenau Ffestiniog, with its slate caverns. Also Welsh Highland Railway. Pottery, craft shops, galleries, maritime museum, car museum. Portmeirion Italianate village and good beaches nearby.

The harbour, Porthmadog

Pwllheli
Map Ref Ac7 ⇌

A small resort big in appeal to sailors; many craft are moored in its attractive 420-berth modern marina. Promenade with 5-mile-long curving sand and shingle beach, shopping, golf, leisure centre. River and sea fishing. Penarth Fawr, an interesting medieval house, north-east of town. Located halfway along Llŷn's south coast – a good centre for exploring the entire peninsula.

Pwllheli Marina

Trefor
Map Ref Ac6

Atmospheric former quarrying village on Llŷn's north coast. Spectacular cliff scenery where Yr Eifl mountains plunge into the sea. Caernarfon, Pwllheli and the superb sands at Nefyn all close by.

Trefriw
Map Ref Bb5

Woollen mill village on the western side of the Conwy Valley, with Trefriw Wells Spa. Lakes at Llyn Geirionydd and Llyn Crafnant are both local beauty spots. Good walking country.

Tywyn
Map Ref Da6 ⇌

Seaside resort on Cardigan Bay, with beach activities, sea and river fishing and golf among its leading attractions. Good leisure centre. Narrow-gauge Talyllyn Railway runs inland from here and St Cadfan's Stone and Llanegryn Church are important Christian monuments. In the hills stand Castell-y-Bere, a native Welsh castle, and Bird Rock, a haven for birdlife.

Tal-y-llyn near Tywyn

Hotels, Guest Houses & Farmhouses

CARREG PLAS GUEST HOUSE

★★★ GUEST HOUSE

ABERDARON, Pwllheli LL53 8LH
Tel: (01758) 760308 Fax: (01758) 760696

17th Century manor house of historic interest, grade 2 listed, in secluded wooded grounds. Two miles from Aberdaron, close to Whistling Sands beach, surrounded by stretches of magnificent coastline largely National Trust owned. Range of room sizes, most having own facilities. Home cooking par excellence. Special childrens' reductions, cots/highchairs provided.

Months open 3-10; B&B p/p £21.00-£27.50. 2 Nights Break D, B&B p/p £67.00-£80.00. Weekly D, B&B p/p £225.00-£270.00.

PANTEIDAL ORGANIC GARDEN RESTAURANT WITH ROOMS

AWAITING GRADING

Panteidal, **ABERDOVEY** LL35 0RG
Tel: (01654) 767322 Fax: (01654) 767322
E-mail: office@panteidalfreeserve.co.uk
Website: www.panteidalorganics.co.uk

Months open 1-12; B&B p/p £45.00-£60.00.

TREM-Y-WAWR

★★ BED & BREAKFAST

GOLD

Cae Groes, **BALA** LL23 7AQ
Tel: (01678) 520994

Private house, elevated position in countryside with a view of Bala town and lake. Five minutes walk to leisure centre, lake, town and restaurants, modern rooms with central heating, radio/alarms, TV, tea and coffee tray. Lovely garden. Ideal centre for touring. A range of outdoor activities including water sports nearby. Lockable garage for cycles. Full Welsh breakfast.

Months open 1-12; B&B p/p £20.00-£24.00.

GARDEN HOTEL

★★★ HOTEL

GOLD

1 High St, **BANGOR** LL57 1DQ
Tel: (01248) 362189 Fax: (01248) 371328
E-mail: bookings@garden-hotel-bangor.co.uk
Website: www.garden-hotel-bangor.co.uk

The Hotel is situated on the High Street, where it is close to the main railway station. The 10 en-suite bedrooms have all facilities you would expect from a first class hotel. Delicious freshly prepared food, fine wines, and a warm welcoming atmosphere where you can feel at home.

Months open 1-12; B&B p/p £35.00-£40.00. 2 Nights Break D, B&B p/p £90.00-£100.00. Weekly D, B&B p/p £270.00-£300.00.

BRYN MELYN HOTEL

★★ HOTEL

SILVER

Panorama Rd, **BARMOUTH** LL42 1DQ
Tel: (01341) 280556 Fax: (01341) 280342
E-mail: bryn.melyn@virgin.net
Website: www.brynmelynhotel.co.uk

Delightful AA 2 Star hotel set on the hillside with stunning views of the Mawddach Estuary, Cader Mountains and sea. Offering a warm welcome, relaxed atmosphere, comfortable en-suite accommodation and the delights of good home cooking. An ideal base to explore Snowdonia and beautiful North and Mid-Wales. Private car parking. Residential License.

Months open 1-12; B&B p/p £25.00-£36.00. 2 Nights Break D, B&B p/p £89.00-£96.00. Weekly D, B&B p/p £295.00-£315.00.

WAVECREST HOTEL

★★★ HOTEL

8 Marine Parade, **BARMOUTH** LL42 1NA
Tel: (01341) 280330 Fax: (01341) 280330
E-mail: thewavecrest@talk21.com
Website: www.lokalink.co.uk/wavecrest.html

Months open 4-10; B&B p/p £20.00-£27.00. 2 Nights Break D, B&B p/p £68.00-£80.00. Weekly D, B&B p/p £240.00-£275.00.

PLAS COLWYN GUEST HOUSE

★★ GUEST HOUSE

BEDDGELERT LL55 4UY
Tel: (01766) 890458

Enjoy a warm welcome whilst exploring Snowdonia's beauty. Delicious fresh home cooked meals served in our intimate licensed restaurant; vegetarians welcome. Guests private lounge with log fire. Non-smoking throughout. Families, walkers and pets welcome. Private parking. All rooms with refreshment facilities, some en-suite. Accommodation for the northern section of the Cambrian Way.

Months open 1-12; B&B p/p £18.00-£21.00.

TANRONNEN INN

INN

BEDDGELERT LL55 4YB
Tel: (01766) 890347 Fax: (01766) 890606
E-mail: tanronneninn@frederic-robinson.co.uk

Situated at the head of the magnificent Glaslyn pass in the heart of the Snowdonia National Park. Fully refurbished to the highest standard with seven en-suite bedrooms. Family rooms available. Sky TV in bedrooms. Two intimate little bars. Mastercard, Eurocheque, Switch, Delta, Visa accepted. Robinsons traditional draught beers.

Months open 1-12; B&B p/p £41.00-£42.00. 2 Nights Break D, B&B p/p £110.00-£115.00. Weekly D, B&B p/p £341.00-£345.00.

THE ROYAL OAK HOTEL

HOTEL

BETWS-Y-COED LL24 0AY
Tel: (01690) 710219 Fax: (01690) 710603
E-mail: royal-oak@betws-y-coed.co.uk

Picturesque former Victorian coaching inn situated at the village centre amidst the charming Snowdonia National Park scenery, and overlooking the River Llugwy. 26 luxury en-suite bedrooms, colour TV/sky and hospitality trays. 'Taste of Wales' restaurant, grill and bistro serving delicious local dishes from 7.30am-9.00pm.

Months open 1-12; B&B p/p £35.00-£46.00.
2 Nights Break D, B&B p/p £90.00.

BRON CELYN GUEST HOUSE

GUEST HOUSE
GOLD

Lôn Muriau, Llanrwst Rd, **BETWS-Y-COED**
LL24 0HD Tel: (01690) 710333 Fax: (01690) 710111
E-mail: broncelyn@betws-y-coed.co.uk
Website: www.betws-y-coed.co.uk/broncelyn/

Months open 1-12; B&B p/p £20.00-£26.00. 2 Nights Break D, B&B p/p £60.00-£73.00. Weekly D, B&B p/p £210.00-£255.50.

PARK HILL HOTEL/GWESTY BRYN PARC

HOTEL

Llanrwst Rd, **BETWS-Y-COED** LL24 0HD
Tel: (01690) 710540 Fax: (01690) 710540
E-mail: parkhill.hotel@virgin.net
Website: www.betws-y-coed.co.uk/acc/parkhill

Our hotel is your castle. Family run country house hotel. Ideally situated in Snowdonia National Park. Breathtaking views on Conwy and Llugwy valleys. Renowned for its cuisine and its teddy bear collection. Indoor heated swimming pool with sauna free and exclusively for our guests. AA/RAC♦♦ Ashley Courteney and WHICH? recommended. Multilingual staff.

Months open 1-12; B&B p/p £27.50-£36.00. 2 Nights Break D, B&B p/p £80.00-£95.00. Weekly D, B&B p/p £276.00-£332.50.

TAN-Y-FOEL COUNTRY HOUSE HOTEL

COUNTRY HOTEL
GOLD

Capel Garmon, nr **BETWS-Y-COED** LL26 0RE
Tel: (01690) 710507 Fax: (01690) 710681
E-mail: enquiries@tyfhotel.co.uk
Website: www.tyfhotel.co.uk

Culinary oasis in Snowdonia. A uniquely tranquil contemporary hotel for the person searching for something different. Traditional values of high service and quality with stunning views. Totally 'No Smoking' establishment. Within easy reach of all the major National Park attractions. The only AA 'Two Red Star' and 'Three Rosette' establishment in the Betws-y-Coed area.

Months open 2-12; B&B p/p £45.00-£75.00. 2 Nights Break D, B&B p/p £148.00-£208.00. Weekly D, B&B p/p £518.00-£728.00.

TY-COCH FARM & TREKKING CENTRE

FARM
AWARD

Penmachno, **BETWS-Y-COED** LL25 0HJ
Tel: (01690) 760248 Fax: (01690) 760266
E-mail: tycoch@amserve.net

Months open 1-12; B&B p/p £17.50. Weekly D, B&B p/p £165.00-£175.00.

LLEUAR FAWR

Penygroes, *CAERNARFON* LL54 6PB
Tel: (01286) 660268 Fax: (01286) 660268

★★★ FARM

GOLD

17th Century listed farmhouse set in peaceful location. Central for exploring mountains of Snowdonia, Llŷn Peninsula, Isle of Anglesey and historic town of Caernarfon. Farm noted for bird and wild life, salmon and trout fishing. Two spacious en-suite bedrooms with colour TV, tea making facilities. Children at reduced rates. Warm Welsh welcome awaits you.

Months open 1-11; Single B&B per night £25.00. Double B&B per night £36.00-£40.00.

LLWYNDU MAWR

Carmel Road, Penygroes,
***CAERNARFON* LL54 6PU**
Tel: (01286) 880419 Fax: (01286) 880845

★★ FARM

Months open 1-11; B&B p/p £16.00-£18.00. 2 Nights Break D, B&B p/p £42.00-£46.00. Weekly D, B&B p/p £154.35-£166.95.

PENGWERN

Saron, Llanwnda, *CAERNARFON* LL54 5UH
Tel: (01286) 831500 Fax: (01286) 830741
E-mail: pengwern@talk21.com
Website: www.smoothhound.co.uk/hotels/pengwern.htm

★★★★

AWARD

GOLD

Charming spacious farmhouse of character situated between mountains and sea with unobstructed views of Snowdonia. Well appointed bedrooms all en-suite. Land runs down to Fory Bay, noted for its bird life. Jane Rowlands has a cookery diploma and provides all the excellent meals with farm house fresh food, including home produced beef and lamb. Excellent access.

Months open 2-11; B&B p/p £22.00-£28.00. 2 Nights Break D, B&B p/p £74.00-£82.00. Weekly D, B&B p/p £231.00-£266.00.

Caernarfon Castle

THE MENAI BANK HOTEL

North Road, *CAERNARFON* LL55 1BD
Tel: (01286) 673297 Fax: (01286) 673297
E-mail: menaibankhotel@tesco.net
Website: www.menaibankhotel.co.uk

★★ HOTEL

GOLD

Family owned period hotel. Original features. Extensive coastal views. Close to castle and Snowdonia National Park. Tastefully decorated comfortable bedrooms, some non-smoking. Colour televisions, teamakers, clock radio alarms. Ground floor bedroom. Attractive restaurant. Bar. Residents lounge, pool table, pay telephone, lawned garden, car parking. Credit cards. Colour brochure. AA 2 Star.

Months open 1-12; B&B p/p £25.00-£30.00. 2 Nights Break D, B&B p/p £74.00-£86.00. Weekly D, B&B p/p £256.00-£295.00.

THE LODGE

Tal-y-Bont, *CONWY* LL32 8YX
Tel: (01492) 660766 Freephone: 0800 9176593
Fax: (01492) 660534
E-mail: bbaldon@lodgehotel.co.uk
Website: www.lodgehotel.co.uk

★★★ HOTEL

GOLD

Our happy family run hotel, nestling against the hills of Snowdonia in the tranquil village of Tal-y-Bont is a real discovery. Much of the fruit and vegetables you will eat in our sunny restaurant, is produced in our gadens. We are proud of our awards for old-fashioned hospitality, warmth and cuisine. Come and discover why so many of our guests return year after year.

Months open 1-12; B&B p/p £30.00-£60.00. 2 Nights Break D, B&B p/p £80.00-£120.00. Weekly D, B&B p/p £240.00-£420.00.

CRAIG-Y-MÔR GUEST HOUSE

West Parade, *CRICCIETH* LL52 0EN
Tel: (01766) 522830
E-mail: enquiries@craig-y-mor-bandb.freeserve.co.uk

★★★ GUEST HOUSE

Months open 3-10; B&B p/p £20.00-£21.00.

Llŷn landscape inland from Porth Neigwl

GLYN Y COED HOTEL
Portmadoc Rd, *CRICCIETH* LL52 0HP
Tel: (01766) 522870 Fax: (01766) 523341

★★ HOTEL

GOLD

AA/RAC ♦♦♦♦
Acclaimed beautiful Victorian house overlooking sea, mountains, castles and near to Portmeirion. Highly recommended home-cooking catering for most diets. Private parking. Cosy bar. All en-suite bedrooms, one ground floor. Seniors rates. Excellent value in superior accommodation. Brochure issued with pleasure.

Months open 1-12; B&B p/p £21.00-£28.00. 2 Nights Break D, B&B p/p £62.00-£76.00. Weekly D, B&B p/p £205.00-£250.00.
🛏10 ⇌10 C 🅘🍽🍷⚡♨ SP ⚓🌺❋☘(FR,GR,SP) P16 🛈

MIN Y GAER HOTEL
Porthmadog Road, *CRICCIETH* LL52 0HP
Tel: (01766) 522151 Fax: (01766) 523540
E-mail: info@minygaerhotel.co.uk
Website: www.minygaerhotel.co.uk

★★ HOTEL

BRONZE

A pleasant licensed hotel, situated near the beach with delightful views of Criccieth Castle and the scenic coastline. Comfortable furnished, non-smoking bedrooms have colour TV and tea/coffee facilities. An ideal base for touring Snowdonia and the Llŷn Peninsula. Private car parking. AA/RAC ♦♦♦♦.

Months open 3-10; B&B p/p £21.00-£25.00.
🛏10 ⇌10 🐾 C 🍷⚡♨❋ P12 🛈

BRYNCELYN FARM
Cwm Cywarch, *DINAS MAWDDWY*,
Machynlleth SY20 9JG
Tel: (01650) 531289

★★★ FARM

GOLD

Beautifully situated in the Cywarch valley at the foot of Aran mountains (3000ft). Spacious en-suite bedrooms from where you will enjoy the views and tranquil peace of Cwm Cywarch. An ideal base for walking, climbing and touring. Warm welcome awaits you.

Months open 1-12; B&B p/p £20.00.
🛏2 ⇌2 🐾 C 🍽♨⚓🌺❋ P

BRYN SION FARM
Cwm Cywarch, *DINAS MAWDDWY*,
Machynlleth SY20 9JG
Tel: (01650) 531251
E-mail: enquiries@brynsion.co.uk
Website: www.brynsion.co.uk

★★★ FARM

Bryn Sion is an attractively decorated old stone farmhouse with oak beams situated in the picturesque Cywarch valley with paths leading from the farmhouse up to the popular Aran mountains (3,000ft). Ideal location for walking, climbing and birdwatching within easy reach of the beach, Snowdonia mountains and Mid Wales. Both en-suite bedrooms are tastefully decorated with colour TV, tea/coffee making facilities, hairdryers and central heating.

Months open 1-12; B&B p/p £18.00-£20.00.
🛏2 ⇌2 🐾 C ♨SP 🎵 P 🛈

DOLSERAU HALL HOTEL

DOLGELLAU LL40 2AG
Tel: (01341) 422522 Fax: (01341) 422400
E-mail: wtb@dhh.co.uk
Website: www.dhh.co.uk

★★★ COUNTRY HOTEL

For 12 years, a haven of peace and tranquility, exclusively for residents, set amidst the most spectacular scenery offering very comfortable accommodation, excellent traditional food and relaxed atmosphere. No wonder 65% of our guests last year had stayed before! Special breaks all year. Christmas and New Year programme. AA 3 Star Rosette.

Months open 1-12; B&B p/p £47.50-£52.50. 2 Nights Break D, B&B p/p £93.00-£120.00. Weekly D, B&B p/p £325.00-£420.00.

VICTORIA INN

LLANBEDR LL45 2LD
Tel: (01341) 241213 Fax: (01341) 241644
E-mail: victoriainn@frederic-robinson.co.uk

★★ INN

Recently refurbished to the highest standard, this cosy inn now offers five en-suite bedrooms tastefully furnished. The Victoria stands in the centre of the village on the banks of the River Artro. Delicious bar meals available. Sky TV in bedrooms. Robinsons traditional draught beers. Mastercard, Visa, Eurocheque, Switch, Delta, accepted.

Months open 1-12; B&B p/p £28.25-£31.50.

ROYAL SHIP HOTEL

Queens Square, *DOLGELLAU* LL40 1AR
Tel: (01341) 422209 Fax: (01341) 421027
E-mail: royalship@frederic-robinson.co.uk

★★ HOTEL

This extensively modernised hotel stands in the centre of Dolgellau with a fine view of Cader Idris. 18 bedrooms en-suite, family rooms available. Sky TV in bedrooms. Full colour brochure on request. AA/RAC ♦♦. Car park. Mastercard, Visa, Eurocheque, Switch, Delta accepted. Robinsons traditional draught beers.

Months open 1-12; B&B p/p £21.00-£36.75. 2 Nights Break D, B&B p/p £67.00-£98.50. Weekly D, B&B p/p £224.00-£297.00.

ROYAL VICTORIA HOTEL

LLANBERIS LL55 4TY
Tel: (01286) 870253 Fax: (01286) 870149
E-mail: info@royalvictoria.fsnet.co.uk
Website: www.royal-victoria-hotel.co.uk

★★★ HOTEL

GOLD

An elegant Victorian Hotel set in 30 acres of gardens at the foot of Snowdon. 111 comfortably appointed bedrooms with full facilities. Two Restaurants serving excellent food, bars and residents' lounge. A peaceful retreat and ideal touring base for North Wales. 'Getaway' Breaks throughout the year. Close to Snowdon Mountain Railway.

Months open 1-12; B&B p/p £25.00-£49.00. 2 Nights Break D, B&B p/p £79.00-£110.00. Weekly D, B&B p/p £276.00.

WALES CYMRU

T W O   H O U R S   A N D   A   M I L L I O N   M I L E S   A W A Y

TYNYCORNEL HOTEL

★★★
HOTEL

GOLD

Talyllyn, *TYWYN* LL36 9AJ
Tel: (01654) 782282 Fax: (01654) 782679
E-mail: tynycornel.co.uk

In an area of outstanding beauty overlooking Talyllyn Lake. Tynycornel Hotel has developed a reputation to match its location with 17 en-suite bedooms. Spectacular views, excellent restaurant, conference and meeting facilities. Relaxed, friendly atmosphere and renowned brown trout fishery.

Months open 1-12; B&B p/p £48.50-£63.50. 2 Nights Break D, B&B p/p £140.00-£170.00. Weekly D, B&B p/p £420.00-£595.00.

🛏17 🛏17 🛉 C 🍽🍷 £ ♿ SP ⌚ 🌲❄P

Bed & Breakfast
£27.50 p.p. is the most you'll pay

BRYNIAU GOLAU

★★★
BED & BREAKFAST

Llangower, *BALA* LL23 7BT
Tel: (01678) 521782 Fax: (01678) 521790
E-mail: emsley@bryniau-golau.fsnet.co.uk
Website: www.bryniau-golau.fsnet.co.uk

Country house with beautiful gardens set on a tranquil hillside in the Snowdonia National Park, overlooking Bala Lake with views of the Arenig mountains and spectacular sunsets. It affords the perfect base for exploring the area and enjoying local sightseeing, hiking and a variety of sporting activities.

Months open 1-12; B&B p/p £22.00-£26.00.

🛏2 🛏2 ♿ SP ⌚❄🍴(CAN) P2 i

ERW FEURIG FARM GUEST HOUSE

★★★
FARM

AWARD

GOLD

***BALA* LL23 7LL**
Tel: (01678) 530262 Fax: (01678) 530262
E-mail: erwfeurig@yahoo.com
Website: www.ukworld.net/erwfeurig

Set on the family farm, with panoramic views, Erw Feurig is ideally situated for activities and attractions. Family, double and twin rooms, some with en-suite shower and toilet. Ground twin room has private facilities. All rooms with tea/coffee tray and colour TV. Hearty breakfasts served in pleasant dining room. Private coarse fishing.

Months open 1-12; Single B&B per night £20.00-£25.00. Double B&B per night £40.00-£44.00.

🛏4 🛏3 C ♿ SP ⌚❄ P7 i

LAST-MINUTE OFFERS

Looking for late availability or last-minute offers? For details of great-value breaks call Central Reservations on freephone 0800 834820 for North Wales, 0800 273747 for Mid Wales or 0800 3289597 for South and West Wales.

PLAS GOWER

★★★★
BED & BREAKFAST

GOLD

Llangower, *BALA* LL23 7BY
Tel: (01678) 520431 Fax: (01678) 520431
E-mail: olwen@plasgower.com
Website: www.plasgower.com

Welcoming Georgian stone house with beautiful views over Bala Lake and surrounding mountains. The lake shore is only two minutes walk away. Peaceful relaxed atmosphere, log fires, lovely garden. Ideal for walking, sailing or exploring the delights of Mid and North Wales. Many eating places in Bala, three miles away.

Months open 1-12; Single B&B per night £20.00-£22.00. Double B&B per night £40.00-£44.00.

🛏2 🛏1 C ♿ SP 🌲❄🏠P4 i

RHYDYDEFAID FARM

★★★
FARM

AWARD

GOLD

Frongoch, *BALA* LL23 7NT
Tel: (01678) 520456 Fax: (01678) 520456
E-mail: olwen@rhydydefaid.freeserve.co.uk
Website: www.bala-wales.com/rhydydefaid

Traditional, Welsh stone-built farmhouse set amidst beautiful countryside, secluded position. Three miles from Bala. Family run mixed farm. Oak beamed lounge with woodburning inglenook fireplace. Comfortable bedrooms, one with exposed beams and trusses. Choice of breakfast. Ideal base for touring Snowdonia National Park, and Mid Wales. Near National White Water Centre. Brochure available.

Months open 1-12; Single B&B per night £20.00. Double B&B per night £38.00-£40.00.

🛏3 🛏3 🛉 C ♿ 🌲❄ P3 i

TREM-Y-WAWR

★★
BED & BREAKFAST

GOLD

Cae Groes, *BALA* LL23 7AQ
Tel: (01678) 520994

Private house, elevated position in countryside with a view of Bala town and lake. Five minutes walk to leisure centre, lake, town and restaurants, modern rooms with central heating, radio/alarms, TV, tea and coffee tray. Lovely garden. Ideal centre for touring. A range of outdoor activities including water sports nearby. Lockable garage for cycles. Full Welsh breakfast.

Months open 1-12; B&B p/p £20.00-£24.00.

🛏3 🛏1 ♿ SP ⌚❄ TW P4 i

Llyn Tegid, Bala, is a popular sailing centre

NANT-Y-FEDW
★★★★ BED & BREAKFAST

Tre Felin, Llandegai, *BANGOR* LL57 4LH
Tel: (01248) 351683
E-mail: davies19@supanet.com

Delightful 150 year old cottage situated in countryside near Penrhyn Castle between Snowdonia and the sea. It has a wealth of charms, enhanced by original beams, open fires, antique furnishings and a restful sitting room for guests. All rooms have tea and coffee facilities, radio alarm clocks, hairdryers, colour TV, door and room keys. AA♦♦♦♦. Grade II listed building.

Months open 1-12; Single B&B per night £23.00-£25.00. Double B&B per night £38.00-£40.00.

YR-ELEN
★★ BED & BREAKFAST

Bryn, Llandegai, *BANGOR* LL57 4LD
Tel: (01248) 364591 Fax: (01248) 362666

Established 1960. Family bungalow. Ground floor bedrooms, washbasins, tea/coffee, TV, hairdryers. Adjacent private bathroom. Panoramic views - Snowdonia, mountains, countryside and sea. Central for Snowdon, beaches, Anglesey, country-mountain walks, National Trust properties, Irish crossings. Keys. Full Welsh breakfast. Vegetarians catered for. On A5122, 1/2 mile from A5/A55 main interchange. Safe parking. Croeso - Welcome.

Months open 3-11; Double B&B per night £30.00-£32.00.

PORTH MYNACH
★★ BED & BREAKFAST

Llanaber Rd, *BARMOUTH* LL42 1YG
Tel: (01341) 280943 Fax: (01341) 280943

Months open 1-12; B&B p/p £15.00-£17.50.

WAVECREST HOTEL
★★★ HOTEL

8 Marine Parade, *BARMOUTH* LL42 1NA
Tel: (01341) 280330 Fax: (01341) 280330
E-mail: thewavecrest@talk21.com
Website: www.lokalink.co.uk/wavecrest-html

Months open 4-10; B&B p/p £20.00-£27.00. 2 Nights Break D, B&B p/p £68.00-£80.00. Weekly D, B&B p/p £240.00-£275.00.

PLAS TAN Y GRAIG GUEST HOUSE
★ GUEST HOUSE

BEDDGELERT LL55 4LT
Tel: (01766) 890310 Fax: (01766) 890629
E-mail: ay.b@virgin.net
Website: www.plastanygraig.co.uk

A warm welcome awaits you at our licensed Guest House in the centre of this award-winning village. Our large bedrooms are great for families and groups. Some are en-suite. Enjoy breakfast/snacks/drinks on our sunny terrace overlooking the river. Evening meals/packed lunches available. Vegetarians welcome.

Months open 1-12; B&B p/p £18.50-£25.00.

PRICES

In this publication we go to great lengths to make sure that you have a clear, accurate idea of prices and facilities. It's all spelled out in the 'Prices' section – and remember to confirm everything when making your booking.

BRON CELYN GUEST HOUSE
★★★ GUEST HOUSE

Lôn Muriau, Llanrwst Rd, *BETWS-Y-COED*
LL24 0HD Tel: (01690) 710333 Fax: (01690) 710111
E-mail: broncelyn@betws-y-coed.co.uk
Website: www.betws-y-coed.co.uk/broncelyn/

GOLD

Months open 1-12; Single B&B per night £20.00-£26.00. Double B&B per night £40.00-£52.00.

BRYN LLEWELYN NON SMOKERS GUEST HOUSE
★★ BED & BREAKFAST

Holyhead Rd, *BETWS-Y-COED* LL24 0BN
Tel: (01690) 710601 Fax: (01690) 710601
Website: www.bangor-uk.com/llewelyn

GOLD

Months open 1-12; B&B p/p £16.50-£27.50.

CWMANOG ISAF FARM
★★★ FARM

BETWS-Y-COED LL24 0SL
Tel: (01690) 710225 Mobile: 07808 421634
E-mail: h.m.hughes.@amserve.net

Peace and tranquility awaits in this homely Welsh farmhouse situated on a small working farm just 1 mile from Betws-y-Coed. Ideal centre for a short break or holiday, walking, sightseeing or simply getting away in the wilds of North Wales. Hearty farmhouse cuisine, vegetarian dishes available. Log fire to relax by on winter evenings.

Months open 1-12; Single B&B per night £23.00-£24.00. Double B&B per night £37.00-£38.00.

FAIRY GLEN HOTEL
★★ HOTEL

Beaver Bridge, *BETWS-Y-COED* LL24 0SH
Tel: (01690) 710269 Fax: (01690) 710269
E-mail: fairyglenhotel@amserve.net

GOLD

A warm, friendly welcome awaits you, at our 17th century family-run hotel, overlooking the River Conwy and close to the famous fairy glen beauty spot. Centrally heated en-suite bedrooms, radio, colour TV, beverage tray, hairdryer. Freshly prepared home-cooked food. Private parking. Residential licensed bar.

Months open 2-10; B&B p/p £21.00-£24.00. 2 Nights Break D, B&B p/p £63.00-£73.00. Weekly D, B&B p/p £222.00-£240.00.

FFERM MAES GWYN
★★★ FARM

Maesgwyn, Pentrefoelas, *BETWS-Y-COED*
LL24 0LR Tel: (01690) 770668

Months open 4-10; Single B&B per night £17.00-£18.00. Double B&B per night £35.00-£36.00.

FRON HEULOG COUNTRY HOUSE
★★★ COUNTRY HOUSE AWARD

BETWS-Y-COED LL24 0BL
Tel: (01690) 710736 Fax: (01690) 710920
E-mail: jean&peter@fronheulog.co.uk
Website: www.fronheulog.co.uk

GOLD

"The country house in the village!" Jean and Peter Whittingham welcome you. Elegant Victorian stone-built home, south-facing in peaceful wooded riverside scenery. Excellent modern accommodation - comfort, warmth, style. Ideal Snowdonia location - tour, walk, relax. Enjoy hosts' personal hospitality, local knowledge and good food! In "Which?". From A5 road, over B5106 bridge, immediately left, 150 yards ahead - welcome!

Months open 1-12; Double B&B per night £40.00-£55.00. Holiday breaks to meet guests' wishes. Please enquire.

Llyn Dinas, Snowdonia

MAIRLYS GUEST HOUSE
★★★
GUEST HOUSE

Holyhead Rd, *BETWS-Y-COED* LL24 0AN
Tel: (01690) 710190 Fax: (01690) 710190
Website: www.betws-y-coed.co.uk/accommodation/mairlys/

Months open 3-11; Single B&B per night £21.00-£24.00. Double B&B per night £42.00-£48.00.

RIVERSIDE GUEST HOUSE RESTAURANT
★★★
RESTAURANT
WITH ROOMS

Holyhead Rd, *BETWS-Y-COED* LL24 0BN
Tel: (01690) 710650 Fax: (01690) 710650
E-mail: riverside4u@talk21.com
Website: www.betwsycoed.net/riverside

Located in the centre of the village. Lovely rooms and a superb restaurant offering local produce with a gourmet twist. Ideal base for Snowdonia. Situated on the A5 running through the village to the west of the Pont y Pair Bridge.

Months open 1-12; Single B&B per night £18.00-£20.00. Double B&B per night £32.00-£42.00.

HAFOTY
★★★★
FARM

Rhostryfan, *CAERNARFON* LL54 7PH
Tel: (01286) 830144 Fax: (01286) 830441
Website: www.accomodata.co.uk/310898.htm

Set on the edge of Snowdonia, Hafoty enjoys magnificent vista of Caernarfon Castle, Menai Strait and Isle of Anglesey. Tastefully decorated en-suite bedooms, separate lounge with beamed ceiling and inglenook fireplace. WTB elected this farmhouse "The Best in Wales" for comfort, quality and true Welsh welcome.Self-catering barns available.

Months open 2-10; Double B&B per night £48.00-£52.00.

HILLCROFT
★★
BED & BREAKFAST

St David's Rd, *CAERNARFON* LL55 1EL
Tel: (01286) 674489

Months open 1-12; B&B p/p £18.00-£20.00.

LLEUAR FAWR
★★★
FARM
GOLD

Lleuar Fawr, Penygroes,
***CAERNARFON* LL54 6PB**
Tel: (01286) 660268 Fax: (01286) 660268

17th Century listed farmhouse set in peaceful location. Central for exploring mountains of Snowdonia, Llŷn Peninsula, Isle of Anglesey and the historic town of Caernarfon. Farm noted for bird and wild life, salmon and trout fishing. Two spacious en-suite bedrooms with colour TV, tea making facilities. Childen at reduced rates. Warm Welsh welcome awaits you.

Months open 1-11; Single B&B per night £25.00. Double B&B per night £36.00-£40.00.

MENAI VIEW GUEST HOUSE & RESTAURANT
★★★
GUEST HOUSE
AWARD
GOLD

North Rd, *CAERNARFON* LL55 1BD
Tel: (01286) 674602 Fax: (01286) 674602
Website: www.smoothhound.co.uk/hotels/menaivie.html

Warm welcome. Attractive guest house overlooking strait. Close to town centre, castle and harbour. Many rooms with sea view. Premier room has 'spa bath' and sea view. Ground floor en-suite available. Lounge bar and restaurant with views. Home cooking, reasonably priced. Small Groups welcome. All major credit cards. Ask about 'winter breaks'.

Months open 1-12; Single B&B per night from £22.50. Double B&B per night £35.00-£50.00.

PENGWERN
★★★★
FARM
AWARD
GOLD

Saron, Llanwnda, *CAERNARFON* LL54 5UH
Tel: (01286) 831500 Fax: (01286) 830741
E-mail: pengwern@talk21.com
Website: www.smoothhound.co.uk/hotels/penwern.htm

Charming spacious farmhouse of character situated between mountains and sea with unobstructed views of Snowdonia. Well appointed bedrooms all en-suite. Land runs down to Fory Bay, noted for its bird life. Jane Rowlands has a cookery diploma and povides all the excellent meals with farm house fresh food, including home produced beef and lamb. Excellent access.

Months open 2-11; Double B&B per night £55.00.

CLASSIFIED ADVERTISING *There's more accommodation to choose from in the classified advertising section of this book. Please see the listing at the end of the 12 Areas display adverts.*

SNOWDONIA MOUNTAINS & COAST

PRINCE OF WALES HOTEL
Bangor St, *CAERNARFON* LL55 1AR
Tel: (01286) 673367 Fax: (01286) 676610
E-mail: princeofwaleshotel@gofornet.co.uk

HOTEL ★★ SILVER

Months open 1-12; Single B&B per night £19.00-£27.50. Double B&B per night £38.00-£55.00.

THE WHITE HOUSE
Llanfaglan, *CAERNARFON* LL54 5RA
Tel: (01286) 673003
E-mail: rwbayles@sjms.co.uk

BED & BREAKFAST ★★★

Large quietly situated country house in own grounds with magnificent views to sea and mountains. All rooms have en-suite or private facilities, colour TV, tea/coffee makers. One bedroom on ground floor. Guests are welcome to use outdoor pool and gardens in summer. Ideal for ornithologists, walkers, golf, visiting Welsh castles and Snowdonia National Park.

Months open 3-11; Single B&B per night £23.50-£25.50.

TYN LLWYN COTTAGE
Llanllyfni, *CAERNARFON* LL54 6RP
Tel: (01286) 881526

BED & BREAKFAST ★★★

Situated on a quiet country road, half a mile off the A487 Caernarfon to Porthmadog Road. Beautiful Welsh stone cottage with exposed beams and attractive garden, ideal for walking, castles, beach. One en-suite is on ground floor, the third bedroom has its own private bathroom. All rooms have colour TV and tea making facilities.

Months open 3-10; Double B&B per night £44.00-£46.00.

FISHERMORE
Llanrwst Rd, *CONWY* LL32 8HP
Tel: (01492) 592891
E-mail: dyers@tesco.net
Website: www.northwalesbandb.co.uk

BED & BREAKFAST ★★★

Months open 4-10; B&B p/p £17.00-£19.00.

CRAIG-Y-MÔR GUEST HOUSE
West Parade, *CRICCIETH* LL52 0EN
Tel: (01766) 522830
E-mail: enquiries@craig-y-mor-bandb.freeserve.co.uk

GUEST HOUSE ★★★

Months open 3-10; B&B p/p £20.00-£21.00.

GLYN Y COED HOTEL
Portmadoc Rd, *CRICCIETH* LL52 0HP
Tel: (01766) 522870 Fax: (01766) 523341

HOTEL ★★ GOLD

Beautiful Victorian house overlooking sea, mountains, castles and near Portmeirion. Cosy bar. Highly recommended home cooking catering for most diets. En-suite bedrooms, one on ground floor. Private parking. Senior rates. AA/RAC Les Routiers Michelin recommended. Most credit cards accepted. Excellent value in superior accommodation ensures perfect holiday. Brochure issued with pleasure.

Months open 1-12; B&B p/p £21.00-£27.50. 2 Nights Break D, B&B p/p £62.00-£76.00. Weekly D, B&B p/p £205.00-£250.00.

MIN Y GAER HOTEL
Porthmadog Rd, *CRICCIETH* LL52 0HP
Tel: (01766) 522151 Fax: (01766) 523540
E-mail: info@minygaerhotel.co.uk
Website: www.minygaerhotel.co.uk

HOTEL ★★ BRONZE

A pleasant, licensed hotel, situated near the beach with delightful views of Criccieth Castle and the scenic Cardigan Bay coastline. The comfortably furnished, non-smoking bedrooms are equipped with colour TV and tea/coffee making facilities. An ideal base for touring Snowdonia and the Llyn Peninsula. Private car parking on the premises. AA/RAC ♦♦♦♦.

Months open 3-10; Single B&B per night £21.00-£25.00. Double B&B per night £42.00-£50.00.

SEASPRAY GUEST HOUSE
4 Marine Terrace, *CRICCIETH* LL52 0EF
Tel: (01766) 522373

GUEST HOUSE ★★

Months open 1-11; B&B p/p £17.50-£19.50. 2 Nights Break D, B&B p/p £50.00-£54.00. Weekly D, B&B p/p £175.00-£189.00.

BRYN SION FARM
Cwm Cywarch, *DINAS MAWDDWY*, Machynlleth SY20 9JG Tel: (01650) 531251
E-mail: enquiries@brynsion.co.uk Website: www.brynsion.co.uk

FARM ★★★

Bryn Sion is an attractively decorated old stone farmhouse with oak beams situated in the picturesque Cywarch valley with paths leading from the farmhouse up to the popular Aran mountains (3,000ft). Ideal location for walking, climbing and birdwatching within easy reach of the beach, Snowdonia mountains and Mid Wales. Both en-suite bedrooms are tastefully decorated with colour TV, tea/coffee making facilities, hairdryers and central heating.

Months open 1-12; Twin B&B per night £36.00-£40.00. Double B&B per night £36.00-£40.00.

RED LION HOTEL/GWESTY'R LLEW COCH
***DINAS MAWDDWY*, nr Machynlleth SY20 9JA**
Tel: (01650) 531247 Fax: (01650) 531247
E-mail: llewcoch@yahoo.com
Website: www.llewcoch.freeserve.co.uk

INN ★

Months open 1-12; Single B&B per night £20.00-£25.00. Double B&B per night £40.00-£50.00.

Mountain road above Dinas Mawddwy

The mountains above Llanberis

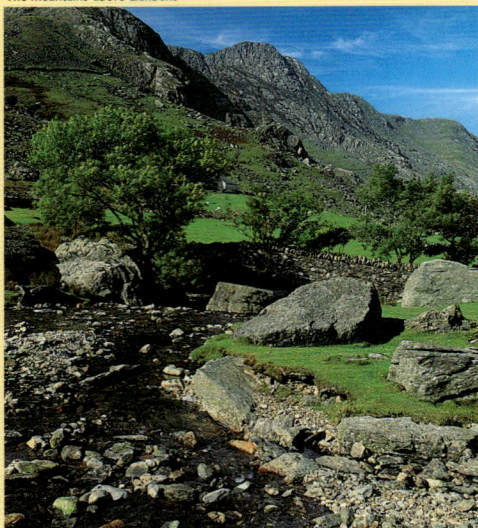

TREM IDRIS
★★ BED & BREAKFAST

Llanelltyd, *DOLGELLAU* LL40 2TB
Tel: (01341) 423776

Situated in an elevated position overlooking the outstanding beautiful Mawddach Estuary, with extensive panoramic views of Cader Idris Mountains. One standard, two en-suite rooms, one ground floor. All rooms with colour TV and tea/coffee facilities. Renowned for scenic walks. Ideally situated for exploring Snowdonia. Seven miles from the coast. Homely, relaxed atmosphere. Non-smokers please.

Months open 1-12; B&B p/p £18.00-£22.00.

Y GOEDLAN
★★★ BED & BREAKFAST

Brihdir, *DOLGELLAU* LL40 2RN
Tel: (01341) 423131 Fax: (01341) 423131

This old vicarage offers peaceful accommodation in pleasant rural surroundings. Ideally placed on B4416 road for walks, sea, mountains and touring. Spacious double, twin and family rooms, all with hot and cold, colour TV, central heating, tea/coffee facilities. Bathroom with shower, two conveniences, lounge. Comfort with homely atmosphere. Hearty breakfast. Reduction for children. Dolgellau two miles.

Months open 2-11; Single B&B per night £18.00-£18.50. Double B&B per night £33.00-£34.00.

HILLCREST GUEST HOUSE
★★★ BED & BREAKFAST **GOLD**

Hillcrest, Pant Llwyd, Bala Rd,
FFESTINIOG LL41 4PW
Tel: (01766) 762787 Fax: (01766) 762787
E-mail: hillcrestjen@talk21.com

A rural setting with a backdrop of mountains, centrally located in an area steeped in history and culture. Excellent accommodation with unrivalled panoramic views from all rooms. Landscaped garden, good food and a haven for relaxation, walking or sight-seeing. A warm welcome guaranteed.

Months open 1-12; Single B&B per night £20.00. Double B&B per night £40.00.

AROSFYR
★★ FARM

Penycefn Rd, *DOLGELLAU* LL40 2YP
Tel: (01341) 422355

Months open 1-12; B&B p/p £15.00-£17.50. Weekly B&B p/p £100.00-£105.00.

DWY OLWYN
★★★ GUEST HOUSE

Coed-y-Fronallt, *DOLGELLAU* LL40 2YG
Tel: (01341) 422822
Website: www.croeso-lynnes-wales.co.uk/acc/dwyolwyn

Situated in an acre of landscaped gardens boasting magnificent views in a peaceful position yet only 8 minutes walk to the town within the Snowdonia National Park. Close to all amenities and numerous walks. Good home cooking (dinner optional) cleanliness and personal attention assured. Ample parking. TV and tea/coffee facilities in all bedrooms. Guest lounge.

Months open 2-12; Single B&B per night £20.00-£22.00.

GLANYGORS
★★★ GUEST HOUSE

Llandanwg, *HARLECH* LL46 2SD
Tel: (01341) 241410

Small friendly guest house near to beach. Beautiful views of mountains. Central location for Snowdonia National Park. Near to train station. Birdwatching; sailing; hill walking and riding all in the area. Presenting good home cooking in a homely and relaxed atmosphere. Central heating and electric blanket for winter months. Open all year. Warm Welsh welcome.

Months open 1-12; Single B&B per night £18.00. Double B&B per night £32.00-£34.00.

TANYFRON
★★★★ BED & BREAKFAST

Arran Rd, *DOLGELLAU* LL40 2AA
Tel: (01341) 422638 Fax: (01341) 421251
E-mail: rowlands@tanyfron.freeserve.co.uk

A warm welcome awaits you in our comfortable, quiet, modernised, 100 year old stone former farmhouse. Half a mile from Dolgellau. Tastefully furnished with matching decor. All rooms have a fridge, hairdryer, heating, clock radio and colour TV. Laundry and telephone for guests' use. Winners of Wales in Bloom 2000.

Months open 2-11; Double B&B per night £40.00-£48.00.

MARTEG
★★★ BED & BREAKFAST **GOLD**

High St, *LLANBERIS* LL55 4HA
Tel: (01286) 870207
E-mail: carol@marteg.freeserve.co.uk

Months open 2-12; Double B&B per night £40.00-£48.00.

SNOWDONIA MOUNTAINS & COAST

PENDRE GUEST HOUSE

★★ GUEST HOUSE

Maengwyn St, *MACHYNLLETH* SY20 8EF
Tel: (01654) 702088

Looking for somewhere to stay within Machynlleth? Pendre is a Georgian style house with en-suite facilities. Ideal base for touring Mid Wales. Homely atmosphere. Plenty to do: golf, walking and fishing. Convenient for Centre for Alternative Technology, Celtica Railway station. Beautiful coast nearby.

Months open 1-12; Single B&B per night £19.00.
Double B&B per night £42.00.

TY NEWYDD

★★ BED & BREAKFAST

30 Dublin St, Tremadog, *PORTHMADOG*
LL49 9RH Tel: (01766) 512553
E-mail: johnjulieo@aol.com
Website: www.porthmadog.co.uk/tynewydd

A small friendly family run B&B in the small village of Tremadog. Just 1 mile from Porthmadog and easy access to all the major attractions in the area by train, road or bus. Colour TVs in all rooms. Good home cooked breakfast to start your day.

Months open 1-12; B&B p/p £18.50-£21.00.

YOKE HOUSE FARM

★★★ FARM

***PWLLHELI* LL53 5TY Tel: (01758) 612621**
E-mail: annwen@iocws.freeserve.co.uk
Website: www.yokehouse.co.uk

A beautifully wooded drive welcomes you to this Georgian farmhouse on a 290 acre working farm where guests are invited to watch the milking, calf feeding etc. Tastefully furnished, the accommodation consists of one double and one twin bedded room all with wash-hand basins, shaver points and welcome tray. Exciting nature trail open to guests.

Months open 3-11; Double B&B per night £40.00-£44.00.

CYNFAL FARM

★★★★ FARM
SILVER

Bryncrug, *TYWYN* LL36 9RB
Tel: (01654) 711703 Fax: (01654) 711703
E-mail: cynfalfrm@aol.com
Website: www.gwynedd.net/croeso.cader.idris

Mixed working farm, magnificently situated with panoramic views of mountains and sea. The Tal-y-Llyn narrow gauge railway runs 150 yards below the house with own halt. Spacious bedrooms tastefully decorated; two doubles, en-suite and one twin with private facilities - beverage tray and TV's. Numerous places for good evening meals. Only two miles from beach. Brochure available from Mrs Carys Evans.

Months open 4-10; Single B&B per night £25.00. Double B&B per night £38.00-£44.00.

EISTEDDFA

★★★ FARM

Abergynolwyn, *TYWYN* LL36 9UP
Tel: (01654) 782385 Fax: (01654) 782228

Eisteddfa is a newly built bungalow in the picturesque Dolgoch Valley, overlooking the Tal-y-llyn narrow gauge railway which runs through our land. En-suite bedrooms with tea/coffee and TV. One room suitable for disabled. Log fires when cold and wet. Within easy reach of beach and mountain. Come and enjoy farm life. AA♦♦♦♦ Enquiries to Gweniona Pugh.

Months open 3-10; Single B&B per night £20.00-£25.00. Double B&B per night £40.00-£48.00.

Holiday Cottages

ABERDOVEY HOLIDAYS LIMITED

★★★★
GOLD

13 Glan Dovey Terrace, *ABERDOVEY* LL35 0EB
Tel: (01654) 767418 Fax: (01654) 767078
E-mail: aberdovey-holidays@msn.com
Website: aberdovey-holidays.com Enquiries: David & Hilary Inman, Hafod, Sea Front, Aberdovey LL35 0EB

Handsome, well equipped, apartments created within four 19th Century Sea Captains' Houses. Spectacular sea and mountain views. 45 paces from golden sands, perfect for families and couples. 85% of guests return year after year. Freephone brochure: 0800 212305.

Months open 1-12; Weekly/unit £157.00-£550.00.
UNITS 13 SLEEPS 1-8

CELTIC HOUSE

★★★★
GOLD

Sea View Terrace, *ABERDYFI/ABERDOVEY* LL35 0LL
Tel: (01654) 767274 Fax: (01654) 767506
E-mail: jreynolds@celtichouse.f9.co.uk
Website: celtichouse.f9.co.uk

Months open 1-12; 3 Nights £150.00-£290.00.
Weekly/unit £250.00-£550.00. UNITS 1 SLEEPS 1-10

TAI GWYLIAU TY'N DON S/C ACCOMMODATION

★★★ UP TO **★★★★**
GOLD

Llanengan, *ABERSOCH*, Pwllheli
LL53 7LG Tel: (01286) 831184
Enquiries: Mrs Elisabeth Evans, Penlan,
Rhos Isaf, Caernarfon LL54 7NG

Months open 2-11; 2 Nights £70.00. 3 Nights £80.00.
4 Nights £90.00. Weekly/unit £119.00-£430.00.
UNITS 10 SLEEPS 2-7

HEN HAFOD / FEDW'R GOG
NR *BALA* / NR MAERDY

★★★★

Enquiries: G. Owen, Penisarmynydd, Maerdy,
Corwen LL21 0NP Tel: (01490) 460448

These are ideal, peaceful private location for the country lover. The properties are surrounded by beautiful countryside with a wealth of wildlife. Idyllic, stone built cottages of charm and character, exposed beams, inglenook fireplace. Situated within the Snowdonia National Park near the market town of Bala.

Months open 1-12; 2 Nights £40.00-£60.00. 3 Nights £50.00-£180.00.
4 Nights £100.00-£200.00. Weekly/unit £90.00-£300.00.
UNITS 3 SLEEPS 2-7

Y BWTHYN

★★★

C/o Tŷ Capel, Llwyn Einion, *BALA* LL23 7PN
Tel: (01678) 520572 Fax: (01678) 520572
Enquiries: Mrs B. Davies

Months open 4-10; 2 Weekly/unit £105.00-£115.00.
UNITS 1 SLEEPS 4

Barmouth

COEDMOR COTTAGE ★★★★
Coedmor, Caerdeon, *BARMOUTH* LL42 1TL
Tel: (01341) 430332

Months open 1-12; 3 Nights £100.00. Weekly/unit £150.00-£250.00.
UNITS 1 SLEEPS 3

TALARFOR ★★★★
Llanaber, *BARMOUTH* LL42 1BQ
Tel: (01341) 280069

Months open 1-12; 3 Nights £50.00. Weekly/unit £120.00-£340.00.
UNITS 1 SLEEPS 5+

TŶ GLAN-YR-AFON ★★★★★
Bontddu, *BARMOUTH* LL40 2UR
Tel: (01341) 242626 Fax: (01341) 242626
E-mail: rowenpark@breathemail.net
Enquiries: Rowen C.P., Talybont,
Barmouth, LL43 2AD

BRONZE

Luxury farmhouse, one mile from Bontddu, in a quiet, peaceful setting overlooking two mountain streams. Completely renovated and refurbished to a very high standard, three bedrooms, two bathrooms, inglenook with woodburner in lounge. Kitchen - dishwasher, microwave, washing machine, tumble dryer. Central heating. All linen, electricity, fuel included.

Months open 1-12; Weekly/unit £365.00-£625.00.
UNITS 1 SLEEPS 1-6

BEACH BUNGALOW ★★★★★
The Beach, Pontllyfni, *CAERNARFON* LL54 5ET
Tel: (01286) 660400

BRONZE

Quiet secluded cove, your own beach, moments from your patio door. Split level lounge-diningroom. Every comfort. 1 to 4 bedrooms. 2 bathrooms, text TV, video, CD music, dishwasher, phone, washer, T dryer. C heating, electric blankets. Boating, bathing, fishing, walk on flat coastal strip. Golf. Nearby shops, restaurants, barsnacks. Tour Snowdonia. View anytime featured by BBC. Try £49 minibreak. Brochure

Months open 1-12; 2 Nights £49.00-£199.00. 3 Nights £59.00-£299.00.
4 Nights £69.00-£399.00. Weekly/unit £79.00-£599.00.
UNITS 1 SLEEPS 8

BEACH VILLA CHALET ★★★
HOLIDAY PARK
West Point, The Beach, Pontllyfni,
***CAERNARFON* LL54 5ET**
Tel: (01286) 660400

BRONZE

Our world by the sea, area of outstanding natural beauty. Detached villa chalets overlooking lawn, beach and sea. Every comfort. Lounge suite, dinette, 2 or 3 bedrooms, bathroom, text TV, microwave, electric blankets, free electric. Central heating. Nearby restaurants, barsnacks. Lots of nice beaches. Adjacent parking. Featured by BBC. View anytime. Try £25 minibreak. Brochure. Also for sale.

Months open 3-10; Weekly/unit (Static) £99.00-£439.00.
No. ON PARK 50 20

BRYN BRAS CASTLE ★★★★★

Llanrug, nr *CAERNARFON* LL55 4RE
Tel: (01286) 870210 Fax: (01286) 870210
E-mail: holidays@brynbrascastle.co.uk
Website: www.brynbrascastle.co.uk

GOLD

Romantic Regency castle centrally situated enjoying N.Wales' mountains, beaches, heritage, restaurants. Selection of beautifully appointed, warm spacious apartments each with distinctive character. Generously enhanced from dishwasher to flowers. Inclusive c.heating. h.water, linen. All highest grade. 32 acres gardens, woodlands, panoramic hillwalk views sea, Anglesey, Snowdon. Privacy, comfort, spaciousness for relaxing in tranquility - ideal for couples.No young children. Short breaks all year. Flexible start/depart days.

Months open 1-12; Weekly/unit £350.00-£620.00.
UNITS 7 SLEEPS 2-4

BRYN GWYN ★★★★

Waunfawr, *CAERNARFON* LL55 4SD
Tel: (01286) 650549
Enquiries: Mrs G. Pierce

Months open 4-10; Weekly/unit £175.00-£300.00.
UNITS 1 SLEEPS 5

TŶ LOWRI ★★★★

13 Menai St, Y Felinheli, *CAERNARFON* LL56 4HX
Tel: (029) 2025 1152 Fax: (07713) 655925
E-mail: huw@jeli-weli.co.uk
Enquiries: 9 Victoria Park Rd West, Caerdydd CF5 1EZ

Months open 1-12; 2 Nights £100.00-£180.00. 3 Nights £120.00-£200.00. 4 Nights £120.00-£250.00. Weekly/unit £180.00-£300.00.
UNITS 1 SLEEPS 5+

TYN Y FFYNNON ★★★★

Nant Peris, *CAERNARFON* LL55 4UH
Tel: (01286) 871723
Enquiries: Mrs S. Kelly

Months open 1-12; 2 Short Breaks £180.00-£280.00. Weekly/unit £325.00-£695.00.
UNITS 1 SLEEPS 2-12

TY'N YR ONNEN MOUNTAIN FARM HOLIDAY PARK ★★

Waunfawr, *CAERNARFON* LL55 4AX
Tel: (01286) 650281 Fax: (01286) 650043
E-mail: tyn-y-onnen@gwynedd.net
Website: www.gwynedd.net/caernarfon/tyn-yr-onnen

A warm welcome to a traditional hill farm, secluded and off the beaten track. Panoramic beauty of Snowdonia, nature trails, walks, friendly animals to cuddle. Ideal touring base camp. Guaranteed clean facilities. WH Railway 5 mins. Caravan woodcabin chalet. Tastefully equipped with mountain views. Brochure on receiving Fax or SAE.

Months open 1-12; Weekly/unit £150.00-£350.00. Short Breaks available.
UNITS 4 SLEEPS 6+

CEFN COED ★★★ UP TO ★★★★

Lon Goed, *CHWILOG* LL53 6NX
Tel: (01766) 810259
Enquiries: Mr & Mrs Hebert

Months open 1-12; 2 Nights £100.00-£125.00. 3 Nights £150.00-£175.00. 4 Nights £200.00-£225.00. Weekly/unit £180.00-£520.00.
UNITS 2 SLEEPS 6&7 (FR)

MUR-CLWT-LLOER ★★★★

CHWILOG, Pwllheli LL53 6NQ
Tel: (01766) 810236
E-mail: mur@talk21.com
Enquiries: Mrs Sian T. Hughes

Peace and quiet in a self contained 2 bedroomed luxury farmhouse. Allowing freedom of self-catering, it is clean, comfortable and carpeted throughout. There is a spacious garden and panoramic views of Cardigan Bay and Snowdonia mountain range. Situated off main Pwllheli/Criccieth Road. Brochure for further details.

Months open 1-12; 2 Nights £30.00. 3 Nights £40.00. 4 Nights £50.00. Weekly/unit £100.00-£375.00.
UNITS 1 SLEEPS 4

YSGUBOR WEN ★★★★

Ysgubor Wen, Bryn Garrog, Eglwysbach, *COLWYN BAY* LL28 5TY
Tel: (01492) 650549
E-mail: bryngarrog@aol.com

Welsh barn tastefully converted. Warm and with all modern conveniences. Central village location. Well placed for beaches, walking, Snowdonia, National Trust venues and local towns.

Months open 1-12; 2, 3 or 4 nights £80.00-£196.50. Weekly/unit £120.00-£295.00.
UNITS 1 SLEEPS 4+ (FR)

ENFYS ★★★

13 Marine Terrace, *CRICCIETH* LL52 0EF
Tel: (01766) 522655
E-mail: walkerjones@lineone.net
Website: www.lineone.net/walkerjones

Two self-contained flats with uninterrupted views across Tremadog Bay leading to Cardigan Bay. Flats are en-suite with fully equipped kitchens and are comfortably furnished. Perfect location for Snowdonia and Llŷn Peninsula. Flatlet also available (no sea view). Enquiries to: Linda Walker Jones.

Months open 1-12; Weekly/unit £180.00-£230.00. Short Breaks available.
UNITS 3 SLEEPS 2-4

NANT-Y-FELIN COTTAGES

AWAITING GRADING

GOLD

Nant-y-Felin, Portmadoc Rd, *CRICCIETH* LL52 0HP
Tel: (01766) 522675 Fax: (01766) 522675
Website: www.accommodation.uk.net/nantyfelin.htm
Enquiries: Mrs A. Reynolds

Beautiful Victorian mansion overlooking sea, mountains and castles. Centrally situated for touring Snowdonia and Portmeirion. House and cottages are set in landscaped gardens, one minute to beach, shops, pub, trains, buses. Sleeping 2-10 with private parking. En-suite bedroom. Linen supplied. Brochure with pleasure send to Mrs Reynolds, Nant-y-Felin 01766-522675.

Months open 1-12; 3 Nights £90.00-£500.00. 4 Nights £120.00-£600.00. Weekly/unit £100.00-£950.00.

UNITS 3 SLEEPS 2-10

TYDDYN FELIN

AWAITING GRADING

Ynys, *CRICCIETH* LL52 0PA
Tel: (01766) 530659/810994 Fax: (01766) 530659
E-mail: MeganJones@gwynedd.gov.uk

Working farm in peaceful setting on the edge of Snowdonia National Park. Convenient for mountains, sandy beaches, popular tourist attractions. Spacious self-contained wing. 4 bedrooms, bathroom, separate shower, extra toilet. Lounge (CTV/video) d/room (CTV), kitchen (d/washer, w/machine, fridge-freezer, microwave). Fishing, rough shooting. Garden furniture, barbeque. Ideal for two families.

Months open 1-12; 2 Nights £90.00-£120.00. 3 Nights £150.00-£180.00. 4 Nights £160.00-£220.00. Weekly/unit £180.00-£390.00.

UNITS 1 SLEEPS 9

WINDSOR HOUSE

★★ UP TO ★★★

12 Marine Terrace, *CRICCIETH* LL52 0EF
Tel: (01766) 522856
E-mail: gweigh3526@aol.com

Months open 1-12; 2 Nights £70.00. 3 Nights £105.00. 4 Nights £140.00. Weekly/unit £120.00-£230.00.

UNITS 3 SLEEPS 4-5

AROSFYR

★★★ UP TO ★★★★

Penycefn Rd, *DOLGELLAU* LL40 2YP
Tel: (01341) 422355
Enquiries: Mrs C.E. Skeel Jones

Months open 1-12; 2 Nights £50.00-£70.00. 3 Nights £75.00-£105.00. 4 Nights £100.00-£140.00. Weekly/unit £100.00-£325.00.

UNITS 3 SLEEPS 2-5

HENDRE GEFEILLIAID

★★★★

Hendre Gefeilliaid, Tabor, *DOLGELLAU* LL40 2RE
Tel: (01341) 423042 Fax: (01341) 423042
Website: www.northwalescottage.co.uk
Enquiries: Mrs M. Lees

Months open 1-12; 2 Nights £50.00-£100.00. 3 Nights £75.00-£150.00. 4 Nights £100.00-£200.00. Weekly/unit £150.00-£350.00.

UNITS 1 SLEEPS 4-5

PENMAENUCHA FARM

★★★★

GOLD

Penmaenpool, *DOLGELLAU* LL40 1YD
Tel: (01341) 423937
Enquiries: Mr & Mrs Owen

Properties situated overlooking the beautiful Mawddach estuary and mountains beyond, on a 600 acre sheep and beef farm extending up to the foothills of Cader Idris. Walking distance to George III hotel and RSPB lookout and reserve. Golden sandy beaches, pony trekking, golf, fishing and mountain biking locally.

Months open 1-12; 2 Nights £60.00-£90.00. 3 Nights £80.00-£110.00. 4 Nights £100.00-£140.00. Weekly/unit £160.00-£420.00.

UNITS 4 SLEEPS 4-6

The Coed y Brenin Forest has many recreational facilities

MELIN LLECHEIDDIOR ★★★★
GARNDOLBENMAEN LL51 9EZ
Tel: (01766) 530635 Fax: (01766) 530635

Situated near the river Dwyfach within easy reach of sea and mountains. One double room, one twin bedded room, sun lounge, bathroom, lounge with colour TV, kitchen fully equipped and microwave. Children welcome. Cot and high chair available. Pets welcome on request. Leisure centre and riding stables nearby.

Months open 1-12; Weekly/unit £125.00-£175.00.
UNITS 1 SLEEPS 4

HEN FFERMDY AWAITING GRADING
Talsarnau, nr **HARLECH** Tel: (01299) 861120
Fax: (01299) 861120 E-mail: enquiries@henffermdy.co.uk
Enquiries: White Lodge, Fenn Green, Alveley, nr Bridgnorth
WV15 6AJ
Peaceful hilltop location to recharge your batteries and soothe your soul. Situated high above the Porthmadog estuary, Hen Ffermdy offers timeless setting with modern comfort. Sleeps ten in bunk beds. Ideal holiday/training/interest groups. Tel/fax 01299-826110 for brochure or e-mail enquiries@henffermdy.co.uk
Months open 1-12; 2 Nights £150.00-£250.00. 3 Nights £175.00-£250.00. 4 Nights £200.00-£300.00. Weekly/unit £300.00-£400.00.
UNITS 1 SLEEPS 10

BODWROG ★★★★
LLANBEDROG, Pwllheli LL53 7RE
Tel: (01758) 740341 Enquiries: Mrs Williams
Farmhouse with superb coastal views. Sandy beach 1½ miles. Three bedrooms. Colour TV, radio, microwave, electric blankets, double-glazing, Children welcome. Free babysitting. Rough shooting, riding, watersports, sporting clays locally. Marina, leisure centre five miles. Spring/Autumn breaks £60-£100. Many returning guests. Croeso.

Months open 4-10; 2 Nights £60.00-£65.00. 3 Nights £75.00-£80.00. 4 Nights £90.00-£100.00. Weekly/unit £160.00-£300.00.
UNITS 1 SLEEPS 5-6

HAULFRYN ★★★
Brynrefail, **LLANBERIS**, Caernarfon LL55 3NR
Enquiries: Mrs Foulkes, 21 Cae'r Garreg,
Caernarfon LL55 3NR

Months open 1-12; Weekly/unit £200.00-£250.00.
UNITS 1 SLEEPS 6

LATE AVAILABILITY For the latest offers call our freephone Central Reservations service. North Wales – 0800 834820 Mid Wales – 0800 273747 South and West Wales – 0800 3289597

2 LLAINWEN UCHAF ★★★
LLANBERIS LL55 4LL Tel: (0151) 724 2154
Fax: (0151) 724 2154 E-mail: sybwilliams@lineone.net
Enquiries: Mrs S.G. Williams,
6 Wyndale Close, Liverpool LI8 7JX

Months open 1-12; Weekly/unit £210.00.
Weekend/midweek breaks available.
UNITS 1 SLEEPS 4

PENDYFFREN HALL ★★
Glan yr Afon Road, **PENMAENMAWR** LL34 6UF
Tel: (01492) 623219

Months open 1-10; 2 Nights £50.00-£60.00. 3 Nights £75.00.
4 Nights £100.00. Weekly/unit £90.00-£250.00.
UNITS 5 SLEEPS 6

CAE EITHIN TEW AWAITING GRADING
Cwmystradllyn, Garndolbenmaen,
porthmadog LL51 9BQ
Enquiries: Bryn Weirglodd, Cwmystradllyn,
Garndolbenmaen, Porthmadog LL51 9AZ
Tel: (01766) 530310

Farmhouse situated in beautiful, peaceful countryside of the Cwmystradllyn valley. Central for touring Snowdonia and Llŷn peninsula within easy reach of beaches and seven miles inland from Porthmadog. Ideal for quiet relaxing holiday. Well equipped kitchen, dining room etc, sitting room, telephone and four bedrooms. Central heating throughout.

Months open 1-12; Weekly/unit £200.00-£400.00.
UNITS 1 SLEEPS 8

TY NEWYDD FLATS ★★
Dublin St, Tremadog, **PORTHMADOG** LL49 9RH
Tel: (01766) 512553 E-mail: johnjulieo@aol.com
Website: www.porthmadog.co.uk/tynewydd/flats
Enquiries: John & Julie Otty
Two flats each sleeping four in the village of Tremadog, which has three pubs and chip shop. 1 mile from Porthmadog. Good location for access to all major attractions by road, train or bus.

Months open 1-12; 3 Nights £100.00-£150.00. 4 Nights £100.00-£150.00.
Weekly/unit £150.00-£200.00.
UNITS 2 SLEEPS 4

PLEASE NOTE
All the accommodation in this publication has applied for grading. With Holiday Cottages it may occasionally not have been possible to undertake a grading. This situation is clearly identified by 'Awaiting Grading' or a provisional Star rating (indicated by the letter P appearing alongside the Stars) within the advertisement/entry.

GWYNFRYN FARM HOLIDAYS

★★★★★

Gwynfryn Farm, *PWLLHELI* LL53 5UF
Tel: (01758) 612536 Fax: (01758) 612536
E-mail: wm@gwynfryn.freeserve.co.uk
Website: www.gwynfrynfarm.co.uk
Enquiries: Mrs Sharon Rees Ellis

GOLD

Come to our organic dairy farm, away from the 'madding crowd', yet only 2 miles Llŷn's Heritage coast. Castles, slate/copper mines, Snowdonia within 25 miles. Quality cottages for romantic couples or parties of 4-8. Beds made up, cooked dishes to order, central storage heating. 3 with open fires, cleanliness and comfort assured. Short breaks. Colour brochure. New 2001 - swimming pool, sauna, jacuzzi. B&B also available.

Months open 1-12; 2, 3 & 4 Nights on request. Weekly/unit £195.00.
UNITS 10 SLEEPS 2-8

RHEDYNOG GANOL

★★★★

Chwilog, *PWLLHELI* LL53 6LQ
Tel: (01766) 810021
Enquiries: Mrs M. E. Hughes

Peace and quiet. Clean and comfortable, well-equipped, 3 bedroom farm house which allows you the freedom of self-catering. Fitted carpet throughout, garden and safe area for children and pets. Within reach of beaches and numerous walks. Guests return year after year.

Months open 5-10; Weekly/Unit £100.00-£350.00.
UNITS 1 SLEEPS 5

WALES CYMRU

TWO HOURS AND A MILLION MILES AWAY

LLWYNDYRUS FARM HOLIDAY COTTAGE

★★★★

Llwyndyrus Farm, Y Ffor, *PWLLHELI* LL53 6RH
Tel: (01766) 810859
Enquiries: Mrs K. Ellis

Character accommodation furnished to a high standard on a 200 acre farm. Situated in an environmentally sensitive area. Great walks from the door and great cycling country. Safe play area with track and pedal tractors etc. All units with own secure gardens and wood-burning stoves. 4 miles from seaside and 20 min drive to Snowdonia.

Months open 1-12; Weekly/unit £120.00-£400.00.
UNITS 3 SLEEPS 2-5

PENLON COTTAGE

★★★

TREFOR, Caernarfon LL54 5AB
Tel: (01286) 660768
Enquiries: M. C. Jones

Detached bungalow-style cottage situated a mile from the little fishing/quarry village of Trefor. Views of the Rivals Mountains and across Caernarfon Bay.

Months open 4-10; Weekly/unit £200.00-£350.00.
UNITS 1 SLEEPS 5

PANT Y NEUADD COTTAGES

★★★★

Aberdyfi Rd, *TYWYN* LL36 9HW
Tel: (01654) 711393
E-mail: pantyneuadd@care4free.net

Cosy, fully-equipped cottages just three miles from Aberdovey. Excellent base for golf/walking. Close to sandy beach and shopping. Brochure with pleasure.

Months open 1-12; 2 Nights £70.00. 3 Nights £85.00. 4 Nights £100.00.
Weekly/unit £160.00-£220.00.
UNITS 2 SLEEPS 2-3

SWN Y NANT & BODNANT FARM COTTAGES ★★★★★

Cynfal Farm, Bryncrug, *TYWYN* LL36 9RB
Tel: (01654) 711703 Fax: (01654) 711703
E-mail: cynfalfrm@aol.com
Website: www.gwynedd.net/croeso.cader.idris
Enquiries: Mrs Carys Evans

GOLD

Two identical luxury stone cottages converted from a former barn. Spacious en-suite family room downstairs with a twin room above, also en-suite. Well equipped pine kitchen includes dishwasher, electric stove, fridge, freezer, washing machine, dryer and microwave. TV and video in open plan lounge/diner. Bedding and towels provided. Two miles from beach. Brochure: Mrs Carys Evans.

Months open 1-12; 2 Nights £90.00. 3 Nights £120.00. 4 Nights £135.00. Weekly/unit £160.00-£450.00.

UNITS 2 SLEEPS 5 ▢ ▣ SP ⤬ ▣ ✻ P4

MENAI HOLIDAY COTTAGES ★★ UP TO ★★★★★

1 Greenfield Terrace, Hill St,
***MENAI BRIDGE* LL59 5AY**
Tel: (01248) 717135 Fax: (01248) 717051
E-mail: wsc@menaiholidays.co.uk
Website: www.menaiholidays.co.uk

GOLD

Guests return year after year to generously equipped, peaceful houses. Choose from a converted chapel, gamekeeper's house, traditional farmhouses, seaside cottages or mountain retreats. Historic sights, fishing, beaches, birdwatching, walking all close by. Choose as carefully as we do from our detailed brochure.

Months open 1-12; 2 Nights £75.00-£920.00. 3 Nights £75.00-£920.00. 4 Nights £88.00-£1050.00. Weekly/unit £110.00-£2000.00.

UNITS 100+ SLEEPS 2-20 ☍ ▢ ⛫ SP ⤬ M ▣ ✻ ⚼ (FR) P

NORTH WALES HOLIDAY COTTAGES & FARMHOUSES ★★ UP TO ★★★★★

39 Station Rd, *DEGANWY* LL31 9DF
Tel: 08707 559888 Fax: (01492) 572504
E-mail: norwal.hols@virgin.net

GOLD

Relax and explore the mountains, vales and beaches from one of our carefully selected properties available throughout this unique area. Contact us for an informative brochure or visit our website: www.northwalesholidaycottages.co.uk

Months open 1-12; 2 Nights from £70.00. 3 Nights from £90.00. 4 Nights from £110.00. Weekly/unit £125.00-£1000.00.

UNITS 180 SLEEPS 2-12 ☍ ▢ ⛫ SP ⤬ M ▣ ✻ P ℹ

Caravan & Camping Parks

PARC CAERELWAN ★★★★ HOLIDAY PARK

Talybont, *BARMOUTH* LL43 2AX
Tel: (01341) 247236 Fax: (01341) 247711
E-mail: parc@holidaysites.co.uk
Website: www.holidaysites.co.uk/parc

GOLD

Top quality caravan bungalows and caravans near sandy beach with mountain views. Indoor pool, health suite, children's activities, launderette, shop. Short breaks available. Pets welcome.

Months open 1-12; Weekly/unit (Static) £145.00-£358.00.

No. ON PARK 150 ⊞ 80 ☍ ☂ ⛫ ▣ ⋔ ▣ ⚄ ✻ ℹ

LAST-MINUTE DEALS

For the latest information and offers on holidays and short breaks in Wales, see: Teletext Page 251

Look out for the Wales Tourist Board grading on Teletext entries to make sure that the accommodation has been checked out by us.

Pwllheli Marina on Llŷn's south coast

ROWEN CARAVAN PARK

Talybont, *BARMOUTH* LL43 2AD
Tel: (01341) 242626 Fax: (01341) 242626
E-mail: rowenpark@breathemail.net
Website: www.ukparks.co.uk/rowen

★★★★ HOLIDAY PARK
BRONZE

A small, quiet family park situated in a tree-lined meadow beside a small stream. Footpath to beach, and Talybont village is a short stroll away. Excellent, well-equipped accommodation comprising two and three bedroom caravans and chalets with all facilities. Shop and launderette on site. Free brochure.

Months open 4-10; Weekly/unit (Static) £115.00-£376.00.
No. ON PARK 35 ⊞ 27 ⛺🏠🚿🛁⛱🏪 P35

SARNFAEN HOLIDAY PARK

Talybont, nr *BARMOUTH* LL43 2AQ
Tel: (01341) 247241 Fax: (01341) 247849
E-mail: robert.gallimore@sarnfaen.force9.net
Website: www.sarnfaen-holiday-park.com

★★★★ HOLIDAY PARK
GOLD

Family holidays to enjoy. Superb quality caravans for hire or sale. Attractive landscaped gardens. Refreshing sea air. New leisure club - sauna, steam, jacuzzi, indoor pool. Coffee shop, dog walk and childrens play area.

Months open 3-12; Weekly/unit (Static) £141.00-£486.00.
No. ON PARK 109 ⊞ 31 ⛺🏪🎮✗🍴⛱ P109

Bryn Gloch

★★★★ HOLIDAY PARK
♿

Caravan & Camping Park within Snowdonia National Park

Award-winning site nestled between Snowdonia mountain ranges and on the banks of the river Gwyrfai with breathtaking views.

Peaceful site, electric hook-ups, shop, off-licence, games room, spacious play area, fishing & mini-golf.

DRAGON AWARD CARAVANS • CHALETS • TOURING PITCHES • TENT PITCHES

01286 650216

www.bryngloch.co.uk   eurig@easynet.co.uk

CAERNARFON BAY CARAVAN PARK & HOLIDAY BUNGALOWS

Dinas Dinlle, *CAERNARFON* LL54 5TW
Tel: (01286) 830492 Fax: (01286) 831037
Enquiries: Mrs C. M. Ashurst

★★★★ HOLIDAY PARK
GOLD

Our small family-run holiday park offers peace and tranquility amid the scenic splendours of Snowdonia. Quality c/h bungalow and caravans yards from award-winning beach, six miles from Caernarfon Castle. We have a small licensed restaurant and many satisfied visitors who return year after year - recommendation indeed. Pets welcome.

Months open 2-12; 2 Nights £50.00-£100.00. 3 Nights £75.00-£150.00. 4 Nights £100.00-£200.00. Weekly/unit £95.00-£375.00.
UNITS 20 SLEEPS 2-6 ⛺🏠🍴 SP🏊 P20 ℹ

PLAS Y BRYN CHALET PARK

Bontnewydd, nr *CAERNARFON* LL54 7YE
Tel: (01286) 672811

★★★ HOLIDAY PARK

This small park is situated two miles from the historic town of Caernarfon. Central to Snowdonia, Anglesey and the Llŷn Peninsula. Beaches within four miles. We offer safety, seclusion and beautiful views of Snowdon. Village pub and shop nearby. Choice of two or three bedrooms. Prices to suit all.

Months open 3-12; Weekly/unit (Static) from £95.00.
No. ON PARK 18 ⊞ 16 ⛺🍴🎮 P20 ℹ

DOLGAMEDD CARAVAN & CAMPING PARK

Bontnewydd/Brithdir, *DOLGELLAU* LL40 2DG
Tel: (01341) 422624 Fax: (01341) 422624
c/o Gwanas, Dolgellau LL40 2SH

AWAITING GRADING
GOLD

Months open 4-10; Weekly/unit (Static) £150.00-£300.00.
Per night (Tourers/Tents) £6.00-£8.00.
No. ON PARK 20 ⊞ 1 🚐 10 🚙 5 ⛺ 50 ⛺🏪🎮⛱ P ℹ

DYFFRYN SEASIDE ESTATE

DYFFRYN ARDUDWY LL44 2HD
Tel: (01341) 247220 Fax: (01341) 247622

HOLIDAY &
BRONZE

Situated five miles north of Barmouth on A496. 400 yards from beautiful beach. For hire six or four berth caravans. Wheelchair accessible caravans, chalets, bungalows, camping field. All facilities - children's playground, chip shop, licensed pub, shop, launderette, leisure complete with heated indoor pool.

Months open 4-10; Weekly/unit (Static) £100.00-£370.00.
Per night (Tents) £5.00-£10.00.
No. ON PARK 248 ⊕ 20 ▲ 200

BEACH HOLIDAY HOMES

West Point, The Beach, Pontllyfni,
NEFYN, Caernarfon LL54 5ET
Tel: (01286) 660400

HOLIDAY PARK
GOLD

Beach holiday homes with your own beach moments from your patio door. Quiet secluded cove with sub-tropical plants. Every comfort, lounge, kitchen, dinette, bathroom, colour TV, microwave, electric blankets, central heating. 2 or 3 bedrooms, nearby restaurants, bar snacks. Tour Snowdonia and famous Llŷn peninsula beaches. Featured by BBC. Adjacent parking. Try £12 minibreak. Brochure. Also for sale.

Months open 3-10; Weekly/unit (Static) £79.00-£399.00.
No. ON PARK 50 ⊕ 20

PRICES

Rates for caravan holiday home rental are PER UNIT PER WEEK or SHORT BREAK (2–4 days). All prices include VAT. Please check all prices and facilities before confirming your booking.

PENDYFFREN HALL

Glan Yr Afon Rd, PENMAENMAWR LL34 6UF
Tel: (01492) 623219

HOLIDAY PARK

Months open 3-10; Per night (Tourers/Tents) £12.00-£15.00.
⊕ 25 ⊕ & ▲ 75

BLACK ROCK SANDS CAMPING & TOURING PARK

Morfa Bychan, PORTHMADOG LL49 9LD
Tel: (01766) 513919

TOURING &
CAMPING PARK
GOLD

A well established park behind the dunes of Black Rock sands. Ideal for bathing, boating and watersports. Your perfect location for touring Snowdonia. Modern heated showers, toilet with free hot water, dish washing and laundry facilities. Children's play area. An ideal family park. Free colour brochure. David Bellamy Conservation Gold Award.

Months open 3-10; Per night (Tourers/Tents) £10.00-£15.50.
⊕ 40 ▲ 100 ⊕ 140

GLYN FARM CARAVANS

TREFRIW, Llanrwst LL27 0RZ
Tel: (01492) 640442

HOLIDAY &
TOURING PARK

Small select family-run site centrally situated Snowdonia and coastal resorts. Lovely walking country, beautiful lakes. Local fishing, boating, skiing, riding and leisure centre.

Months open 3-10; Weekly/unit (Static) £200.00-£250.00.
Per night (Tourers) £6.50-£8.00.
No. ON PARK 10 ⊕ 4 ⊕ 28

Snowdonia National Park near Dolgellau

Mid Wales Lakes & Mountains

Pen-y-Garreg reservoir, Elan Valley

This large area embraces the green, rural heartlands of Wales. It extends from the unexplored Berwyn Mountains in the north to the grassy heights and wide, open spaces of the 519-square-mile Brecon Beacons National Park in the south. Along the way there's more undisturbed countryside – scenic lakelands rich in wildlife, remote hill sheep farmlands and the timeless, tranquil hills of the border country.

On Your Travels ...

Celtica, Machynlleth

Number one on the list is the National Showcaves Centre for Wales at Dan-yr-Ogof in the Brecon Beacons National Park. There are three separate caves to visit – the main Showcaves complex, the Cathedral Cavern with its stunning light-and-sound show, and the archaeological Bone Cave. And that's not all. This popular family attraction also has a Dinosaur Park, Iron Age Farm, Shire Horse Centre with covered play area, museum, pony trekking and dry slope skiing. Another enterprising Brecon Beacons attraction is the Llangorse Rope Centre, with large natural and artificial rock surfaces – all under cover, so you can climb in relative comfort, whatever the weather!

Central Wales is home to the rare red kite – you might see one in the skies above the peaceful Elan Valley lakes. Call in at the Elan Valley Visitor Centre for information on these beautiful lakes and the rich wildlife which flourishes here. Wales's Celtic heritage is the theme at Celtica, Machynlleth, where state-of-the-art technology brings the past to life in an exciting way.

For further information please tel (01938) 551255; e-mail: tourism@powys.gov.uk

Where to Stay
Wales

Brecon
Map Ref Ge6

Main touring centre for the Brecon Beacons National Park. Handsome old town with thriving market, ruined castle, cathedral (with imaginative Heritage Centre), priory, theatre and three interesting museums (Brecknock, Jazz and South Wales Borderers'). Wide range of inns and good shopping. Centre for walking and pony trekking. Golf, fishing and canal cruising. Hosts major international Jazz Festival in summer.

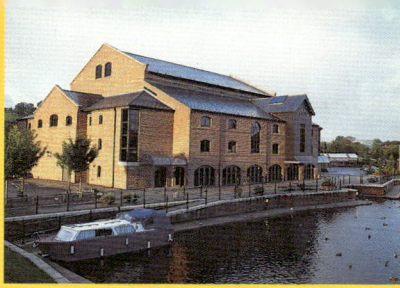

Theatr Brycheiniog, Brecon

setting on the River Wye amid beautiful hills. Lively sheep and cattle markets. Good shopping for local products, touring centre for Mid Wales and border country. River walk, Wyeside Arts Centre.

Crickhowell
Map Ref Hb7

Small, pleasant country town beautifully situated on River Usk. Good for walking, fishing, pony trekking and riding. Remains of Norman castle. Nearby 14th-century Tretower Court and Castle also worth visiting.

Elan Valley
Map Ref Gc3

The first – and possibly the most scenic – of Wales's man-made lakelands. The string of reservoirs is set in high moor and mountain, an area rich in wildlife. Elan Valley Visitor Centre at Elan village.

Crickhowell

Hay-on-Wye
Map Ref Hb5

Small market town on the borderland Offa's Dyke Path, nestling below the Black

The 'town of books'

Builth, on the River Wye

Builth Wells
Map Ref Ge4

Solidly built old country town which plays host every July at the Llanelwedd Showground to the Royal Welsh Show, Wales's largest farming gathering. Lovely

Elan Valley, Mid Wales's 'lakelands'

Mountains beside a picturesque stretch of the River Wye. This world-famous 'town of books' is a mecca for book lovers – Hay is filled with antiquarian and second-hand bookshops, some huge. Attractive crafts centre and interesting speciality shops too. Literature Festival in early summer attracts big names.

Knighton
Map Ref Hb2 ⇌

Tref-y-Clawdd, the 'town on the dyke', stands in a deep wooded valley where the 8th-century Offa's Dyke defines the ancient border between Wales and England. Some of the best-preserved stretches of the earthen dyke can be found in

Lake Vyrnwy, deep in the mountains

The border town of Knighton

the undisturbed hills near the town's Offa's Dyke Centre. Walk the Offa's Dyke Path or Glyndŵr's Way. Peaceful countryside, dotted with hidden villages, all around.

Lake Vyrnwy
Map Ref Ea3

Dramatically beautiful man-made lake ringed by forests and mountains. Neo-Gothic water tower adds to the spectacle. Wonderful birdwatching and wildlife in vast RSPB nature reserve. Nature trails, Vyrnwy Visitor Centre, craft shops.

Llanbadarn Fynydd
Map Ref Ge1

Village in peaceful rolling hills between Llandrindod Wells and Newtown. Don't miss the little church at nearby Llananno with

its elaborately carved rood screen, possibly the finest in Wales.

Llandrindod Wells
Map Ref Ge3 ⇌

Victorian spa town with spacious streets and impressive architecture. Victorian-style visitor centre and excellent museum tracing history of the spa. Also has an intriguing museum dedicated to the bicycle. A popular inland resort with golf, fishing, bowling, boating and tennis available. Excellent touring centre for Mid Wales hills and lakes. Annual Victorian Festival in August.

Llangammarch Wells
Map Ref Gd5 ⇌

Sleepiest of the old Mid Wales spa towns, set in peaceful spot on the northern approaches to wild Mynydd Eppynt. Wonderful walking, fishing country all around, Builth Wells nearby.

Victorian Llandrindod Wells

Llangorse
Map Ref Ha6

Village at edge of Llangorse Lake in lovely pastoral setting in Brecon Beacons National Park. Attractive country inns and ancient church. Popular with pony trekkers, walkers and sailors. Indoor climbing centre.

Llanidloes
Map Ref Gd1

Historic and attractive market town at confluence of Severn and Clywedog rivers; excellent touring centre. Noted for its 16th-century market hall and other fine half-timbered buildings. Interesting shops and local museum. Massive Clywedog dam and lake 3 miles away on B4518. Take the scenic drive around lakeside and visit the Bryn Tail Lead Mine beneath the dam.

Llangorse Lake in the Brecon Beacons National Park

Market hall, Llanidloes

Llanwddyn
Map Ref Ea3

Settlement spectacularly located at approach to mountain-ringed Lake Vyrnwy. A country-lover's paradise – lake is surrounded by a vast nature reserve rich in wildlife. Close to Bala and southern Snowdonia National Park.

Llanwrtyd Wells
Map Ref Gc5 ⇌

One-time spa encircled by wild, beautiful countryside, now centre for pony trekking, walking, fishing and mountain biking. Cambrian Woollen Mill a popular attraction; 'Red Kite Country' information point. Explore spectacular Abergwesyn Pass and Llyn Brianne.

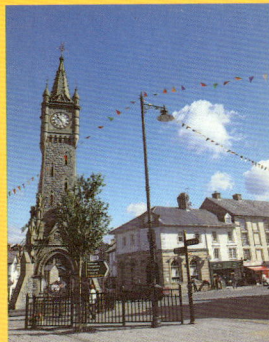
Machynlleth

Llyswen
Map Ref Ha5

Village in a lovely stretch of the upper Wye Valley between Builth Wells and Brecon. Good fishing locally and wonderful walking country – the Brecon Beacons are on doorstep. Hay-on-Wye nearby.

Machynlleth
Map Ref Dc5 ⇌

Historic market town near beautiful Dovey Estuary. Owain Glyndŵr's Parliament House in the wide, handsome main street is now a museum and brass-rubbing centre. Superbly equipped Bro Ddyfi Leisure Centre offers wide range of activities. Celtica centre tells the story of Celtic myth and legend. Outstanding art gallery. On Glyndŵr's Way long-distance walk. The inventive Centre for Alternative Technology is 3 miles away.

Rhayader, gateway to the Elan Valley lakes

Montgomery
Map Ref Ec6

Hilltop market town of distinctive Georgian architecture beneath the ruins of a 13th-century castle. Offa's Dyke, which once marked the border, runs nearby. Not far from Welshpool and Powis Castle.

New Radnor
Map Ref Hb3

Historic village in sleepy border country close to Offa's Dyke Path. Remnants of a medieval castle. Interesting old church at nearby Old Radnor. Radnor Forest to the north, Hay-on-Wye, the 'town of books', to the south.

Pandy
Map Ref Hc7

Village in green, rolling border country north of Abergavenny. Excellent walking centre – long-distance Offa's Dyke Path passes close by, and the Brecon Beacons and Black Mountains are on the doorstep.

Presteigne
Map Ref Hc2

Typical black-and-white half-timbered border town with ancient inns; the Radnorshire Arms has secret passages. Judge's Lodging attraction recreates the past. Pony trekking available. Offa's Dyke Path nearby.

Rhayader
Map Ref Gd2

Country market town full of character, with inviting inns and Welsh craft products in the shops. Excellent base for exploring mountains and lakes (Elan Valley and Claerwen), with opportunities for pony trekking, mountain biking and fishing. Welsh Royal Crystal Visitor Centre. Small museum. An interesting walk through the country on the nearby Gigrin Farm Trail, a 'Red Kite Country' visitor centre.

Welshpool
Map Ref Ec5 ≥

Old market town of the borderlands, with half-timbered buildings and welcoming inns. Attractive canalside museum. Good shopping centre – especially at the Old Station, a major shopping venue; also golf and angling. Powis Castle an impressive stately home with a Clive of India Museum and outstanding gardens. Ride the narrow-gauge Welshpool and Llanfair Railway, visit the Moors Wildlife Collection, walk Offa's Dyke and Glyndŵr's Way.

Welshpool's attractive main street

Hotels, Guest Houses & Farmhouses

THE BEACONS

★★★ GUEST HOUSE

GOLD

16 Bridge St, **BRECON** LD3 8AH
Tel: (01874) 623339 Fax: (01874) 623339
E-mail: beacons@brecon.co.uk
Website: www.beacons.brecon.co.uk

Recently restored listed Georgian house offering beautifully appointed standard, en-suite and luxury period rooms. The candlelit restaurant offers fine food and wines (5 nights). Cosy cellar bar, elegant lounge, private parking and bike lock-up. Excellently situated for Brecon's historic centre and National Park exploration and activities.

Months open 1-12; B&B p/p £18.00-£29.50.
2 Nights Break D, B&B p/p £65.90-£88.90.

🛏14 🛌11 🐂 C ⛄♥⛄ SP ⛲🚲 P16 ℹ

CWMCAMLAIS UCHAF FARM

★★★★ FARM

AWARD

GOLD

Cwmcamlais, Sennybridge, **BRECON** LD3 8TD
Tel: (01874) 636376 Fax: (01874) 636376
E-mail: phillipsj2@talk21.com
Website: www.bbfa.co.uk

A warm Welsh welcome is assured at Cwmcamlais Uchaf. Peacefully situated in a quiet valley in the Brecon Beacons National Park. Most guests are returning or recommended to our 16th century farmhouse which is full of charm and character. Our breakfasts are truly a 'Taste of Wales' with spring water on tap.

Months open 1-12; B&B p/p £21.00-£22.00. Weekly B&B p/p £145.00.

🛏3 🛌2 🐂♥⛲🚲 TW P4 ℹ

PLEASE NOTE that all prices are PER PERSON, based on TWO PEOPLE sharing a double or twin room. SINGLE OCCUPANCY will usually be charged extra, and there may be supplements for private bath/shower. Daily rates are for bed and breakfast. Weekly rates are for dinner, B&B. All prices quoted include VAT. Please check all prices and facilities before confirming your booking.

PETERSTONE COURT

SILVER

Llanhamlach, **BRECON** LD3 7YB
Tel: (01874) 665387 Fax: (01874) 665376

Peterstone Court is a privately owned 18th Century Country House, full of charm and history, with stunning views of the Brecon Beacons and the River Usk. There are 12 beautifully proportioned period style en-suite bedrooms. Extensive leisure facilities and exquisite dining make this the ideal venue for that special break.

Months open 1-12; B&B p/p £89.25-£120.75.
2 Nights Break D, B&B p/p £136.50.

🛏12 🛌12 🐂 C ⛄♥⛄ SP ⛲🚲🎵 P70

DISSERTH MILL

★★ BED & BREAKFAST

GOLD

BUILTH WELLS LD2 3TN
Tel: (01982) 553217

250 metres off A483 north of Builth Wells. 2½ miles to Royal Welsh Showground. 4 miles to Llandrindod. Swimming and sports facilities 13 miles. Elan Valley reservoirs and beautiful hills and walks close at hand. Also garden to relax in during your stay. Cycle hire shop at Builth for more energetic guests.

Months open 1-12; B&B p/p £20.00-£25.00. 2 Nights Break B&B p/p £40.00-£50.00. Weekly B&B p/p £130.00-£140.00.

🛏3 🛌2 🐂 C ♥⛄ P4 ℹ

The borderland Black Mountains

BEAR HOTEL

★★★
HOTEL

High St, *CRICKHOWELL* NP8 1BW
Tel: (01873) 810408 Fax: (01873) 811696
E-mail: bearhotel@aol.com
Website: www.bearhotel.co.uk

A quaint, individually furnished 15th century hotel, unique in its appealing atmosphere. The most popular hotel in the area. It is very much the hub of the community. Bar meals and the à la carte restaurant have received great acclaim internationally. **Best Pub in Britain 2000.**

Months open 1-12; B&B p/p £32.50-£60.00. 2 Nights Break D, B&B p/p £115.00-£170.00. Weekly D, B&B p/p £321.00-£486.00.

DRAGON HOTEL

★★
HOTEL

BRONZE

CRICKHOWELL, Brecon Beacons National Park
NP8 1BE Tel: (01873) 810362 Fax: (01873) 811868
E-mail: dragon-hotel@crickhowell10,freeserve.co.uk
Website: www.dragonhotel.co.uk

A small and friendly, pretty pink-washed, 18thC hotel in an enticing market town. Surrounded by magnificent countryside where there are many interesting things to do and see. The most popular walking and outdoor activity hotel in the area. Guided and self-guided walks programme. Traditional and interesting tea-room, a-la-carte and bistro menus. Non-residents welcome.

Months open 1-12; B&B p/p from £27.00. 2 Nights Break D, B&B p/p £86.00-£95.00.

THE MANOR HOTEL

★★★
HOTEL

Brecon Rd, *CRICKHOWELL* NP8 1SE
Tel: (01873) 810212 Fax: (01873) 811938
E-mail: themanorhotel@talk21.com

In a stunning location, perched on a hillside of the Usk Valley way above the town, this impressive manor house was the birthplace of Sir George Everest. The recently refurbished bedrooms and public areas retain an elegant yet relaxed atmosphere, and there are extensive leisure facilities. The restaurant has panoramic views and is the setting for some bold modern cooking. Guests also have the option of eating in the informal atmosphere of the nearby Nantyffin Cider Mill, the hotel's sister operation.

Months open 1-12; B&B p/p £30.00-£50.00. 2 Nights Break D, B&B p/p £120.00-£170.00. Weekly D, B&B p/p £770.00-£1090.00.

TY CROESO HOTEL

★★★
HOTEL

BRONZE

The Dardy, Llangattock, *CRICKHOWELL* NP8 1PU
Tel: (01873) 810573 Fax: (01873) 810573
E-mail: tycroeso@ty-croeso-hotel.freeserve.co.uk
Website: www.wiz.to/tycroeso

Delightful country hotel on hillside above Monmouth-Brecon canal in Brecon Beacons National Park. Magnificent views over Black Mountains. A warm welcome, log fires, candlelit restaurant, fine wines and delicious food including speciality 'Taste of Wales' menu. Charming bedrooms and elegant fourposter. Perfect base for walkers, Cardiff and tourist attractions.

Months open 1-12; B&B p/p £30.00-£37.50. 2 Nights Break D, B&B p/p £87.00-£97.00. Weekly D, B&B p/p £250.00-£280.00.

ELAN VALLEY HOTEL

★★
COUNTRY HOTEL

GOLD

ELAN VALLEY, Rhayader LD6 5HN
Tel: (01597) 810448 Fax: (01597) 810448
E-mail: <hotel@elanvalley.demon.co.uk
Website: www.elanvalleyhotel.co.uk

At the heart of the spectacular, undiscovered lakeland of Wales. Informal, friendly, family-run hotel, offering a delicious home cooked and imaginative menu, real ales, good wines and affordable, comfortable accommodation. Children made very welcome. Perfect spot for walking, fishing, cycling, birdwatching, photography, or just relaxing and indulging yourselves.

Months open 1-12; B&B p/p £27.50-£50.00. 2 Nights Break D, B&B p/p £85.00-£100.00.

THE OLD POST OFFICE

★★★
GUEST HOUSE

Llanigon, *HAY-ON-WYE* HR3 5QA
Tel: (01497) 820008
Website: www.hay-on-wye.co.uk/oldpost

Months open 1-12; B&B p/p £18.00-£27.00.

CLASSIFIED ADVERTISING *There's more accommodation to choose from in the classified advertising section of this book. Please see the listing at the end of the 12 Areas display adverts.*

MID WALES LAKES & MOUNTAINS

LAKE VYRNWY HOTEL
LLANWDDYN SY10 0LY
Tel: (01691) 870692 Fax: (01691) 870259
E-mail: res@lakevyrnwy.com
Website: www.lakevyrnwy.com

★★★★
COUNTRY HOTEL

Set high in the Hills of the Berwyn Mountains, this Hotel commands breathtaking views over Lake Vyrnwy and its surrounding countryside. Bedrooms are individually decorated and furnished. The Restaurant is a delight, food delicious, the view fantastic. The perfect setting for an activity filled holiday or just a relaxing weekend away.

Months open 1-12; B&B p/p £55.00-£91.00.
2 Nights Break D, B&B p/p £73.00-£105.00.

🛏 35 🛏 35

THE PADDOCK
Shobdon, **PRESTEIGNE**, Leominster HR6 9NQ
Tel: (01568) 708176 Fax: (01568) 708829
E-mail: thepaddock@talk21.com

★★★★
GUEST HOUSE

Delightful ground floor accommodation situated in the border region between Wales and England, known as The Marches. This outstandingly beautiful area is popular with walkers and garden lovers. Centrally positioned for many historical attractions. Delicious home-cooked food and a warm welcome. En-suite rooms. Large garden, parking, drying facilities.

Months open 1-12; B&B p/p £22.00-£23.50. 2 Nights Break D, B&B p/p £72.00-£75.00. Weekly D, B&B p/p £252.00-£262.50.

🛏 5 🛏 5

BRYNAFON COUNTRY HOUSE HOTEL
South St, **RHAYADER** LD6 5BL
Tel: (01597) 810735 Fax: (01597) 810111
E-mail: info@brynafon.co.uk
Website: www.brynafon.co.uk

★★★
COUNTRY HOTEL

BRONZE

Set amid glorious hills and mountains ¹/₂ mile away from Rhayader and modern leisure centre and near the beautiful Elan Valley and reservoirs. Discover this former workhouse, famed for its comfort, charm, renowned friendliness and excellent bar and restaurant food.

Months open 1-12; B&B p/p £25.00-£35.00. 2 Nights Break D, B&B p/p £75.00-£95.00. Weekly D, B&B p/p £202.50-£256.50.

🛏 16 🛏 16

Lake Vyrnwy is surrounded by ruggedly beautiful countryside

Bed & Breakfast
£27.50 p.p. is the most you'll pay

11, THE WATTON
BRECON LD3 7ED
Tel: (01874) 625650

Months open 4-10; Single B&B per night £18.00-£20.00.

ASHGROVE
Llanspyddid, *BRECON* LD3 8PB
Tel: (01874) 622833
E-mail: ashgrove@btclick.com

Large Dower House dating from early 1800's is situated 2 miles from Brecon, and provides a warm, relaxed, informal atmosphere for your stay. Spacious B&B. WTB approved for walkers and cyclists. Colour TV, radio/alarm and refreshments in all rooms. Packed lunches, flasks filled, drying facilities. No smoking. Large garden. Off-road parking. O.S.Grid 009282. Brochure available.

Months open 3-12; B&B p/p £15.00-£16.00. 2 Nights Break D, B&B p/p £40.00-£50.00.

THE BEACONS
16 Bridge St, *BRECON* LD3 8AH
Tel: (01874) 623339 Fax: (01874) 623339
E-mail: beacons@brecon.co.uk
Website: www.beacons.brecon.co.uk

Recently restored listed Georgian house offering beautifully appointed standard, en-suite rooms. The candlelit restaurant offers fine food and wines (5 nights). Cosy cellar bar, elegant lounge, private parking and bike lock-up. Excellently situated for Brecon's historic centre and National Park exploration and activities.

Months open 1-12; B&B p/p from £18.00. 2 Nights Break D, B&B p/p £65.90-£88.90.

BLAENCAR FARM
Sennybridge, *BRECON* LD3 8HA
Tel: (01874) 636610 Fax: (01874) 636610

Enjoy the warmth and quality of a true Welsh welcome on a working farm in the heart of Brecon Beacons National Park. 8 miles west of Brecon, the charming farmhouse, recently refurbished, offers superior accommodation and comfort for discerning guests looking for something special. Country pub pleasant 15 minute walk.

Months open 1-12; Double B&B per night £40.00-£50.00.

BRYN-Y-FEDWEN FARM
Trallong Common, Sennybridge, *BRECON* LD3 8HW Tel: (01874) 636505
Fax: (01874) 636505 Website: www.bbfa.co.uk

Bryn-y-Fedwen, situated high above the river Usk valley amidst lovely countryside, overlooking the Brecon Beacons. 1½ miles north of the A40 between Brecon and Sennybridge. Enjoy a warm, friendly atmosphere. Spacious en-suite bedrooms and cosy lounge with log fire. Good home cooking. Great for walking and birdwatching. Many attractions and activities close by.

Months open 1-12(except March); Single B&B per night £25.00. Double B&B per night £44.00.

COUNTY HOUSE
100 The Struet, *BRECON* LD3 7LS
Tel: (01874) 625844 Fax: (01874) 625844
E-mail: countyhouse@ukworld.net
Website: www.ukworld.net/countyhouse

Months open 1-12; Double B&B per night £55.00.

THE FLAG & CASTLE GUEST HOUSE
11 Orchard St, Llanfaes, *BRECON* LD3 8AN
Tel: (01874) 625860

Months open 1-12; B&B p/p £19.00-£25.00.

MAESWALTER
Heol Senni, nr *BRECON* LD3 8SU
Tel: (01874) 636629
E-mail: maeswalter@talk21.com

Months open 1-12; Single B&B per night £20.00-£25.00. Double B&B per night £36.00-£45.00.

OLD VICARAGE
Erwood, *BUILTH WELLS* LL2 3SZ Tel: (01982) 560680 /0808 1980319 E-mail: linda@oldvic43.fsnet.co.uk
Website: www.oldvic43.fsnet.co.uk

Beautiful setting, peaceful grounds overlooking the stunning Wye Valley from spacious attractive bedrooms with double aspects. Period furnishings. Welcome trays, easychairs, TV's. central heating. Period beds have Welsh blankets and throws spun in Welsh mills. Guests' own bathroom, separate wc. Private lounge. Elan Valley, Hay-on-Wye book town, Brecon Beacons all nearby. True traditional farmhouse cooking with homemade preserves always available.

Months open 1-12; B&B p/p £16.00-£17.00. 2 Nights Break D, B&B p/p £46.00-£48.00. Weekly D, B&B p/p £132.00-£138.00.

CASTELL CORRYN
Llangenny, *CRICKHOWELL* NP8 1HE
Tel: (01873) 810327 Fax: (01873) 810327
E-mail: 113114.2610@compuserve.com

Situated above the Usk Valley within the Brecon Beacons National Park. Outstanding views. Beautiful, restful gardens. Children welcome. Special diets. All rooms en-suite, colour TV, tea-making facilities, hairdryer. Take A40 west from Abergavenny for 5 miles. Turn right into Llangenny. Winding lane to village. Turn right before river bridge up right. First house right.

Months open 1-12; B&B p/p £20.00-£25.00.

THE FIRS
★★★ GUEST HOUSE

Tretower, *CRICKHOWELL* NP8 1RF
Tel: (01874) 730780 Fax: (01874) 730780
Website: www.holiday-wales.com

Months open 1-12; B&B p/p £19.00-£23.50.
2 Nights Break D, B&B p/p on request.

TY-NANT
★★★ BED & BREAKFAST

ELAN VALLEY, nr Rhayader LD6 5HN
Tel: (01597) 811412 Fax: (01597) 811412

Months open 2-11; B&B p/p £20.00.

TY-BACH
★★★ BED & BREAKFAST

Llowes, *HAY-ON-WYE* HR3 5JE
Tel: (01497) 847759 Fax: (01497) 847940
E-mail: charles.bradfield@farmline.com
Website: www.hay-on-wye.co.uk/tybach

Relax in our home nestling under the Begwyns, enjoying breathtaking views across the river Wye to the Black Mountains. Three miles from the book-lover's Hay-on-Wye. Roam our gardens, ornamental ponds and woodlands, experiencing warm, country hospitality. Perfect location for wildlife, bird-watching, canoeing, gliding, golf, riding, cycling, fishing, walking, relaxing etc.

Months open 1-12; B&B p/p £22.50-£25.00.

OFFA'S DYKE HOUSE
★★ BED & BREAKFAST

4 High St, *KNIGHTON* LD7 1AT
Tel: (01547) 528634 Fax: (01547) 528634
Mobile: 0780 8090549

Months open 1-12; B&B p/p £16.00.

CEFNSURAN FARM
★★★ FARM BRONZE

Llangunllo, *KNIGHTON* LD7 1SL
Tel: (01547) 550219 Fax: (01547) 550348
E-mail: cefn@suran.freeserve.co.uk
Website: www.farmbreaks.org.uk

16th Century farmhouse set in extremely picturesque valley with rolling hills. Woodburning inglenook fireplaces and exposed beams retaining a farmhouse feel. 5 Star Self-catering available in our Finn Lodge. Enjoy the peace and wildlife on our farm walks, or just relax in this perfect setting. Where a warm welcome awaits you.

Months open 1-12; Single B&B per night £20.00-£25.00.
Double B&B per night £45.00-£50.00.

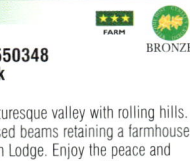

THE OAKS
AWAITING GRADING

LAKE VYRNWY, Llanwddyn, Nr Oswestry SY10 0LZ
Tel: (01691) 870250 Fax: (01691) 870250
E-mail: Mdug99@cs.com

Located by unforgettable Lake Vyrnwy. Sensational scenery and a warm welcome into a comfortable family home. En-suite/private bathrooms, TV, tea/coffee, private parking and garden. Fantastic base for walking, birdwatching, relaxing or exploring Mid and North Wales.

Months open 5-11; Double B&B per night £41.00-£49.00.

HILLSIDE LODGE GUEST HOUSE
★★★ GUEST HOUSE

LLANBADARN FYNYDD LD1 6TU
Tel: (01597) 840364

Spacious and peaceful, this family-run guest house offers excellent accommodation in an outstanding position standing alone on the hillside overlooking the Ithon valley. Ideal for long holidays or short peaceful breaks. Families welcome. Pets by arrangement. All rooms en-suite, tea/coffee, hairdryers, ironing facilities. Elan Valley fishing, birdwatching. Totally non-smoking.

Months open 1-12; Single B&B per night £25.00.
Double B&B per night £40.00.

HOLLY FARM
★★★ FARM
GOLD

Howey, *LLANDRINDOD WELLS* LD1 5PP
Tel: (01597) 822402 Fax: (01597) 822402
Website: www.ukword.net/hollyfarm

Working farm with charming old farmhouse. Dates back to Tudor times; country lovers retreat, glorious unspoilt countryside. Near scenic lakes and mountains; ideal for walking, birdwatching or relaxing. En-suite rooms with colour TV and beverage trays. Two lounges with TV and log fires. Home cooking a speciality, using farm produce. Tourism award. Safe parking. AA ◆◆◆◆. Evening meal by arrangement. Brochure - Mrs Ruth Jones

Months open 1-12; B&B p/p £20.00-£25.00. 2 Nights Break D, B&B p/p £60.00-£70.00. Weekly D, B&B p/p £195.00-£220.00.

NEUADD FARM COUNTRY GUEST HOUSE
★★★★ FARM
AWARD
GOLD

Penybont, *LLANDRINDOD WELLS* LD1 5SW
Tel: (01597) 822571 Fax: (01597) 824295
Website: www.smoothhound.co.uk

Enjoy a relaxing break in our comfortably furnished 16th century farmhouse overlooking the lovely Ithon valley, separate guest sitting and dining room both with inglenook fireplaces. Central heating. Good traditional home cooking. Ideal for exploring Mid Wales and Elan Valley or walk direct from our door. No traffic. Fishing. Brochure Jackie and Peter Longley.

Months open 1-12; Single B&B per night £22.00-£25.00.
Double B&B per night £40.00-£48.00.

HILLVIEW
★★★ BED & BREAKFAST

LLANGAMMARCH WELLS LD4 4AA
Tel: (01591) 620711

Months open 3-11; B&B p/p £19.00-£22.00. 2 Nights Break D, B&B p/p £27.00-£30.00. Weekly D, B&B p/p £153.00-£171.00.

GLANIRFON FARMHOUSE BED & BREAKFAST
★★ BED & BREAKFAST
GOLD

Abernant, *LLANWRTYD WELLS* LD5 4AF
Tel: (01591) 610604 Fax: (01591) 610604
E-mail: info@glanirfon.co.uk
Website: www.glanirfon.co.uk

A warm welcome awaits at Glanirfon, a spacious modernised Welsh longhouse, retaining period atmosphere, in peaceful countryside, one mile from Llanwrtyd. Separate guest sitting and dining rooms. TV in all bedrooms. Llanwrtyd, Britain's smallest town, is an ideal centre for walking, cycling or enjoying the many attractions of Mid Wales.

Months open 1-12; Single B&B per night £17.00-£18.50.
Double B&B per night £34.00-£37.00.

OAKFIELD HOUSE
★★★ BED & BREAKFAST
GOLD

**Dol-y-Coed Rd, *LLANWRTYD WELLS*
LD5 4RA Tel: (01591) 610605**

Months open 4-11; B&B p/p £19.00-£21.00.

ORLESWELL
★★★★ BED & BREAKFAST

**Erw Haf, Ffos Rd, *LLANWRTYD WELLS*
LD5 4RT Tel: (01591) 610747**

Months open 1-12; Twin B&B per night £36.00-£40.00.

OAKFIELD
★★★ BED & BREAKFAST

***LLYSWEN*, Brecon LD3 0UR
Tel: (01874) 754301**

Months open 3-10; Single B&B per night £16.00-£18.00.
Double B&B per night £32.00-£36.00.

DREWIN FARM
★★★ FARM
AWARD

**Churchstoke, *MONTGOMERY* SY15 6TW
Tel: (01588) 620325 Fax: (01588) 620325
E-mail: ceinwen@drewin.freeserve.co.uk**

Relax in this peaceful setting overlooking panoramic views. The Drewin is a 17th century famhouse, retaining much of its original character - oak beams and inglenook fireplace. Two well furnished en-suite bedrooms with modern amenities and colour TV. Fully centrally heated. Wonderful area for wildlife. On Offa's Dyke footpath. Good home cooking and a very warm welcome awaits our visitors. AA Selected 4 diamonds. AA winner of Best Breakfast award for Wales 1999-2000. FHB.

Months open 4-10; Single B&B per night £22.00-£25.00.
Double B&B per night £40.00-£44.00.

LITTLE BROMPTON FARM
★★★★ FARM
AWARD
GOLD

***MONTGOMERY* SY15 6HY
Tel: (01686) 668371 Fax: (01686) 668371
E-mail: gaynor.brompton@virgin.net**

Country lover's retreat; glorious unspoilt countryside, quiet roads. Stay at our idyllic 17th century farmhouse on a working farm. Traditionally furnished oak beamed rooms. En-suites, quality prevails - colour TV, beverage trays, radios and hairdryer. Traditional farmhouse cooking, vegetarians catered for. Payphone. On Offa's Dyke, we are situated on the B4385, two miles east of Georgian Montgomery. Croeso.
Months open 1-12; Single B&B per night £22.00-£24.00.
Double B&B per night £40.00-£44.00.

WALKERS REST
AWAITING GRADING

**Glannant House, *PANDY*, Abergavenny NP7 8DN
Tel: (01873) 890088 Fax: (01873) 890088**

Situated on the Offa's Dyke path, The Walkers Rest is an ideal stop-off point offering friendly accommodation with a hearty breakfast and packed lunch to help you on your way. Overlooking the Black Mountains with tea gardens and private car park. We also offer organised weekends should you wish to stay a bit longer.

Months open 1-12; B&B p/p £15.00-£20.00.
2 Nights Break D, B&B p/p £40.00-£50.00.

THE PADDOCK
AWAITING GRADING

**Shobdon, *PRESTEIGNE*, Leominster HR6 9NQ
Tel: (01568) 708176 Fax: (01568) 708829
E-mail: thepaddock@talk21.com**

Months open 1-12; Double B&B per night £44.00-£47.00.

BRYNAFON COUNTRY HOUSE HOTEL
★★★ COUNTRY HOTEL
BRONZE

**South St, *RHAYADER* LD6 5BL
Tel: (01597) 810735 Fax: (01597) 810111
E-mail: info@brynafon.co.uk
Website: www.brynafon.co.uk**

Set amid glorious hills and mountains, yet only half a mile from Rhayader and modern leisure centre. A few miles away lies the beautiful Elan Valley and reservoirs. Discover this family run, former workhouse, famed for its comfort, charm, renowned friendliness and excellent bar and restaurant.

Months open 1-12; B&B p/p from £25.00. 2 Nights Break D, B&B p/p £75.00-£95.00. Weekly D, B&B p/p £202.50-£256.50.

BRYNTEG B&B
★★★ BED & BREAKFAST

**Brynteg, East St, *RHAYADER* LD6 5EA
Tel: (01597) 810052
E-mail: brynteg@hotmail.com**

Months open 1-12; Single B&B per night £17.00.
Double B&B per night £34.00.

LIVERPOOL HOUSE
★★ GUEST HOUSE
GOLD

**East St, *RHAYADER* LD6 5EA
Tel: (01597) 810706 Fax: (01597) 810964
E-mail: ann@liverpoolhouse.net
Website: www.liverpoolhouse.net**

Superior en-suite accommodation and delicious Welsh food await you at this spacious guest house and annexe. Secure car park. Two lounges. Snacks, cream and Welsh teas available. All bedrooms have television, beverage tray, hairdryer and iron. Two 4-poster beds. Families and groups welcome. Excellent value. Short breaks available. Brochure on request.

Months open 1-12; B&B p/p £16.00-£20.00. 2 Nights Break D, B&B p/p £52.00.

RIVERSIDE LODGE
★★ GUEST HOUSE

**Elan Valley, nr *RHAYADER* LD6 5HL
Tel: (01597) 810770 Fax: (01597) 810770
E-mail: info@riverside-lodge.com
Website: www.riverside-lodge.com**

Set in spectacular surroundings in a peaceful location on the banks of the river Elan, gateway to the lakelands of Wales. Riverside walks, cosy log fires and good home cooking. Friendly family-run guest house. Perfect for fishing, walking and birdwatching. En-suite accommodation available. Fully licensed restaurant with panoramic views over river Elan.
Months open 1-12; Single B&B per night £17.50-£20.00.
Double B&B per night £35.00-£40.00.

LAST-MINUTE OFFERS
Looking for late availability or last-minute offers? For details of great-value breaks call Central Reservations on freephone 0800 834820 for North Wales, 0800 273747 for Mid Wales or 0800 3289597 for South and West Wales.

MID WALES LAKES & MOUNTAINS

TREGWYNT
★★★
BED & BREAKFAST

Mutton Dingle, *NEW RADNOR* LD8 2IL
Tel: (01544) 350409
E-mail: m.haines@ukgateway.net

Discover the Radnor Hills! Set on a hillside above the village, Tregwynt offers a warm welcome in a peaceful setting with magnificent views. Ideal for touring, and the perfect base for walkers and cyclists. Lounge with TV. Single room on ground floor. Pub ½ mile.

Months open 3-11; Single B&B per night £18.00-£20.00.
Double B&B per night £36.00-£40.00.

HAFREN
★★
BED & BREAKFAST

38 Salop Rd, *WELSHPOOL* SY21 7EA
Tel: (01938) 554112 Fax: (01938) 554112
E-mail: hafren@tinyworld.co.uk

Months open 1-12; B&B p/p £17.00-£20.00. 2 Nights Break D, B&B p/p £52.00-£58.00. Weekly D, B&B p/p £168.00-£189.00.

THE HAVEN
★★★
BED & BREAKFAST

Winllan Rd, Llansantffraid, *WELSHPOOL*
SY22 6TR Tel: (01691) 828101 Fax: (01691) 828101
E-mail: thehaven@ukworld.net
Website: www.ukworld.net/thehaven

Months open 3-12; Single B&B per night £21.00-£23.00.
Double B&B per night £36.00-£40.00.

TYNLLWYN FARM
★★★
FARM
AWARD
GOLD

WELSHPOOL SY21 9BW
Tel: (01938) 553175

Tynllwyn is a family farm and farmhouse with a friendly welcome. Good farmhouse food and bar licence. All bedrooms have central heating, colour TV, tea/coffee facilities, hot and cold wash units. One mile from lovely market town of Welshpool on the A490 North. Very quiet and pleasantly situated on a hillside with beautiful views. Two day short break available October to March. Pets by arrangement.

Months open 1-12; Single B&B per night £18.00-£20.00.
Double B&B per night £32.00-£38.00.

Holiday Cottages

TYCERRIG
★★★★★

Trallong, nr *BRECON* LD3 8HP
Tel: (01874) 638848 Fax: (01874) 638848
E-mail: anthbryer@excite.co.uk
Website: www.cottageguide.co.uk/tycerrig

Months open 1-12; Weekly/unit £130.00-£220.00.
UNITS 1 SLEEPS 4

OAKVIEW
★★★★★

Graig Barn Farm, Llangenny Lane, *CRICKHOWELL* NP8 1HB
Tel: (01873) 810275
E-mail: johng.morris@virgin.net
Website: www.ukworld.net/oakview

Barn conversion to two luxury apartments on a small family run farm. A superb quiet location with magnificent views over the Usk Valley. A wide variety of leisure pursuits available locally. Kitchens are well-equipped with many labour saving devices including washing machine, dishwasher, fridge/freezer and microwave. Ideal touring/walking base.

Months open 1-12; 2 Nights £120.00-£140.00. 3 Nights £180.00-£210.00. 4 Nights £220.00-£280.00. Weekly/unit £250.00-£400.00.
UNITS 2 SLEEPS 1-6

PREGGE MILL
★★★★

Pregge Lane, *CRICKHOWELL* NP8 1SE
Tel: (01873) 811157 Fax: (01873) 811157
E-mail: preggemill@btinternet.com
Website: www.btinternet.com/~preggemill

Months open 1-12; 2 Nights £85.00-£90.00. 3 Nights £115.00-£130.00. 4 Nights £140.00-£160.00. Weekly/unit £180.00-£270.00.
UNITS 1 SLEEPS 2-4

PIPPINS
★★★★★
GOLD

Neuadd Farm, Penybont, *LLANDRINDOD WELLS* LD1 5SY
Tel: (01597) 822571 Fax: (01597) 824295
Website: www.smoothhound.co.uk

Months open 1-12; 2 Nights £60.00-£90.00. 3 Nights £90.00-£130.00. 4 Nights £110.00-£200.00. Weekly/unit £180.00-£360.00.
UNITS 1 SLEEPS 4

OLD VICARAGE COTTAGE
★★★★

The Old Vicarage, *LLANGORSE*, Brecon LD3 7UB
Tel: (01874) 658639

Months open 1-12; 2 Nights £60.00-£80.00. 3 Nights £75.00-£95.00. 4 Nights £85.00-£105.00. Weekly/unit £130.00-£265.00.
UNITS 1 SLEEPS 4

POWELLS COTTAGE
★★★★

LLANGORSE, nr Brecon LD3 7UE
Enqiries: Jill and Mike Jones, Oak Cottage, Llangorse, Brecon, Powys LD3 7UE
Tel: (01874) 658672 Fax: (01874) 658699
E-mail: m.g.jones@lineone.net

Fully equipped old cottage on edge of attractive village overlooks hills with use of large secluded garden. Short walk to village. Facilities include lake, climbing centre, riding, fishing and walking. Bed linen and towels provided. CH, parking, TV, video, within National Park. Quiet and relaxing.

Months open 1-12; 2 Nights £60.00. 3 Nights £90.00-£120.00. 4 Nights £120.00-£150.00. Weekly/unit £125.00-£250.00.
UNITS 1 SLEEPS 3

BRELGWYN & TY BYCHAN ★★★★

1&2 The Rank, Cwmbelan, _LLANIDLOES_ SY18 6QA
Enquiries: J. Barratt, 18 Meadow Road, Aldridge,
Walsall WS9 0ST Tel: (01922) 452687

Tastefully restored cottages with open fires, beamed ceilings and lawned gardens. Riverbank setting. Leisure facilities, shopping close by, superb for fishing, sailing, golf and walking. Renowned Red Kite country waiting to be discovered. Ideal family accommodation. SAE for brochure.

Months open 3-11; 2 Nights £75.00. Weekly/unit £120.00-£210.00.
UNITS 2 SLEEPS 4-5 ▭ Ⓜ 🍴 P5

CWMIRFON LODGE ★★★★

LLANWRTYD WELLS LD5 4TN
Tel: (01591) 610849 Fax: (01591) 610750
E-mail: karin@cwmirfon.co.uk
Website: www.cwmirfon.co.uk

Three cosy cottages with terraces and garden and stunning views down the Irfon Valley. Ideal for walking, cycling and wildlife. 3 acres of woods. 100 yards to a safe and natural swimming pool in the River Irfon. Large recreation room with wood burner. Three miles to all amenities. Spoil yourself!

Months open 1-12; 2 Nights £80.00-£150.00. 3 Nights £115.00-£255.00.
4 Nights £150.00-£260.00. Weekly/unit £160.00-£350.00.
UNITS 3 SLEEPS 2-6 ▭ 🔥 SP 🍴 ✗ (GR) P10 ℹ

BRYNLLWYDWYN HALL ★★★

Uwchygarreg, _MACHYNLLETH_ SY20 8RR
Tel: (01654) 702042

Machynlleth 3 miles. Brynllwydwyn Hall. Private drive. Part of large country farmhouse. Relax in peaceful spacious surroundings. Lovely views, walks (Glyndwrs Way). Oak panelled hall, bay windows, log fires, c/h. 4 bedrooms with wash basins. Comfortable beds. Off peak short breaks.

Months open 1-12; Rates/unit £100.00-£300.00.
UNITS 4 SLEEPS 5-9 ▭ SP 🍴 P3-4

MIN AFON (RIVERSIDE) ★★★★★

Pantperthog, _MACHYNLLETH_ SY20 9AR
Enquiries: Mr.Mrs. A. Britton, 'Pentir', Pantperthog,
Machynlleth SY20 9AR
Tel: (01645) 702070 Fax: (01654) 702070

Months open 1-12; 2 Nights £100.00-£140.00. 3 Nights £125.00-£180.00.
4 Nights £150.00-£200.00. Weekly/unit £180.00-£380.00.
UNITS 1 SLEEPS 4 ▭ SP 🍴 P ℹ

MOELFRE COTTAGE ★★★

Rhosdyrnog, Talywern, _MACHYNLLETH_ SY20 8NU
Tel: (01650) 511288 Fax: (01650) 511288

Cottage of character situated in a quiet rural village amongst glorious unspoilt countryside. Seven miles from Machynlleth. Ideal base for walking, birdwatching and exploring Mid Wales. Well equipped kitchen has microwave, cooker, fridge. Sky digital TV in lounge. Garden with barbeque and picnic table. Bed linen provided. Brochure.

Months open 1-12; 2 Nights £50.00-£60.00. 3 Nights £75.00-£85.00.
4 Nights £90.00-£110.00. Weekly/unit £130.00-£195.00.
UNITS 1 SLEEPS 4 ⏰ ▭ SP Ⓜ 🍴 ✹ P2 ℹ

ROSE COTTAGE ★★★★

Llandyssil, _MONTGOMERY_ SY15 6LQ
Enquiries: Mrs S. Ralph, Garreg, Llandyssil,
Montgomery SY15 6LQ Tel: (01686) 668364
Website: www.powysguest.co.uk

Guests return each year to comfortable, clean cottage in small village near shop, P.O., bakery, pub. Ideal walking, touring or just relaxing. Details available.

Months open 1-12; 2 Nights £60.00. 3 Nights £90.00.
4 Nights £120.00. Weekly/unit £125.00-£200.00.
UNITS 1 SLEEPS 4-5 ⏰ ▭ SP Ⓜ 🖥 P2 ℹ

HAINES MILL ★★★★

NEW RADNOR, Presteigne LD8 2TN
Tel: (01544) 350327 Fax: (01544) 350327

Tastefully restored self-contained flat in old mill has two double bedrooms, shower room, kitchenette, lounge area with television. The mill nestles alongside its stream at the base of beautiful Harley Valley, close to Radnor Forest which provides great pleasure for walkers, cyclists, bird watchers and all nature lovers alike.

Months open 1-12; 3 Nights £90.00-£105.00.
Weekly/unit £163.00-£215.00.
UNITS 1 SLEEPS 4-5 ⏰ ▭ SP 🍴 P2

CORNER HOUSE COTTAGE ★★★★

c/o Upper House, Kinnerton,
PRESTEIGNE LD8 2PE
Tel: (01547) 560207

Delightful cottage in Radnor Valley on mixed working farm. Refurbished lounge with picturesque inglenook, wood-burner (logs available), CTV. Pine furnished kitchen, electric cooker, microwave, washing machine. Sun-trap garden secure for children/pets. Short breaks available. Within easy reach of Hay-on-Wye, Ludlow, and Kite Country. Ideal for exploring Mid Wales' beautiful borderland.

Months open 1-12; 2 Nights £65.00-£70.00. 3 Nights £75.00-£100.00.
4 Nights £85.00-£120.00. Weekly/unit £100.00-£250.00.
UNITS 1 SLEEPS 5+2 ⏰ ▭ SP 🍴 P3

DERWEN HOUSE ★★★★

Derwen Garden Centre, Guilsfield,
WELSHPOOL **SY21 9PH**
Tel: (01938) 553015 Fax: (01938) 556170

A large gracious estate dower house, comprising two self-contained units, set in glorious Mid Wales countryside. Powis Castle, Llanfair light railway and Lake Vyrnwy are amongst numerous local attractions. Good walking area. Shop, post office, two pubs nearby. Adjacent to owner's garden centre. 10% discount throughout for house visitors.

Months open 1-12; 3 Nights £145.00-£325.00. 4 Nights £195.00-£405.00. Weekly/unit £225.00-£485.00.

UNITS 2 SLEEPS 6-16

BRECON BEACONS HOLIDAY COTTAGES ★★ UP TO ★★★★★

Brynoyre, Talybont-on-Usk, ***BRECON*** **LD3 7YS**
Tel: (01874) 676446 Fax: (01874) 676416
E-mail: enquiries@breconcottages.com
Website: www.breconcottages.com

GOLD

Over 200 cottages and farmhouses, some sleeping up to 40 people in the Brecon Beacons, Black Mountains, Wye Valley and South Wales Valleys. Excellent locations for touring, hill walking, pony trekking, mountain biking, bird watching, fishing, sailing, climbing, golf and a great many other types of outdoor pursuits. Free colour brochure.

Months open 1-12; 2 Nights £95.00-£575.00. 3 Nights £105.00-£675.00. Weekly/unit £135.00-£1350.00.

UNITS 230 SLEEPS 2-50 (FR,I)

VALLEY VIEW & DINGLE COTTAGE ★★★★★

Tynllwyn Farm, ***WELSHPOOL*** **SY21 9PG**
Tel: (01938) 553175 Fax: (01938) 555306
E-mail: caroline.emberton@cp-ltd.co.uk

GOLD

Two beautifully restored, fully-equipped farm cottages. Sleep 4-6. Panoramic views, lovely walks, close to Powis Castle. Fishing, golf, quad and pony trekking all nearby. Both cottages furnished to high standard with pine furniture. Fitted kitchen including microwave, washing machine and dryer facilities. Lawns to rear with own patio furniture.

Months open 1-12; 2 Nights £60.00-£110.00. 3 Nights £80.00-£125.00. 4 Nights £95.00-£200.00. Weekly/unit £125.00-£400.00.

UNITS 2 SLEEPS 4-6

CALL IN AT A TOURIST INFORMATION CENTRE

Wales's network of TICs helps you get the best out of your holiday.

- Information on what to see and where to go ● Local events
- Brochures, maps and guides ● And a Bed Booking Service

Properties displaying the ℹ️ *symbol can be booked through any networked Tourist Information Centre – this service is especially handy when you're out and about in Wales.*

The Offa's Dyke Path runs through rolling border country

Ceredigion – Cardigan Bay

Llangrannog, tucked away amongst the cliffs

*T*he southern arc of Cardigan Bay, dotted with pretty little resorts and stretches of spectacular Heritage Coast, is home to a prolific marine life including porpoises and dolphins. Inland, traditional farming country matched by traditional country towns rise into the wildernesses of the Cambrian Mountains. The Teifi Valley, in contrast, is a gentle, leafy landscape famous for its beautiful river scenery and falls.

On Your Travels ...

Vale of Rheidol Railway

Travelling is pure pleasure on the narrow-gauge Vale of Rheidol Railway. You set off from the coast at Aberystwyth and climb through a lovely wooded valley to the spectacular chasm and waterfalls at Devil's Bridge. Deeper in the Cambrian Mountains seek out Strata Florida Abbey, near Pontrhydfendigaid. Although now a ruin, a magical atmosphere envelopes this serene spot, an echo of its medieval status as the 'Westminster Abbey of Wales'.

Back along the coast, visit Aberaeron's Georgian-style harbour. This architectural gem is full of interest. There's a Sea Aquarium here which displays Cardigan Bay's rich marine life, and an unusual Honey Bee Exhibition – not to mention the chance to taste delicious honey ice-cream. For more of the 'coast and country' theme, travel inland from Aberaeron to the Teifi Valley, one of Wales's loveliest vales. Cenarth Falls is a famous beauty spot where you can learn about traditional fishing methods at the National Coracle Centre, a museum dedicated to the ancient one-man crafts still used on the Teifi.

For further information please tel (01970) 612125;
e-mail: econ@ceredigion.gov.uk
website: www.ceredigion.gov.uk

Where to Stay
Wales

Sandy Aberporth

Aberporth
Map Ref Fa5

Popular seaside village. Two attractive beaches and good sea fishing. Scenic cliff walks. Convenient for visiting other coastal villages along Cardigan Bay. Felinwynt Rain Forest and Butterfly Centre nearby.

Aberystwyth
Map Ref Fe2 ⇌

Premier resort on the Cardigan Bay coastline. Fine promenade, cliff railway, camera obscura, harbour and many other seaside attractions. Excellent museum in restored Edwardian theatre. University town, lively arts centre with theatre and concert hall. National Library of Wales stands commandingly on hillside. Good shopping. Vale of Rheidol narrow-gauge steam line runs to Devil's Bridge falls.

Cardigan
Map Ref Fa5

Bustling market town on mouth of the River Teifi close to beaches and resorts. Good

Cardigan, at the mouth of the Teifi

shopping facilities, accommodation, inns. Golf and fishing. Popular base for Cardigan Bay and for exploring inland along wooded Teifi Valley and west to the Pembrokeshire Coast National Park. Y Felin Corn Mill and ruined abbey at neighbouring St Dogmael's. Welsh Wildlife Centre nearby.

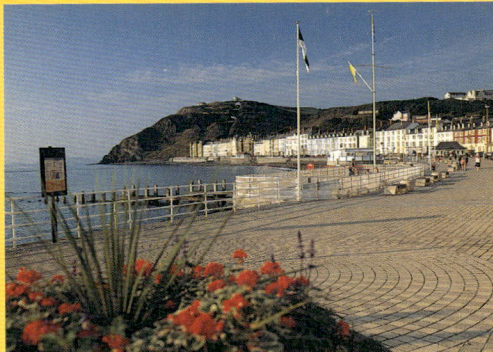
The promenade, Aberystwyth

The Vale of Rheidol Railway runs to Devil's Bridge

picturesque Teifi Valley. St David's University College founded in 1822 is modelled on the Oxford colleges' quadrangle layout. Concerts are often held here and visitors are welcome. Golf and angling, range of small shops and some old inns. Visit the landscaped hillside Cae Hir Gardens, Cribyn.

Devil's Bridge
Map Ref Ga2

Small mountain resort in beautiful wooded setting. Famous for its spectacular gorge and falls, accessible by steep footpath. At terminus of narrow-gauge Vale of Rheidol Railway which runs along lovely valley from Aberystwyth.

Lampeter
Map Ref Fe5

Farmers and students mingle in this distinctive old market and university town in the

Llangeitho
Map Ref Fe4

Village in farming country at the western approach to the wild, remote Cambrian Mountains. Handy for coast and country – Aberaeron, Cors Caron Nature Reserve (birdwatching) and Devil's Bridge all nearby.

Llanon
Map Ref Fd3

Cardigan Bay village well placed for touring the entire coast – halfway between Aberystwyth and New Quay, with attractive sand and pebble beach. Much to

see locally, including the Llanerchaeron Estate (National Trust).

Llanybydder
Map Ref Fd5

Small market town in the heart of the country beside the River Teifi. Holds a famous horse fair the last Thursday of each month which attracts people from far and wide.

Newcastle Emlyn
Map Ref Fb6

Traditional market town on the River Teifi. Teifi Valley Railway and Museum of the Welsh Woollen Industry are nearby attractions. A good base for touring north Pembrokeshire and Teifi Valley.

New Quay
Map Ref Fc4

Picturesque little resort with old harbour on Cardigan Bay. Lovely beaches and coves around and about. Good for sailing and fishing. Resort sheltered by protective headland.

Harbour and sheltered beach, New Quay

Devil's Bridge Falls

Hotels, Guest Houses & Farmhouses

BELLE VUE ROYAL HOTEL

★★★
HOTEL

Marine Terrace, *ABERYSTWYTH* SY23 2BA
Tel: (01970) 617558 Fax: (01970) 612190
E-mail: reception@bellevueroyalhotel.fsnet.co.uk
Website: www.bellevueroyal.co.uk

Situated on the seafront, the hotel is only a minute from the town centre. It is personally run by the proprietors. Decorated to a high standard resulting in individuality. It has both AA/RAC♦♦♦ and an AA Rosette for its cuisine.

Months open 1-12; B&B p/p £43.50-£45.00. 2 Nights Break D, B&B p/p £123.00-£125.00. Weekly D, B&B p/p £415.00-£430.00.

MARINE HOTEL & RESTAURANT

★★
HOTEL

The Promenade, *ABERYSTWYTH* SY23 2BX
Tel: (01970) 612444 Fax: (01970) 617435
Website: www.marinehotelaberystwyth.com

GOLD

Months open 1-12; B&B p/p £25.00-£50.00. 2 Nights Break D, B&B p/p £89.00-£115.00. Weekly D, B&B p/p £280.00-£385.00.

HAFOD ARMS HOTEL

★★
HOTEL

***DEVIL'S BRIDGE*, nr Aberystwyth SY23 3JL**
Tel: (01970) 890232 Fax: (01970) 890394
E-mail: enquiries@hafodarms.co.uk
Website: www.hafodarms.co.uk

Come and relax in this historic former shooting lodge. The only hotel at Devil's Bridge. Unique location overlooking wooded gorge and waterfalls. Splendid views of Red Kite country. Six acres of natural gardens. Private parking. Fully licensed. Elegant restaurant. Short breaks and themed weekends. Enquire direct.

Months open 1-12; B&B p/p £27.50-£40.00. 2 Nights Break D, B&B p/p £80.00. Weekly D, B&B p/p £280.00.

Bed & Breakfast
£27.50 p.p. is the most you'll pay

BRENDAN GUEST HOUSE

★
GUEST HOUSE

19 Marine Terrace, *ABERYSTWYTH* SY23 2AZ
Tel: (01970) 612252
E-mail: ivor.williams@virgin.net

Occupying a prime seafront position and a listed building. The Brendan is a comfortable family-run guest house with colour television, central heating, wash basins and tea/coffee-making facilities in all rooms, a number of which have en-suite amenities and extensive sea views.

Months open 1-12; Single B&B per night £20.00-£22.00. Double B&B per night £40.00-£44.00.

LLETY CEIRO COUNTRY GUEST HOUSE

★★★
GUEST HOUSE

Lôn Ceiro, Llandre, Bow St,
***ABERYSTWYTH* SY24 5AB**
Tel: (01970) 821900 Fax: (01970) 820966
E-mail: MarineHotel@Barbox.net

Luxury guest house set in beautiful surroundings on working sheep farm. Ideal location for walkers, bird watchers or activity holidays. All bedrooms are equipped to the highest standard. Fantastic home cooked food in our stylish restaurant with stunning views. Ideal for touring or corporate parties. Relax and enjoy. AA ♦♦♦♦.

Months open 1-12; B&B p/p from £20.00. 2 Nights Break D, B&B p/p £79.00-£110.00. Weekly D, B&B p/p £245.00-£325.00.

MARINE HOTEL & RESTAURANT

The Promenade, *ABERYSTWYTH* SY23 2BX
Tel: (01970) 612444 Fax: (01970) 617435
Website: www.marinehotelaberystwyth.com

Large seafront hotel. Superb ocean views from our refurbished bedrooms, bar, restaurant and bistro. Fantastic home-cooked traditional Welsh cuisine. A family run hotel highly recommended for our friendly atmosphere and every attention to guests' needs. 44 en-suite bedrooms. Lift to all floors. Disabled facilities. Leisure and gym facilities. Special bargain breaks.

Months open 1-12; B&B p/p from £25.00. 2 Nights Break D, B&B p/p £89.00-£115.00. Weekly D, B&B p/p £280.00-£350.00.

TYCAM FARM

Capel-Bangor, *ABERYSTWYTH* SY23 3NA
Tel: (01970) 880662

Peaceful dairy and sheep farm in glorious Rheidol Valley. Seven and a half miles from Aberystwyth, two and a half miles from A44. Real home comforts are offered in traditional Cardiganshire farmhouse. Lounge, dining room, separate tables, colour TV. Perfect walking, birdwatching (Red Kite area), sightseeing. Half a mile of superb salmon, sewin, trout fishing on farm plus nearby lake. Golf, leisure centre.

Months open 4-10; Double B&B per night £36.00-£42.00.

BRYNHYFRYD GUEST HOUSE

Gwbert Rd, *CARDIGAN* SA43 1AE
Tel: (01239) 612861 Fax: (01239) 612861
E-mail: garcus@btinternet.com

AA ♦. RAC ♦.
Months open 1-12; Single B&B per night £18.00-£25.00.
Double B&B per night £36.00-£40.00.

BRYNOWEN BED & BREAKFAST

Brynowen, Sarnau, Llandysul,
***CARDIGAN* SA44 6QT**
Tel: (01239) 654456 Fax: (01239) 654456

Close to the clean sandy beaches of the Ceredigion Heritage Coast, Brynowen is convenient for both sea and country. Easy access to the southern half of Cardigan Bay, historic Cardigan itself, and the beautiful Teifi Valley. All these, added to hearty breakfasts, are good reasons for temporarily making our home your home.

Months open 3-11; B&B p/p £15.00-£18.00.

HAFOD ARMS HOTEL

***DEVIL'S BRIDGE*, nr Aberystwyth SY23 3JL**
Tel: (01970) 890232 Fax: (01970) 890394
E-mail: enquiries@hafodarms.co.uk
Website: www.hafodarms.co.uk

Come and relax in this historic former shooting lodge. The only hotel at Devil's Bridge. Unique location overlooking wooded gorge and waterfalls. Splendid views of Red Kite country. Six acres of natural gardens. Private parking. Fully licensed, elegant restaurant. Short breaks and themed weekends. Enquire direct.

Months open 1-12; Double B&B per night £55.00.

BRYNOG MANSION

Felinfach, *LAMPETER* SA48 8AQ
Tel: (01570) 470266

Secluded spacious 250 year old mansion. 170 acre grazing farm, situated in the beautiful Vale of Aeron. Three quarters of a mile off the A482 midway between Lampeter and Aberaeron - a unique seaside resort just ten minutes by car. Full Welsh breakfast in the grand old furnished dining room. Separate guest's lounge. Garden for guest's use. Rough shooting, birdwatching and riverside walks. Welsh spoken.

Months open 1-12; Single B&B per night £22.50-£25.00.
Double B&B per night £45.00-£50.00.

HAULFAN

6 Station Terrace, *LAMPETER* SA48 7HH
Tel: (01570) 422718

Months open 1-12; B&B p/p £18.00-£20.00.

PANTYCELYN GUEST HOUSE

Llanwnnen, *LAMPETER* SA48 7LW
Tel: (01570) 434455 Fax: (01570) 434455
E-mail: huwannj@aol.com
Website: www.pantycelyn.co.uk

Relax and unwind in this peaceful unspoiled branch of the Teifi Valley. Pantycelyn, in 11 acres of meadows 5 miles west of Lampeter, is ideally situated for enjoying Cardigan Bay's Heritage Coast and Ceredigion's many other attractions. You are assured of a warm welcome, memorable breakfasts, plus friendly Welsh Cobs.

Months open 2-10; Single B&B per night £20.00-£22.00.
Double B&B per night £40.00-£44.00.

PENLANMEDD

Llanfair Rd, *LAMPETER* SA48 8JZ
Tel: (01570) 493438 Fax: (01570) 493438
E-mail: penlanmedd@coombes-e.freeserve.co.uk

If the idea of seclusion, comfort, good food, log fires, pretty gardens and wonderful views appeals - then stay with us in our 18th century farmhouse. Set in farmland overlooking the tranquil River Teifi Valley, we are just ½ hour from Cardigan Bay, Cambrian Mountains and all that this unspoilt area has to offer.

Months open 1-12; Single B&B per night £25.00.
Double B&B per night £38.00-£40.00.

FRONDOLAU FARM GUEST HOUSE

Heol Llain Prysg, *LLANON* SY23 5HZ
Tel: (01974) 202354

Months open 1-12; B&B p/p £16.00-£18.00.
Weekly D, B&B p/p £166.00-£178.00.

SLIDE SETS

Ask about our attractive range of 35mm colour slides showing views of Wales, available at 75p per slide.

For a complete list of subjects please contact the Photography Library, Wales Tourist Board, Brunel House, 2 Fitzalan Road, Cardiff CF24 0UY. Tel: (029) 2047 5215.

CLASSIFIED ADVERTISING There's more accommodation to choose from in the classified advertising section of this book. Please see the listing at the end of the 12 Areas display adverts.

Plynlimon's remote high country rises above Aberystwyth

Mwnt near Cardigan

Holiday Cottages

GORSLWYD FARM
★★★★

Tan-y-Groes, *ABERPORTH*, Cardigan SA43 2HZ
Tel: (01239) 810593 Fax: (01239) 811569
Enquiries: Jennie Donaldson

Attractive comfortable cottages set in beautiful gardens with stream, nature trail, adventure playground, barbecue, games room and farm animals. Close to many sandy beaches. In quiet safe seclusion but not remote - an ideal base for exploring Wales. Holidays for all ages to enjoy in every season. Wheelchair user access throughout. John Ch14 V27.

Months open 3-10; 2 Nights £60.00-£140.00. 3 Nights £90.00-£210.00.
4 Nights £120.00-£280.00. Weekly/unit £150.00-£350.00.
UNITS 8 SLEEPS 6

PENFFYNNON PROPERTIES
★★★★ UP TO ★★★★★
SILVER

Penffynnon, *ABERPORTH* SA43 2DA
Tel: (01239) 810387 Fax: (01239) 811401
E-mail: tt@lineone.net
Enquiries: Mrs Jann Tucker

Our comfortable, self contained and fully equipped properties are adjacent to the safe bathing of Aberporth's Blue Flag Beach. We have sea views, ample parking, and dogs are welcome by arrangement. Aberporth has several pubs and a full range of shops. Local attractions include Cardigan Bay Dolphins and water sports.

Months open 1-12; 2 Nights on request. 3 Nights on request.
4 Nights on request. Weekly/unit £150.00-£850.00.
UNITS 7 SLEEPS 5-8

PRICES

In this publication we go to great lengths to make sure that you have a clear, accurate idea of prices and facilities. It's all spelled out in the 'Prices' section – and remember to confirm everything when making your booking.

ABERLERI FARM COTTAGES
★★★★★
GOLD

Cambrian Coast Park, Borth,
nr *ABERYSTWYTH* SY24 5JU
Enquiries: Freepost Department WB
Tel: (01970) 871233 Fax: (01970) 871124
Website: www.sunbourne.co.uk

Re-built farmhouse and four cottages in landscaped grounds. Very close to sandy beaches, golf course, nature reserve. Borth village 1 mile. Luxuriously appointed accommodation. Satellite TV, central heating, wonderful kitchens and bathrooms. Indoor swimming pool and jacuzzi. Use of facilities at nearby top graded holiday park, with shop, bar, catering, clubroom, entertainment, children's activities.

Months open 1-12; Weekly/unit £145.00-£659.00.
UNITS 5 SLEEPS 2-10

ABERCEIRO BUNGALOW
★★★★
GOLD

Lôn Ceiro, Llandre, Bow St, *ABERYSTWYTH*
SY24 5AB Freephone: 0800 0190020

Months open 1-12; Weekly/unit £250.00-£375.00.
UNITS 1 SLEEPS 6

GEUALLT COTTAGE
★★★★

Old Goginan, *ABERYSTWYTH* SY23 3PD
Tel: (01562) 885097 Fax: (01562) 886838
Enquiries: Mrs G. Duffield, 28 Newfield Rd,
Hagley, Stourbridge DY9 0JR

Months open 5-10; Weekly/unit £225.00-£265.00.
UNITS 1 SLEEPS 4

APARTMENT 1, GLANAFON COURT
★★★★

Gwbert-on-Sea, *CARDIGAN* SA43 1PP
Tel: (01239) 612873
Enquiries: Mrs J. Roberts, Awel-y-nant,
Melin-y-Coed, Cardigan SA43 1PQ

Months open 1-12; 3 Nights £120.00-£200.00.
4 Nights £130.00-£250.00. Weekly/unit £200.00-£350.00.
UNITS 1 SLEEPS 4-6

CEREDIGION - CARDIGAN BAY

THREE HORSESHOE INN ★★★★
LLANGEITHO, Tregaron SY25 6TW
Tel: (01974) 821244
E-mail: jane.williams6@virgin.net
Enquiries: J. Williams

Months open 1-12; 2 Nights £50.00-£80.00. 3 Nights £75.00-£120.00.
4 Nights £100.00-£160.00. Weekly/unit £175.00-£280.00.
UNITS 1 SLEEPS 3-4

3 BELLE VUE ★★★
New Rd, *NEW QUAY*
Tel: (01545) 580686 Fax: (01545) 580686
E-mail: hencaliban@hotmail.com
Enquiries: Mrs Watson, Blaenddol, Gilfachreda,
New Quay SA45 9ST

Months open 3-9; 2 Nights £90.00-£140.00. Weekly/unit
£170.00-£380.00. UNITS 1 SLEEPS 5

FFOSFFALD ISAF / HEN DY PAIR ★★★★
Ffosffald, Drefeau, *LLANYBYDDER* SA40 9TA
Tel: (01570) 434200
Enquiries: Mrs M. Thomas

GOLD

Two cottages in rural setting facing panoramic views. Fully equipped warm, very comfortable with private patios barbecues. Swings, croquet pitch for children. Roam in our fields. Observe wildlife and starry skies in seclusion. Convenient to coast and hills. Regret no pets. Send for detailed information in our illustrated brochure.

Months open 3-12; 2 Nights £55.00-£90.00. 3 Nights £80.00-£110.00.
4 Nights £95.00-£130.00. Weekly/unit £170.00-£320.00.
UNITS 2 SLEEPS 4-5

YSBYTTY ★★★★
Llwyndyfydd, *NEW QUAY*, Llandysul SA44 6LF
Tel: (0116) 2675834
Enquiries: Margaret King

Beamed stone cottage set in woodland in valley leading to Cwmtudu cove and National Trust coastline. Area rich in animal and bird life. Picturesque harbours and beaches within easy reach. The mediaeval gardens of Aberglasney and the new National Botanical Garden of Wales are about a pleasant hour's drive away.

Months open 1-12; 3 Nights £105.00-£150.00.
Weekly/unit £210.00-£395.00.
UNITS 1 SLEEPS 6-8

THE COTTAGE ★★★★
Llain Brongwyn, Cwm-Cou, *NEWCASTLE EMLYN*
SA38 9PR Tel: (01239) 711024
E-mail: bruce@brongwyn.freeserve.co.uk
Enquiries: Bruce Wilson

Charming stone cottage sleeping 6. All modern conveniences. 8 miles from sandy coves of Cardigan Bay. Warm welcome from neighbouring owners, very private and peaceful, south facing with own 'secret garden', beamed ceilings and inglenook open fireplace. 3 miles NW Newcastle Emlyn with its good shops and pubs. Local fishing, golf and walking.

Months open 1-12; 2 Nights £80.00-£185.00. 3 Nights £104.00-£240.00.
4 Nights £128.00-£296.00. Weekly/unit £160.00-£370.00.
UNITS 1 SLEEPS 4-6

Cardigan Bay is dotted with many excellent beaches

Pembrokeshire

Saundersfoot, a popular sailing centre

*P*embrokeshire is one of Europe's finest stretches of coastal natural beauty and a haven for wildlife. The park, running for 225 square miles around the south-western tip of Wales, contains all the classic coastal features – huge beaches, tiny bays, towering headlands, wooded creeks, sheltered harbours and exposed headlands. Pembrokeshire's stunning coastal beauty extends inland to the Preseli Hills, grassy uplands scattered with mysterious prehistoric sites.

Oakwood Park

On Your Travels ...

Wales's most successful modern attraction must surely be Oakwood, near Narberth.

Styled on an American theme park, Oakwood packs in everything from white-knuckle rides to furry farm animals. Don't miss Megafobia, Britain's largest wooden rollercoaster, or – if you have the nerve – the heart-stopping Vertigo. Another highly popular family attraction in these parts is Folly Farm near Kilgetty, a large working farm which has thrown its doors open to visitors with huge success.

Yet another big success story in recent years has been the revival of traditional Welsh cheeses. See – and taste – what it's all about at the Llangloffan Farmhouse Cheese Centre near Mathry, where cheese is hand-made from the milk of the farm's own cows. Travel further west and you come to St Davids, the tiny cathedral city founded by Wales's patron saint. You'll be following in the footsteps of medieval travellers who were also drawn to this beautiful spot on pilgrimage to its purple-stoned cathedral, one of Christendom's great shrines.

For further information please tel (01646) 682278; e-mail: tourism@pembrokeshire.gov.uk

Amroth
Map Ref Ka3

Popular Carmarthen Bay village with sand and pebble beach. Starting point of the 186-mile-long Pembrokeshire Coast Path. Some attractive inns. National Trust's Colby Woodland Garden in hills above.

Boncath
Map Ref Fa6

Small village on eastern approach to Preseli Hills and Pembrokeshire Coast National Park. Good base for southern Cardigan Bay, north Pembrokeshire and lovely Teifi Valley with its coracles and woollen mills.

Broad Haven
Map Ref Jb5

Sand and green hills cradle this holiday village on St Bride's Bay in the far west of the Pembrokeshire Coast National Park. Beautiful beach and coastal walks. National Park Information Centre.

South-facing Amroth, at the start of the Pembrokeshire Coast National Park

Broad Haven beach

Cardigan
Map Ref Fa5

Bustling market town on mouth of the River Teifi close to beaches and resorts. Good shopping facilities, accommodation, inns. Golf and fishing. Popular base for Cardigan Bay and for exploring inland along wooded Teifi Valley and west to the Pembrokeshire Coast National Park. Y Felin Corn Mill and ruined abbey at neighbouring St Dogmael's. Welsh Wildlife Centre nearby.

Cilgerran
Map Ref Fa6

Village tucked away on a loop in the River Teifi. Spectacular views from ramparts of its romantic ruined castle. Plenty of local attractions, including the Wales Wildlife Centre. Close to Cardigan Bay and Pembrokeshire coast.

Cardigan, at Pembrokeshire's northern gateway

Clynderwen
Map Ref Je4 ⇌

Centrally located for all of Pembrokeshire, the village stands in countryside just south of the Preseli Hills. Llawhaden Castle, Black Pool Mill and Caverns and Oakwood Park all close by.

Croes-goch
Map Ref Jb3

Small village, useful spot for touring Pembrokeshire Coast National Park – especially its peaceful, rugged northern shores and nearby centres of St Davids and Fishguard. Llangloffan Farmhouse Cheese Centre nearby.

The harbour at Lower Fishguard

grounds. Attractive redeveloped riverside and old wharf buildings. Picton Castle a few miles to the east. Many attractions nearby, including Scolton Manor and Country Park, Pembrokeshire Motor Museum and Nant-y-Coy Mill. Centrally located for exploring all of Pembrokeshire Coast National Park.

Haverfordwest, a centrally located touring centre

Fishguard
Map Ref Jc2 ≈

Lower Fishguard is a cluster of old wharves and cottages around a beautiful sheltered harbour. Shopping in Fishguard town. Good walks along Pembrokeshire Coast Path and in the country. Nearby Goodwick is the Irish ferry terminal, with a direct rail link from London. Excellent range of craft workshops in area including Tregwynt Woollen Mill. Music Festival in summer.

The castle by the sea at Manorbier

Freshwater East
Map Ref Jd6

Sheltered sandy bay south-east of Pembroke with excellent beach backed by dunes. Magnificent walking on the coastal footpath to some of Pembrokeshire's most spectacular cliff scenery. Manorbier and Tenby close by.

Haverfordwest
Map Ref Jc5 ≈

Ancient town, administrative and shopping centre for the area. Medieval churches and narrow streets. Museum in castle

Little Haven
Map Ref Jb5

Combines with Broad Haven – just over the headland – to form a family seaside holiday centre. The village dips down to pretty sandy beach. A popular spot for sailing, swimming and surfing.

Manorbier
Map Ref Jd6 ≈

Described as 'the most pleasant spot in Wales' by much-travelled priest Gerald of Wales 800 years ago, this unspoilt village has an imposing Norman castle, sandy bay and fine coastal walks.

Newgale
Map Ref Jb4

Holiday village on extensive 2-mile west-facing beach within the Pembrokeshire Coast National Park. Excellent for windsurfing and central for beaches on St Bride's Bay. Solva and St Davids close by.

There's an attractive, spacious beach at Newgale

Newport, one of Pembrokeshire's many small resorts

Newport
Map Ref Jd2

Historic castled village on north Pembrokeshire coast. Fine beaches, sea fishing. Pentre Ifan Burial Chamber is nearby. Backed by Preseli Hills and overlooked by Carn Ingli Iron Age Fort.

Pembroke
Map Ref Jd6 ⇌

Ancient borough built around Pembroke Castle, birthplace of Henry VII. In addition to its impressive castle, well-preserved sections of old town walls. Fascinating Museum of the Home. Sandy bays within easy reach, yachting, fishing – all the coastal activities associated with estuaries. Plenty of things to see and do in the area, including visit to beautiful Upton Castle Grounds.

St Davids
Map Ref Ja4

Smallest cathedral city in Britain, shrine of Wales's patron saint. Magnificent ruins of a Bishop's Palace beside ancient cathedral nestling in hollow. Set in Pembrokeshire Coast National Park, with fine beaches nearby; superb scenery on nearby headland. Craft shops, sea life centres, boat trips to Ramsey Island, farm park; ideal for walking and birdwatching.

St Davids Cathedral

Sandy Haven
Map Ref Jb6

Hamlet west of Milford Haven near the entrance to the sheltered waters of the Haven. Overlooks inlet of Sandyhaven Pill. Promontory of Great Castle Head to the south.

Pembroke Castle

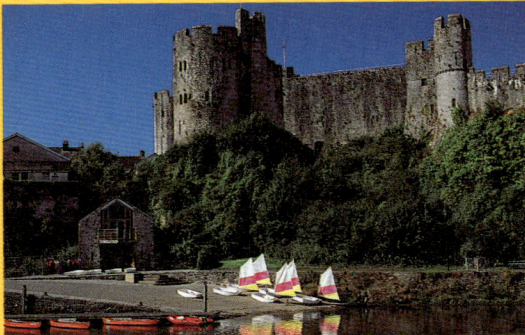

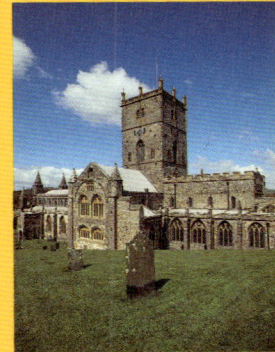

Saundersfoot, on Pembrokeshire's south coast

Saundersfoot

Map Ref Je6 ≷

Very attractive resort and sailing centre on the south Pembrokeshire coast within the national park. Good sandy beach and pretty harbour filled with colourful holiday craft. Excellent sea fishing. Tenby and a host of places to visit nearby, including Stepaside Bird and Animal Park, Stepaside Craft Village and Folly Farm, a family attraction based at a large working farm.

Solva

Map Ref Jb4

Pretty coastal village on St Bride's Bay with small, perfectly sheltered harbour and excellent range of quality craft shops. Pembrokeshire Coast Path offers good walking. Famous cathedral at nearby St Davids.

Tenby

Map Ref Je6 ≷

Picturesque south Pembrokeshire resort with two wide beaches. Fishing trips from attractive Georgian harbour and boat trips to nearby Caldy Island. The medieval walled town has a maze of narrow streets and fine old buildings, including Tudor Merchant's House. Galleries, craft shops, museum on headland. Attractions include Manor House Leisure Park and 'Silent World' Aquarium. Wales in Bloom award winner in 2000.

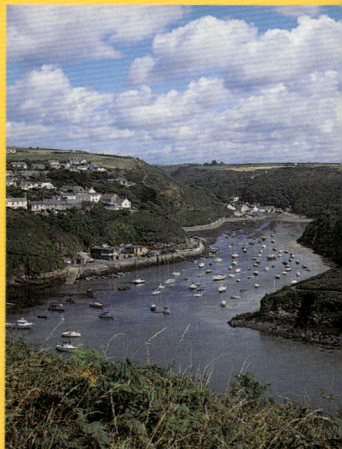

Solva's sheltered inlet

Trefin

Map Ref Jb3

Village between St Davids and Fishguard just a stone's throw from some of the most wildly beautiful – and remote – stretches of north Pembrokeshire coast. Wonderful walking on the coast path.

Tenby's handsome Georgian harbour

Hotels, Guest Houses & Farmhouses

WOLFSCASTLE COUNTRY HOTEL
★★★ HOTEL
GOLD

Wolfscastle, *HAVERFORDWEST* SA62 5LZ
Tel: (01437) 741688 Fax: (01437) 741383
E-mail: andy741225@aol.com

Friendly hotel sited only ten minutes from the coast and the ferry to Ireland. After twenty years under the same management, it has developed into one of Wales' most popular eating establishments, with 20 comfortable en-suite bedrooms and a bar and restaurant offering interesting local produce.

Months open 1-12; B&B p/p £39.00-£42.00. 2 Nights Break D, B&B p/p £106.00-£120.00.

THE BOWER FARM
★★★ FARM
AWARD
GOLD

***LITTLE HAVEN*, Haverfordwest SA62 3TY**
Tel: (01437) 781554 Fax: (01437) 781940
E-mail: bowerfarm@lineone.net
Website: www.a1tourism.com/uk/bower.html

Months open 1-12; B&B p/p £22.00-£29.00. 2 Nights Break D, B&B p/p £88.00-£102.00. Weekly D, B&B p/p £275.00-£339.00.

WHITEGATES
★★ GUEST HOUSE
GOLD

***LITTLE HAVEN*, Haverfordwest SA62 3LA**
Tel: (01437) 781552 Fax: (01437) 781552

Overlooking St Brides Bay and fishing village, conservatory, bar overlooking pool-bay, bird islands, wild flowers, golf, diving, windsurfing, close by. Choice eating places within easy walking.

Months open 1-12; B&B p/p £18.00-£27.00. 2 Nights Break D, B&B p/p POA. Weekly D, B&B p/p POA.

THE COACH HOUSE HOTEL
★★★ HOTEL

116 Main St, *PEMBROKE* SA71 4HN
Tel: (01646) 684602 Fax: (01646) 687456
E-mail: griffin@coachhouse-hotel.co.uk
Website: www.pembrokeshire.co.uk

A traditional coaching inn situated in the medieval castle town of Pembroke. Tastefully refurbished throughout to provide 16 comfortable en-suite bedrooms. Family rooms available, tea/coffee making facilities, colour TV's. Excellent restaurant, dine in style beside open log fire. Patio area for warmer nights. 5 mins to beaches and coastal paths.

Months open 1-12; B&B p/p £25.00-£35.00. 2 Nights Break D, B&B p/p £69.50.

POYERSTON FARM
★★★★ FARM
GOLD

Cosheston, *PEMBROKE* SA72 4SJ
Tel: (01646) 651347 Fax: (01646) 651347
E-mail: poyerston@pfh.co.uk
Website: www.pfh.co.uk/poyerston

Enjoy luxury accommodation on our family run working farm. Nestled between medieval Pembroke and historic Carew. Minutes away from beautiful south Pembrokeshire coastline, sandy beaches and scenic walks in National Park. En-suite bedrooms (some ground floor). Relaxing conservatory overlooking gardens. 'Taste of Wales' hospitality and cuisine. Colour brochure from Sheila Lewis.

Months open 1-12; B&B p/p £24.00-£27.00. 2 Nights Break D, B&B p/p £78.00-£85.00. Weekly D, B&B p/p on request.

WHITESANDS BAY HOTEL
★ HOTEL

***ST DAVIDS* SA62 6PT**
Tel: (01437) 720403 Fax: (01437) 720403

Wales most westerly family hotel. Panoramic views over St David's Head, Whitesands Bay and Ramsey Island, close to coastal path, environmentally clean beach. Concessional green fees, several local golf courses, excellent food and wines in restaurant and licensed bars, en-suite rooms with usual facilities, colour TV's. Short breaks off season. Quiet parkland setting, swimming pool, sauna.

Months open 1-12; B&B p/p £35.00-£43.00. 2 Nights Break D, B&B p/p £97.00-£109.50. Weekly D, B&B p/p £330.00-£388.50.

Milford Haven Waterway, a major coastal feature, is used by crafts large and small

BAY VIEW HOTEL

★★ HOTEL

Pleasant Valley, Stepaside,
***SAUNDERSFOOT* SA67 8LR**
Tel: (01834) 813417

Family hotel with friendly atmosphere. Children welcome. Situated in private peaceful surroundings away from crowded places, within easy reach of beaches, attractions and beautiful walks. Cots, high chairs, baby listening, washing facilities. Crazy golf, mini golf, swings, outdoor heated swimming pool. TV lounge, residential licence, lunchtime snacks. Entertainment weekly main season. Ample parking.

Months open 4-9; B&B p/p £15.25-£19.25.
Weekly D, B&B p/p £145.00-£170.00.

MERLEWOOD HOTEL

★★ HOTEL

St. Brides Hill, *SAUNDERSFOOT* SA69 9NP
Tel: (01834) 812421 Fax: (01834) 814886
E-mail: merlewood@saundersfoot.freeserve.co.uk
Website: www.merlewood.co.uk

Ideally positioned with superb views of Saundersfoot beach and Carmarthen Bay. Excellent table d'hote menu (children's choice menu). Sea view, lounge bar and verandah. Heated outdoor swimming pool (open whitsun to mid Sept), play area, table tennis, launderette, mini-golf, entertainment main season. Groups welcome. Family suites. Ample parking. No pets. AA/RAC♦♦. Online brochure request.

Months open 4-10; B&B p/p £25.00-£27.00.
Weekly D, B&B p/p £195.00-£245.00.

BOOK DIRECT

Just pick up the phone and talk direct to your chosen accommodation. You'll receive personal attention – and will be speaking to someone who can answer all your questions so you can make your booking there and then. Nothing could be simpler.

In looking through these pages you'll also find that much of the accommodation can also be contacted by e-mail.

ATLANTIC HOTEL

★★★★ HOTEL SILVER

The Esplanade, *TENBY* SA70 7DU
Tel: (01834) 842881 Fax: (01834) 842881 Ex. 256
E-mail: enquiries@atlantic-hotel.uk.com
Website: www.atlantic-hotel.uk.com

The Atlantic Hotel has spectacular views of the sea. Relax in the indoor heated pool, spa bath and steam room. Choice of restaurants. Private car park. Lift.

Months open 1-12; B&B p/p £42.00-£65.00.

CLARENCE HOUSE HOTEL

★★ HOTEL

Esplanade, *TENBY* SA70 7DU
Tel: (01834) 844731 Fax: (01834) 844372
E-mail: clarencehotel@freeuk.com
Website: www.clarencehotel-tenby.co.uk

Comfortable south-facing seafront hotel close to walled town with superb views of Caldey Island and the Pembrokeshire coast. Renowned for carefree relaxed holidays. Ground floor sea view dining room, excellent cuisine. Cliff gardens opposite with access to South Beach. Residents' bar. Rose garden, patio. Lift to all en-suite bedrooms which have colour TV and teamaker. Send now for free colour brochure/tariff.

Months open 2-12; B&B p/p £20.00-£50.00. 2 Nights Break D, B&B p/p £52.00-£100.00. Weekly D, B&B p/p £182.00-£392.00.

THE KINLOCH COURT HOTEL

★★★ HOTEL BRONZE

Queens Parade, *TENBY* SA70 7EG
Tel: (01834) 842777 Fax: (01834) 843097
E-mail: kinlochhotel@aol.com

Kinlock Court is excellently positioned above South Beach yet only three minutes from the town centre and harbour. Fourteen well appointed bedrooms, all en-suite, with private facilities. TV lounge, licensed bar. Welcoming atmosphere, superb restaurant, private car park. Please telephone for brochure.

Months open 1-12; B&B p/p £29.00-£33.00. 2 Nights Break D, B&B p/p £86.00-£94.00. Weekly D, B&B p/p £294.00-£322.00.

LAMPHEY COURT HOTEL

★★★★
HOTEL

BRONZE

Lamphey, **PEMBROKE** SA71 5NT
Tel: (01646) 672273 Fax: (01646) 672480
E-mail: info@lampheycourt.co.uk
Website: www.lampheycourt.co.uk

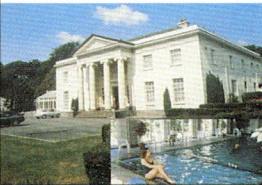

One of Wales' leading country hotels. Beautifully restored Georgian mansion in quiet grounds near coast, renowned for award-winning food and warm hospitality. Spacious bedrooms - complemented by attractive courtyard studios - ideal for families. Children share free. Superb leisure centre, swimming pool, jacuzzi, saunas, gym, tennis, beautician. Corporate and Leisure rates. Conference rates. Best Western.

Months open 1-12; B&B p/p £42.00-£65.00. 2 Nights Break D, B&B p/p £90.00-£146.00. Weekly D, B&B p/p £270.00-£499.00.

🛏37 ⇌37 📶 C 🍴🍷✿💷 ♿ SP ✿🏤 ✕ (FR,GR,I,D) TW P50 ℹ

TENBY HOUSE HOTEL

★★★
HOTEL

Tudor Square, **TENBY** SA70 7AJ
Tel: (01834) 842000 Fax: (01834) 844647
E-mail: tenbyhouse@virgin.net
Website: www.tenbyhousehotel.com

Tenby House has been recently renovated, preserving many of the fine features incorporated by Sir William Paxton. Winners of the prestigious National Park 2000 Award for enhancement within the historical core of Tenby. 18 quality en-suite bedrooms. Lesley and Griff Fisher extend a warm welcome.

Months open 1-12; B&B p/p £35.00-£45.00.
2 Nights Break D, B&B p/p £110.00-£150.00.

🛏18 ⇌18 C 🍴🍷💷 ♿ SP ⊿🏤 TW P14 ℹ

ROYAL LION HOTEL

★★★
HOTEL

BRONZE

North Beach, **TENBY** SA70 7EX
Tel: (01834) 842127 Fax: (01834) 842441
E-mail: royal-liontenby@hotmail.com

Originally a Coaching Inn but today it enjoys completely refurbished bedrooms, ground floor bars, restaurant, foyer and reception areas. The Royal Lion has a proud reputation for good food and the restaurant and many bedrooms command spectacular views of Tenby Harbour. Exclusive use of indoor pool next door. Full colour brochure and tariff available.

Months open 1-12; B&B p/p £30.00-£45.00.
2 Nights Break B&B p/p £50.00-£80.00.

🛏21 ⇌21 C 🍴🍷💷 ♿ SP ⊿ TW P

LAST-MINUTE DEALS

For the latest information and offers on holidays and short breaks in Wales, see: Teletext Page 251

Look out for the Wales Tourist Board grading on Teletext entries to make sure that the accommodation has been checked out by us.

Bed & Breakfast
£27.50 p.p. is the most you'll pay

BEACHAVEN GUEST HOUSE

★★
GUEST HOUSE

Amroth Sea Front, **AMROTH**,
Narberth SA67 8NG
Tel: (01834) 813310

Months open 4-10; Single B&B per night £15.00. Double B&B per night £30.00-£34.00.

🛏3 ⇌3 📶 🍴🍷 ♿ SP ℹ

ANCHOR GUEST HOUSE

★★
GUEST HOUSE

Enfield Rd, **BROAD HAVEN** SA62 3JN
Tel: (01437) 781051 Fax: (01437) 781050
E-mail: anch@bdhn.fsnet.co.uk
Website: www.anchor-guesthouse.co.uk

Months open 1-12; Single B&B per night £18.00-£27.50.
Double B&B per night £36.00-£55.00.

🛏8 ⇌8 📶 C ♿✿P ℹ

ATLANTIC VIEW

★★★
BED & BREAKFAST

BRONZE

Settlands Hill, **BROAD HAVEN**,
Haverfordwest SA62 3JY Tel: (01437) 781589
E-mail: enquiries@atlantic-view.co.uk
Website: www.atlantic-view.co.uk

Comfort and a warm welcome await you with un-interrupted panoramic views of the beach and the whole of St Brides bay. Perfectly situated for the coast path and just a few minutes' walk from Broad Haven and Little Haven, both of which have a good choice of pubs, restaurants and shops.

Months open 1-12; Double B&B per night £40.00-£50.00.

🛏5 ⇌5 C ♿✿P

CLASSIFIED ADVERTISING

There's more accommodation to choose from in the classified advertising section of this book.
Please see the listing at the end of the 12 Areas display adverts.

BARLEY VILLA

★★★ FARM

Walwyns Castle, nr *BROAD HAVEN*, Haverfordwest SA62 3EB
Tel: (01437) 781254
E-mail: barley-villa@pfh.co.uk

GOLD

Months open 4-10; Single B&B per night £25.00. Double B&B per night £37.00-£44.00.

LION ROCK

★★★ GUEST HOUSE

***BROAD HAVEN*, Haverfordwest SA62 3JP**
Tel: (01437) 781645 Fax: (01437) 781203
E-mail: lion.rock@btinternet.com
Website: www.jpmarketing.co.uk/lionrock

GOLD

Quiet cliff top position with stunning views over St. Bride's Bay. Own access to Pembrokeshire coastal path. Three minutes' walk to safe, sandy beach with windsurfing, surfing and diving facilities available locally. Ideal for walkers, bird watchers, short distance to boats for bird islands. Excellent breakfasts are our speciality.

Months open 3-10; Single B&B per night £20.00-£25.00. Double B&B per night from £40.00.

WYNDARRA B&B

★★ BED & BREAKFAST

Wyndarra, *CILGERRAN* SA43 2RY
Tel: (01239) 621243

Wyndarra B&B is adjoining the Welsh Wildlife centre. Just a few minutes walk to Cilgerran Castle and the River Teifi which runs through a beautiful gorge with woodland walks and nearby beaches. Only four miles from Cardigan market town and many places of historical interest nearby.

Months open 1-11; B&B p/p £16.00-£18.00.

BANK HOUSE FARM

★★ FARM

***CROESGOCH*, Haverfordwest SA62 5LF**
Tel: (01348) 831305

Months open 3-11; Single B&B per night £17.00-£19.00. Double B&B per night £34.00-£38.00.

DOLWERN

★★ BED & BREAKFAST

Feidr Fawr, Dinas Cross, Newport, *FISHGUARD* SA42 0UY Tel: (01348) 811266
Mobile: 07949 523131
E-mail: annette-keylock@lineone.net

'Dolwern' is a ten minute walk from the coastal path and fifteen minutes from Pwllgwaelod and Cwm-yr-Eglwys beaches. We are on the edge of the Preseli Mountains, an ideal base for walkers, cyclists and tourists. A quiet comfortable, hundred year old house. Come and enjoy the magical beauty of Pembrokeshire with us.

Months open 1-12; Single B&B per night £17.00. Double B&B per night £36.00-£38.00.

HEATHFIELD MANSION

★★★ GUEST HOUSE

Mathry Rd, Letterston, *FISHGUARD* SA62 5EG
Tel: (01348) 840263 Fax: (01348) 840263
Central Reservations Tel: (01348) 873484
E-mail: heathfield@p.net.co.uk or angelica.rees@virgin.net
Website: www.p-net.co.uk/heathfield

GOLD

Georgian country house within its own grounds of pastures and woodland. A perfect place to relax, it is also ideally suited to explore Pembrokeshire's treasures. The guest rooms are comfortable and spacious with beautiful views over rolling countryside. Golf, horse-riding, sailing, coastal and hill walking nearby. Self-catering available. French & German spoken.

Months open 3-10; Single B&B per night £22.00-£25.00. Double B&B per night £44.00-£50.00.

SEALYHAM FARM GUEST HOUSE

★★★ FARM

Wolfscastle, Haverfordwest, *FISHGUARD* SA62 5NE
Tel: (01348) 840512 Fax: (01348) 840512
E-mail: lindaroche@uk.packardbell.org
Website: www.pembrokeshireholidays.co.uk

AWARD

Months open 1-12; B&B p/p £20.00-£24.00. 2 Nights Break D, B&B p/p £55.00-£65.00. Weekly D, B&B p/p £190.00-£218.00.

CUCKOO MILL FARM

★★★ FARM

Pelcomb Bridge, St Davids Rd, *HAVERFORDWEST* SA62 6EA
Tel: (01437) 762139

GOLD

Genuine welcome to our working family farm. Comfortable Edwardian house set in peaceful countryside in central Pembrokeshire. Perfect situation for touring Pembrokeshire especially coastline, beaches, historical places. Comfortable, relaxed, quality accommodation. En-suite bedrooms with TV, teatray, radio. Excellent, plentiful, varied home cooking. Unrestricted access. Apply Margaret Davies.

Months open 1-12; Single B&B per night £20.00-£25.00. Double B&B per night £40.00-£50.00.

THE FOLD

★★ BED & BREAKFAST

Cleddau Lodge, Camrose, *HAVERFORDWEST* SA62 6HY
Tel: (01437) 710640 Fax: (01437) 710663
E-mail: cleddau.lodge@btinternet.com

Converted 17th century farmhouse in secluded garden, overlooking River Cleddau. Private fishing available. Central to Pembrokeshire coast - six miles. Double bedroom with wash basin, private shower room with WC. Homely welcome. Part of 50 acre estate with gardens. Woodlands and river with otters. Views of the Preseli Hills.

Months open 3-10; Single B&B per night £16.50-£18.50. Double B&B per night £33.00-£37.00.

THE BOWER FARM

★★★ FARM

***LITTLE HAVEN*, Haverfordwest SA62 3TY**
Tel: (01437) 781554 Fax: (01437) 781940
E-mail: bowerfarm@lineone.net
Website: www.a1tourism.com/uk/bower.html

AWARD / GOLD

Months open 1-12; Single B&B per night £22.00-£27.00. Double B&B per night £44.00-£54.00.

PRICES

Single rates are for ONE PERSON in a single room. Double rates are for TWO PEOPLE sharing a double or twin room. There may be supplements for private bath/shower and single occupancy of a double/twin room. All prices quoted include VAT. Please check all prices and facilities before confirming your booking.

BWRDD CROESO CYMRU
WALES TOURIST BOARD
Quality Inspected

WHITEGATES
★★ BED & BREAKFAST

LITTLE HAVEN, Haverfordwest SA62 3LA
Tel: (01437) 781552 Fax: (01437) 781552

Overlooking St Brides Bay and fishing village, conservatory, bar overlooking pool-bay, bird island, wild flowers, golf, diving, windsurfing, close-by, Choice eating places within easy walking.

Months open 1-12; B&B p/p £18.00-£27.00.

🛏4 ➡4 🍴♦🐾✕🖶 SP ⛄❄ TW P 🅹

HONEYHILL B&B
★★ BED & BREAKFAST

Warlows Meadow, *MANORBIER* SA70 7SX
Tel: (01834) 871906 Fax: (01834) 871293

Months open 1-12; B&B p/p £18.00-£22.00.

🛏2 ➡2 C ♦🖶❄✕(FR) P2 🅹

WYNDHURST
★★★★ BED & BREAKFAST

NEWGALE, Haverfordwest SA62 6AS
Tel: (01437) 720162

Months open 1-12; Single B&B per night £18.00-£25.00. Double B&B per night £35.00-£40.00.

🛏3 ➡1 ♦🖶✕❄(FR,GR,PGS) P6

LLYS DEWI
★★ BED & BREAKFAST

Fishguard Rd, *NEWPORT* SA42 0UF
Tel: (01239) 820177

Months open 3-10; Single B&B per night from £25.00. Double B&B per night £36.00-£40.00.

🛏3 ➡3 🐾♦🖶❄🎏 P2 🅹

SOAR HILL
★★★ BED & BREAKFAST

Cilgwyn Rd, *NEWPORT* SA42 0QG
Tel: (01239) 820506
E-mail: soarhill@hotmail.com

Months open 1-12; B&B p/p £20.00-£25.00. 2 Nights Break B&B p/p £36.00-£45.00. Weekly B&B p/p £96.00-£120.00.

🛏3 ➡2 C ♦ SP ✕🐾❄🎏 P4 🅹

TREE TOPS
★★★★ GUEST HOUSE

West St, *NEWPORT* SA42 0TD
Tel: (01239) 820048 Fax: (01239) 820048
E-mail: bandbtreetops@talk21.com

Months open 1-12; B&B p/p £22.00-£25.00. 2 Nights Break B&B p/p £44.00-£50.00. Weekly B&B p/p £150.00.

🛏3 ➡3 C ♦ SP 🖶❄ P3 🅹

Still Undecided?

Then call Central Reservations on freephone 0800 834820 for North Wales, 0800 273747 for Mid Wales or 0800 3289597 for South and West Wales – and you'll be plugged into a great choice of places to stay.

HALF-PINT COTTAGE
★★★ BED & BREAKFAST

Merrion Village, *PEMBROKE* SA71 5HT
Tel: (01646) 661278 & 07979 535623

GOLD

Charming cottage with interesting history, set in delightful garden. Guests' own lounge to relax by log fire. Close to spectacular Pembrokeshire coast path and beautiful beaches. An ideal base for walkers, cyclists, and people seeking a warm welcome and somewhere to unwind from stressful reality. We have something special here.

Months open 1-12; B&B p/p £18.00-£20.00.
2 Nights Break D, B&B p/p £54.00-£60.00.

🛏3 🍴♦🖶❄✕ P2 🅹

MIDDLEGATE HOTEL
★ HOTEL

43 Main St, *PEMBROKE* SA71 4JS
Tel: (01646) 622442 Fax: (01646) 622442

Months open 1-12; B&B p/p £20.00-£22.00.

🛏4 ➡4 🍴♟♦🎵❄ P20+ 🅹

POYERSTON FARM
★★★★★ FARM

Cosheston, *PEMBROKE* SA72 4SJ
Tel: (01646) 651347 Fax: (01646) 651347
E-mail: poyerston@pfh.co.uk
Website: www.pfh.co.uk/poyerston

GOLD

Enjoy luxury accommodation on our family run working farm. Nestled between medieval Pembroke and historic Carew. Minutes away from beautiful South Pembrokeshire coastline, sandy beaches and scenic walks in National Park. En-suite bedrooms (some ground floor). Relaxing conservatory overlooking gardens. 'Taste of Wales' hospitality and cuisine. Colour brochure from Sheila Lewis.

Months open 1-12; Single B&B per night £24.00-£27.00. Double B&B per night £48.00-£54.00.

🛏5 ➡5 C 🍴♦ SP 🖶❄ TW P12 🅹

ROSEDENE LICENSED GUEST HOUSE
★★★ GUEST HOUSE

Rosedene, Hodgeston, nr Freshwater East, *PEMBROKE* SA71 5JU
Tel: (01646) 672586 Fax: (01646) 672855
E-mail: eileen@rosedene85.freeserve.co.uk
Website: www.rosedene85.freeserve.co.uk

SILVER

Months open 2-11; Double B&B per night £44.00-£54.00.

🛏7 ➡7 C 🍴♟♦🖶 SP 🖶❄ TW P7 🅹

SEAHORSES
★★ BED & BREAKFAST

Freshwater East, *PEMBROKE* SA71 5LA
Tel: (01646) 672405

Months open 5-9; Single B&B per night £16.00-£18.00. Double B&B per night £32.00-£36.00.

🛏2 ♦P 🅹

MURMUR-Y-MOR

BED & BREAKFAST ★★★

Abereiddy, *ST DAVIDS*, Haverfordwest SA62 6DS
Tel: (01348) 381670

Months open 3-10; Single B&B per night £20.00.
Double B&B per night £36.00-£40.00.

TORBANT FARMHOUSE

★★ FARM GOLD

Croesgoch, *ST DAVIDS*, Haverfordwest SA62 5JN
Tel: (01348) 831276 Fax: (01348) 831276
E-mail: torbant@pfh.co.uk
Website: www.pfh.co.uk/torbant

A warm welcome awaits you at Torbant, a peacefully situated farmhouse near St Davids and Pembrokeshire Coast National Park. The sea is 1.5 miles away with beautiful beaches and magnificent scenery. Both en-suite rooms have TV and beverage trays. Hearty breakfasts with local produce. Lounge always available, also useful utility room.

Months open 3-10; B&B p/p £20.00-£22.00.

SKERRYBACK

★★★ FARM AWARD GOLD

SANDY HAVEN, Haverfordwest SA62 3DN
Tel: (01646) 636598 Fax: (01646) 636595
E-mail: skerryback@pfh.co.uk
Website: www.pfh.co.uk/skerryback

Months open 3-11; Single B&B per night £20.00-£25.00. Double B&B per night £40.00-£50.00.

VALLEY FARMHOUSE

BED & BREAKFAST ★★

Valley Rd, *SAUNDERSFOOT* SA69 9BX
Tel: (01834) 813388
E-mail: gpearson@farmvalley.co.uk

A warm welcome awaits you at our 19thc farmhouse with log fires and original beams. One mile sandy beaches and coastal path. Comfortable en-suite double room with TV and tea-making facilities (cot available). Also separate bunk bedded room. Special nightly family rates from £50. Vegetarians welcome. Home made bread and cakes.

Months open 4-10; Double B&B per night £35.00-£40.00.

PENTIGILI

BED & BREAKFAST ★★★

Carnhedryn, nr *ST DAVIDS*,
Haverfordwest SA62 6XT
Tel: (01437) 720692 Fax: (01437) 721014
E-mail: Shaun-Rhian@Pentigili-bed-and-breakfast.co.uk
Website: www.pentigili-bed-and-breakfast.co.uk

Months open 4-10; B&B p/p £18.00-£20.00.

LLANDDINOG HOUSE

BED & BREAKFAST ★★★★

Llandelog, nr *SOLVA*, St Davids, Haverfordwest SA62 6NA Tel: (01348) 831467 Fax: (01348) 831467
E-mail: llanddinoghouse@solvawales.freeserve.co.uk
Website: www.stdavids.co.uk

Months open 1-12; Double B&B per night £50.00-£55.00.

CLARENCE HOUSE HOTEL

HOTEL ★★

Esplanade, *TENBY* SA70 7DU
Tel: (01834) 844371 Fax: (01834) 844372
E-mail: clarencehotel@freeuk.com
Website: www.clarencehotel-tenby.co.uk

Months open 2-12; Single B&B per night from £20.00. Double B&B per night from £36.00.

THE DIGGINS

BED & BREAKFAST ★★★

The Diggins, Lawrenny, *TENBY* SA68 0PW
Tel: (01646) 651235
E-mail: alisonlewis@thediggins.freeserve.co.uk
Website: www.ukbnb.net/diggins

Months open 1-12; B&B p/p £18.00-£24.00.

FLEMISH COURT

GUEST HOUSE ★★★ GOLD

St Florence, *TENBY* SA70 8LS
Tel: (01834) 871413

Here you will find a real Welsh welcome. All rooms en-suite. Sumptuous breakfasts. All day access. Parking. Situated in floral village with Norman church opposite. Easy access to all attractions, coastal walks, etc. Try us first for that restful, relaxing holiday you deserve. Evening meals available. Telephone for brochure. Safe parking.

Months open 1-12; Single B&B per night £25.00.
Double B&B per night £40.00.

GWYNNE HOUSE

GUEST HOUSE ★★★

Bridge St, *TENBY* SA70 7BU
Tel: (01834) 842862 Fax: (01834) 842862
E-mail: gwynnehouse@email-msn.com

For all year round holidays and short breaks. This elegant Georgian grade II listed building, situated above the harbour, enjoys picturesque views across the bay. Conveniently situated to enjoy a leisurely stroll around the walled town or to explore the Pembrokeshire Coast National Park. Brochure on request. Grading AA ◆◆◆◆. Open all year.

Months open 1-12; Single B&B per night from £25.00. Double B&B per night from £40.00.

HAMMONDS PARK HOTEL

HOTEL ★★ GOLD

Narberth Rd, *TENBY* SA70 8HT
Tel: (01834) 842696

Months open 1-12; Double B&B per night £38.00-£55.00.

PEN-MAR HOTEL

HOTEL ★★ BRONZE

New Hedges, *TENBY* SA70 8TL
Tel: (01834) 842435 Fax: (01834) 842435
E-mail: penmarhotel@jhurton.freeserve.co.uk
Website: www.s-h-systems.co.uk/a15498.html/

Months open 1-12; Single B&B per night £12.00-£18.00. Double B&B per night £36.00-£50.00.

SEA BREEZES HOTEL
★★ BED & BREAKFAST

18 The Norton, _TENBY_ SA70 8AA
Tel: (01834) 842753

All our comfortable rooms are en-suite and situated on the first floor with all modern amenities and a choice menu for breakfast. Approx 30 metres from Tenby's award-winning North beach and picturesque harbour. A short stroll from the unique town centre. Our breaks from autumn to early summer are excellent excellent value!

Months open 3-11; Single B&B per night £16.50-£22.00. Double B&B per night £33.00-£44.00.

SUTHERLANDS
★★ BED & BREAKFAST

3 Picton Rd, _TENBY_ SA70 7DP
Tel: (01834) 842522

Months open 1-12; Single B&B per night £18.00-£24.00. Double B&B per night £36.00-£48.00.

THE OLD COURT HOUSE VEGETARIAN GUEST HOUSE
★★★ BED & BREAKFAST
GOLD

TREFIN, nr St Davids, Haverfordwest
SA62 5AX Tel: (01348) 837095
E-mail: oldcourthouse@netscapeonline.co.uk
Website: www.pembrokeshire-online.co.uk/courthouse

Enjoy a relaxing break in our 200 year old cosy cottage offering en-suite rooms, open fire and delicious freshly prepared vegetarian/vegan food. Situated in the village of Trefin just 2 minutes from the spectacular Pembrokeshire coast footpath. Cookery courses and demonstrations also available from October-March.

Months open 1-12; B&B p/p £22.50. 2 Nights Break D, B&B p/p £37.00. Weekly D, B&B p/p £245.00.

Holiday Cottages

IVY COURT COTTAGES
★★★★ UP TO ★★★★★
BRONZE

Ivy Court, Llys-y-Fran, nr _HAVERFORDWEST_
SA63 4RS Tel: (01437) 532473 Fax: (01437) 532346
E-mail: holidays@ivycourt.co.uk
Website: www.ivycourt.co.uk

Months open 1-12; Short Breaks from £90.00.
Weekly/unit £170.00-£625.00.

UNITS 10

FRON FAWR
★★★★★
BRONZE

BONCATH SA37 0HS
Tel: (01239) 841285 Fax: (0870) 1209175
E-mail: cottages@fronfawr.co.uk
Website: www.fronfawr.co.uk

48-acre property with views across the Pembrokeshire countryside. Its cottages are converted traditional stone and slate barns. See web site for full details or phone for brochure.

Months open 1-12; 3 Nights £95.00-£160.00. 4 Nights £105.00-£190.00. Weekly/unit £140.00-£750.00.

UNITS 4 SLEEPS 2-8

CLASSIFIED ADVERTISING There's more accommodation to choose from in the classified advertising section of this book. Please see the listing at the end of the 12 Areas display adverts.

HAVEN COTTAGES
★★★ GOLD

Whitegates, _LITTLE HAVEN_, Haverfordwest
SA62 3LA Tel: (01437) 781386 Fax: (01437) 781386
E-mail: welshhaven@aol.com Enquiries: Richard Llewellin

Situated 200m from sandy beach and coastal path on edge of village. Ideal windsurfing, golf, riding, bird islands, family beach holidays, easy walk to eating places.

Months open 1-12; 2 Nights £115.00-£245.00.
Weekly/unit £160.00-£555.00.

UNITS 2 SLEEPS 2-8

MILLMOOR COTTAGES & ROCKSDRIFT APARTMENTS
★★★★ GOLD

BROAD HAVEN, Haverfordwest SA62 3JH
Tel: 0800 0199930 Fax: (01437) 781002
E-mail: vw@millmoor.co.uk
Website: www.millmoor.co.uk

Prince of Wales Award winning accommodation in heart of Pembrokeshire Coast National Park. Superb beach and heritage coastline 200 yards. Well kept garden and play area. Personally run and supervised by owners who care! WTB gold medal winners. Write or phone (Freephone 0800 019930) anytime for free colour brochure.

Months open 1-12; 2 Nights £84.00-£175.00. 3 Nights £84.00-£175.00. 4 Nights £96.00-£195.00. Weekly/unit £120.00-£720.00.

UNITS 24 SLEEPS 2-8

TRENEWYDD FARM COTTAGES
★★★★★ BRONZE

St Dogmael's, _CARDIGAN_ SA43 3BJ
Tel: (01239) 612370 Fax: (01239) 621040
E-mail: cherylhyde@trenewyddfarm.fsnet.co.uk
Website: www.trenewyddfarm.fsnet.co.uk

Months open 1-12; 2 Nights £72.00-£153.00. 3 Nights £87.00-£200.00. 4 Nights £112.00-£260.00. Weekly/unit £179.00-£800.00.

UNITS 5 SLEEPS 13

Newgale, in the far west of Pembrokeshire

GWARMACWYDD FARM COTTAGES ★★★★

Llanfallteg, *CLYNDERWEN*, nr Whitland SA34 0XY
Tel: (01437) 563260 Fax: (01437) 563839
E-mail: info@a-farm-holiday.org
Website: www.a-farm-holiday.org
Enquiries: Mrs A. Colledge

A working farm of 400 acres, Gwarmacwydd is idyllically situated in the wooded Vale of the River Taf, within 25 minutes of the sandy beaches of Saundersfoot and Tenby. Gwarmacwydd's character stone cottages are a comfortable, centrally heated base from which to explore West Wales.

Months open 1-12; 2 Nights £50.00-£100.00. 3 Nights £75.00-£150.00. 4 Nights £100.00-£200.00. Weekly/unit £200.00-£460.00.

UNITS 5 SLEEPS 23

GARN-Y-MÛL ★★★

***CROESGOCH*, nr St Davids SA62 3JP**
Tel: (01959) 562972 Fax: (01959) 565365
Enquiries: Mrs Flynn, Froglets, Brasted Chart, Westerham TN16 1LY

Months open 1-12; 2 Nights £80.00-£150.00. 3 Nights £100.00-£190.00. 4 Nights £120.00-£250.00. Weekly/unit £160.00-£250.00.

UNITS 1 SLEEPS 4-6

PARK VIEW ★★

2 Park View, Ropewalk, *FISHGUARD* SA65 9BT
Tel: (01348) 873685 Enquiries: Mrs Beryl Badland, Llain yr Esgob, Dwrbach, Fishguard SA65 9RR

Cosy stone cottage close to centre of Fishguard. Overlooks attractive park with children's play facilities. Free parking at rear. Short breaks available. Brochure on request.

Months open 1-12; 2 Nights £60.00-£90.00. 3 Nights £90.00-£120.00. 4 Nights £120.00-£200.00. Weekly/unit £175.00-£275.00.

UNITS 1 SLEEPS 4

TREWEN PARK HOLIDAY VILLAGE ★★

***FRESHWATER EAST*, Pembroke SA71 5LP**
Tel: (01646) 672001 Fax: (01646) 672779
E-mail: holidays@ajemholidays.co.uk
Website: www.ajemholidays.co.uk
Enquiries: AJEM Holidays, 8 Whiteshott, Basildon SS16 5HF

All-year-round holidays and short breaks. 100yds wide sandy beach, situated in the Pembrokeshire Coast National Park. Comfortable holiday homes. Beautiful scenery. Good walking.

Months open 1-12; Weekly/unit £140.00-£280.00. Short Breaks available.

UNITS 10 SLEEPS 4-6

CLEDDAU LODGE ★★

Camrose, *HAVERFORDWEST* SA62 6HY
Tel: (01437) 710226/640 Fax: (01437) 710663
E-mail: claddau.lodge@btinternet.com
Enquiries: Mrs N. Tudor-Williams

Part of Georgian manor house on quiet country estate with private fishing. Coast 6 miles. Beautiful rural setting with views of Preseli hills. Central to beaches, horse riding, golf, sailing, etc. Woodlands with abundant wildlife and otter reserve.

Months open 3-10; 2, 3 & 4 Nights on request. Weekly/unit £105.00-£270.00.

UNITS 1 SLEEPS 7

NEW HOUSE FARM

AWAITING GRADING

GOLD

Little Treffgarne, *HAVERFORDWEST* SA62 5DD
Tel: (01437) 741754 Fax: (01437) 741754
E-mail: newhousefarm@compuserve.com
Website: www.data-wales.co.uk

Enjoy a warm welcome in this rural hideaway with stunning views. In an idyllic setting from which to explore Pembrokeshire's spectacular coastal path, our cosily restored 19th Century cottages - one with woodburner - are convenient for watersports, walking, fishing, wildlife, golf, pony trekking. Haverfordwest 10mins away.

Months open 1-12; 2 Nights £50.00-£90.00. 3 Nights £70.00-£130.00. 4 Nights £90.00-£170.00. Weekly/unit £150.00-£260.00.

UNITS 3 SLEEP UP TO 15

WALES CYMRU

TWO HOURS AND
A MILLION MILES AWAY

LANDWAY FARMHOUSE ★★★★

MANORBIER, nr Tenby
Tel: (01834) 871264 Fax: (01834) 871264
Enquiries: Park Farm, Manorbier, Tenby,
Pembrokeshire SA70 7SU

Traditional farmhouse sleeps 6/8. Sunlounge, colour TV, freezer, microwave, automatic washing machine, telephone, central heating, walled garden. Pets allowed. Suitable disabled. Near coastal path for walking. Easy distance for beaches, shops, castles and many other activities. Working farm. Personally run and supervised by owner who cares.

Months open 5-9; Weekly/unit £200.00-£520.00.

UNITS 1 SLEEPS 2-8

LITTLE HAVEN COTTAGES ★★★★

Woodlands Farm, Blocketts Lane, **LITTLE HAVEN**, Haverfordwest SA62 3UH Tel: (01291) 623337
Fax: (01291) 627631 Website: www.littlehavencottages.com
Enquiries: Mrs Judith Stephens, Grey Rocks, Woodcroft, Chepstow NP16 7HY

Walk down to superb beaches from a group of holiday cottages perched above the fishing village of Little Haven. Converted from stone-built and slated barns and farm buildings. Each with a private garden. Some with a beautiful sea view.

Months open 1-12; 2 Nights £75.00-£150.00. 3 Nights £100.00-£200.00.
4 Nights £150.00-£300.00. Weekly/unit £125.00-£625.00.

UNITS 9 SLEEPS 4-6

BEATTIES COTTAGE ★★★★

No 10 Wood Village, **NEWGALE**, Haverfordwest
SA62 6AR Tel: (01244) 300343 or (01437) 710381
E-mail: powysguest@btinternet.co.uk
Website: www.powysguest.co.uk Enquiries: Mrs M. Moreton, Primrose Cottage, Green Lane, Picton, Chester CH2 4HG

Beautiful cosy cottage. All year comforts. Sea views. Lovely peaceful position close to sea and coastal path. Excellent amenities including washing machine, microwave, fridge/freezer, heating, safe play area. 3 bedrooms. No pets.

Months open 1-12; 3 Nights £112.50. 4 Nights £150.00.
Weekly/unit £160.00-£400.00.

UNITS 1 SLEEPS 6

CELTIC HAVEN & IVY TOWER VILLAGES

Enquiries to:
The Holiday
Information Centre,
Tudor Square,
Tenby SA70 7AD
Tel: 01834 844000
Fax: 01834 844124

E-mail: news-desk@activitywales.co.uk
Website: www.activitywales.co.uk or www.celtichaven.co.uk

Set in 25 acres of parkland with private beach access, Celtic Haven is the ultimate in cottage holidays. Luxury graded accommodation with tennis, indoor swimming pool, golf, health suite, sauna and solarium. 10 free activities including go-karts, shooting, archery, bumper boats - also enjoy the stunning scenery whilst walking or horse riding. The Manor House sleeps 12, the fabulous cottages are for 2 to 8.

OPEN 1-12 **SLEEPS 2-12** **WEEKLY MIN:** £193 **WEEKLY MAX:** £1504
FARMHOUSES, COTTAGES

Marloes Sands, one of Pembrokeshire's finest beaches

TY GWYN

★★★★ UP TO ★★★★★

Whitesands, *ST DAVIDS*
Tel: (01348) 837871 Fax: (01348) 837876
Website: www.qualitycottages.co.uk
Enquiries: Quality Cottages, Cerbid, Solva,
Haverfordwest, Pembrokeshire SA62 6YE

WTB Tourism Award winners. One of a selection of quality cottages with exceptionally high residential standards. Log fires. Pets welcome free. All around the magnificent Welsh coastline with its numerous sandy beaches and superb scenic walks - a naturalist's, paradise. Free colour brochure.

Months open 1-12; 3 Nights £239.00. Weekly/unit £485.00-£1220.00.
UNITS 160 SLEEPS 2-14

PRETTY COTTAGE

★★★★ UP TO ★★★★★

***SOLVA* Enquiries: Quality Cottages,
Cerbid, Solva, Haverfordwest SA62 6YE**
Tel: (01348) 837871
Website: www.qualitycottages.co.uk

WTB Tourism Award winners. One of a selection of quality cottages with exceptionally high residential standards. Log fires. Pets welcome free. All around the magnificent Welsh coastline with its numerous sandy beaches and superb scenic walks - a naturalist's, paradise. Free colour brochure.

Months open 1-12; 3 Nights £144.00. Weekly/unit £240.00-£710.00.
UNITS 160 SLEEPS 2-14

WYNCLIFFE COTTAGE

★★★★

Quickwell Hill, *ST DAVIDS* SA62 6PD
Tel: (01437) 720447

Wyncliffe Cottage sleeps 4. There are sandy beaches, coves and cliff walks within easy walking distance. St David's Peninsula is renowned for its natural beauty. Brochure from Mrs Glenys James.

Months open 3-11; Weekly/unit £175.00-£395.00. Short Breaks available.

UNITS 1 SLEEPS 4

CHARACTER COTTAGES

★★★★ UP TO ★★★★★

Llaethdy, Whitesands, *ST DAVIDS* SA62 6PR
Tel & Fax: (01437) 721831
E-mail: Peter-Anna@eggconnect.net
Website: www.character-cottages-st-davids.co.uk
Enquiries: Peter Davies (Chris Smith)

A small portfolio of owner-run cottages, sympathetically renovated to the highest standard. Set amongst spectacular scenery in prime locations on the St Davids peninsular.

Months open 1-12; 4 Nights £150.00-£180.00. Weekly/unit £210.00-£560.00.
5 COTTAGES SLEEPS 4-6+

LLANDDINOG OLD FARMHOUSE & COTTAGES

AWAITING GRADING

Llandeloy, *SOLVA* SA62 6NA
Tel: (01348) 831224
E-mail: stpcastl@aol.com
Website: www.pembrokeshireholidays.co.uk
Enquiries: Stephanie Castle

Delightful farm cottages set down a quiet country lane 3 miles from sandy beaches, numerous coves and coastal paths. The picturesque harbour of Solva, St David's Cathedral, Preseli Mountains close by. Water sports, walking, riding, cycling and golf. Cot and high chair provided. Short breaks available.

Months open 1-12; 2 Nights £110.00-£130.00. 3 Nights £120.00-£135.00.
4 Nights £135.00-£160.00. Weekly/unit £170.00-£500.00.
UNITS 3 SLEEPS 4-6+

TY HIR

★★★

Twr-y-Felin, *ST DAVIDS* SA62 6QS
Tel: (01437) 721678 Fax: (01437) 721838
E-mail: stay@tyf.com Website: www.tyf.com
Enquiries: Tyf, 1 High St, St Davids,
Pembrokeshire SA62 6SA

A converted stone barn of great character situated in a quiet location 5 minutes walk from the heart of St Davids and 10 minutes from the coastal path. Well equipped with all modern conveniences, Ty Hir offers a fantastic base for families and groups to explore Pembrokeshire.

Months open 1-12; 2 Nights £80.00. 3 Nights £89.00.
4 Nights £99.00. Weekly/unit £99.00-£575.00.
UNITS 1 SLEEPS 6

Y BWTHYN ★★★★

9 New St, _ST DAVIDS_ SA62 6SW
Tel: (01437) 720511 Fax: (01437) 720511
Enquiries: Pam Wilcox, 27 Nun St, St Davids SA62 6NT

Cosy Welsh cottage modernised but retains olde worlde charm. Sleeps 6, kitchen/dining room, fridge, microwave, washer/dryer. Bath/shower room. Lounge with TV, gas fire, central heating, ample parking. In St Davids centre close to cathedral shops, golf, beaches, cliff-walks. Linen and towels supplied.

Months open 1-12; Weekly/unit £110.00-£395.00.

UNITS 1 SLEEPS 6 🛏 ⬜ Ⓜ 🍽 ❄ P2

LATE AVAILABILITY For the latest offers call our freephone Central Reservations service. North Wales – 0800 834820 Mid Wales – 0800 273747 South and West Wales – 0800 3289597

PLEASE NOTE

All the accommodation in this publication has applied for grading. With Holiday Cottages it may occasionally not have been possible to undertake a grading. This situation is clearly identified by 'Awaiting Grading' or a provisional Star rating (indicated by the letter P appearing alongside the Stars) within the advertisement/entry.

CARNOCK HOUSE ★★

Carnock House, Esplanade, _TENBY_ SA70 7DU
Tel: (01834) 844371 Fax: (01834) 844372

Superb seafront location offers studio accommodation for couples/small families. Top floor two bedroom flat sleeps 5. With steps opposite to beach and close to town, harbour, golf course and all amenities. Carnock provides an ideal base for enjoying Tenby and exploring Pembrokeshire. Clarence Hotel facilities available to all residents.

Months open 1-12. 2 Nights £30.00-£140.00. 3 Nights £45.00-£210.00. 4 Nights £60.00-£280.00. Weekly/unit £100.00-£350.00.

UNITS 10 SLEEPS 2-5 🛏 ⬜ 📺 SP Ⓜ 🍽 ℹ

NYTH ADERYN FLAT ★★★

North Cliffe, _TENBY_ SA70 8AT
Tel: (01834) 842842
E-mail: nythaderyntenby@beeb.net
Enquiries: Mrs J.W. Morgan

Spacious, self-contained, well equipped flat. Overlooking north beach, harbour, picturesque walled town and Caldey Island. Superb views. Washing/drying facilities, fridge/freezer, microwave plus conventional cooker. Access to private open air heated swimming pool. Close to beaches and coastal path. Leisure facilities in nearby area. Children welcome.

Months open 5-9; Weekly/unit £160.00-£500.00.

UNITS 1 SLEEPS 4-6 ⬜ ❌ Ⓜ 🍽 P1

Spectacular walking along the long-distance Pembrokeshire Coast Path

PEMBROKESHIRE

The National Park extends inland to the Preseli Hills

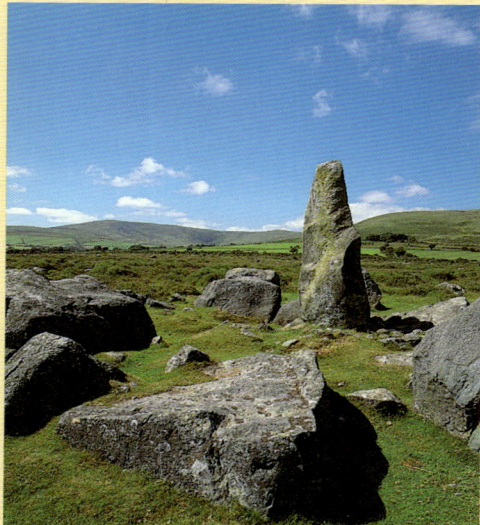

Caravan & Camping Parks

FISHGUARD BAY CARAVAN & CAMPING PARK

Garn Gelli, *FISHGUARD* SA65 9ET
Tel: (01348) 811415 Fax: (01348) 811425
E-mail: neil@fishguardbay.com
Website: www.fishguardbay.com

HOLIDAY &
TOURING PARK
★★★★
AWARD
BRONZE

Enjoy superb views along unspoilt coastline within the Pembrokeshire National Park. Situated in an area of outstanding natural beauty, you will be ideally positioned to walk and tour this beautiful corner of Wales. Spacious Dragon Award caravans. Pitches and hook-ups available for touring caravans, motor caravans and tents.

Months open 3-1; Weekly/unit (Static) £145.00-£365.00.
Per night (Tourers/Tents) £8.50-£11.50.

No. ON PARK 50 ⊕10 ⊕20 ⊕20 ▲30 ⊨⚷⊡⌂⏣⏚☗⌕⏁⏚P

CAERFAI BAY CARAVAN & TENT PARK

ST DAVIDS SA62 6QT
Tel: (01437) 720274 Fax: (01437) 720274
E-mail: info@caerfaibay.co.uk
Website: www.caerfaibay.co.uk

TOURING &
CAMPING PARK
★★★
GOLD

Months open 4-10; Weekly/unit (Static) £150.00-£350.00.
Per night (Tourers/Tents) £5.50-£11.50.

No. ON PARK 33 ⊕5 ⊕27 ⊕15 ▲75 ⊨⊡⌂⏣⏚⏁⏚⌕

SAUNDERSFOOT BAY LEISURE PARK

Broadfield, *SAUNDERSFOOT* SA69 9DG
Tel: (01834) 812284 Fax: (01834) 813387
E-mail: saundersfoot.bay@business.ntl.com
Website: www.saundersfootbay.co.uk

★★★★★
HOLIDAY PARK
AWARD

Award-winning park on the beautiful Pembrokeshire National Park coastline near Tenby, about 10 minutes stroll from the beach with magnificent views over Carmarthen Bay. Luxurious holiday homes with heating throughout, colour TV with video player and free video library. Past winner of Calor Gas 'Best Park in Britain' award.

Months open 3-11; Weekly/unit (Static) £115.00-£465.00.

No. ON PARK 169 ⊕55 ⊨⏣⊡⌂⏚☗⏚P ℹ

KILN PARK HOLIDAY CENTRE

TENBY Enquiries: British Holidays, Normandy Court, 1 Wolsey Rd, Hemel Hempstead HP2 4TU Tel: (0845) 607 8099 Quote WTB
Fax: (01442) 254956
Website: www.british-holidays.co.uk

★★★
HOLIDAY PARK

Kiln Park offers superb facilities and a choice of quality caravan accommodation. A family park with excellent cabaret entertainment, kids club, indoor/outdoor heated pools, restaurants and bars. British Holidays also offers 4 similar family holiday parks throughout Wales. All facilities as for Kiln Park plus mini golf, bowling greens, rope course and climbing walls. David Bellamy Silver Award.

Months open 3-10; Weekly/unit £207.50-£750.00.

No. ON PARK 620 ⊕305 ⊨▮⊡⏚⏣⊡⌂✕♫⏚⌂⏚🖫⏚ ℹ

SALTERN CARAVAN PARK

The Green, *TENBY* SA70 8EP
Tel: (01834) 842157

★★★★
HOLIDAY PARK

Months open 4-10; Weekly/unit (Static) £130.00-£315.00.

No. ON PARK 58 ⊕58 ⊨⊡🖫⏚P ℹ

Dramatic seascapes at Stack Rocks south of Pembroke

Carmarthenshire –
Beautiful Coast &
Countryside in West Wales

*D*ylan Thomas *captured the essence of this timeless part of Wales in his short stories and poems. It's an area of sweeping sands backed by green farmland, fertile vales and forests. Explore the huge beaches along Carmarthen Bay, the lovely Vale of Towy, the moors of Mynydd Llanybydder, the glades of the Brechfa Forest and the mountainous western corner of the Brecon Beacons National Park.*

Carreg Cennen Castle near Llandeilo

On Your Travels ...

The big news story here is the opening of the National Botanic Garden of Wales in the Vale of Towy near Carmarthen. This major Millennium

National Botanic Garden

Project, costing over £40 million, has transformed a vast, 568-acre slice of countryside. The Great Glasshouse, its stunning centrepiece, houses plants from all over the world. The verdant Vale of Towy is matched in beauty by the wooded Teifi Valley to the north, where Wales's traditional woollen industry once flourished. Bygone times are recalled at the Museum of the Welsh Woollen Industry at Dre-fach Felindre, a living museum with a working mill on site.

Carmarthenshire's green landscapes and 'heron-priested shore' inspired poet and writer Dylan Thomas's greatest works – as you'll discover when you visit his beloved Boathouse at Laugharne. If you've time to visit just one castle in these parts make sure it's Carreg Cennen, perched precipitously on a cliff near Llandeilo. Carreg Cennen is the ultimate romantic ruin – weatherbeaten, atmospheric and spectacular, with an overpowering sense of the past.

For further information please tel (01269) 590223;
e-mail: tourism@carmarthenshire.gov.uk
website: www.carmarthenshire.gov.uk

Where to Stay **Wales**

102

Ammanford
Map Ref Ke2 ⇌

Bustling valley town, good for Welsh crafts and products, on western edge of Brecon Beacons National Park. Spectacular mountain routes over nearby Black Mountain to Llangadog.

Carmarthen
Map Ref Kc2 ⇌

Prosperous county town in pastoral Vale of Towy. Lively market and shops, new livestock mart. Remnants of medieval castle in town centre. Heritage Centre in riverside location. Golf, fishing, tennis and well-equipped leisure centre. Remains of Roman amphitheatre. Immaculate museum in beautiful historic house on outskirts of

Carmarthen, in the Vale of Towy

town. Gwili Railway, delightful Aberglasney Garden and magnificent National Botanic Garden of Wales, a major Millennium Project, all nearby.

Llandeilo
Map Ref Ga7 ⇌

Country town and touring base for beautiful Vale of Towy and Carreg Cennen Castle, impressively set on a high crag. Dinefwr (National Trust) on edge of town contains magnificent landscaped parklands with ruined

Llandeilo, overlooking the River Towy

castle. Wonderful gardens nearby: Gelli Aur Country Park with its arboretum and deer herd, charming Aberglasney, the 'garden lost in time' and the superb £43-million National Botanic Garden of Wales.

The traditional market town of Llandovery

Llandovery
Map Ref Gb6 ⇌

An important market town on the A40 – its Welsh name Llanymddyfri means 'the church among the waters'. Ruined castle, good craft shops and excellent local museum/information centre with details on 'Red Kite Country'. In the hills to the north is the cave of Twm Siôn Cati – the Welsh Robin Hood. Good touring centre for Brecon Beacons and remote Llyn Brianne area.

Llanelli
Map Ref Kd4 ⇌

Bustling town with good shopping, covered market and pleasant parklands. Wildfowl and Wetlands Centre on estuary

modelled on Slimbridge. Millennium Coastal Park scheme is a far-reaching development which is transforming the waterfront. Nearby Pembrey Country Park, adjoining 7 miles of sandy beach, has a visitor centre and many attractions. The Welsh Motor Sports Centre also close by.

Pembrey
Map Ref Kc4

Lots of places to visit locally – Pembrey Country Park with its many attractions and vast, 7-mile beach, Kidwelly Castle, Llanelli's Wildfowl and Wetland Centre, Gower and Swansea. Also convenient for Welsh Motor Sports Centre.

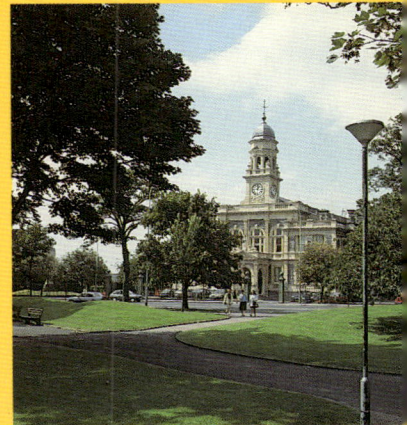
Llanelli's town centre parklands

CARMARTHENSHIRE - BEAUTIFUL COAST & COUNTRYSIDE IN WEST WALES

Hotels, Guest Houses & Farmhouses

BRYNCOCH FARM

Llandyfan, *AMMANFORD* SA18 2TY
Tel: (01269) 850480 Fax: (01269) 850888
E-mail: bryncoch@tesco.net

★★ BED & BREAKFAST

Bryncoch Farm, built in the 17th century, is situated high above the Amman Valley in the Brecon Beacons National Park. Golf course, riding centre and National Botanic Gardens only minutes away. Hosts Mary and Graham Richardson offer large comfortably furnished bedrooms, having en-suite bathrooms and unspoilt views over the valley. English breakfast cooked by your host served in a warm and friendly atmosphere.

Months open 1-12; B&B p/p £17.00-£20.00.
Weekly B&B p/p £100.00-£120.00.

LAST-MINUTE OFFERS

Looking for late availability or last-minute offers? For details of great-value breaks call Central Reservations on freephone 0800 834820 for North Wales, 0800 273747 for Mid Wales or 0800 3289597 for South and West Wales.

GLASFRYN GUEST HOUSE & RESTAURANT

★★★ GUEST HOUSE   GOLD

Brechfa, *CARMARTHEN* SA32 7QY
Tel: (01267) 202306 efax: 0870 1341770
E-mail: joyce.glasfryn@clara.co.uk
Website: www.carmarthenonline.co.uk/glasfryn

Friendly guest house situated on the edge of the Brechfa Forest. Ideally situated for touring South West and Mid Wales. 15 mins from Carmarthen, 15 mins from National Botanic Gardens. Licensed, conservatory, restaurant, excellent home cooking. A la carte menu. All rooms en-suite. Ideal for walking, cycling, etc.

Months open 1-12; B&B p/p £22.50-£25.00. Weekly D, B&B p/p £238.00.

WHITE HART INN

★★ INN

36 Carmarthen Rd, *LLANDEILO* SA19 6RS
Tel: (01558) 823419 Fax: (01558) 823089
E-mail: therese@whitehartinn.co.uk
Website: www.whitehartinn.fsnet.co.uk

A warm and friendly welcome awaits at this comfortable inn set in the picturesque Towy valley. Good food available from 12 noon to 11pm.

Months open 1-12; B&B p/p £26.00-£40.00.

LLANERCHINDDA FARM

★★ GUEST HOUSE

Cynghordy, *LLANDOVERY* SA20 0NB
Tel: (01550) 750274 Fax: (01550) 750300
E-mail: nick@cambrianway.com
Website: www.cambrianway.com

Voted 'Best B&B in Wales 1997' and 'Best Hospitality off the Beaten Track 1998' our farm in the middle of nowhere is the perfect place to stay. Fabulous location. Excellent home made food. Walking, fishing and miles of peace and quiet; also cottages.

Months open 1-12; B&B p/p £24.00. Weekly D, B&B p/p £252.00.

Llansteffan Castle, perched on a bluff above Carmarthen Bay

Bed & Breakfast
£27.50 p.p. is the most you'll pay

GLASFRYN GUEST HOUSE & RESTAURANT
Brechfa, *CARMARTHEN* SA32 7QY
Tel: (01267) 202306 efax: 0870 1341770
E-mail: joyce.glasfryn@clara.co.uk
Website: www.carmarthenonline.co.uk/glasfryn
Friendly guest house situated in the beautiful village of Brechfa on the edge of the Brechfa forest. Ideally situated for touring South West and Mid Wales. 15 minutes from Carmarthen, 15 minutes from National Botanic Gardens, 1¼ hours Fishguard ferry. Licensed conservatory restaurant. Excellent home cooking, a la carte menu. All rooms en-suite. Ideal for walking, birdwatching, biking - cycle hire available. Phone for brochure.

Months open 1-12; B&B p/p £22.50-£25.00. Weekly D, B&B p/p £238.00.

PLAS FARM
Llangynog, *CARMARTHEN* SA33 5DB
Tel: (01267) 211492 Fax: (01267) 211492
Family run, working farm. Spacious farmhouse, quiet location. Ideal touring base. Nearest beach is six miles. Golf course one mile. Farmhouse situated six miles from Carmarthen market town along A40 West towards St Clears, en route to Fishguard and Pembroke ferries. Warm welcome assured at all times. All rooms en-suite. Tea/coffee and TV in all rooms. Contact Mrs Margaret Thomas.

Months open 1-12; Single B&B per night £20.00-£25.00. Double B&B per night £36.00-£40.00.

TREBERSED FARM
**St Peters, Travellers Rest, *CARMARTHEN*
SA31 3RR** Tel: (01267) 238182
Fax: (01267) 223633
E-mail: trebersed.farm@farmline.com

Months open 1-12; Single B&B per night £25.00. Double B&B per night £40.00.

PANT Y BAS
Pentrefelin, *LLANDEILO* SA19 6SD
Tel: (01558) 822809

Full British breakfast served in friendly establishment having lawned gardens in delightful riverside setting. The bedrooms are separate twin/double units on the ground floor. Fully en-suite, set to a high standard. Convenient for Aberglasny Gardens, National Botanic Garden of Wales. Beautiful coastlines and much more. Off road parking.

Months open 1-12; Single B&B per night £15.00-£25.00. Double B&B per night £35.00-£40.00.

PENHILL
Trap, *LLANDEILO* SA19 6UB
Tel: (01558) 823060 Fax: (01558) 823060
E-mail: simon@thane1.freeserve.co.uk
Website: www.thane1.freeserve.co.uk/penhill.htm

Months open 1-12; B&B p/p £21.00.

CLASSIFIED ADVERTISING There's more accommodation to choose from in the classified advertising section of this book. Please see the listing at the end of the 12 Areas display adverts.

WHITE HART INN
36 Carmarthen Rd, *LLANDEILO* SA19 6RS
Tel: (01558) 823419 Fax: (01558) 823089
E-mail: therese@whitehartinn.fsnet.co.uk
Website: www.whitehartinn.fsnet.co.uk
A warm and friendly welcome awaits at this comfortable inn set in the picturesque Towy Valley. Good food available from 12 noon to 11pm.

Months open 1-12; B&B p/p min £26.00.

CWMGWYN FARM
Llangadog Rd, *LLANDOVERY* SA20 0EQ
Tel: (01550) 720410 Fax: (01550) 720262
E-mail: cwmgwyn@waitrose.com
Warm welcome to enjoy the country on our livestock farm overlooking the River Towy, two miles from Llandovery on A4069. The 17th century farmhouse is full of charm and character with inglenook fireplace, exposed stonework and beams. Spacious luxury en-suite bedrooms with hairdryer, colour TV, tea/coffee,. Centrally situated for touring, near Aberglasney and the National Botanic Garden for Wales.

Months open 4-11; Single B&B per night £21.00-£26.00. Double B&B per night £40.00-£44.00.

LLANERCHINDDA FARM
Cynghordy, *LLANDOVERY* SA20 0NB
Tel: (01550) 750274 Fax: (01550) 750300
E-mail: nick@cambrianway.com
Website: www.cambrianway.com
Voted 'Best B&B in Wales 1997' and 'Best Hospitality off the Beaten Track 1998". Our nine bedrooms (all en-suite) farmhouse, in the middle of nowhere, is the perfect place to stay. Wonderful location, excellent home made food round the farmhouse table. Walks, nature trails and peace and quiet. We also have cottages available.

Months open 1-12; B&B p/p £24.00. Weekly D, B&B p/p £252.00.

FOUR SEASONS GUEST HOUSE
**62 Gwscwm Rd, *PEMBREY*,
Burry Port SA16 0YU**
Tel: (01554) 833367 Fax: (01554) 833367

Months open 1-12; Single B&B per night £20.00-£25.00. Double B&B per night £38.00-£50.00.

THE PREMIER GARDENS OF WALES

There's a major new addition to Welsh gardens following the opening of the magnificent National Botanic Garden of Wales in the Vale of Towy near Carmarthen. The National Botanic joins many beautiful gardens throughout Wales – those at Aberglasney (near Llandeilo), Dyffryn (Vale of Glamorgan), Portmeirion, the Museum of Welsh Life (near Cardiff), Bodnant (Vale of Conwy), Chirk Castle, Erddig (Wrexham), Penrhyn Castle (Bangor), Powis Castle (Welshpool) and Plas Newydd (Anglesey).

All are members of the Premier Gardens of Wales. For a copy of the Premier Gardens brochure, please see 'Free Publications' on page 183.

Holiday Cottages

CWMDWYFRAN FARM COTTAGE ★★★★

Cwmdwyfran Farm, Cwmdwyfran,
Bronwydd Arms, *CARMARTHEN* SA33 6JF
Tel: (01267) 281419
E-mail: joan@jbrandrick.freeserve.co.uk
Enquiries: Mrs Joan brandrick

A superb holiday cottage converted from a stone farm building, fully equipped, and tastefully furnished to a high standard. A south facing verandah with beautiful views. An idyllic quiet setting, with abundant birdlife. Ample parking. Gwili railway, fishing within 1 mile. Golf, pony trekking and beaches, a short drive away.

Months open 3-11; 2 Nights £50.00-£60.00. 3 Nights £75.00-£90.00.
4 Nights £100.00-£120.00. Weekly/unit £109.00-£229.00.

UNITS 1 SLEEPS 4-5 🐾 ⬜ Ⓜ 🔌 P2+ ℹ

CAE'R BEILI ★★★★★

Pen y Fedw, Cil-y-Cwm, *LLANDOVERY* SA20 0UF
Tel: (01550) 720622
E-mail: tomos@s01416a.force9.co.uk
Enquiries: Mrs Meryl Tomos

GOLD

Luxurious well-equipped barn set in its own private and secluded grounds with panoramic views of the Cambrian Mountains and Brecon Beacons. Ideal base for relaxing or exploring by foot, cycle or car. Excellent birdwatching (Red kite) and abundant wildlife. Castles, crafts, beaches and family attractions within easy travelling. Croeso!

Months open 1-12; 2 Nights £80.00-£106.00. 3 Nights £120.00-£159.00.
4 Nights £160.00-£212.00. Weekly/unit £240.00-£570.00.

UNITS 1 SLEEPS 6+ 🛏 ⬜ Ⓖ SP 🔌 ☀ P6 ℹ

BRYNGWENYN FARM AWAITING GRADING

Pontyberem, *LLANELLI* SA15 5NG
Tel: (01269) 843990
Enquiries: Marilyn Breheny

Overlooking the Gwendraeth Valley, stay with us on a working sheep farm. Ideal spot for quiet holidays, walks or a base for off road cycle path to Llanelli's coastal park. Easily reached from the M4 and Swansea and the market town of Carmarthen.

Months open 1-12; 2 Nights £90.00. 3 Nights £135.00.
4 Nights £180.00-£320.00. Weekly/unit £245.00-£345.00.

UNITS 2 SLEEPS 5 🐾 ⬜ Ⓖ SP 🔌 ☀ P10 ℹ

DYTHEL FARM HOLIDAY FLATS ★★★

Trimsaran Rd, *LLANELLI* SA15 4LR
Tel: (01554) 810815 or 0411 280294
Enquiries: Chris Franklin

Quiet private site. Comfortable, well-equipped accommodation. Free entry to Pembrey Country Park. Ideal location for walking, biking, riding. Panoramic views of Gower peninsula, beaches and harbour.

Months open 3-12; 2 Nights £150.00. 3 Nights £175.00-£250.00.
4 Nights £200.00-£300.00. Weekly/unit £200.00-£400.00.

UNITS 4 SLEEPS 4-12 🐾 ⬜ SP ☀ 🔌 P8 ℹ

The Vale of Towy near Dryslwyn

Dylan Thomas's Boathouse, Laugharne

Swansea Bay
including Mumbles, Gower, Afan & the Vale of Neath

Mumbles, at the gateway to Gower

*S*wansea enjoys an enviable location on a wide, sandy bay. It's a fresh, friendly city – an appealing blend of old and new, with a traditional market and modern Maritime Quarter. Close by there's Mumbles, a pretty sailing resort, and the Gower Peninsula, Britain's first 'Area of Outstanding Natural Beauty'. Inland, explore the forests and waterfalls of the Afan Valley and Vale of Neath.

On Your Travels ...

Dylan Thomas had a deep affection for his birthplace, Swansea. The city celebrates its most famous son at the Dylan Thomas Centre, the National Literature Centre for Wales, home

Swansea Marina

to a permanent exhibition on the poet's life and work. Swansea's modern Maritime Quarter is an object lesson in creative waterfront redevelopment. A red-bricked former warehouse on the marina today houses the excellent Maritime and Industrial Museum, where old Swansea lives on – and where a woollen mill continues to produce traditional Welsh cloth.

It's worth taking a trip into the nearby hills and vales. Margam

Country Park, near Port Talbot, is a expansive area of grassland, lake and wooded hillside. It's a very popular family attraction packed with things to see and do, including an elegant 18th-century orangery, giant maze, nature and farm trails, adventure playground, boating and mountain biking. The valleys are full of unexpected sights. There's the National Trust's Aberdulais Falls, near Neath, for example, a strange combination of industrial heritage and great natural beauty.

For further information please tel (01792) 468321; e-mail: tourism@swansea.gov.uk

Where to Stay
Wales

Afan Argoed Country Park near Cymmer

Pwll-du, one of Gower's many beautiful beaches

Caswell Bay
Map Ref Ke5

Pretty little bay with south-facing sands on the Gower Peninsula. Attractive coastal and woodland footpaths through Bishop's Wood Nature Reserve. Cliff walks to Langland Bay and Brandy Cove.

Cymmer
Map Ref Lc4

Attractively set in the steep-sided and wooded 'Little Switzerland' of the Afan Valley. Afan Argoed Country Park has excellent walking and mountain biking, together with the fascinating Welsh Miners' Museum.

Mumbles
Map Ref La4

Small resort on Swansea Bay with attractive waterfront and pier; centre for watersports and sailing. On fringe of Gower Peninsula. Oystermouth Castle and Clyne Valley Country Park and Gardens nearby.

Three Cliffs Bay, on Gower's sheltered south coast

Worms Head, Rhossili

Swansea
Map Ref La4 ⇌

Wales's second city. Superb marina complex and Maritime Quarter – excellent leisure centre, with Maritime and Industrial Museum alongside. Art gallery, Dylan Thomas Centre at Tŷ Llên, Superbowl, dry ski slope and 'Plantasia' exotic plants attraction. Good shopping. Covered market with distinctively Welsh atmosphere. Swansea Festival and 'Fringe' Festival in October. Theatres and cinemas, parks and gardens, restaurants and wine bars. Wales in Bloom award winner 2000.

City centre, Swansea

Reynoldston
Map Ref Kd5

Centrally located Gower Peninsula village only a few miles from the magnificent beaches and coastal scenery at Oxwich, Port Eynon and Rhossili. Moorlands to the north with superb viewpoint across peninsula.

Rhossili
Map Ref Kc5

Gower's spectacular 'Land's End', a village set on headland above stunning 3 miles of sandy beach. Surfing, hang gliding, coastal walking. Worms Head juts into sea. National Trust Visitor Centre.

Tŷ Llên, Swansea

SWANSEA BAY INCLUDING MUMBLES, GOWER, AFAN & THE VALE OF NEATH

Hotels, Guest Houses & Farmhouses

ST ANNE'S HOTEL
★★★ HOTEL
BRONZE

Western Lane, MUMBLES SA3 4EY
Tel: (01792) 369147 Fax: (01792) 360537
E-mail: info@stanneshotel-mumbles.com

Months open 1-12; B&B p/p from £35.00. 2 Nights D, B&B p/p £100.00.
Weekly D, B&B p/p £275.00.
🛏 33 ➡ 33 🅲 🍽🍷 £ ♿ SP 💻 TV P i

SHORELINE HOTEL
★★ HOTEL

648 Mumbles Rd, MUMBLES, Swansea SA3 4QZ
Tel: (01792) 366233
Website: www.shorelinehotel.co.uk

Months open 1-12; B&B p/p £25.00-£30.00.
🛏 12 ➡ 12 🅲 🍷 £ ♿ SP 💻 i

Aberdulais Falls in the Vale of Neath

CLASSIFIED ADVERTISING There's more accommodation to choose from in the classified advertising section of this book. Please see the listing at the end of the 12 Areas display adverts.

WORM'S HEAD HOTEL
★★ HOTEL

RHOSSILI, Swansea SA3 1PP
Tel: (01792) 390512 Fax: (01792) 391115

Cliff top hotel with spectacular views of the famous Worm's Head and Rhossili Bay from our bars and restaurant serving local produce. Ideally situated for most outdoor pursuits. We specialise in private parties, weddings, conferences and family breaks.

Months open 1-12; B&B p/p £33.00-£35.00. 2 Nights Break D, B&B p/p £95.00-£103.00. Weekly D, B&B p/p £285.00-£309.00.
🛏 19 ➡ 19 🅲 🍽🍷 £ ♿ SP 💻 🎵 ✿ P i

BEST WESTERN ABERAVON BEACH HOTEL
★★★ HOTEL

Neath Port Talbot, SWANSEA BAY SA12 6QP
Tel: (01639) 884949 Fax: (01639) 897885
E-mail: sales@aberavonbeach.com
Website: www.aberavonbeach.com

Modern hotel close to M4, 7 miles from Swansea. Convenient for Gower Peninsula, Welsh valleys and tourist attractions of South Wales. Seafront location opposite a wide sandy beach with panoramic views across Swansea Bay. Elegant restaurant with fine food, comfortable bedrooms with all facilities, all-weather leisure centre with pool, spa and sauna. Welcoming staff.

Months open 1-12; B&B p/p £34.50-£39.50. 2 Nights Break D, B&B p/p £99.00. Weekly D, B&B p/p £297.00.
🛏 52 ➡ 52 🅲 🍽🍷 £ ♿ SP 💻 ✿ (FR) TV P i

Margam Country Park, near Port Talbot, attracts many visitors

SWANSEA BAY INCLUDING MUMBLES, GOWER, AFAN & THE VALE OF NEATH

THE BEAUMONT HOTEL
★★ HOTEL

72-73 Walter Rd, SWANSEA SA1 4QA
Tel: (01792) 643956 Fax: (01792) 643044
E-mail: info@beaumonthotel.co.uk
Website: www.beaumonthotel.co.uk

A charming and welcoming family-run 16 en-suite room hotel. A short walk from city centre. Conservatory Restaurant, executive rooms with sunken baths available. Comfortable bar area.

Months open 1-12; B&B p/p £32.50-£42.50. 2 Nights Break D, B&B p/p £85.50-£103.50. Weekly D, B&B p/p £299.25-£367.50.

THE GROSVENOR HOUSE
★★★ GUEST HOUSE

Mirador Crescent, Uplands, SWANSEA SA2 0QX
Tel: (01792) 461522 Fax: (01792) 461522
E-mail: grosvenor@ct6.com
Website: www.ct6.com/grosvenor

Grosvenor House warmly welcomes non-smoking business and holiday visitors. All bedrooms en-suite, colour television, clock/radio, hairdryer, trouser press, welcome tray and many 'home from home' touches. Comfortable lounge, separate dining room, small secure car park. AA ◆◆◆◆. RAC ◆◆◆ and sparkling diamond award. Brochure available from Proprietors Ellen and Tim Lowen.

Months open 1-12; B&B p/p £23.00-£27.00.

HENDREFOELAN HOLIDAY APARTMENTS
★★★ CAMPUS

University of Wales Swansea, Gower Rd, Sketty, **SWANSEA SA2 7PG** Enquiries: Accommodation Office, University of Wales Swansea, Singleton Park, Swansea SA2 8PP Tel: (01792) 208929/295101 Fax: (01792) 295327 E-mail: n.s.edmonds@swansea.ac.uk or conferences@swansea.ac.uk Website: www.swan.ac.uk/conferences

Swansea University's student village offers apartments, bungalows and houses sleeping 4-11. Located at the gateway to beautiful Gower with wonderful beaches and surfing and great opportunities for scenic hikes both coastal and inland. Shop, tennis courts on site. Excellent sports centre and pub/restaurant nearby.

Months open 7-9; 3 Nights £130.00-£230.00.
4 Nights £130.00-£230.00. Weekly £220.00-£460.00.
Breaks available 7.7.01-9.9.01 including Bank Holiday.
UNITS 230 SLEEPS 4-11

THE JARVIS INTERNATIONAL SWANSEA
★★★ HOTEL SILVER

Phoenix Way, The Lakeside Park,
SWANSEA SA7 9EG
Tel: (01792) 310330 Fax: (01792) 797535

Ideal for exploring Swansea and West Wales. Comfortable rooms, carvery restaurant, and lounge bar, ample free parking. One mile from M4, 10 mins from City. AA/RAC graded.

Months open 1-12; B&B p/p £34.00-£44.00.
2 Nights Break D, B&B p/p £78.00. Weekly D, B&B p/p £234.00.

Cockle pickers at Penclawdd on Gower's north shore

Bed & Breakfast
£27.50 p.p. is the most you'll pay

Holiday Cottages

BRYN TEG HOUSE ★★ BED & BREAKFAST
9 Craig-y-Fan, *CYMMER*, Port Talbot SA13 3LN
Tel: (01639) 851820 Fax: (01639) 851820

Months open 1-12; B&B p/p £16.00. 2 Nights Break D, B&B and use of mountain bike p/p £30.00. 3 course evening meal pp £8.00.

GREENWAYS ★★ FARM
Hills Farm, *REYNOLDSTON*, Swansea SA3 1AE
Tel: (01792) 390125

Months open 2-11; Single B&B per night £18.00-£25.00.
Double B&B per night £36.00-£40.00.

STONEY-FORGE GUEST HOUSE ★★★★ GUEST HOUSE
**Knelston, *REYNOLDSTON*,
Swansea SA31 1AR**
Tel: (01792) 390920

Months open 2-11; Single B&B per night £22.00-£25.00. Double B&B per night £36.00-£40.00.

SUNNYSIDE ★ FARM
**Llanddewi Castle Farm, Llanddewi,
REYNOLDSTON SA3 1AU**
Tel: (01792) 390194

Months open 1-11; Single B&B per night £18.00.
Double B&B per night £36.00.

SHORELINE HOTEL ★★ HOTEL
648 Mumbles Rd, *MUMBLES*, Swansea SA3 4QZ
Tel: (01792) 366233
Website: www.shorelinehotel.co.uk
A warm and friendly welcome awaits you at this family run, fully licensed hotel. Situated on the seafront in the beautiful village of Mumbles. Sample the many restaurants and bars located in the heart of the village. The hotel is ideally situated for the Gower Peninsula and Swansea city centre.

Months open 1-12; B&B p/p from £25.00.

CALL IN AT A TOURIST INFORMATION CENTRE

Wales's network of TICs helps you get the best out of your holiday.

- Information on what to see and where to go
- Local events
- Brochures, maps and guides
- And a Bed Booking Service

Properties displaying the 𝒊 symbol can be booked through any networked Tourist Information Centre – this service is especially handy when you're out and about in Wales.

CASWELL BAY COURT ★★★★★
CASWELL BAY, Gower, Swansea SA3 3BP
Tel: (01792) 775395 Fax: (01792) 790970
E-mail: peterjfrost@aol.com
Enquiries: 221 Clasemont Rd, Morriston, Swansea SA6 6BT

Months open 1-12; 2 Nights £180.00-£198.00. 3 Nights £270.00-£297.00.
4 Nights £360.00-£396.00. Weekly/unit £630.00-£694.00.
UNITS 1 SLEEPS 4

THE SLOPE *AWAITING GRADING*
Middleton, *RHOSSILI*, Swansea SA3 1PJ
Tel: (01792) 390500 E-mail: berylhowe@aol.com
Enquiries: Mrs B Howe, Oldfarmhouse, Middleton,
Rhossili, Swansea SA3 1PJ
Small well-equipped cottage, sympathetically converted from traditional farm buildings. Views over cliff and sea. 750m to safe clean beach. Under personal supervision of owners.

Months open 1-12; Short Break prices on request.
Weekly/unit £170.00-£230.00.
UNITS 1 SLEEPS 2

BANK FARM HOLIDAY BUNGALOWS ★★★
Bank Farm, Horton, *SWANSEA* SA3 1LL
Tel: (01792) 390228 Fax: (01792) 391282
E-mail: bankfarmleisure@cs.com
Website: www.bankfarmleisure.co.uk
Brick built holiday bungalow, sleeping four/five. Within easy walking distance of golden sandy beach. Stunning views over Bristol Channel. Sixteen miles from Swansea shopping centre. Many scenic walks on the Gower Peninsula, both coastal and inland.

Months open 3-12; Weekly/unit £120.00-£350.00.
UNITS 6 SLEEPS 4-5

REDCLIFFE APARTMENTS *AWAITING GRADING*
**6A Redcliffe Apartments, Caswell Bay,
SWANSEA Tel: (01792) 234586
Enquiries: Mrs P. Morgan, 44 Kilfield Rd, Bishopston,
Swansea SA3 3DN**

Holiday flat. Unique position in Caswell Bay with private access to beach. Close to Mumbles and Swansea. First floor apartment, fully-fitted kitchen, freezer, microwave, bathroom, bath, shower, living room, dining area, colour TV, double bed settee, twin bedroom with fitted wardrobes, folding bed, duvets. Sorry no pets.

Months open 1-12; 2 Nights £50.00-£100.00. 3 Nights £70.00-£120.00.
4 Nights £100.00-£125.00. Weekly/unit £90.00-£240.00.
UNITS 1 SLEEPS 4-5

The Valleys of South Wales

*T*he Valleys are full of surprises – dramatic natural beauty, country parks and lakes, forest and cycle trails. Although best known for their industrial past, the Valleys are green and attractive, their steep hillsides rising to breezy, untouched mountaintops with wide views across a roller-coaster landscape. Another surprise is their wealth of attractions – everything from castles to fascinating reminders of a rich industrial heritage.

Cwmcarn Forest Drive

On Your Travels ...

Llancaiach Fawr historic house

Take a trip on the narrow-gauge Brecon Mountain Railway from Merthyr Tydfil into the foothills of the Brecon Beacons, with wonderful lake and mountain views en route. It's one of this area's many unexpected delights. Another is Caerphilly Castle. It's only now that Caerphilly's true stature as one of Europe's finest medieval monuments is becoming recognised. The castle's sprawling stone and water defences – complete with tipsy tower which out-leans Pisa's – cover 30 acres, completely dominating their surroundings.

History of a more recent kind is the theme at Blaenavon's Big Pit Mining Museum. The coalmine itself is the exhibit, preserved much as it was when the miners clocked off for the last time in 1980. The highlight here is the underground tour, during which visitors descend 300ft by pit cage. The mining of 'black gold' was at its most intense in the Rhondda Valleys. The Rhondda Heritage Centre near Pontypridd brings the past imaginatively to life through multi-media displays, a reconstructed village street and exciting underground experience.

For further information please tel (01792) 781212; e-mail: valleys@tsww.com website: www.valley-breaks.co.uk

Where to Stay
Wales

114

Aberdare
Map Ref Le3

Town on fringe of Brecon Beacons National Park. Attractive town park with woodlands and boating lake. Dare Valley Country Park on western outskirts. Golf courses, sports centre and swimming pool.

The Brecon Mountain Railway runs from the 'Heads of the Valleys'

Blackwood
Map Ref Mb3

Southern valley town close to hills and forests. Pen-y-fan Pond Country Park, Parc Cwm Darran and Sirhowy Valley Country Park all nearby. Visit Llancaiach Fawr 'living history' manor house.

Bridgend
Map Ref Ld5 ⇌

Bustling commercial and market town bordering rural Vale of Glamorgan. Close to lively Porthcawl, unspoilt Heritage Coast, Bryngarw Country Park, Ewenny Priory and ruins of Coity, Newcastle and Ogmore castles.

Caerphilly
Map Ref Ma4 ⇌

A sight not to be missed – 13th-century Caerphilly Castle, which dominates the town centre, is one of Europe's finest surviving medieval strongholds and has a famous leaning tower. Golf course, shopping, good centre for exploring the Valleys and visiting Cardiff. Fine views and pleasant walks from Caerphilly Mountain. Visit nearby Nantgarw China Works shop and museum in restored 18th-century house.

Cross Keys
Map Ref Mb4

Located beneath forested slopes at the southern end of the Ebbw Valley – the scenic 7-mile Cwmcarn Forest Drive has panoramic views. Also close by is the Sirhowy Valley Country Park with woodland and riverside walks.

Caerphilly Castle's formidable stone and water defences

Rhondda Heritage Park near Pontypridd

Cyfarthfa Castle, Merthyr Tydfil

Pontypridd
Map Ref Le4 ⇝

Busy Valleys town which recalls its past at the Pontypridd Historical and Cultural Centre and nearby Rhondda Heritage Park. Visit John Hughes's famous Grogg Shop. Home town of Tom Jones.

Merthyr Tydfil
Map Ref Le2 ⇝

Once the 'iron capital of the world'. Cyfarthfa Castle's museum and Ynysfach Iron Heritage Centre tell of those times. Also visit the birthplace of hymn-writer Joseph Parry. Town is on the doorstep of Brecon Beacons National Park. Narrow-gauge Brecon Mountain Railway runs north into the mountains. Garwnant Visitor Centre set amongst forests and scenic lakes in hills close by.

Pontypool
Map Ref Mc3 ⇝

Historic metal-producing town on eastern edge of South Wales Valleys. Attractive park contains Valley Inheritance Museum and dry ski slope. Big Pit Mining Museum and rurally located Llandegfedd reservoir nearby.

Tredegar
Map Ref Ma2

Former ironmaking town in hilly 'Heads of the Valleys' close to the Brecon Beacons National Park – town's clock tower is made of iron. Attractive Parc Bryn Bach and Parc Cwm Darran both nearby.

Nelson
Map Ref Ma3

Located between Taff and Rhymney valleys. Attractive walks in open countryside to the north. Close to the major attraction of Llancaiach Fawr, a 'living history' manor house.

Bryn Bach Park

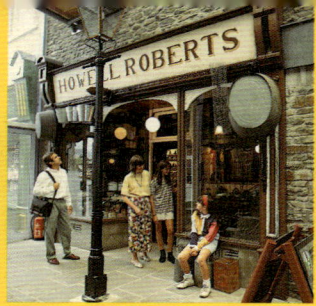

Stone circle, Pontypridd

Hotels, Guest Houses & Farmhouses

DARE VALLEY COUNTRY PARK COUNTRYSIDE RESIDENTIAL CENTRE
ABERDARE CF44 7RG
Tel: (01685) 874672 Fax: (01685) 882919

★★ HOTEL

GOLD

Less than two miles from Aberdare town centre and in 200 hectares of beautiful parkland you will find a cosy, modern hotel ideal for country-loving families and groups. Dare Valley is a great base for exploring the region or walking the hills. We happily cater for special dietary needs.

Months open 1-12; B&B p/p £18.75. 2 Nights Break D, B&B p/p £57.50-£80.00. Weekly D, B&B p/p £191.19-£266.00.

🛏15 🛌15 🕮❄ P40 i

HERITAGE PARK HOTEL
Coed Cae Rd, Trehafod, **PONTYPRIDD** CF37 2NP
Tel: (01443) 687057 Fax: (01443) 687060
E-mail: heritageparkhotel@talk21.com
Website: www.heritageparkhotel.co.uk

★★★ HOTEL

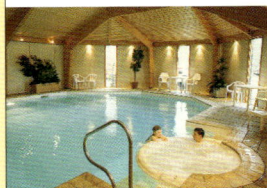

Set in the beautiful Rhondda Valleys and only 10 miles north of Cardiff. A modern, but traditionally built, hotel adjacent to the Rhondda Heritage Museum. The hotel also boasts a leisure complex, 44 spacious newly refurbished en-suite bedrooms, a fine restaurant and a warm Welsh welcome.

Months open 1-12; B&B p/p £37.50-£40.00. 2 Nights Break D, B&B p/p £90.00-£100.00. Weekly D, B&B p/p £315.00-£350.00.

🛏44 🛌44 SP (FR,SP) P150 i

SLIDE SETS

Ask about our attractive range of 35mm colour slides showing views of Wales, available at 75p per slide.

For a complete list of subjects please contact the Photography Library, Wales Tourist Board, Brunel House, 2 Fitzalan Road, Cardiff CF24 0UY. Tel: (029) 2047 5215.

YE OLDE RED LION
97 Queen Victoria St, **TREDEGAR** NP22 3PX
Tel: (01495) 724449 Fax: (01495) 711699

★ HOTEL

Family-run hotel with home from home welcome. Ideal for sightseeing and business people. Lively atmosphere and good food all year round.

Months open 1-12; B&B p/p £45.00-£52.00.
Weekly B&B p/p £165.00-£312.00. Call for group bookings.

🛏10 🛌10 P6 i

Bed & Breakfast
£27.50 p.p. is the most you'll pay

DARE VALLEY COUNTRY PARK COUNTRYSIDE RESIDENTIAL CENTRE
ABERDARE CF44 7RG
Tel: (01685) 874672 Fax: (01685) 882919

★★ HOTEL

GOLD

A modern hotel set in 200 hectares of beautiful and accessible parkland. All twin and family rooms can be adapted to take up to four persons, making them ideal for large families, school parties and groups seeking a central base for exploring South Wales. We are happy to cater for guests with special dietary needs.

Months open 1-12; Single B&B per night from £18.75.
Double B&B per night £37.50.

🛏15 🛌15 P40 i

WYRLOED GUEST HOUSE
Manmoel, **BLACKWOOD** NP12 0RW
Tel: (01495) 371198 Fax: (01495) 371198

★★★ BED & BREAKFAST

Victorian-style home with beautiful views, situated in mountain hamlet of Manmoel. Peaceful but not isolated, with small village pub and church. Excellent for touring South Wales Valleys and walking. M4 get off junction 28 - sign for Brynmawr. Turn at Crumlin for Oakdale. Top of hill - right turn for Manmoel. Follow signs into village.

Months open 1-11; Single B&B per night £20.00.
Double B&B per night £36.00.

🛏4 🛌4 SP P6 i

117

THE VALLEYS OF SOUTH WALES

WERN GANOL FARMHOUSE
Nelson, Treharris, *CAERPHILLY* CF46 6PS
Tel: (01443) 450413

★★ FARM / BRONZE

Months open 1-12; Single B&B per night £25.00.
Double B&B per night £40.00.

🛏6 🛌6 ♿ 🐕 ⚙ P7 ℹ

THE CASTLE HOTEL
Castle St, *MERTHYR TYDFIL* CF47 8BG
Tel: (01685) 386868 Fax: (01685) 383898
E-mail: enquiries@castlehotelwales.com

★★★ HOTEL

Months open 1-12; Double B&B per night from £45.00.

🛏40 🛌40 🐕 C 🍴♱ ♿ SP ℹ

FAIRMEAD GUEST HOUSE
24 Gelligaer Rd, Trelewis, *NELSON* CF46 6DN
Tel: (01443) 411174 Fax: (01443) 411430
E-mail: fairmead@21.com
Website: www.fairmeadhouseaol.com

★★★★ GUEST HOUSE / GOLD

Months open 1-12; Single B&B per night from £27.50.
Double B&B per night from £55.00.

🛏3 🛌3 🐕 C ♿ ✕ ⚙ P5 ℹ

TYN-Y-WERN
Ynysybwl, *PONTYPRIDD* CF37 3LY
Tel: (01443) 790551 Fax: (01443) 790551

★★★ COUNTRY HOUSE / GOLD

A Victorian mine manager's residence lovingly restored, only 30 minutes from Cardiff's many attractions. Seaside just 40 minutes and surrounded by miles of hills and forestry - makes 'Tyn-y-Wern' attractive for country and city visitors. Most food obtained from organic sources, all tastes catered for, Italian cuisine a speciality. Tea/coffee facilities and colour TV in all rooms. Colour brochure available.

Months open 1-12; Single B&B per night £23.50.
Double B&B per night £39.00-£44.00.

🛏3 🛌1 🐕 C 🍴♱ SP ⚙🐎 🎵(i) P100 ℹ

YE OLDE RED LION
97 Queen Victoria St, *TREDEGAR* NP22 3PX
Tel: (01495) 724449 Fax: (01495) 711699

★ HOTEL

Months open 1-12; Single B&B per night £27.50.
Double B&B per night £45.00-£52.00.

🛏10 🛌10 C 🍴♱ ♿ 🎵 P6

Decorative ironwork at former 'iron capital' of Merthyr Tydfil

---

Holiday Cottages

GELLIGOEDIOG HOLIDAY COTTAGES
Manmoel, *BLACKWOOD* NP12 0RH
Tel: (01495) 371097/246844
Fax: (01495) 249102

★★★★

Situated near a sleepy hamlet, these homely decorated cottages offer a peaceful atmosphere. Ideal base for exploring South Wales. Log burning stoves with fuel provided.

Months open 1-12; Weekly/unit £175.00-£200.00.

UNITS 2 SLEEPS 6 🐕 🖥 📺 SP 🍽 P

WYRLOED LODGE GUEST HOUSE & HOLIDAY COTTAGES
Wyrloed Lodge Guest House, Manmoel, *BLACKWOOD* NP12 0RW
Tel: (01495) 371198 Fax: (01495) 371198
Enquiries: Mrs Norma James

★★★★

Months open 1-12; 3 Nights £75.00-£95.00. 4 Nights £95.00-£115.00. Weekly/unit £150.00-£200.00.

UNITS 2 SLEEPS 5-4 🐕 🖥 📺 SP M 🍽 P6

TY MAEN FARM
Llangynwyd, Maesteg, nr *BRIDGEND* CF34 0EH
Tel: (01656) 733505
Enquiries: Olwen or David Jones

★★★★

Tastefully converted cottage, in beautiful hill and natural oak woodland conservation area. Ideal for walking. An abundance of wildlife and freedom of 470 acres working hill farm. Within 5 miles of M4 and only 12 miles from the coast. Cardiff, Swansea, historic and beauty spots within easy reach.

Months open 1-12; 2 Nights £85.00-£115.00. 3 Nights £105.00-£140.00. 4 Nights £120.00-£160.00. Weekly/unit £160.00-£300.00.

UNITS 1 SLEEPS 6 🐕 🖥 SP ✕ 🍽 P3 ℹ

JUNCTION COTTAGE
★★★★

Canal Basin, Off Fountain Rd, Pontymoile,
PONTYPOOL NP4 8ER Tel: (0800) 5422663
Fax: (01495) 755877 E-mail: junctioncottage@messages.co.uk
Website: www.junctioncottage.co.uk
Enquiries: Mrs Appleby, Ty Siân, 27 Top Rd, Garndiffaith, Pontypool

Historic Toll house on the Monmouthshire and Brecon Canal. Picturesque location ideal for touring Wales. Stroll, cycle or watch the barges pass by at Junction Cottage.

Months open 1-12; 2 Nights £80.00-£100.00. 3 Nights £120.00-£140.00. 4 Nights £150.00-£160.00. Weekly/unit £150.00-£275.00.

UNITS 1 SLEEPS 6

Caravan & Camping Parks

CWMCARN FOREST DRIVE CAMPSITE
★★★★
TOURING &
CAMPING PARK
GOLD

Cwmcarn, **CROSS KEYS**, Newport NP11 7FA
Tel: (01495) 272001 Fax: (01495) 272001
E-mail: tic@caerphilly.gov.uk
Website: www.caerphilly.gov.uk

Months open 1-12; Per night (Tourers/Tents) £7.20-£9.00.

No. ON PARK 40 40 40 40

Wales on the Web

www.visitwales.com

Make the most of your visit to Wales by calling into the Wales Tourist Board website. It's your easy route to up-to-date information on attractions and events in Wales, as well as lots of holiday ideas, itineraries and themes to explore.

Book Online! The website is also your gateway to online booking. Just key in your details and we'll come up with options tailored to your needs and budget.

PRICES

Touring caravan and camping park rates are for TWO PEOPLE and their caravan, motor home or tent PER NIGHT. All prices include VAT. Please check all prices and facilities before confirming your booking.

CLASSIFIED ADVERTISING *There's more accommodation to choose from in the classified advertising section of this book. Please see the listing at the end of the 12 Areas display adverts.*

Llyn Fawr on the approach to the Rhondda Valleys

Cardiff. The Glamorgan Heritage Coast & Countryside

*C*ardiff, Wales's cosmopolitan capital, is welcoming the 21st century in style. A futuristic Cardiff is emerging along the Bay, while in the city itself the castle and Civic Centre have been joined by a major new landmark, the Millennium Stadium. Close by there's attractive coast and countryside. The pastoral Vale of Glamorgan, dotted with picturesque villages, leads to a beautiful Heritage Coast shoreline and popular seaside resorts.

Civic Centre, Cardiff

Pendoylan, Vale of Glamorgan

On Your Travels ...

Cardiff just gets bigger and better. The Cardiff Bay development is transforming the old docklands into a modern waterfront for the new millennium with a huge freshwater lake and all kinds of bayside attractions. Already, there's much to see, including Techniquest, an endlessly entertaining – and educational – 'hands-on' science discovery centre. In the heart of the city you'll find the National Museum and Gallery of Wales, part of Cardiff's elegant neoclasssical Civic Centre. Its many treasures include a world-class collection of French Impressionist paintings.

The Museum of Welsh Life at St Fagans on the outskirts of Cardiff allows you to travel around Wales – and back into bygone times – all in a day. Farmhouses, workshops, a school, chapel, bakehouse and village store are some of the many old buildings that have been re-erected here stone-by-stone in a beautiful parkland setting. If gardens and exotic plants are your interest don't miss Dyffryn in the pastoral Vale of Glamorgan, one of Wales's finest landscaped gardens.

For further information on *CARDIFF* please tel (029) 2022 7281; e-mail: enquiries@cardifftic.co.uk website: www.cardiffmarketing.co.uk For the *VALE OF GLAMORGAN AND HERITAGE COAST* please tel (01446) 709328; e-mail: tourism@valeofglamorgan.gov.uk website: www.valeofglamorgan.gov.uk

Where to Stay
Wales

Cardiff Bay

Bridgend
Map Ref Ld5 ⇌

Bustling commercial and market town bordering rural Vale of Glamorgan. Close to lively Porthcawl, unspoilt Heritage Coast, Bryngarw Country Park, Ewenny Priory and ruins of Coity, Newcastle and Ogmore castles.

Cardiff
Map Ref Mb5 ⇌

Capital of Wales. Splendid Civic Centre, lovely parkland, excellent shopping, entertainment and sporting centre. St David's Hall and International Arena provide top-class venues. Ornate castle, National Museum and Gallery and new Millennium Stadium all in city centre. Techniquest science discovery centre on exciting new Cardiff Bay waterfront development, where the city of the 21st century is taking shape. Llandaff Cathedral and Museum of Welsh Life, St Fagans. Wales in Bloom award winner 2000.

Cowbridge
Map Ref Le6

Picturesque town with wide main street and pretty houses – centre of the Vale of Glamorgan farming community. Fine old inns, shops selling high-class clothes and country wares. Fourteenth-century town walls.

Penmark
Map Ref Le6

Vale of Glamorgan village in countryside scattered with historic sites. Close to Porthkerry County Park, the Glamorgan Heritage Coast and Cardiff International Airport. Resort of Barry Island just a few miles away.

Porthcawl
Map Ref Lc6

Traditional seaside resort – beaches, funfair, promenade. Attractive harbour and quieter coast along Rest Bay. Summer entertainment at the Grand Pavilion. Sailing and windsurfing. Famous links golf course. Kenfig Pool and Dunes National Nature Reserve. Convenient for visiting unspoilt South Wales countryside – Bryngarw Country Park and Vale of Glamorgan with its pretty villages set amid leafy lanes.

The seafront, Porthcawl

Hotels, Guest Houses & Farmhouses

COURT COLMAN MANOR
Pen-y-Fai, *BRIDGEND* CF31 4NG
Tel: (01656) 720212 Fax: (01656) 724544
E-mail: experience@court-colman-manor.com
Website: court-colman-manor.com

★★ HOTEL
GOLD

Grade II Georgian Manor set in 6 acres of landscaped gardens. 34 en-suite rooms with TV, trouser press, ironing set, hot beverage making facilities, many having panoramic views over beautiful countryside. Unique to Court Colman, various themed rooms including Welsh, Gothic, Indian, Moroccan and Mediterranean. Bar and restaurant facilities available.

Months open 1-12; B&B p/p £25.00-£45.00. 2 Nights Break D, B&B p/p £88.00-£163.00. Weekly D, B&B p/p £294.00-£570.50.
🛏34 🛏34 C ⓣⓞⓘⓎ🅔♿SP⌕❀🅗 ✕(FR,GR,SP,IN) TW P250

AUSTINS
11 Coldstream Terrace, City Centre, *CARDIFF*
CF11 6LJ Tel: (029) 2037 7148 Fax: (029) 2037 7158
E-mail: austins@hotelcardiff.com
Website: www.hotelcardiff.com

★★ GUEST HOUSE

Small friendly, family run hotel. 300m from Cardiff Castle overlooking the river Taff. All central attractions are within a few minutes walk. Cardiff Central station is 10 minutes walk along the river. All rooms have tea/coffee and colour TV. En-suite rooms available. A warm welcome offered to all nationalities. Come and enjoy Cardiff this year.
Months open 1-12; B&B p/p £15.00-£19.50. 2 Nights Break B&B p/p £30.00-£38.00. Weekly B&B p/p £90.00-£117.00.
🛏11 🛏4 ♿C🅔♿P7 ℹ

THE BIG SLEEP HOTEL
Bute Terrace, *CARDIFF* CF10 2FE
Tel: (029) 2063 6363 Fax: (029) 2063 6364
E-mail: bookings.cardiff@thebigsleephotel.com
Website: www.thebigsleephotel.com

★★ HOTEL

Months open 1-12; B&B p/p £22.50-£42.50.
🛏81 🛏81 ♿CⓎ🅔♿⌕P30 ℹ

BOOK DIRECT

Just pick up the phone and talk direct to your chosen accommodation. You'll receive personal attention – and will be speaking to someone who can answer all your questions so you can make your booking there and then. Nothing could be simpler.

In looking through these pages you'll also find that much of the accommodation can also be contacted by e-mail.

THE GREENDOWN INN HOTEL
Drope Rd, St Georges-super-Ely,
nr *CARDIFF* CF5 6EP
Tel: (01446) 760310 Fax: (01446) 760937
Website: greendownhotel.co.uk

★★★ INN
BRONZE

The Greendown dates from the 15th Century and is a privately run Inn/Hotel set in peaceful rural surroundings offering good food and excellent en-suite accommodation, minutes from St Fagans castle which houses the Welsh Folk Museum. 15 minutes Cardiff City Centre, 5 minutes M4 Junction 33.

Months open 1-12; B&B p/p £39.95-£42.00. 2 Nights Break D, B&B p/p £90.00-£150.00. Weekly D, B&B p/p £294.00-£343.00.
🛏15 🛏♿CⓣⓞⓘⓎ🅔♿SP⌕♫❀🅗P100 ℹ

HILTON CARDIFF
Kingsway, *CARDIFF* CF10 3HH
Tel: (029) 2064 6300 Fax: (029) 2064 6333
E-mail: cwlhitwgm@hilton.com
Website: www.hilton.com

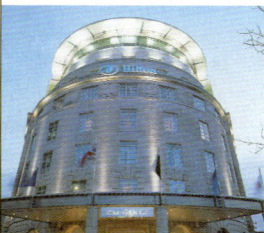

★★★★★ HOTEL

Hilton Cardiff is situated in the heart of the Welsh capital city, overlooking Cardiff Castle, extensive shopping facilities on the doorstep and close to the Millennium Stadium. The hotel offers luxury king size bedrooms, a Patisserie, *Razzi* Restaurant & Bar, the Living Well healthclub, featuring a 20m stainless steel pool, steam room, spa, sauna and beauty rooms.

Months open 1-12; B/B per room per night £99.00-£210.00. 2 Nights B&B p/p £99.00-£210.00.
🛏197 🛏197 ⓣⓞⓘⓎ🅔♿SP⌕✾✕(FR,GR,I,D,N,SW,GK,DSH) TW P80

THE TOWNHOUSE
70 Cathedral Rd, *CARDIFF* CF11 9LL
Tel: (029) 2023 9399 Fax: (029) 2022 3214
E-mail: thetownhouse@msn.com
Website: www.thetownhousecardiff.co.uk

★★ HOTEL

Experience the delights of this elegant classic town house situated 10 minutes walk from the city centre. All rooms include en-suite bathroom, rc television, tea and coffee making facilities, and direct dial telephone. Car parking is available. All major credit cards are accepted.

Months open 1-12; B&B p/p £24.75-£29.75.
🛏9 🛏9 ♿C🅔♿SP✕P8 ℹ

Bed & Breakfast
£27.50 p.p. is the most you'll pay

MAIR'S BED & BREAKFAST
★★★ BED & BREAKFAST BRONZE

9 Coychurch Rd, *BRIDGEND* CF31 3AR
Tel: (01656) 654838 Fax: (01656) 654838
E-mail: mairbb@euphony.net

A warm Welsh welcome awaits you at Mair's. It is situated two minutes walk from the town centre and is just three miles from the heritage coast. Ideal for holidays or business. The house was opened by Graham Henry, the Welsh rugby coach, in November 1999.

Months open 1-12; Single B&B per night £18.00-£20.00. Double B&B per night £36.00-£40.00. ⇔6 ⇔3 🐕 C ♿ ⚭ 🎣 P12 i

AUSTINS
★★ GUEST HOUSE

11 Coldstream Terrace, City Centre, *CARDIFF*
CF11 6LJ Tel: (029) 2037 7148 Fax: (029) 2037 7158
E-mail: austins@hotelcardiff.com
Website: www.hotelcardiff.com

Small friendly, family run hotel. 300m from Cardiff Castle overlooking the river Taff. All central attractions are within a few minutes walk. Cardiff Central station is 10 minutes walk along the river. All rooms have tea/coffee and colour TV. En-suite rooms available. A warm welcome offered to all nationalities. Come and enjoy Cardiff this year.

Months open 1-12; Single B&B per night £20.00-£27.50. Double B&B per night £30.00-£39.00. ⇔11 ⇔4 🐕 C ♿ P7 i

CARDIFF UNIVERSITY
★★ UP TO ★★★★ CAMPUS BRONZE

Southgate House, Bevan Place,
PO Box 533, *CARDIFF* CF14 3XZ
Tel: (029) 2087 5508 Fax: (029) 2087 4990
E-mail: groups@cardiff.ac.uk Website: www.cf.ac.uk

Between June and September Cardiff University has more than 3000 en-suite rooms available at very competitive rates. Ten minutes from the city centre, the University can provide bed and breakfast for individuals, groups and families. Extensive parking and sporting facilities make the University an ideal choice for touring Cardiff and South Wales.

Months open 6-9; Single room B&B £17.00-£21.00.
⇔2500 ⇔2000 🍴♿♿ ⚭ ⚭ P100

FARTHINGS
★★★ BED & BREAKFAST

Lisvane Rd, Lisvane, *CARDIFF* CF14 0SG
Tel: (029) 2075 6404 Fax: (029) 2075 6404

Close to Cardiff centre yet in the heart of the village of Lisvane, 'Farthings' offers single and double, cottage-style accommodation with private lounge plus secure parking. A short walk from the local inn serving meals. Close to bus and train services to Cardiff centre and beyond.

Months open 1-12; Single B&B per night £27.50.
Double B&B per night £45.00. ⇔3 ⇔0 ♿ ⚭ ❄ ✿(FR) P4

CLASSIFIED ADVERTISING *There's more accommodation to choose from in the classified advertising section of this book. Please see the listing at the end of the 12 Areas display adverts.*

Norwegian Church, Cardiff Bay, now an arts centre and café

PLAS-Y-BRYN

★★
BED & BREAKFAST

93 Fairwater Rd, Llandaff, *CARDIFF* CF5 2LG
Tel: (029) 2056 1717

Months open 1-12; Single B&B per night £18.00-£24.00.
Double B&B per night £34.00-£48.00.

🛏3 ☕ 🐎♿✕✿ ℹ

RAMBLER COURT HOTEL

★★
HOTEL

188 Cathedral Rd, *CARDIFF* CF11 9JE
Tel: (029) 2022 1187 Fax: (029) 2022 1187

Friendly family-run hotel situated in one of the finest examples of Victorian streets. Fifteen minutes walk to Millennium Stadium and city centre. Ideally situated for most of Cardiff's main attractions. Close to parks, good restaurants and bistros.

Months open 1-12; Single B&B per night £18.00-£25.00.
Double B&B per night £36.00-£40.00.

🛏9 ➡4 ♿ SP 🎱 P4

PRICES

Single rates are for ONE PERSON in a single room. Double rates are for TWO PEOPLE sharing a double or twin room. There may be supplements for private bath/shower and single occupancy of a double/twin room. All prices quoted include VAT. Please check all prices and facilities before confirming your booking.

Part of Cardiff Castle is an opulent Victorian mansion

CENTRAL RESERVATIONS

Your free one-stop shop for holiday accommodation. A wide choice of places to stay, last-minute offers, late availability, bargain breaks.

Call freephone 0800 834820 for North Wales, 0800 273747 for Mid Wales or 0800 3289597 for South and West Wales.

WESTWINDS

★★
BED & BREAKFAST

4 Heol-y-Delyn, Lisvane, *CARDIFF* CF14 0SQ
Tel: (029) 2068 9228

Months open 1-12; Single B&B per night £24.00.
Double B&B per night £36.00.

🛏2 ♿✕✿ P2 ℹ

WYNFORD HOTEL

★★
HOTEL
GOLD

Clare St, *CARDIFF* CF11 6BD
Tel: (029) 2037 1983 Fax: (029) 2034 0477

Months open 1-12; Single B&B per night £27.50.
Double B&B per night £48.00-£54.00.

🛏18 ➡18 C 🍴♥♿♨♪🎵✕⚒(FR,GR,SP) P15

THE OLD BARN BED & BREAKFAST

★★★
BED & BREAKFAST
GOLD

The Croft, *PENMARK*, nr Cardiff CF62 3BP
Tel: (01446) 711352 Fax: (01446) 711352
E-mail: enquiries@theoldbarnbedandbreakfast.co.uk
Website: www.theoldbarnbedandbreakfast.co.uk

Set in the heart of the village. 'The Old Barn' is a recently converted 17th century farm building, retaining many original features and charm yet providing modern, comfortable facilities. 13 miles from Cardiff and ideally situated for exploring heritage coast, Brecon Beacons and other areas of South Wales. Guest kitchen and lounge facilities.

Months open 1-12; Single B&B per night £25.00-£27.50. Double B&B per night £40.00-£45.00.

🛏2 ➡2 🐎 C ♿ SP ✕🎱 P2 ℹ

EDMON HOUSE

★★★
GUEST HOUSE
GOLD

33 Esplanade Avenue, *PORTHCAWL* CF36 3YS
Tel: (01656) 788102 Fax: (01656) 783682
E-mail: edmonhouse@edmonhouse.force9.co.uk
Website: www.bridgend.gov.uk

Welcome to our totally renovated mid-terraced guest house where you can relax and enjoy luxury en-suite accommodation. On the doorstep to the beautiful heritage coastline. All amenities are conveniently situated close by. Located 100 yards from the seafront. We offer discounts for short breaks and have Christmas and New Year packages available.

Months open 1-12; B&B p/p min £25.00. 2 Nights Break D, B&B p/p £80.00-£100.00. Weekly D, B&B p/p £245.00-£315.00.

🛏3 ➡3 🐎🍴♿ SP ✕✿ ℹ

ROSSETT GUEST HOUSE

★★
GUEST HOUSE
GOLD

1 Esplanade Avenue, *PORTHCAWL* CF36 3YS
Tel: (01656) 771664 Fax: (01656) 771664
E-mail: rossettgh@netscapeonline.co.uk

Months open 1-12; Single B&B per night £17.00-£20.00.
Double B&B per night £34.00-£40.00.

🛏3 ➡2 🐎 C 🍴♿ SP 🎱🎱 ⚒(FR,GR) P2 ℹ

Holiday Cottages

WALES CYMRU
TWO HOURS AND
A MILLION MILES AWAY

CARDIFF UNIVERSITY

★★ UP TO ★★★★

BRONZE

Southgate House, Bevan Place, PO Box 533,
CARDIFF CF14 3XZ
Tel: (029) 2087 5508 Fax: (029) 2087 4990
E-mail: groups@cardiff.ac.uk
Website: www.cf.ac.uk

Between June and September Cardiff University has more than 3000 en-suite rooms available at very competitive rates. Ten minutes from the city centre, the University has self-catering services for individuals, groups, families. Extensive parking and sporting facilities make the University an ideal choice for touring Cardiff and South Wales.

Months open 6-9; 2 Nights £32.00. 3 Nights £48.00. 4 Nights £64.00.
Weekly/unit £288.00-£578.00.
UNITS 300 SLEEPS 4-8

PENTWYN COTTAGE (THE ANNEX)

★★★★

St Mellons Rd, Lisvane, *CARDIFF* CF14 0SH
Tel: (029) 2075 8393 or 07989 637582
Enquiries: Mrs Rosemary Rayner

Comfortable well equipped annex for 2 people adjoining part of owners cottage. Very spacious lounge/diner designed to excellent standards with delightful patio overlooking large well tended gardens. Fully equipped modern kitchen, spacious and well presented bedroom, en-suite bath/shower. Country views from all windows. Excellent location adjacent M4/city centre.

Months open 1-12; 2 Nights £60.00-£80.00. Weekly/unit £180.00-£220.00.
UNITS 1 SLEEPS 2

PLEASE NOTE

All the accommodation in this publication has applied for grading. With Holiday Cottages it may occasionally not have been possible to undertake a grading. This situation is clearly identified by 'Awaiting Grading' or a provisional Star rating (indicated by the letter P appearing alongside the Stars) within the advertisement/entry.

TREGUFF FARM COTTAGES

AWAITING GRADING

Treguff Farm, nr *COWBRIDGE* CF71 7LT
Tel: (01446) 751342 or (01446) 860350

Stone cottages converted from a group of farm buildings, adjacent to an Elizabethan farmhouse on a four hundred acre working stock farm. Specimen carp fishing available on farm lake. The interiors of the cottages have sympathetically retained most of the original architectural features. Excellent touring centre.

Months open 1-12; Weekly/unit £250.00-£550.00.
UNITS 5 SLEEPS 2-8

TY TANGLWYST FARM HOLIDAY COTTAGES

★★★★

Ty Tanglwyst Farm, Pyle,
PORTHCAWL, Bridgend CF33 4SA
Tel: (01656) 745635/740224 Fax: (01656) 745635
E-mail: tytanglwystholidaycottages@hotmail.com
Enquiries: Mr & Mrs John Lougher

Two beautiful cottages converted from traditional stone farm building. Flagstone floors, whitewashed walls and exposed beams. Furnished and equipped to a high standard. Central heating and log fires. Ideally situated on dairy farm 30 mins from both Cardiff and Swansea. Ten minutes to beaches. Numerous attractions nearby. Colour brochure available.

Months open 1-12; 2 Nights £120.00. 3 Nights £150.00. 4 Nights £180.00.
Weekly/unit £200.00-£300.00.
UNITS 2 SLEEPS 4-5

Wye Valley & Vale of Usk

*T*hese two lovely valleys, close to the border, serve as the best possible introduction to Wales. The thickly wooded Wye Valley, an 'Area of Outstanding Natural Beauty', is a walker's paradise. Rolling green hills separate the Wye from the Usk, another beautiful river valley – like the Wye, famous for its fishing – which flows through rich countryside on its way to the sea at Newport.

Tintern in the Wye Valley

On Your Travels ...

Tredegar House, Newport

The beauty of Tintern Abbey has been an inspiration to artists and visitors to the Wye Valley for many centuries.

This evocative historic site, with its soaring arches and elaborate decorative stonework, is undoubtedly the best-preserved medieval abbey in Wales. Architecture and landscape are at one here, the abbey blending harmoniously with its idyllic riverbank setting.

These borderlands are dotted with historic sites. At Chepstow there's a famous landmark – Britain's first stone-built castle, dating back to the Norman Conquest. If Chepstow was the first, than Raglan was one of the last. Handsome Raglan Castle, built more as a palace than military fortification, marked the end of the troublesome medieval period. While there's plenty of evidence of home comforts at Raglan, it doesn't begin to rival Tredegar House on the outskirts of Newport. Tredegar is a magnificent 17th-century mansion with glittering state rooms. In contrast to this opulent 'upstairs', you can also see the not-quite-so-glamorous 'downstairs' where the servants lived and worked.

For further information please tel (01633) 644842; e-mail: tourism@monmouthshire.gov.uk

Where to Stay
Wales

Abergavenny
Map Ref Mc1

Flourishing market town with backdrop of mountains at south-eastern gateway to Brecon Beacons National Park. Pony trekking in nearby Black Mountains. Castle and museum; leisure centre, excellent local theatre housed in grand Victorian Town Hall. Monmouthshire and Brecon Canal runs just to the west of the town. Good touring base for the lovely Vale of Usk and Brecon Beacons. Wales in Bloom award winner 2000.

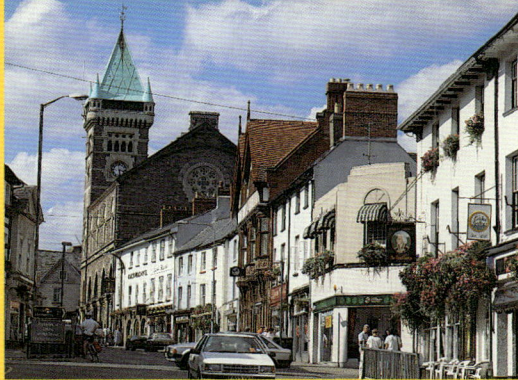
Attractive Abergavenny stands in the Usk Valley

Chepstow
Map Ref Me4

Attractive hilly town with substantial remains of a great stone castle – reputedly the first to be built in Britain – above the River Wye. Fortified gate still stands in main street and medieval walls remain. Good shopping. Museum, Stuart Crystal Engraving Workshop. Sunday market, fine racecourse, excellent walks – beginning of Wye Valley Walk and Offa's Dyke Path. Ideal for touring Wye Valley. Wales in Bloom award winner 2000.

Magor
Map Ref Md4

On coastal plain of Severn Estuary in countryside full of historic interest – castles at Chepstow, Caldicot and Penhow, Roman remains at Caerleon and Caerwent. Easy access by Second Severn Crossing.

Monmouth
Map Ref Me1

Historic market town in picturesque Wye Valley. Birthplace of Henry V, who was born in Monmouth Castle in 1387, and Charles Rolls (of Rolls-Royce) – the ruined castle is close to town centre. Interesting local history museum with collection of Nelson memorabilia. Rare fortified gateway still spans the River Monnow. Well located for touring Wye Valley and borderland Wales.

Monnow Bridge, Monmouth

Newport
Map Ref Mc4

Busy industrial, commercial and shopping centre. Newport Museum and Art Gallery in John Frost Square (named after Chartist leader) and leisure centre with wave machine. St Woolos Cathedral on hill overlooking

Chepstow, gateway to Wales

town. Ruined castle on riverside near shops and attractive Victorian market hall. On the outskirts, magnificently restored Tredegar House set in extensive grounds, and 14 Locks Canal Visitor Centre. Wales in Bloom award winner 2000.

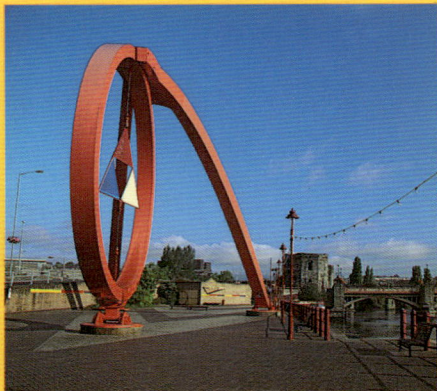

Newport, at the mouth of the Usk

Raglan
Map Ref Md2

Historic village dominated by handsome Raglan Castle, noted for its impressive Great Tower of Gwent. Convenient for touring the Usk and Wye valleys and eastern Brecon Beacons. Wales in Bloom award winner 2000.

Tintern
Map Ref Me3

Riverside village in particularly lovely stretch of Wye Valley. Impressive ruins of Tintern Abbey not to be missed. Tintern Old Station has visitor centre. Excellent woodland walks and good fishing.

Trellech
Map Ref Me2

Picturesque village on the 'B' road from Chepstow to Monmouth, set in the heart of beautiful border country. Lovely Wye Valley a few miles to the east.

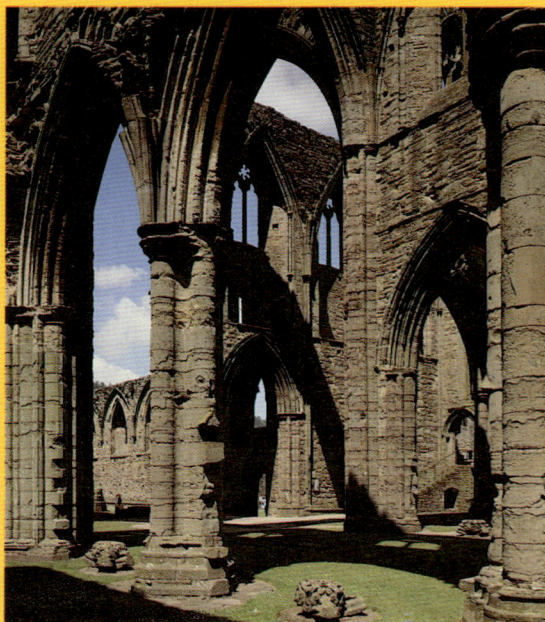

Tintern Abbey, founded in medieval times

Abergavenny
Map Ref Mc1 ≷

Flourishing market town with backdrop of mountains at south-eastern gateway to Brecon Beacons National Park. Pony trekking in nearby Black Mountains. Castle and museum; leisure centre, excellent local theatre housed in grand Victorian Town Hall. Monmouthshire and Brecon Canal runs just to the west of the town. Good touring base for the lovely Vale of Usk and Brecon Beacons. Wales in Bloom award winner 2000.

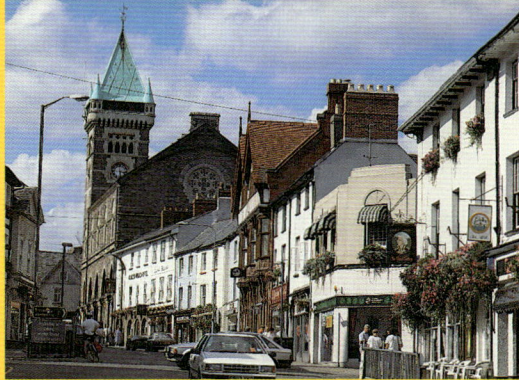
Attractive Abergavenny stands in the Usk Valley

Chepstow
Map Ref Me4 ≷

Attractive hilly town with substantial remains of a great stone castle – reputedly the first to be built in Britain – above the River Wye. Fortified gate still stands in main street and medieval walls remain. Good shopping. Museum, Stuart Crystal Engraving Workshop. Sunday market, fine racecourse, excellent walks – beginning of Wye Valley Walk and Offa's Dyke Path. Ideal for touring Wye Valley. Wales in Bloom award winner 2000.

Magor
Map Ref Md4

On coastal plain of Severn Estuary in countryside full of historic interest – castles at Chepstow, Caldicot and Penhow, Roman remains at Caerleon and Caerwent. Easy access by Second Severn Crossing.

Monmouth
Map Ref Me1

Historic market town in picturesque Wye Valley. Birthplace of Henry V, who was born in Monmouth Castle in 1387, and Charles Rolls (of Rolls-Royce) – the ruined castle is close to town centre. Interesting local history museum with collection of Nelson memorabilia. Rare fortified gateway still spans the River Monnow. Well located for touring Wye Valley and borderland Wales.

Monnow Bridge, Monmouth

Chepstow, gateway to Wales

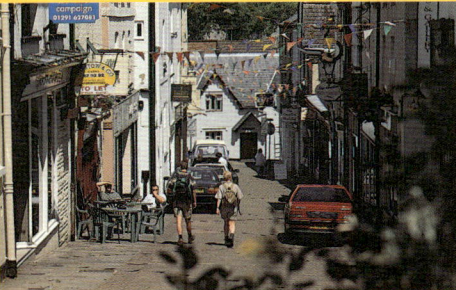

Newport
Map Ref Mc4 ≷

Busy industrial, commercial and shopping centre. Newport Museum and Art Gallery in John Frost Square (named after Chartist leader) and leisure centre with wave machine. St Woolos Cathedral on hill overlooking

Newport, at the mouth of the Usk

town. Ruined castle on riverside near shops and attractive Victorian market hall. On the outskirts, magnificently restored Tredegar House set in extensive grounds, and 14 Locks Canal Visitor Centre. Wales in Bloom award winner 2000.

Raglan
Map Ref Md2

Historic village dominated by handsome Raglan Castle, noted for its impressive Great Tower of Gwent. Convenient for touring the Usk and Wye valleys and eastern Brecon Beacons. Wales in Bloom award winner 2000.

Tintern
Map Ref Me3

Riverside village in particularly lovely stretch of Wye Valley. Impressive ruins of Tintern Abbey not to be missed. Tintern Old Station has visitor centre. Excellent woodland walks and good fishing.

Trellech
Map Ref Me2

Picturesque village on the 'B' road from Chepstow to Monmouth, set in the heart of beautiful border country. Lovely Wye Valley a few miles to the east.

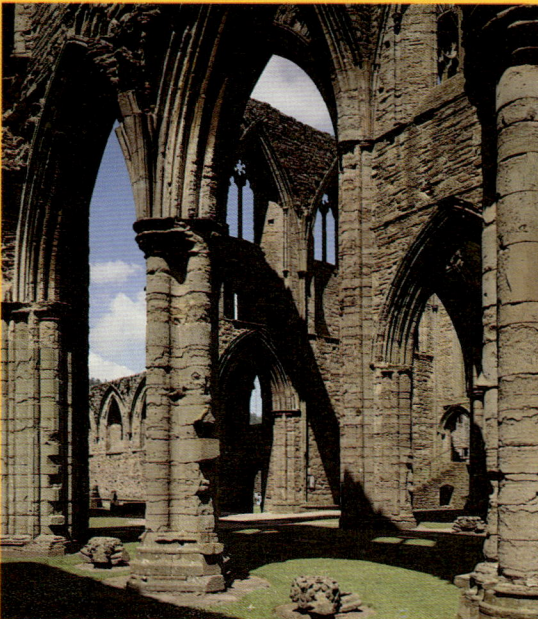

Tintern Abbey, founded in medieval times

Hotels, Guest Houses & Farmhouses

PENTRE COURT

★★ BED & BREAKFAST

Llanwenarth Citra, *ABERGAVENNY* NP7 7EW
Tel: (01873) 853545
E-mail: judith@pentrecourt.com
Website: pentrecourt.com

Charming, spacious Georgian country home, relaxing atmosphere, log fires and antiques, set in 3½ acres of beautifully stocked gardens/paddock, bulbs, shrubs, roses etc. with wonderful views over Usk Valley. Just inside the National Park, 1 mile from town. Ideal for walkers.

Months open 1-12; B&B p/p £18.00-£25.00. 2 Nights Break D, B&B p/p £70.00-£85.00. Weekly D, B&B p/p £245.00-£299.00.

🛏3 🚪3 🖪 C 🍴❀✿🏠 P5 i

LLANSANTFFRAED COURT HOTEL

★★★★ COUNTRY HOTEL

Llanvihangel Gobion,
nr *ABERGAVENNY* NP7 9BA
Tel: (01873) 840678 Fax: (01873) 840674
E-mail: reception@llch.co.uk
Website: www.llch.co.uk

SILVER

A timeless landscape steeped in history awaits the traveller to this stunning Georgian country house. Set in 20 acres amid the hills and mystical valleys of the Wye and Usk. Nationally acclaimed for its cuisine and hospitality. Exquisitely furnished, log fires and a Welsh welcome. Spoil yourself!

Months open 1-12; B&B p/p £44.00-£77.50.
2 Nights Break D, B&B p/p £136.00-£190.00.

🛏21 🚪21 🖪 C 🍴❀✿🏠 ✕(GR,SP) TW P250 i

Llandegfedd reservoir near Usk

CASTLE VIEW HOTEL

★★ HOTEL

16 Bridge St, *CHEPSTOW* NP6 5EZ
Tel: (01291) 620349 Fax: (01291) 627397
E-mail: info@hotelschepstow.co.uk
Website: www.hotelschepstow.co.uk

BRONZE

Historic 300 year old hotel, opposite one of Britain's oldest stone built castles. Antique wall paintings in some bedrooms, carved oak staircase, totally refurbished, many large family rooms. Commended cuisine in restaurant and bar, malts, 4ch. Sky, family run. 5mins M4/M5/M48. Ideal Cardiff, Bristol, Caerleon (Roman remains), Wye Valley, Tintern, Forest of Dean.

Months open 1-12; B&B p/p £30.00-£38.00. 2 Nights Break D, B&B p/p £86.00-£96.00. Weekly D, B&B p/p £258.00-£288.00.

🛏13 🚪13 🍴❤🚭👶SP✿🏠 i

COMFORT INN

★★ LODGE

Comfort Inn, Jnc 23A, M4 Motorway,
***MAGOR* NP26 3YL**
Tel: (01633) 881515 Fax: (01633) 881896

A modern 43 bed lodge. All rooms en-suite with TV. An ideal location for touring the Wye Valley and South East Wales. Coach parties welcome.

Months open 1-12; B&B p/p £22.50-£26.50. 2 Nights Break D, B&B p/p £40.00-£45.00.

🛏43 🚪43 🍴🚭👶 P250 i

THE RIVERSIDE HOTEL

★★ HOTEL

Cinderhill St, *MONMOUTH* NP25 5EY
Tel: (01600) 715577 Fax: (01600) 712668

BRONZE

A privately-owned hotel with modern en-suite bedrooms, all recently redecorated. Our restaurants offer superb home-cooked meals using local fresh produce. Within easy reach of beauty spots, located in the beautiful Wye Valley in an area to take your breath away. Traditional hospitality with professional service.

Months open 1-12; B&B p/p £25.00-£34.00. 2 Nights Break D, B&B p/p £70.00-£95.00. Weekly D, B&B p/p £490.00-£650.00.

🛏17 🚪17 🖪 C 🍴❤🚭👶SP P30 i

THE INN AT THE ELM TREE
St Brides Wentloog, _NEWPORT_ NP10 8SQ
Tel: (01633) 680225 Fax: (01633) 681035
E-mail: inn@the-elm-tree.co.uk
Website: www.the-elm-tree.co.uk

★★★★★
INN

Wales' first 5-star Inn. Two miles from M4(J28) in peaceful rural village close to capitol. A unique blend of traditional values and understated elegance.
Some bedrooms have 4-posters, waterbeds, jacuzzis. Enviable reputation for excellent cuisine. Ideal for short breaks, sightseeing, country pursuits, relaxing, romancing, wining and dining. RAC/AA ◆◆◆◆◆.

Months open 1-12; B&B p/p £30.00-£40.00.
2 Nights Break D, B&B p/p £90.00-£110.00.

🛏10 ⬥10 ⬥ 🍴♥ ⬥ SP 🔲 ※✿🏦 ✗ (FR,SP,TH) TW P23 _i_

Bed & Breakfast
£27.50 p.p. is the most you'll pay

KINGS HEAD HOTEL
59 Cross St, _ABERGAVENNY_ NP7 5EU
Tel: (01873) 853575 Fax: (01873) 853575

★★
INN

Months open 1-12; Single B&B per night £25.00.
Double B&B per night £50.00.

🛏5 ⬥4 🍴♥ ⬥ TW P _i_

ROCK & FOUNTAIN HOTEL
Clydach North, nr _ABERGAVENNY_ NP7 0LL
Tel: (01873) 830393 Fax: (01873) 830393
E-mail: archer@rockandfountain.fsnet.co.uk
Website: www.rockandfountain.fsnet.co.uk

★★★
INN

Months open 1-12; Single B&B per night £27.50.
Double B&B per night £45.00-£50.00.

🛏6 🍴♥ ⬥ ♪✿ P22 _i_

PENTRE HOUSE
Brecon Rd, _ABERGAVENNY_ NP7 7EW
Tel: (01873) 853435 Fax: (01873) 852321

★★★
BED & BREAKFAST

AWARD   SILVER

Attractive, small Georgian country house, set in 1 acre of award-winning gardens. Very comfortably furnished. Antiques, beamed ceilings, log fires. Sugar Loaf Mountain and River Usk nearby.

Months open 1-12; Single B&B per night £20.00-£25.00.
Double B&B per night £34.00-£35.00.
2 Nights Break by arrangement.

🛏3 ⬥ SP 🔲 ※✿🏦 P5 _i_

CLASSIFIED ADVERTISING _There's more accommodation to choose from in the classified advertising section of this book. Please see the listing at the end of the 12 Areas display adverts._

YEW TREE FARM
Llanellen, nr _ABERGAVENNY_ NP7 9LB
Tel: (01873) 854307 Fax: (01873) 854307
E-mail: groseandeollanellen@ukonline.co.uk

★★
FARM

Months open 4-10; B&B p/p £20.00.

🛏1 ⬥1 🐾 ⬥ C ⬥ SP 🗴 ※✿🏦 P2 _i_

BRIDGE HOUSE
Pwllmeyric, _CHEPSTOW_ NP16 6LF
Tel: (01291) 622567

★★
BED & BREAKFAST

Months open 1-12; Single B&B per night £19.00-£20.00.
Double B&B per night £37.00-£38.00.

🛏2 🔲 P3 _i_

CASITA ALTA
15 Toynbee Close, Osbaston, _MONMOUTH_ NP25 3NU
Tel: (01600) 713023

★★
BED & BREAKFAST

GOLD

Months open 1-12; Single B&B per night £22.50-£27.50.
Double B&B per night £33.00-£42.00.

🛏2 ⬥1 ⬥✿ (FR,GR,SP) P2

CHURCH FARM GUEST HOUSE
Mitchel Troy, _MONMOUTH_ NP25 4HZ
Tel: (01600) 712176

★★★
GUEST HOUSE

GOLD

A spacious and homely 16th century former farmhouse with oak beams and inglenook fireplaces. Set in large attractive garden with stream. Easy access to A40 and only two miles from historic Monmouth. Excellent base for Wye Valley, Forest of Dean and Black Mountains. Large car park. Terrace, barbeque. Colour TV, central heating and tea/coffee making facilities.

Months open 1-12; B&B p/p £20.00-£23.50. 2 Nights Break D, B&B p/p £66.00-£73.00. Weekly D, B&B p/p £224.00-£248.50.

🛏8 ⬥6 ⬥ C 🍴♥ ⬥ ※✿🏦 ✗ (FR) P12 _i_

The remains of Newport's ancient castle

Tranquil border country, Wye Valley

Holiday Cottages

CHAPEL GUEST HOUSE

GUEST HOUSE ★★★

Church Rd, St Brides Wentloog, nr NEWPORT
NP10 8SN Tel: (01633) 681018 Fax: (01633) 681431
E-mail: chapelguesthouse@hotmail.com

BRONZE

Comfortable en-suite accommodation in a converted chapel situated in a village between Newport and Cardiff. Inn/restaurant adjacent. Tredegar House nearby. Guest lounge. TV and beverage trays in all bedrooms. Children welcome - special rates. Leave M4 at junction 28, take A48 towards Newport, at roundabout take third exit B4239 to St Brides. In village turn right (Church Road), then left, entrance off inn car park.

Months open 1-12: Single B&B per night £22.00-£25.00. Double B&B per night £38.00-£44.00.

ELM TREE HOUSE

BED & BREAKFAST ★★

St Brides Wentloog, NEWPORT NP10 8SQ
Tel: (01633) 680384

Months open 1-12; B&B p/p from £20.00.

KNOLL GUEST HOUSE

GUEST HOUSE ★★★

145 Stow Hill, NEWPORT NP20 4FZ
Tel: (01633) 263557 Fax: (01633) 212168
Website: www.knollguesthouse@activebooking.com

The Knoll is a period Victorian house, furnished to an excellent standard, and has been a family-run business since 1987. Our aim is to maintain a high standard of accommodation and meals in a friendly and hospitable atmosphere. Our rooms offer en-suite facilities, tea/coffee making, TV, radio/alarm and telephone.

Months open 1-12; Double B&B per night £48.00.

BROOKLANDS FARM

FARM ★★

GOLD

Chepstow Rd, RAGLAN NP15 2EN
Tel: (01291) 690782 Fax: (01291) 690782
E-mail: brooklands-farm@raglanf.sbusiness.co.uk

Working dairy farm with sheep and cattle. Situated close to Raglan Castle and within 200 metres of Raglan village with its shops and pubs. Large spacious garden. All rooms have wash hand basin, tea/coffee making facilities. Local golf course, walking, fishing and horse riding all within a short distance. Local touring centre.

Months open 1-12; B&B p/p £15.00-£18.00. 2 Nights Break D, B&B p/p £30.00-£36.00. Weekly D, B&B p/p £150.00-£175.00.

SUGAR LOAF COTTAGES

★★★★★

Dunmar Farm, Pentre Lane,
ABERGAVENNY NP7 7LA
Tel: (01873) 858675 Fax: (01873) 858675
E-mail: rmhofayz@aol.com

GOLD

Tastefully converted barns well furnished and equipped. One mile from Abergavenny on the south facing slopes of the Sugar Loaf mountain. An area of outstanding natural beauty and spectacular views. Ideal for country sports and leisure activities. Taste our wine or follow the vineyard and woodland trail. Ring for brochure.

Months open 3-12; 3 Nights £80.00-£172.00. 4 Nights £105.00-£220.00. Weekly/unit £120.00-£345.00.

UNITS 5 SLEEPS 2-5

STEPPES FARM COTTAGES

★★★★★

Rockfield, MONMOUTH NP25 5SW
Tel: (01600) 716273 Fax: (01600) 715257
Website: steppesfarmcottages.co.uk

The perfect country holiday. Our tiny hamlet of top quality stone and oak beamed cottages are superbly situated 2 miles from Monmouth in the Wye Valley. Cottages furnished to highest standards. Beautiful landscaped gardens, lawns, pond and individual patio furniture. Ideal for Wye Valley, Brecon Beacons, Forest of Dean, Herefordshire. Suitable elderly and semi-disabled.

Months open 1-12; Weekly/unit £250.00-£470.00.

UNITS 6 SLEEPS 4-6

LAST-MINUTE DEALS

For the latest information and offers on holidays and short breaks in Wales, see: Teletext Page 251

Look out for the Wales Tourist Board grading on Teletext entries to make sure that the accommodation has been checked out by us.

WYE VALLEY & VALE OF USK

UPPER GRIPPATH FARM ★★★★

Risca, nr *NEWPORT* NP11 6JB
Tel: (01633) 615000 Fax: (01633) 615000
E-mail: louise.saunders@ic24.net
Website: www.grippath.ic24.net

Warm welcome awaits at comfortable well-equipped cottage on working sheep farm. Offering peace and outdoors yet close to Newport, Cardiff and Valley attractions.

Months open 1-12; 2 Nights £100.00. 3 Nights £150.00. 4 Nights £200.00. Weekly/unit £245.00-£295.00.

UNITS 1 SLEEPS 4 🐴 ▢ ⓖ SP ⤵ 🖥 P2 *i*

BERLLANDERI COACH HOUSE ★★★★★

Usk Rd, *RAGLAN* NP15 2HR
Tel: (01291) 690268 Fax: (01291) 690268
E-mail: coachhouse@berllanderi.freeserve.co.uk
Website: www.villarama.com/1495.html

Luxury 17th century coach house conversion by artist and architect, incorporating traditional and contemporary design. Complete comfort with underfloor heating, slate and oak floors, spiral staircase, 2 bedrooms, en-suite, large oak-beamed living room. Set in the Usk Valley between the Brecon Beacons and the Wye Valley.

Months open 1-12; 2 Nights £150.00-£210.00. 3 Nights £200.00-£260.00. 4 Nights £250.00-£310.00. Weekly/unit £325.00-£450.00.

UNITS 1 SLEEPS 8 🐴 ▢ ⓖ SP ⤵ 🖥 P *i*

CRAIGO BARN ★★★★

Craigo Farm, Botany Bay, *TINTERN*, Chepstow
NP16 6SN Tel: (01291) 689757 Fax: (01291) 689365
E-mail: sheron@hassell.com Website: www.tintern.org.uk

Tintern: in the heart of the beautiful Wye Valley. Comfortable, well-equipped detached stone cottage, nestling peacefully on smallholding in forests above Tintern Abbey, amidst 1000's of acres of picturesque woodland walks. Visit Tintern Abbey, local castles, medieval market towns, something to suit all interests. Idyllic location throughout all seasons.

Months open 1-12; 2 Nights £85.00-£168.00. 3 Nights £110.00-£216.00. 4 Nights £126.00-£248.00. Weekly/unit £175.00-£345.00.

UNITS 1 SLEEPS 6 🐴 ▢ ⓖ SP 🖥 🎾 (FR) *i*

THE OLD RECTORY AWAITING GRADING

TINTERN, nr Chepstow NP16 6SG Tel: (01291) 689519
Fax: (01291) 689939 E-mail: old.rectory@vizzavi.co.uk
Website: www.tinternoldrectory.co.uk

Comfortable self-contained apartment in charming former Rectory overlooking beautiful River Wye. Accommodation tastefully decorated and equipped to highest standard. Heating and linen included. Children welcome. Breakfast available. Excellent base for walking, sightseeing or relaxing. Pubs, shops, restaurants and Tintern Abbey within easy walking distance. Short breaks available. Ring for brochure.

Months open 1-12; 2 Nights £75.00. 3 Nights £100.00-£150.00. 4 Nights £100.00-£175.00. Weekly/unit £150.00-£300.00.

UNITS 1 SLEEPS up to 4 🐴 ▢ ⓖ SP ⤵ 🖥 🎾 (FR,GR,I) P3 *i*

THE CROFT ★★★★★

TRELLECH NP25 4PA
Tel: (01600) 860681/207

Centre of historic village, near church. Set high above Wye Valley amidst outstanding scenery. Self contained wing of 1686 stone house. Much character and interest including secret bedroom. Conservatory, walled front garden. Well appointed kitchen/dining room, large comfortable lounge with french doors opening onto secluded patio. 3 bedrooms. Pets welcome.

Months open 1-12; Weekly/unit £120.00-£450.00.

UNITS 1 SLEEPS 6 🐴 ▢ SP M 🖥 P3 *i*

The Second Severn Crossing

QUALITY COTTAGES ★★★★ UP TO ★★★★★

Cerbid, *SOLVA,* Haverfordwest SA62 6YE
Tel: (01348) 837871
Website: www.qualitycottages.co.uk

WTB Tourism Award winners. 34 years experience in self catering. We offer a selection of quality cottages with exceptionally high residential standards. Log fires etc. Pets welcome free. Around the magnificent Welsh coastline with its numerous sandy beaches and super scenic walks. A naturalist's paradise. Free colour brochure.

Months open 1-12; 3 Nights £108.00-£270.00.
Weekly/unit £199.00-£1350.00.

UNITS 160 SLEEPS 2-14

Still Undecided?

Then call Central Reservations on freephone 0800 834820 for North Wales, 0800 273747 for Mid Wales or 0800 3289597 for South and West Wales – and you'll be plugged into a great choice of places to stay.

WALES CYMRU
WDA

TASTE OF WALES IS FINANCED WITH THE ASSISTANCE OF THE EUROPEAN COMMUNITY

W here you see the sign, you're in for a sweet dining experience. Taste of Wales is a sign of quality. Wherever it is displayed it means you can expect the highest quality service, and the finest food made from the best Welsh produce. For our latest guide call 029 2082 8984

BLAS AR CYMRU
A TASTE OF WALES

Your guide to finding good food
Eich canllaw er mwyn dod o hyd i fwyd da

"THE PROOF OF THE PUDDING"

WALES CYMRU

TWO HOURS AND A MILLION MILES AWAY

In addition to the 12 Areas display adverts, there's more accommodation to choose from in the following classified listing. As with the display advertising, it's divided into Wales's 12 Areas. Within each area the listings appear alphabetically by placename.

ISLE OF ANGLESEY
AREA 1

Hotels, Guest Houses & Farmhouses

AMLWCH *Map Ref: Ac1*

PENYCEFN HOUSE Salem St, Amlwch LL68 9DD
Tel: (01407) 832122 Fax: (01407) 832122 ⊨5 Open: 1-12;
2 Star B&B

BEAUMARIS *Map Ref: Ae3*

PLAS CICHLE Beaumaris LL58 8PS Tel: (01248) 810488
Website: www.globalvillas.com/plascichle.html ⊨3 ⇥3
Open: 2-11; 3 Star Farm

BENLLECH BAY *Map Ref: Ad2*

BELVOIR 8 Lon Fferam, Benllech Bay LL74 8RL
Tel: (01248) 852907 ⊨2 ⇥2 Open: 3-10; 4 Star B&B

BRYNSIENCYN *Map Ref: Ad4*

TYDDYN GOBLET Brynsiencyn, Anglesey LL61 6TZ
Tel: (01248) 430296 ⊨2 ⇥2 Open: 1-11; 3 Star Farm

CEMAES BAY *Map Ref: Ac1*

GADLYS COUNTRY HOUSE HOTEL Cemaes Bay
Tel: (01407) 710227 Fax: (01407) 711404
E-mail: pva@gadlys.com Website: www.gadlys.com
⊨13 ⇥13 Open: 1-12; 2 Star Hotel

DWYRAN *Map Ref: Ac4*

TAL-Y-FOEL Dwyran LL61 6LQ Tel: (01248) 430377
Fax: (01248) 430977 E-mail: hutchings@talyfoel.u.net.com
Website: www.tal-y-foel.co.uk ⊨4 ⇥4 Open: 1-12; 3 Star
Farm

HOLYHEAD *Map Ref: Aa2*

VALLEY HOTEL London Rd, Valley, Holyhead LL65 3DU
Tel: (01407) 740203 Fax: (01407) 740686
E-mail: valleyhotel@tinyworld.co.uk
Website: www.valley-hotel-hotel-anglesey.co.uk
⊨20 ⇥18 Open: 1-12; 2 Star Hotel

LLANNERCH-Y-MEDD *Map Ref: Ac2*

DRWS-Y-COED Llannerch-y-Medd LL71 8AD
Tel: (01248) 470473 Fax: (01248) 470473 ⊨3 ⇥3
Open: 1-12; 4 Star Farm

MENAI BRIDGE *Map Ref: Ad3*

BWTHYN B&B Brynafon, Menai Bridge LL59 5HA
Tel: (01248) 713119 Fax: (01248) 713119 ⊨2 ⇥2
Open: 1-12; 4 Star B&B

TREARDDUR BAY *Map Ref: Aa3*

THE BEACH HOTEL Trearddur Bay LL65 2YT
Tel: (01407) 860332 Fax: (01407) 861140 ⊨27 ⇥27
Open: 1-12; 3 Star Hotel

INGLEDENE B&B Ravenspoint Rd, Trearddur Bay LL65 2YU
Tel: (01407) 861026 Fax: (01407) 861026
E-mail: ingledene@hotmail.com ⊨3 ⇥2 Open: 1-12;
2 Star B&B

MORANEDD GUEST HOUSE Trearddur Rd, Trearddur Bay
LL65 2UE Tel: (01407) 860324 Fax: (01407) 860324
⊨6 Open: 1-12; 2 Star B&B

Holiday Cottages

BENLLECH BAY *Map Ref: Ad2*

PENTITH SELF-CATERING HOLIDAYS Kingslea,
42 Bay View Rd, Benllech Bay LL74 8TT
Tel: (01248) 853537 Houses/Flats/Bungalows:
UNITS: 10 SLEEPS: 4-8 Open: 1-12

BODORGAN *Map Ref: Ac3*

TIR NA NOG COTTAGES Bodorgan LL62 5BN
Tel: (01407) 840054 Fax: (01407) 840873
E-mail: tnnog@aol.com UNITS: 2 SLEEPS: 5
Open: 1-12; 4 Star

BULL BAY *Map Ref: Ac1*

RHIANFA HOLIDAY APARTMENTS Rhianfa, Bull Bay, Amlwch
LL68 9SU Tel: (01407) 830557 Fax: (01407) 830557
E-mail: timothyronhill@hotmail.com
Website: absolute.com/rhianfa UNITS: 7 SLEEPS: 2-6+⊨
Open: 3-11; 3 Star

LLIGWY *Map Ref: Ad2*

**MINFFORDD CARAVAN PARK & LUXURY HOLIDAY
PROPERTIES** Lligwy, Dulas LL70 9HJ Tel: (01248) 410678
Fax: (01248) 410378 E-mail: hhughesroberts@talk21.com
UNITS: 5 Caravans, 2 Cottages SLEEPS: 2-9
Open: 1-12 (cottages) 3-11 (caravans); 5 Star

MARIANGLAS *Map Ref: Ad2*

HAFAN Marianglas, LL73 8NY Tel: (01942) 715518 or 0468
601655 Fax: (01942) 718714 UNITS: 1
Open: 1-12; 4 Star

PENTRAETH *Map Ref: Ad2*

PEN-Y-GARNEDD FARM nr Pentraeth LL75 8YW
Tel: (01248) 450580 UNITS: 1 SLEEPS: 5+⊨
Open: 1-12; 3 Star

TREARDDUR BAY *Map Ref: Aa3*

TREARDDUR HOLIDAY BUNGALOWS Lon Isallt, Trearddur
Bay LL65 2UP Tel: (01407) 860494 Fax: (01407) 861133
E-mail: stuartconradsmith@freenet.co.uk
UNITS: 50 SLEEPS: 2-7 Open: 3-10

Caravan & Camping Park

BEAUMARIS
Map Ref: Ae3

KINGSBRIDGE CARAVAN & CAMPING PARK Llanfaes, Beaumaris LL58 8LR Tel: (01248) 490636 Fax: (01248) 490636 No. ON PARK 27 ⌂ 2 ⌂ 48 ⛺ 100 Open: 3-10: 2 Star Holiday, Touring & Camping Park

LLANDUDNO, COLWYN BAY, RHYL & PRESTATYN
AREA 2

Hotels, Guest Houses & Farmhouses

COLWYN BAY
Map Ref: Bc4

CROSSROADS GUEST HOUSE 15 Coed Pella Rd, Colwyn Bay LL29 7AT Tel: (01492) 530736 E-mail: wte@crossroadsguesthouse.co.uk Website: www.crossroadsguesthouse.co.uk ⌂5 ⌂13 Open: 1-12; 3 Star Guest House

EDELWEISS HOTEL Off Lawson Rd, Colwyn Bay LL29 8MD Tel: (01492) 532314 Fax: (01492) 534707 E-mail: edelweisshotel@hotmail Website: www.hotelvenues.com/edelweiss ⌂26 ⌂26 Open: 1-12; 2 Star Hotel

LLYSFAEN HOUSE 58 Llysfaen Rd, Colwyn Bay LL29 9HB Tel: (01492) 517859 E-mail: views@compuserve.com Website: www.marl.com/lds/llysfaenhouse/llysfaenhouse.html ⌂3 Open: 1-12; 2 Star B&B

NORFOLK HOUSE HOTEL 39 Prince's Drive, Colwyn Bay LL29 8PE Tel: (01492) 531757 Fax: (01492) 533781 E-mail: bodrings@norfolkhousehotel.fsnet.co.uk Website: www.wow-cymru.com ⌂21 ⌂21 Open: 1-12; 3 Star Hotel

NORTHWOOD HOTEL 47 Rhos Rd, Rhos on Sea, Colwyn Bay LL28 4RS Tel: (01492) 549931 E-mail: mail@northwoodhotel.co.uk Website: www.northwoodhotel.co.uk ⌂12 ⌂11 Open: 1-12; 3 Star Hotel

QUALITY HOTEL Penmaenhead, Old Colwyn, Colwyn Bay LL29 9LD Tel: (01492) 516555 Fax: (01492) 515565 E-mail: colwynbayhotel@cwcom.net Website: www.choiceeurope ⌂43 ⌂43 Open: 1-12; 2 Star Hotel

SUNNYSIDE 146 Dinerth Rd, Rhos-on-Sea, Colwyn Bay LL28 4YF Tel: (01492) 544048 ⌂2 Open: 3-11; 2 Star B&B

THE WHITEHALL HOTEL 51 Cayley Promenade, Rhos-on-Sea, Colwyn Bay LL28 4EP Tel: (01492) 547296 Fax: (01492) 543160 E-mail: whitehallhotel@talk21.co Website: www.whitehall-hotel.co.uk ⌂12 ⌂12 Open: 1-12; 3 Star Hotel

CONWY
Map Ref: Bb4

CAERLYR HALL HOTEL Conwy Old Rd, Dwygyfylchi, Conwy LL34 6SW Tel: (01492) 623518 Fax: (01492) 622070 ⌂9 ⌂9 Open: 1-12; 3 Star Hotel

GLAN HEULOG GUEST HOUSE Llanrwst Rd, Conwy LL32 8LT Tel: (01492) 593845 E-mail: glanheulog@nolguesthousefreeserve.co.uk ⌂6 ⌂6 Open: 1-12; 3 Star Guest House

SYCHNANT PASS HOUSE Sychnant Pass Rd, Conwy LL32 8B Tel: (01497) 596868 Fax: (01492) 596868 E-mail: bresykes@sychnant-pass-house.co.uk Website: www.sychnant-pass-house.co.uk ⌂10 ⌂10 Open: 1-12; 4 Star Country House

LLANDUDNO
Map Ref: Bb3

BELLE VUE HOTEL 26 North Parade, Llandudno LL30 2LP Tel: (01492) 879547 Fax: (01492) 870001 ⌂13 ⌂13 Open: 1-12; 3 Star Hotel

CARMEL PRIVATE HOTEL 17 Craig-y-Don Parade, Promenade, Llandudno LL30 1BG Tel: (01492) 877643 ⌂9 ⌂6 Open: 1-12; 2 Star Hotel

GLENORMES HOTEL 11 Mostyn Crescent, Central Promenade, Llandudno LL30 1AR Tel: (01492) 876643 Fax: (01492) 876643 ⌂12 ⌂12 Open: 2-12; 3 Star Hotel

HEATHERDALE 30 St Davids Rd, Llandudno LL30 2UL Tel: (01492) 877362 Fax: 0870 125-8167 E-mail: heatherdale@btinternet.com Website: www.heatherdale.btinternet.co.uk ⌂6 ⌂6 Open: 1-12; 3 Star Guest House

THE IMPERIAL HOTEL The Promenade, Llandudno LL30 1PS Tel: (01492) 877466 Fax: (01492) 878043 E-mail: imphotel@btinternet.com Website: www.theimperial.co.uk ⌂100 ⌂100 Open: 1-12; 3 Star Hotel

KINMEL HOTEL 12 Mostyn Crescent, Central Promenade, Llandudno LL30 1AB Tel: (01492) 876171 Fax: (01492) 876171 ⌂12 ⌂12 Open: 2-11; 2 Star Hotel

LYNTON HOUSE HOTEL 80 Church Walks, Llandudno LL30 2HD Tel: (01492) 875009/875057 Fax: (01492) 875057 E-mail: jfair75440@aol.com Website: www.smoothhound.co.uk/hotels/lyntonho.html ⌂14 ⌂14 Open: 1-12; 2 Star Hotel

THE MIN-Y-DON HOTEL North Parade, Llandudno LL30 2LP Tel: (01492) 876511 Fax: (01492) 878169 ⌂30 ⌂25 Open: 2-12; 2 Star Hotel

THE MONTCLARE HOTEL 4 North Parade, Llandudno LL30 2LP Tel: (01492) 877061 ⌂9 ⌂9 Open: 3-10; 2 Star Hotel

QUEENS HOTEL Promenade, Llandudno LL30 2LE Tel: (01492) 877218 Fax: (01492) 877218 ⌂81 ⌂81 Open: 1-12; 2 Star Hotel

SHERWOOD HOTEL Craig y Don Parade, The Promenade LL30 1BG Tel: (01492) 875313 Fax: (01492) 875313 ⌂8 ⌂8 Open: 3-11; 2 Star Hotel

WESTDALE HOTEL 37 Abbey Rd, Llandudno LL30 2EH
Tel: (01492) 877996 Fax: (01492) 877996 ⨝ 12 🛏 3
Open: 2-10; 2 Star Hotel

PRESTATYN   Map Ref: Be3

TRAETH GANOL HOTEL 41 Beach Rd West,
Prestatyn LL19 7LL Tel: (01745) 853594
Fax: (01745) 886687 E-mail: hotel@dnetw.co.uk ⨝ 9 🛏 9
Open: 1-12; 3 Star Hotel

Holiday Cottages

COLWYN BAY   Map Ref: Bc4

BRON-Y-WENDON HOLIDAY COTTAGES Wern Rd,
Llanddulas, Colwyn Bay LL22 8HG
Tel: (01492) 512903 Fax: (01492) 512903
E-mail: bron-y-wendon@northwales-holidays.co.uk
Website: www.northwales-holidays.co.uk UNITS: 5;
SLEEPS: 2-5+⛢ Open: 1-12; 5 Star

NANT-Y-GLYN HOLIDAY PARK The Lodge, Nant-y-Glyn Rd,
Colwyn Bay LL29 7RD
Tel: (01492) 512282 Fax: (01492) 512903
E-mail: nant-y-glyn@northwales-holidays.co.uk
Website: www.northwales-holidays.co.uk UNITS: 12;
SLEEPS: 2-9+⛢ Open: 1-12; 3,4&5 Star

CONWY   Map Ref: Bb4

7 STRYD Y GWYNT Conwy LL32 8PB Tel: (01492) 680659
E-mail: cottage@northstar.u-net.com
Website: www.northstar.u-net.com/cottagepage
Enq: Mrs M Rowlands, 'Llety'r Adar', Llanelian, Colwyn Bay
LL29 6AT UNITS: 1; SLEEPS: 4 Open: 1-12

LLANDUDNO   Map Ref: Bb3

AUGUSTA HOLIDAY FLATS 7 Augusta St, Llandudno LL30
2AE Tel: (01492) 878330 Fax: (01492) 878330 UNITS: 40;
SLEEPS: 2-8 Open 1-12

BALMORAL SELF-CATERING APARTMENTS 6 Trinity Sqare,
Llandudno LL30 2RA Tel: (01492) 544018
Fax: 020 8903 0763 E-mail: N.Wales@btinternet.com
Website: www.baalmoral.fsnet.co.uk UNITS: 14;
SLEEPS: 2-7 Open: 1-12; 2 Star

RHOS-ON-SEA   Map Ref: Bb3

ST DAVID'S HOLIDAY APARTMENTS 68 Colwyn Avenue,
Rhos-on-Sea, Colwyn Bay LL28 4NN
Tel: (01492) 548576 Fax: (01492) 533322
E-mail: enquiries@stdavidsapartments.com
Website: www.stdavidsapartments.com UNITS: 8; SLEEPS:
2 Open 1-12; 3/5 Star

WALES CYMRU

TWO HOURS AND
A MILLION MILES AWAY

Caravan & Camping Park

COLWYN BAY   Map Ref: Bc4

BRON-Y-WENDON TOURING CARAVAN PARK Wern Rd,
Llanddulas, Colwyn Bay LL22 8HG
Tel: (01492) 512903 Fax: (01492) 512903
E-mail: bron-y-wendon@northwales-holidays.co.uk
Website: www.northwales-holidays.co.uk
No. ON PARK 130 ⛺ 120 🚐 10; Open 3-10; 5 Star Touring
Park

PENMAENMAWR   Map Ref: Ba4

PENDYFFREN HALL Glan yr Afon Rd, Penmaenmawr LL34
6UF Tel: (01492) 623219 No. ON PARK, ⛺ 25 🚐 & ⛺ 75;
Open 3-10

PRESTATYN   Map Ref Be3

LIDO BEACH HOLIDAY PARK Central Beach, Bastion Rd,
Prestatyn LL19 7E Tel: (01745) 855626
Fax: (01745) 887123 No. ON PARK 650 ⛺ 50; Open 4-9;
4 Star Holiday Park

THE NORTH WALES
BORDERLANDS
AREA 3

Hotels, Guest Houses & Farmhouses

CHIRK   Map Ref: Ed1

MORETON PARK LODGE Gledrid, Chirk, nr Wrexham LL14
5DG Tel: (01691) 776666 Fax: (01691) 776655
E-mail: enquiries@moretonparklodge.com
Website: www.moretonpark.com ⨝ 46 🛏 46 Open: 1-12;
Hotel

CORWEN   Map Ref: Be7

PEN-Y-BONT FAWR Cynwyd, Corwen LL21 0ET
Tel: (01490) 412663 ⨝ 3 🛏 2 Open: 1-12; 3 Star B&B

DENBIGH   Map Ref: Be5

BERLLAN BACH Ffordd Las, Llandyrnog, Denbigh LL16 4LF
Tel: (01824) 790725 ⨝ 3 🛏 3 Open: 1-12; 3 Star B&B

CAYO GUEST HOUSE 74 Vale St, Denbigh LL16 3BW
Tel: (01745) 812686 ⨝ 6 🛏 4 Open: 1-12; 2 Star

LLANARMON DYFFRYN CEIRIOG   Map Ref: Eb2

GUEST HOUSE GWYNFA Llanarmon Dyffryn Ceiriog,
nr Llangollen LL20 7LF Tel: (01691) 600287 ⨝ 3 🛏 1
Open: 2-11; 3 Star Guest House

WEST ARMS HOTEL Llanarmon DC, Llangollen LL20 7LD
Tel: (01691) 600665 Fax: (01691) 600622
E-mail: gowestarms@aol.com
Website: www.hotelwalesuk.com ⨝ 16 🛏 16 Open: 1-12;
3 Star Hotel

LLANGOLLEN   Map Ref: Ec1

GOLDEN PHEASANT HOTEL Glyn Ceiriog, nr Llangollen LL20
7BB Tel: (01691) 718281 Fax: (01691) 718479 ⨝ 19
🛏 19 Open: 1-12; 3 Star Country Hotel

Ceiriog Valley

TY ISAR PLWYF Glyndyfrdwy LL21 9HW
Tel: (01490) 430342 E-mail: jenny.carpenter3@virgin.net
🛏2 🚶2 Open: 1-12

WHITEGATE Grange Rd, Llangollen LL20 8AP
Tel: (01978) 860960 Fax: (01978) 861699 🛏3 🚶3
Open: 1-12; 3 Star B&B

WILD PHEASANT HOTEL Berwyn Rd, Llangollen LL20 8AD
Tel: (01978) 860629 Fax: (01978) 861837
E-mail: wild.pheasant@talk21.com
Website: www.wildpheasanthotel.co.uk
🛏34 🚶34 Open: 1-12; 3 Star Hotel

MALPAS   Map Ref: Ce7

MILL HOUSE Higher Wick, Malpas SY14 7JR
Tel: (01948) 780362 Fax: (01948) 780566
E-mail: chris.smith@videoactive.co.uk 🛏2 🚶1
Open: 1-11; 3 Star Guest House

NORTHOP   Map Ref: Cb5

HIGHFIELD HALL HOTEL Northop CH7 6AX
Tel: (01352) 840221 Fax: (01352) 840221
Website: confetti.co.uk(accommodation) 🛏14 🚶14
Open: 1-12; Awaiting Grading

RUABON   Map Ref: Cc7

TIR Y FRON Ruabon, Wrexham LL14 6RW
Tel: (01978) 821633 Fax: (01978) 810690
E-mail: g.manuel@micro-plus-web.net 🛏2; Guest
Bathroom; Open: 1-12; 3 Star B&B

RUTHIN   Map Ref: Be6

PANT GLAS CANOL Bont Uchef, Ruthin LL15 2BS
Tel: Day (01824) 710241, Eve (01824) 710639 Fax: (01824)
710639 🛏3 🚶3 Open: 4-12; 3 Star Farm

WREXHAM   Map Ref: Cc6

ALYN LODGE Pont-y-Capel Lane, Gresford, Wrexham LL12
8SA Tel: (01978) 855811 Fax: (01978) 855729
E-mail: info@alynlodge.co.uk
Website: www.alynlodge.co.uk 🛏7 🚶7 Open: 1-12;
2 Star Conference Centre

BETTISFIELD HALL Bettisfield, Whitchurch SY13 2LB
Tel: (01948) 710525 Fax: (01948) 710819
E-mail: g.springett@aol.com
Website:
www.hometown.aol.com/gspringett/myhomepage/business.html
🛏1 🚶1 Open: 1-12; Guest House

Holiday Cottages

CARROG   Map Ref: Ca7

CARROG MILL COTTAGES Y Felin, Carrog LL21 9AL
Tel: (01490) 430640 Fax: (01490) 430572
E-mail: carrogmill@lineone.net
Website: www.carrogmill.com/carrogmill.co.uk UNITS: 3;
SLEEPS: 2-6; Open: 1-12; 5 Star

RUTHIN   Map Ref: Be6

THE COACH HOUSE Maes-y-Llan Farm, Llanarmon-yn-Ial
CH7 4QF Tel: (01824) 780429 Fax: (01824) 780434
E-mail: vector.partnerships@virgin.net UNITS: 1; SLEEPS 2
adults & 2 children under 5 years; Open 1-12;
5 Star

WREXHAM   Map Ref: Cc6

CORNER HOUSE LUXURY HOLIDAY HOUSES Parkside,
Rossett, Wrexham LL12 0BW Tel: (01829) 270452
Fax: (01829) 271260 UNITS: 9; SLEEPS: 4; Open 1-12;
5 Star

Caravan & Camping Park

WREXHAM   Map Ref: Ce7

THE PADDOCK CARAVAN PARK North Bank, Riverside,
Farndon, Chester CH3 6PU Tel: (01792) 802298
Enquiries: Amanda Jones, 15 March Hywel, Rhos,
Pontardawe, Swansea SA8 3HF No. ON PARK 2 🏠2 🚐2

SNOWDONIA MOUNTAINS & COAST
AREA 4

Hotels, Guest Houses & Farmhouses

ABERDARON   Map Ref: Aa5

CARREG PLAS GUEST HOUSE Aberdaron, Pwllheli LL53 8LH
Tel: (01758) 760308 Fax: (01758) 760696
🛏6 🚻5 Open: 3-10; 3 Star Guest House

ABERDOVEY/ABERDYFI   Map Ref: Db6

PANTEIDAL GARDEN RESTAURANT WITH ROOMS
Panteidal, Aberdovey LL35 0RG Tel: (01654) 767322
Fax: (01654) 767322
E-mail: office@panteidal.freeserve.co.uk
Website: www.panteidalorganics.co.uk 🛏3 🚻3
Open: 1-12;

BALA   Map Ref: De2

BRYNIAU GOLAU Llangower, Bala LL23 7BT
Tel: (01678) 521782 Fax: (01678) 521790
E-mail: emsley@bryniau-golau.fsnet.co.uk
Website: www.bryniau-golau.fsnet.co.uk 🛏2 🚻2
Open: 1-12; 3 Star B&B

ERW FEURIG FARM GUEST HOUSE Cefnddwysarn, Bala
LL23 7LL Tel: (01678) 530262 Fax: (01678) 530262
E-mail: erwfeurig@yahoo.com
Website: www.ukworld.net/erwfeurig 🛏4 🚻3
Open: 1-12; 3 Star Farm

PLAS GOWER Llangower, Bala LL23 7BY
Tel: (01678) 520431 Fax: (01678) 520431
E-mail: olwen@plasgower.com
Website: www.plasgower.com 🛏2 🚻1 Open: 1-12;
4 Star B&B

RHYDYDEFAID FARM Frongoch, Bala LL23 7NT
Tel: (01678) 520456 Fax: (01678) 520456
E-mail: olwen@rhydydefaid.freeserve.co.uk
Website: www.bala-wales.com/rhydydefaid 🛏3 🚻3
Open: 1-12; 3 Star Farm

TREM-Y-WAWR Cae Groes, Bala LL23 7AQ
Tel: (01678) 520994 🛏3 🚻1 Open: 1-12; 2 Star B&B

BANGOR   Map Ref: Ae3

GARDEN HOTEL 1 High St, Bangor LL57 1DQ
Tel: (01248) 362189 Fax: (01248) 371328
E-mail: bookings@garden-hotel-bangor.co.uk
Website: www.garden-hotel-bangor.co.uk 🛏11 🚻10
Open: 1-12; 3 Star Hotel

NANT Y FEDW Trefelin, Llandegai, Bangor LL57 4LD
Tel: (01248) 351683 E-mail: davies19@supanet.com
🛏2 🚻2 Open: 1-12; 4 Star B&B

YR-ELEN Bryn, Llandegai, Bangor, LL57 4LD
Tel: (01248) 364591 Fax: (01248) 362666 🛏2 🚻2
Open: 3-11; 2 Star B&B

BARMOUTH   Map Ref: Db4

BRYN MELYN HOTEL Panorama Rd, Barmouth, LL42 1DQ
Tel: (01341) 280556 Fax: (01341) 280342
E-mail: bryn.melyn@virgin.net
Website: www.brynmelynhotel.co.uk 🛏9 🚻8 Open: 1-12;
2 Star Hotel

PORTH MYNACH Llanaber Rd, Barmouth LL42 1YG
Tel: (01341) 280943 Fax: (01341) 280943 🛏3 Open: 1-12;
2 Star B&B

WAVECREST HOTEL 8 Marine Parade, Barmouth LL42 1NA
Tel: (01341) 280330 Fax: (01341) 280330
E-mail: thewavecrest@talk21.com
Website: www.lokalink.co.uk/wavecrest. 🛏9 🚻9
Open: 4-10; 3 Star Hotel

BEDDGELERT   Map Ref: Ae6

PLAS COLWYN GUEST HOUSE Beddgelert LL55 4UY
Tel: (01766) 890458 E-mail: plascolwyn@hotmail.com
🛏6 🚻3 Open: 1-12; 2 Star Guest House

PLAS TAN Y GRAIG GUEST HOUSE Beddgelert LL55 4LT
Tel: (01766) 890310 Fax: (01766) 890629
E-mail: ay.b@virgin.net Website: www.plastanygraig.co.uk
🛏5 🚻1 Open: 1-12; 1 Star Guest House

TANRONNEN INN Beddgelert LL55 4YB
Tel: (01766) 890347 Fax: (01766) 890606
E-mail: tanronneninn@frederic-robinson.co.uk 🛏7 🚻7
Open: 1-12; 3 Star Inn

BETWS-Y-COED   Map Ref: Bb6

BRON CELYN GUEST HOUSE Lôn Muriau, Llanrwst Rd,
Betws-y-Coed LL24 0HD Tel: (01690) 710333
Fax: (01690) 710111 E-mail: broncelyn@betws-y-coed.co.uk
Website: www.betws-y-coed.co.uk/broncelyn/
🛏5 🚻4 Open: 1-12; 3 Star Guest House

BRON ERYRI GUEST HOUSE Capel Curig, Betws-y-Coed
LL24 0EE Tel: (01690) 720240
E-mail: bron.eryri@lineone.net
Website: www.betws-y-coed.co.uk/acc/bron-eryri/
🛏5 🚻5 Open: 1-12; 2 Star Guest House

BRYN LLEWELYN NON SMOKERS GUEST HOUSE
Holyhead Rd, Betws-y-Coed LL24 0BN Tel: (01690) 710601
Fax: (01690) 710601 Website: www.bangor-uk.com/llewelyn
🛏7 🚻4 Open: 1-12; 2 Star B&B

CWMANOG ISAF FARM Betws-y-Coed LL24 0SL
Tel: (01690) 710225 Mobile: 07808 421634
E-mail: h.m.hughes@amserve.net 🛏3 🚻3 Open: 1-12;
3 Star Farm

FAIRY GLEN HOTEL Beaver Bridge, Betws-y-Coed LL24 0SH
Tel: (01690) 710269 Fax: (01690) 710269
E-mail: fairyglenhotel@amserve.net 🛏8 🚻7
Open: 2-10; 2 Star Hotel

THE FERNS NON SMOKING GUEST HOUSE Holyhead Rd,
Betws-y-Coed LL24 0AN Tel: (01690) 710587
Fax: (01690) 710587 E-mail: ferns@betws-y-coed.co.uk
Website: www.betws-y-coed.co.uk/accommodation/ferns/
🛏9 🚻9 Open: 1-12; 2 Star B&B

FFERM MAES GWYN Pentrefoelas, Betws-y-Coed LL24 0LR
Tel: (01690) 770668 🛏2 Open: 4-10; 3 Star Farm

FRON HEULOG COUNTRY HOUSE Betws-y-Coed LL24 0BL
Tel: (01690) 710736 Fax: (01690) 710920
E-mail: jean&peter@fronheulog.co.uk
Website: www.fronheulog.co.uk 🛏3 ➡3 Open: 1-12;
3 Star Country House

MAIRLYS GUEST HOUSE Betws-y-Coed LL24 0AN
Tel: (01690) 710190 Fax: (01690) 710190 🛏9 ➡9
Open: 1-12; 3 Star Guest House

PARK HILL HOTEL/GWESTY BRYN PARC Llanrwst Rd,
Betws-y-Coed LL24 0HD Tel: (01690) 710540
Fax: (01690) 710540 E-mail: parkhill.hotel@virgin.net
Website: www.betws-y-coed.co.uk/acc/parkhill 🛏9 ➡9
Open: 1-12; 3 Star Hotel

RIVERSIDE GUEST HOUSE/RESTAURANT Holyhead Rd,
Betws-y-Coed LL24 0BN Tel: (01690) 710650
Fax: (01690) 710650 E-mail: riverside4u@talk21.com
Website: www.betws-y-coed.net/riverside 🛏4 ➡1
Open: 1-12; 3 Star Restaurant with Rooms

THE ROYAL OAK HOTEL Betws-y-Coed LL24 0AY
Tel: (01690) 710219 Fax: (01690) 710603
E-mail: royal-oak@betws-y-coed.co.uk 🛏26 ➡26
Open: 1-12; 3 Star Hotel

TAN-Y-FOEL COUNTRY HOUSE HOTEL Capel Garmon, nr
Betws-y-Coed LL26 0RE Tel: (01690) 710507
Fax: (01690) 710681 E-mail: enquiries@tyfhotel.co.uk
Website: www.tyfhotel.co.uk 🛏7 ➡7 Open: 2-12;
4 Star Country Hotel

TY COCH FARM & TREKKING CENTRE Penmachno, Betws-y-Coed LL25 0HJ Tel: (01690) 760248 Fax: (01690) 760266
E-mail: tycoch@amserve.net
🛏3 ➡3 Open: 1-12; 2 Star Farm

BLAENAU FFESTINIOG   *Map Ref: Ba7*

BRYN ELLTYD Tanygrisiau, Blaenau Ffestiniog LL41 3TW
Tel: (01766) 831356 Fax: (01766) 831356
E-mail: bob&annie9@aol.com
Website: www.mtn.co.uk/bobcole 🛏4 ➡4 Open: 1-12;
2 Star B&B

CAERNARFON   *Map Ref: Ad4*

HAFOTY Rhostryfan, Caernarfon LL54 7PH
Tel: (01286) 830144 Fax: (01286) 830441
Website: www.accomodata.co.uk/310898.htm 🛏4 ➡4
Open: 2-10; 4 Star Farm

HILLCROFT St David's Rd, Caernarfon LL55 1EL
Tel: (01286) 674489 🛏4 ➡3 Open: 1-12; 2 Star B&B

LLEUAR FAWR Penygroes, Caernarfon LL84 6PB
Tel: (01286) 660268 Fax: (01286) 660268 🛏2 ➡2
Open: 1-11; 3 Star Farm

LLWYNDU MAWR Carmel Rd, Penygroes LL54 6PU
Tel: (01286) 880419 Fax: (01286) 880845 🛏4 ➡1
Open: 1-12; 2 Star Farm

MENAI BANK HOTEL North Rd, Caernarfon LL55 1BD
Tel: (01286) 673297 Fax: (01286) 673297
E-mail: menaibankhotel@tesco.net
Website: www.menaibankhotel.co.uk 🛏16 ➡16
Open: 1-12; 3 Star Hotel

MENAI VIEW GUEST HOUSE & RESTAURANT
North Rd, Caernarfon LL55 1BD Tel: (01286) 674602
Fax: (01286) 674602
Website: www.ukworld-int.co.uk/menaiview.htm
🛏9 ➡8 Open: 1-12; 3 Star Guest House

PENGWERN Saron, Llanwnda, Caernarfon LL54 5UH
Tel: (01286) 831500 Fax: (01286) 830741
E-mail: pengwern@talk21.com
Website: www.smoothhound.co.uk/hotels/pengwern.htm
🛏3 ➡3 Open: 2-11; 4 Star Farm

PRINCE OF WALES HOTEL Bangor St, Caernarfon LL55 1AR
Tel: (01286) 673367 Fax: (01286) 676610
E-mail: princeofwaleshotel@gofornet.co.uk
Website: www.smoothhound.co.uk/hotels/princeofwales
🛏21 ➡19 Open: 1-12; 2 Star Hotel

THE WHITE HOUSE Llanfaglan, Caernarfon LL54 5RA
Tel: (01286) 673003 E-mail: rwbayles@sjms.co.uk
3 Star B&B

TYN LLWYN COTTAGE Llanllyfni, Caernarfon LL54 6RP
Tel: (01286) 881526 3 Star B&B

TY'N RHOS COUNTRY HOTEL Seion, Llanddeiniolen,
Caernarfon LL55 3AE Tel: (01248) 670489
Fax: (01248) 670079 🛏14 ➡14 Open: 1-12; 4 Star Hotel

CONWY   *Map Ref: Bb4*

THE LODGE Tal-y-Bont, Conwy LL32 8YX
Tel: (01492) 660766 Freephone: 0800 9176593
Fax: (01492) 660534 E-mail: bbaldon@lodgehotel.co.uk
Website: www.lodgehotel.co.uk 🛏14 Open: 1-12;
3 Star Hotel

FISHERMORE Llanrwst Rd, Conwy LL32 8HP
Tel: (01492) 592891 E-mail: dyers@tesco.net
Website: www.northwalesbandb.co.uk 🛏3 ➡3
Open: 4-10; 3 Star B&B

CRICCIETH   *Map Ref: Ad7*

CRAIG-Y-MÔR GUEST HOUSE West Parade, Criccieth
LL52 0EN Tel: (01766) 522830
E-mail: enquiries@craig-y-mor-bandb.freeserve.co.uk
🛏6 ➡6 Open: 3-10; 3 Star Guest House

GLYN Y COED HOTEL Portmadoc Rd, Criccieth LL52 0HP
Tel: (01766) 522870 Fax: (01766) 523341 🛏10 ➡10
Open: 1-12; 2 Star Hotel

MIN Y GAER HOTEL Porthmadog Rd, Criccieth LL52 0HP
Tel: (01766) 522151 Fax: (01766) 523540
E-mail: info@minygaerhotel.co.uk
Website: www.minygaerhotel.co.uk 🛏10 ➡10
Open: 3-10; 2 Star Hotel

SEASPRAY GUEST HOUSE 4 Marine Terrace, Criccieth
LL52 0EF Tel: (01766) 522373 🛏3 ➡2 Open: 1-11;
2 Star Guest House

DINAS MAWDDWY
Map Ref: Dd4

BRYNCELYN FARM Cwm Cywarch, Dinas Mawddwy, Machynlleth SY20 9JG Tel: (01650) 531289 🛏2 🍴2
Open: 1-12; 3 Star Farm

BRYN SION FARM Cwm Cywarch, Dinas Mawddwy SY20 9JG
Tel: (01650) 531251 E-mail: enquiries@brynsion.co.uk
Website: www.brynsion.co.uk 🛏2 🍴2 Open: 1-12;
3 Star Farm

RED LION HOTEL/GWESTY'R LLEW COCH Dinas Mawddwy
SY20 9JA Tel: (01650) 531247 Fax: (01650) 531247
E-mail: llewcoch@yahoo.co.uk
Website: www.llewcoch.freeserve.co.uk 🛏6 🍴3
Open: 1-12; 1 Star Inn

DOLGELLAU
Map Ref: Dc4

AROSFYR Penycefn Rd, Dolgellau LL40 2YP
Tel: (01341) 422355 🛏3 🍴- Open: 1-12; 2 Star Farm

DOLSERAU HALL HOTEL Dolgellau LL40 2AG
Tel: (01341) 422522 Fax: (01341) 422400
E-mail: wtb@dhh.co.uk Website: www.dhh.co.uk
🛏15 🍴15 Open: 2-11; 3 Star Country Hotel

DWY OLWYN Coed-y-Fronallt, Dolgellau LL40 2YG
Tel: (01341) 422822
Website: www.croeso-lynnes-wales.co.uk/acc/dwyolwyn
🛏3 Open: 2-12; 3 Star Hotel

ROYAL SHIP HOTEL Queens Square, Dolgellau LL40 1AR
Tel: (01341) 422209 Fax: (01341) 421027
E-mail: royalship@frederic-robinson.co.uk 🛏24 🍴18
Open: 1-12; 2 Star Hotel

TANYFRON Arran Rd, Dolgellau LL40 2AA
Tel: (01341) 422638 Fax: (01341) 421251
E-mail: rowlands@tanyfron.freeserve.co.uk 🛏3 🍴3
Open: 2-11; 3 Star B&B

TREM IDRIS Llanelltyd, nr Dolgellau LL40 2TB
Tel: (01341) 423776 🛏3 🍴2 Open: 1-12; 2 Star B&B

Y GOEDLAN Brithdir, Dolgellau LL40 2RN
Tel: (01341) 423131 Fax: (01341) 423131 🛏3
Open: 2-11; 3 Star B&B

FFESTINIOG
Map Ref: Dc1

HILLCREST GUEST HOUSE Hillcrest Pant Llwyd, Bala Rd
LL41 4PW Tel: (01766) 762787 Fax: (01766) 762787
E-mail: hillcrestjen@talk21.com 🛏3 🍴3 Open: 1-12;
3 Star B&B

HARLECH
Map Ref: Da2

GLANYGORS GUEST HOUSE Llandanwg, Harlech LL46 2SD
Tel: (01341) 241410 🛏3 🍴1 Open: 1-12; 3 Star Guest
House

TYDDYN GWYNT Harlech LL46 2TH Tel: (01766) 780298
🛏2 Open: 1-12; 2 Star Farm

LLANBEDR
Map Ref: Da3

VICTORIA INN Llanbedr LL45 2LD
Tel: (01341) 241213 Fax: (01341) 241644
E-mail: victorianinn@frederic-robinson.co.uk 🛏5 🍴5
Open: 1-12; 2 Star Inn

LLANBERIS
Map Ref: Ae4

MARTEG High St, Llanberis LL55 4HA Tel: (01286) 870207
E-mail: carol@marteg.freeserve.co.uk 🛏3 🍴3
Open: 2-12; 3 Star B&B

MOUNT PLEASANT HOTEL High St, Llanberis LL55 4HA
Tel: (01286) 870395 Fax: (01286) 870395
E-mail: mph@waterton.org.uk Website: www.waterton.org.uk
🛏7 🍴1 Open: 1-12; 1 Star Hotel

ROYAL VICTORIA HOTEL Llanberis LL55 4TY
Tel: (01286) 870253 Fax: (01286) 870149
E-mail: info@royalvictoria.fsnet.co.uk
Website: www.royal-victoria-hotel.co.uk 🛏111 🍴111
Open: 1-12; 3 Star Hotel

MACHYNLLETH
Map Ref: Dc5

PENDRE GUEST HOUSE Pendre, Maengwyn St, Machynlleth
SY20 8EF Tel: (01654) 702088 🛏3 🍴2 Open: 1-12;
2 Star Guest House

PORTHMADOG
Map Ref: Ae7

TY NEWYDD 30 Dublin St, Tremadog, Porthmadog LL49 9RH
Tel: (01766) 512553 E-mail: johnjulie0@aol.com
Website: www.porthmadog.co.uk/tynewydd 🛏4
Open: 1-12; 2 Star B&B

PWLLHELI
Map Ref: Ac7

YOKE HOUSE FARM Pwllheli LL53 5TY
Tel: (01758) 612621 E-mail: annwen@iocws.freeserve.co.uk
Website: www.yokehouse.co.uk 🛏1 🍴1 Open: 3-11;
3 Star Farm

TYWYN
Map Ref: Da6

CYNFAL FARM Bryncrug, Tywyn LL36 9RB
Tel: (01654) 711703 Fax: (01654) 7117032122
E-mail: cynfalfrm@aol.com
Website: www.gwynedd.net/croeso.cader.idris 🛏3 🍴3
Open: 4-10; 4 Star Farm

EISTEDDFA Abergynolwyn, Tywyn LL36 9UP
Tel: (01654) 782385 Fax: (01654) 782228
Open: 3-10; 3 Star Farm

TYNYCORNEL HOTEL Talyllyn, Tywyn LL36 9AJ
Tel: (01654) 782282 Fax: (01654) 782679
E-mail: tynycornel.co.uk 🛏17 🍴17 Open: 1-12;
3 Star Hotel

Holiday Cottages

ABERDOVEY/ABERDYFI
Map Ref: Db6

ABERDOVEY HOLIDAYS LIMITED 13 Glan Dovey Terrace,
Aberdovey LL35 0EB Tel: (01654) 767418
Fax: (01654) 767078 E-mail: aberdovey-holidays@msn.com
Website: aberdovey-holidays.com UNITS: 13; SLEEPS: 1-8;
Open: 1-12; 4 Star

CELTIC HOUSE Sea View Terrace, Aberdyfi LL35 0LL
Tel: (01654) 767274 Fax: (01654) 767506
E-mail: jreynolds@celtichouse.f9.co.uk
Website: celtichouse.f9.co.uk No UNITS: 1; SLEEPS: 1-10;
Open: 1-12; 4 Star

ABERSOCH
Map Ref: Ac5

ABERSOCH HOLIDAYS Tyddyn Talgoch Uchaf, Bwlchtocyn,
Abersoch LL53 7BT   Tel: (01758) 712285
E-mail: abersoch.holidays@virgin.net
Website: www.abersochholidays.co.uk   UNITS: 4;
SLEEPS: 2-10; Open: 1-12; 3/4 Star

TAI GWYLIAU TY'N DON SELF-CATERING ACCOMMODATION
Llanengan, Pwllheli LL53 7LG   Tel: (01286) 831184
Enquiries: Mrs Elizabeth Evans, Penlan, Rhos Isaf,
Caernarfon LL54 7NG   UNITS: 10; SLEEPS: 2-8; Open: 2-11;
3/4 Star

BALA
Map Ref: De2

BRYN TEG BACH Cae Groes, Bala LL23 7AQ   Tel: (01678)
521480 Fax: (01678) 521481   E-mail: info@balawales.com
Website: www.balawales.com/bryntegbach   UNITS: 1;
SLEEPS: 1-2; Open 3-11; 5 Star

HEN HAFOD, NR BALA & FEDW'R GOG NR MAERDY
Enquiries: G. Owen, Penisarmynydd, Maerdy, Corwen
LL21 0NP   Tel: (01490) 460448   UNITS: 3; SLEEPS: 2-7;
Open 1-12; 4 Star

Y BWTHYN C/o Tŷ Capel, Llwyn Einion, Bala LL23 7PN
Tel: (01678) 520572 Fax: (01678) 520572   UNITS: 1;
SLEEPS: 4; Open: 4-10; 3 Star

BARMOUTH
Map Ref: Db4

COEDMOR COTTAGE Coedmor, Caerdeon, Barmouth
LL42 1TL   Tel: (01341) 430332   UNITS: 1; SLEEPS: 3; Open:
1-12; 4 Star

TALARFOR Llanaber, Barmouth LL42 1BQ
Tel: (01341) 280069   UNITS: 1; SLEEPS: 5+▦; 4 Star

TŶ GLAN-YR-AFON Bontddu, Barmouth LL40 2UR
Tel: (01341) 242626 Fax: (01341) 242626
E-mail: rowenpark@breathemail.net Enquiries: Rowan
UNITS: 1; SLEEPS: 1-6; Open: 1-12; 5 Star

BETWS-Y-COED
Map Ref: Bb6

DOLWEN & HAFAN BACH COTTAGES Penmachno,
nr Betws-y-Coed. Enquiries: Mr T.O. Tottle, 3 Newgate St,
Penmachno LL24 0UT   UNITS: 2; SLEEPS: 2-5;
Open: 1-12; 3 Star

CAERNARFON
Map Ref: Ad4

BEACH BUNGALOW The Beach, Pontllyfni LL54 5ET
Tel: (01286) 660400   UNITS: 1; SLEEPS: 8; Open: 1-12;
Self-Catering

BEACH VILLA CHALET West Point, The Beach, Pontllyfni
LL54 5ET   Tel: (01286) 660400   No. of Caravans: 50;
No. for Hire: 20; Open: 1-12

BRYN BEDDAU Bontnewydd, Caernarfon LL54 7YE
Tel: (01286) 830117 Fax: (01407) 832122
E-mail: eleri.carrog@virgin.net   UNITS: 1; SLEEPS: 5; Open:
1-12; 4 Star

BRYN BRAS CASTLE Llanrug, nr Caernarfon LL55 4RE
Tel: (01286) 870210 Fax: (01286) 870210
E-mail: holidays@brynbrascastle.co.uk
Website: www.brynbrascastle.co.uk   UNITS: 7;
SLEEPS: 2-4; No Children; Open:1-12; 5 Star

BRYN GWYN Waunfawr, Caernarfon LL55 4SD
Tel: (01286) 650549   UNITS: 1; SLEEPS: 5; Open: 4-10;
4 Star

TŶ LOWRI 13 Menai St, Y Felinheli,Caernarfon LL56 4HX
Enquiries: 9 Victoria Park Rd West, Caerdydd CF5 1EZ
Tel: (029) 2025 1152 Fax: (07713) 655925
E-mail: huw@jeli-weli.co.uk   UNITS: 1; SLEEPS: 5+▦
Open: 1-12; 4 Star

TY'N YR ONNEN MOUNTAIN FARM HOLIDAY PARK
Waunfawr, Caernarfon LL55 4AY   Tel: (01286) 650281
Fax: (01286) 650043 E-mail: tyn-yr-onnen@gwynedd.net
Website: www.gwynedd.net/caernarfon/tyn-yr-onnen
UNITS: 4; SLEEPS: 6+▦+⚲

TY SIDAN & HAFOD AUR 12 & 16 Stryd Fawr (High St),
Caernarfon LL55 1RN   Tel: (01286) 830117
Fax: (01286) 675664   E-mail: eleri.carrog@virgin.net
Enquiries: E Carrog, Bryn Beddau, Bontnewydd, Caernarfon
LL54 7YE   UNITS: 2; SLEEPS: 4+6; Open: 1-12; 4 Star

CHWILOG
Map Ref: Ac7

CEFN COED Lon Goed, Chwilog LL53 6NX
Tel: (01766) 810259   UNITS: 2; SLEEPS: 6&7;
Open: 1-12; 3/4 Star

MUR CLWT LLOER Chwilog, Pwllheli LL53 6NQ
Tel: (01766) 810236   E-mail: mur@talk21.com
UNITS : 1; SLEEPS: 4; Open: 1-12; 4 Star

CRICCIETH
Map Ref: Ad7

ENFYS 13 Marine Terrace, Criccieth LL52 0EF
Tel: (01766) 522655   E-mail: walkerjones@lineone.net
Website: www.lineone.net/walkerjones   UNITS: 3;
SLEEPS: 2-4; Open: 1-12; 3 Star

NANT-Y-FELIN COTTAGES Nant-y-Felin, Portmadoc Rd,
Criccieth LL52 0HP   Tel: (01766) 522675
Fax: (01766) 522675
Website: www.accommodation.uk.net/nantyfelin.html
UNITS: 3; SLEEPS: 2-10; Open: 1-12

TYDDYN FELIN Ynys, Criccieth LL52 0PA
Tel: (01766) 530659/810994 Fax: (01766) 530659
E-mail: MeganJones@gwynedd.gov.uk   UNITS: 1;
SLEEPS: 9; Open: 1-12

WINDSOR HOUSE 12 Marine Terrace, Criccieth LL52 0EF
Tel: (01766) 522856   E-mail: gweigh3526@ao2.com
UNITS: 3; SLEEPS: 4-5; Open: 1-12; 2&3 Star

DOLGELLAU
Map Ref: Dc4

AROSFYR Penycefn Rd, Dolgellau LL40 2YP
Tel: (01341) 422355   UNITS: 3; SLEEPS: 2-5; Open: 1-12;
3&4 Star

HENDRE GEFEILLIAID Hendre Gefeilliaid, Tabor, Dolgellau
LL40 2RE   Tel: (01341) 423042 Fax: (01341) 423042
Website: www.northwalescottage.co.uk
UNITS: 1; SLEEPS: 4-5; Open: 1-12; 4 Star

PENMAENUCHA FARM Penmaenpool, Dolgellau LL40 1YD
Tel: (01341) 423937   UNITS: 4; SLEEPS: 4&6;
Open: 1-12; 4 Star

DYFFRYN ARDUDWY   *Map Ref: Da3*

RHINOG PARK Beach Rd, Dyffryn Ardudwy LL44 2HA
Tel: (01341) 247652 Fax: (01531) 640669
E-mail: rhinogpark@countryparks.com
Website: www.countryparks.com UNITS: 6;
SLEEPS: 4-5+▥ Open: 3-10; 4 Star Holiday Park

EGLWYSBACH   *Map Ref: Bb5*

YSGUBOR WEN Bryn Garrog, Eglwysbach, Colwyn Bay
LL28 5TY Tel: (01492) 650549
E-mail: bryngarrog@aol.com UNITS: 1; SLEEPS: 4+▥
Open: 1-12; 4 Star

GARNDOLBENMAEN   *Map Ref: Ad6*

MELIN LLECHEIDDIOR Garndolbenmaen LL51 9EZ
Tel: (01766) 530635 Fax: (01766) 530635 UNITS: 1;
SLEEPS: 4; Open: 1-12; 4 Star

HARLECH   *Map Ref: Da2*

HEN FFERMDY Talsarnau, nr Harlech Tel: (01299) 861120
Fax: (01299) 861120
E-mail: enquiries@henffermdy.co.uk
Enquiries: White Lodge, Fenn Green, Alveley, nr Bridgnorth
WV15 6AJ UNITS: 1; SLEEPS: 10; Open: 1-12

'TY'R FELIN' Pen Llech, Harlech LL46 2YL
Tel: (01189) 871159 E-mail: g.dugdale@btinternet.com
Enquiries: D. Dugdale, 16 Shinfield Rd, Reading RG2 7DA
UNITS: 1; SLEEPS: 5; Open: 3-10; 2 Star

LLANBEDROG   *Map Ref: Ab7*

BODWROG Llanbedrog, Pwllheli LL53 7RE
Tel: (01758) 740341 UNITS: 1; SLEEPS: 5-6; Open: 4-10;
4 Star

LLANBERIS   *Map Ref: Ae4*

2 LLAINWEN UCHAF Llanberis LL55 4LL
Tel: (01517) 242154 Fax: (01517) 242154
E-mail: sybwilliams@lineone.net
Enquiries: Mrs S.G. Williams, 6 Wyndale Close, Liverpool
L18 7JX UNITS: 1; SLEEPS: 4; Open: 1-12; 3 Star

HAULFRYN Brynrefail, Caernarfon LL55 3NR Enquiries:
Mrs Foulkes, 21 Cae'r Garreg, Caernarfon LL55 2DT
UNITS: 1; SLEEPS: 6; Open: 1-12; 3 Star

LLANFAIRFECHAN   *Map Ref: Ba4*

PLAS HEULOG Mount Rd, Llanfairfechan LL33 0HA
Tel: (01248) 680019 Fax: (01248) 680074
E-mail: plas.heulog@btinternet.com
Website: www.plas.heulog.btinternet.co.uk UNITS: 4;
SLEEPS: 2-4; Open: 1-12; 4 Star

NANT PERIS   *Map Ref: Ae4*

TYN Y FFYNNON Nant Peris, Caernarfon LL55 4UH
Tel: (01286) 871723 UNITS: 1; SLEEPS: 2-12;
Open: 1-12; 4 Star

PENMAENMAWR   *Map Ref: Ba4*

PENDYFFREN HALL Glan Yr Afon Rd, Penmaenmawr, Conwy
LL34 6UF Tel: (01492) 623219 Open: 1-10; 2 Star

PORTHMADOG   *Map Ref: Ae7*

CAE EITHIN TEW Cwmystradllyn, Garndolbenmaen,
Porthmadog LL51 9BQ Enquiries: M. Lloyd Evans, Bryn
Weinglodd, Cwmystradllyn, Garndolbenmaen, Porthmadog
LL51 9AZ Tel: (01766) 530310

TY NEWYDD FLATS Dublin St, Tremadog, Porthmadog
LL49 9RH Tel: (01766) 512553 E-mail: johnjulieo@aol.com
Website: www.porthmadog.co.uk/tynewydd/flats
UNITS: 2; SLEEPS: 4-4; Open: 1-12; 2 Star

PWLLHELI   *Map Ref: Ac7*

GWYNFRYN FARM HOLIDAYS Gwynfryn Farm, Pwllheli
LL53 5UF Tel: (01758) 612536 Fax: (01758) 612536
E-mail: wm@gwynfryn.freeserve.co.uk
Website: www.gwynfrynfarm.co.uk UNITS: 10; SLEEPS: 2-8;
Open 1-12

LLWYNDYRUS FARM HOLIDAY COTTAGE Llwyndyrus Farm,
Y Ffôr, Pwllheli LL53 6RH Tel: (01766) 810859
UNITS: 3; SLEEPS: 2,4,5; Open: 1-12; 4 Star

RHEDYNOG GANOL Chwilog, Pwllheli LL53 6LQ
Tel: (01766) 810021 UNITS: 1; SLEEPS: 5; Open: 5-10;
4 Star

TREFOR   *Map Ref: Ac6*

'PENLON COTTAGE' Trefor, Caernarfon LL54 5AB
Tel: (01286) 660768 Enquiries: M.C.Jones, Merbwll, Penlon,
Trefor, Caernarfon LL54 5AB UNITS: 1; SLEEPS: 5;
Open: 4-10; 3 Star

TYWYN   *Map Ref: Da6*

PANT Y NEUADD COTTAGES Aberdyfi Rd, Tywyn LL36 9HW
Tel: (01654) 711393 E-mail: pantyneuadd@care4free.net
UNITS: 2; SLEEPS: 2/3; Open 1-12; 4 Star

SWN Y NANT & BODNANT FARM COTTAGES Cynfal Farm,
Bryncrug, Tywyn LL36 9RB Tel: (01654) 711703
Fax: (01654) 711703 E-mail: cynfalfrm@aol.com
Website: www.gwynedd.net/croeso.cader.idris
UNITS: 2; SLEEPS: 5 per cottage; Open:1-12; Short Breaks:
Nov-March; 5 Star

Walking in Snowdonia

142

Caravan & Camping Park

ABERSOCH
Map Ref: Ac5

BRYN BACH CARAVAN & CAMPSITE Tyddyn Talgoch Uchaf, Bwlchtocyn, Abersoch LL53 7BT Tel: (01758) 712285
E-mail: brynbach.abersoch@virgin.net
Website: www.abersochholidays.co.uk
No. ON PARK 2 ⊡ 2 ⊞ 25 ⊞ 25 ▲ 25; Open: 3-10; 2 Star; Touring & Camping Park

BARMOUTH
Map Ref: Db4

PARC CAERELWAN Talybont, Barmouth LL43 2AX
Tel: (01341) 247236 Fax: (01341) 247711
E-mail: parc@holidaysites.co.uk
Website: www.holidaysites.co.uk/parc
No. ON PARK 150 ⊡ 80; Open: 1-12; 4 Star; Holiday Park

ROWEN CARAVAN PARK Talybont, Barmouth LL43 2AD
Tel: (01341) 242626 Fax: (01341) 242626
E-mail: rowenpark@breathemail.net
Website: www.ukparks.co.uk/rowen
No. ON PARK 35 ⊡ 27; Open: 4-10; 4 Star; Holiday Park

SARNFAEN HOLIDAY PARK Talybont, nr Barmouth LL43 2AQ
Tel: (01341) 247241 Fax: (01341) 247849
E-mail: robert.gallimore@sarnfaen.force9.net
Website: www.sarnfaen-holiday-park.com
No. ON PARK 109 ⊡ 31; Open: 3-12; 4 Star; Holiday Park

CAERNARFON
Map Ref: Ad4

BRYN GLOCH CARAVAN & CAMPING PARK Betws Garmon, Caernarfon LL54 7YY Tel: (01286) 650216
Fax: (01286) 650591 E-mail: eurig@easynet.co.uk
Website: www.bryngloch.co.uk
No. ON PARK 15 ⊡ 15 ⊞ 80 ⊞ 80 ▲ 80; Open: 1-12; 4 Star; Holiday Park

CAERNARFON BAY CARAVAN PARK & HOLIDAY BUNGALOWS Dinas Dinlle, Caernarfon LL54 5TW
Tel: (01286) 830492 Fax: (01286) 831037
No. ON PARK 20; Open: 2-12; 3 Star; Holiday Park

PLAS Y BRYN CHALET PARK Bontnewydd, nr Caernarfon LL54 7YE Tel: (01286) 672811
No. ON PARK 18 ⊡ 16; Open: 3-12; 3 Star; Holiday Park

DOLGELLAU
Map Ref: Dc4

DOLGAMEDD CARAVAN AND CAMPING PARK Bontnewydd/Brithdir, Dolgellau LL40 2DG
Tel: (01341) 422624 Fax: (01341) 422624
c/o Gwanas, Dolgellau LL40 2SH
No. ON PARK 20 ⊡ 1 ⊞ 10 ⊞ 5 ▲ 50; Open: 4-10; Holiday Park

DYFFRYN ARDUDWY
Map Ref: Da3

DYFFRYN SEASIDE ESTATE Dyffryn Ardudwy LL44 2HD
Tel: (01341) 247220 Fax: (01341) 247622
No. ON PARK 248 ⊡ 20 ⊞ ▲ 200; 4 Star; Holiday & Camping Park

NEFYN
Map Ref: Ab6

BEACH HOLIDAY HOMES West Point, The Beach, Pontllyfni LL54 5ET Tel: (01286) 660400
No. ON PARK 50 ⊡ 20; Open: 3-10; 3 Star; Holiday Park

PENMAENMAWR
Map Ref: Ba4

PENDYFFREN HALL Glan Yr Afon Rd, Penmaenmawr LL34 6UF Tel: (01492) 623219
⊞ 25 ⊞ or ▲ 75; Open: 3-10

PORTHMADOG
Map Ref: Ae7

BLACK ROCK SANDS CAMPING & TOURING PARK Morfa Bychan, Porthmadog LL49 9LD Tel: (01766) 513919
⊞ 20 ▲ 120; Open: 3-10; 3 Star; Touring & Camping Park

TREFRIW
Map Ref: Ab5

GLYN FARM CARAVANS Trefriw, Llanrwst LL27 0RZ
Tel: (01492) 640442 No. ON PARK 10 ⊡ 4 ⊞ 28; Open: 3-10; 4 Star; Holiday & Touring Park

MID WALES LAKES & MOUNTAINS
AREA 5

Hotels, Guest Houses & Farmhouses

BRECON
Map Ref: Ge6

11, THE WATTON Brecon LD3 7ED Tel: (01874) 625650
⊨ 4 ⊯ 1 Open: 4-10; 3 Star B&B

ASHGROVE Llanspyddid, Brecon LD3 8PB
Tel: (01874) 622833 E-mail: ashgrove@btclick.com
⊨ 3 Open: 3-12; 2 Star B&B

THE BEACONS 16 Bridge St, Brecon LD3 8AH
Tel: (01874) 623339 Fax: (01874) 623339
E-mail: beacons@brecon.co.uk
Website: www.beacons.brecon.co.uk ⊨ 14 ⊯ 11
Open: 1-12; 3 Star Guest House

BISHOP'S MEADOW Hay Rd, Brecon LD3 9SW
Tel: (01874) 622051 Fax: (01874) 614922 ⊨ 12 ⊯ 12
Open: 1-12; 2 Star Lodge

BLAENCAR FARM Sennybridge, Brecon LD3 8HA
Tel: (01874) 636610 Fax: (01874) 636610 ⊨ 3 ⊯ 13
Open: 1-12; 5 Star Farm

BRYN-Y-FEDWEN Trallong Common, Sennybridge, Brecon LD3 8HW Tel: (01874) 636505 Fax: (01874) 636505
Website: www.bbfa.co.uk ⊨ 2 ⊯ 2 Open: 1-12 (except March); 4 Star Farm

COUNTY HOUSE 100 The Struet, Brecon LD3 7LS
Tel: (01874) 625844 Fax: (01874) 625844
E-mail: countyhouse@ukworld.net
Website: www.ukworld.net/countyhouse ⊨ 3 ⊯ 3
Open: 1-12; 4 Star B&B

CWMCAMLAIS UCHAF FARM Cwmcamlais, Sennybridge, Brecon LD3 8TD Tel: (01874) 636376 Fax: (01874) 636376
E-mail: phillipsj2@talk21.com
Website: www.bbfa.co.uk ⊨ 3 ⊯ 2 Open: 1-12; 4 Star Farm

THE FLAG & CASTLE GUEST HOUSE 11 Orchard St, Llanfaes, Brecon LD3 8AN Tel: (01874) 625860 ⊨3 ⊷3 Open: 1-12; 3 Star Guest House

MAESWALTER Heol Senni, nr Brecon LD3 8SU Tel: (01874) 636629 E-mail: maeswalter@talk21.com ⊨4 ⊷2 Open: 1-12; 2 Star B&B

PETERSTONE COURT Llanhamlach, Brecon LD3 7YB Tel: (01874) 665387 Fax: (01874) 665376 ⊨12 ⊷12 Open: 1-12

BUILTH WELLS   Map Ref: Ge4

DISSERTH MILL Builth Wells LD2 3TN Tel: (01982) 553217 ⊨3 ⊷2 Open: 1-12; 2 Star B&B

OLD VICARAGE Erwood, Builth Wells LD2 3SZ Tel: (01982) 560680 or 0808 1980319 E-mail: linda@oldvic43.fsnet.co.uk Website: www.oldvic43.fsnet.co.uk ⊨3 Open: 1-12; 3 Star Guest House

RHYDFELIN FARM GUEST HOUSE Builth Rd, Cwmbach, Builth Wells LD2 3RT Tel: (01982) 552493 E-mail: liz@rhydfelinguesthouse.freeserve.co.uk Website: www.rhydfelinguesthouse.freeserve.co.uk ⊨4 ⊷1 Open: 1-12; 3 Star Guest House

CRICKHOWELL   Map Ref: Hb7

BEAR HOTEL High St, Crickhowell NP8 1BW Tel: (01873) 810408 Fax: (01873) 811696 E-mail: bearhotel@aol.com Website: www.bearhotel.co ⊨36 Open: 1-12; 3 Star Hotel

CASTELL CORRYN Llangenny, Crickhowell NP8 1HE Tel: (01873) 810327 Fax: (01873) 810327 E-mail: 113114.2610@compuserve.com ⊨3 ⊷3 Open: 1-12; 3 Star B&B

DRAGON HOTEL Crickhowell, Brecon Beacons National Park NP8 1BE Tel: (01873) 810362 Fax: (01873) 811868 E-mail: dragon-hotel@crickhowell10.freeserve.co.uk Website: www.dragonhotel.co.uk ⊨15 ⊷15 Open: 1-12; 2 Star Hotel

Llantony Valley in the Black Mountains

THE FIRS Tretower, Crickhowell, Brecon NP8 1RF Tel: (01874) 730780 Fax: (01874) 730780 Website: www.holiday-wales.com ⊨5 ⊷2 Open: 1-12; 3 Star Guest House

THE MANOR HOTEL Brecon Rd, Crickhowell NP8 1SE Tel: (01873) 810212 Fax: (01873) 811938 E-mail: themanorhotel@talk21.com ⊨22 ⊷22 Open: 1-12; 3 Star Hotel

TY CROESO HOTEL The Dardy, Llangattock, Crickhowell NP8 1PU Tel: (01873) 810573 Fax: (01873) 810573 E-mail: tycroeso@ty-croeso-hotel.freeserve.co.uk Website: www.wiz.to/tycroeso ⊨8 ⊷8 Open: 1-12; 3 Star Hotel

ELAN VALLEY   Map Ref: Gd3

TY NANT BED & BREAKFAST Elan Valley, nr Rhayader LD6 5HN Tel: (01597) 811412 Fax: (01597) 811412 ⊨2 Open: 2-11; 2 Star B&B

ELAN VALLEY HOTEL Elan Valley, Rhayader LD6 5HN Tel: (01597) 810448203 Fax: (01597) 810448 E-mail: <hotel@elanvalley.demon.co.uk Website: www.elanvalleyhotel.co.uk ⊨11 ⊷11 Open: 1-12; 2 Star Country Hotel

HAY-ON-WYE   Map Ref: Hb5

THE OLD POST OFFICE Llanigon, Hay-on-Wye HR3 5QA Tel: (01497) 820008 Website: www.hay-on-wye.co.uk/oldpost ⊨3 ⊷2 Open: 1-12; 3 Star Guest House

TY BACH Llowes, Hay-on-Wye HR3 5JE Tel: (01497) 847759 Fax: (01497) 847940 E-mail: charles.bradfield@farmline.com Website: www.hay-on-wye.co.uk/tybach ⊨2 ⊷2 Open: 1-12 (not xmas); 3 Star B&B

KNIGHTON   Map Ref: Hb2

CEFNSURAN FARM Llangunllo, Knighton LD7 1SL Tel: (01547) 550219 Fax: (01547) 550348 E-mail: cefn@suran.freeserve.co.uk Website: www.farmbreaks.org.uk ⊨2 ⊷2 Open: 1-12; 3 Star Farm

OFFA'S DYKE HOUSE 4 High St, Knighton LD7 1AT Tel: (01547) 528634 Mobile: 0780 8090549 Fax: (01547) 527634 ⊨6 Open: 1-12 (except xmas week); 2 Star B&B

LAKE VYRNWY   Map Ref: Ea3

THE OAKS Llanwddyn, Nr Oswestry SY10 0LZ Tel: (01691) 870250 Fax: (01691) 870250 E-mail: Mdug99@cs.com ⊨3 ⊷3 Open: 5-11; Awaiting Grading

LLANBADARN FYNYDD   Map Ref: Ge1

HILLSIDE LODGE GUEST HOUSE Llanbadarn Fynydd LD1 6TU Tel: (01597) 840364 ⊨3 ⊷3 Open: 1-12; 3 Star Guest House

LLANDRINDOD WELLS
Map Ref: Ge3

HOLLY FARM Howey, Llandrindod Wells LD1 5PP
Tel: (01597) 822402 Fax: (01597) 822402
Website: www.ukword.net/hollyfarm ⌂5 ⇌3 Open: 1-12;
3 Star Farm

NEUADD FARM COUNTRY GUESTHOUSE Penybont,
Llandrindod Wells LD1 5SW Tel: (01597) 824295
Fax: (01597) 822571 Website: www.smoothhound.co.uk
⌂3 ⇌3 Open: 1-12; 4 Star Farm

LLANGAMMARCH WELLS
Map Ref: Gd4

HILLVIEW Llangammarch Wells LD4 4AA
Tel: (01591) 620711 ⌂2 ⇌2 Open: 3-11; 3 Star B&B

LLANWDDYN
Map Ref: Ea3

LAKE VYRNWY HOTEL Llanwddyn SY10 0LY
Tel: (01691) 870692 Fax: (01691) 870259
E-mail: res@lakevyrnwy.com Website: www.lakevyrnwy.com
⌂35 ⇌35 Open: 1-12; 4 Star Country Hotel

LLANWRTYD WELLS
Map Ref: Gc5

GLANIRFON FARMHOUSE BED & BREAKFAST Abernant,
Llanwrtyd Wells LD5 4AF Tel: (01591) 610604
Fax: (01591) 610604 E-mail: info@glanirfon.co.uk
Website: www.glanirfon.co.uk ⌂4 Open: 1-12; 2 Star B&B

OAKFIELD HOUSE Dol-y-Coed Rd, Llanwrtyd Wells LD5 4RA
Tel: (01591) 610605 Fax: (01591) 610605 ⌂3 Open: 4-11;
3 Star B&B

ORLESWELL Erw Haf, Ffos Rd, Llanwrtyd Wells LD5 4RT
Tel: (01591) 610747 ⌂2 ⇌1 Open: 1-12; 4 Star B&B

LLYSWEN
Map Ref: Ha5

OAKFIELD Brecon LD3 0UR Tel: (01874) 754301
⌂2 ⇌1 Open: 3-10; 3 Star B&B

MONTGOMERY
Map Ref: Ec6

DREWIN FARM Churchstoke, Montgomery SY15 6TW
Tel: (01588) 620325 Fax: (01588) 620325
E-mail: ceinwen@drewin.freeserve.co.uk ⌂2 ⇌2
Open: 4-10; 3 Star Farm

LITTLE BROMPTON FARM Montgomery SY15 6HY
Tel: (01686) 668371 Fax: (01686) 668371
E-mail: gaynor.brompton@virgin.net ⌂3 ⇌3 Open: 1-12;
4 Star Farm

NEW RADNOR
Map Ref: Hb3

TREGWYNT Mutton Dingle, New Radnor LD8 2IL
Tel: (01544) 350409 E-mail: m.haines@ukgateway.net
⌂3 Open: 3-11; 3 Star B&B

PANDY
Map Ref: Mc1

WALKERS REST Glannant House, Pandy, Abergavenny
NP7 8DN Tel: (01873) 890088 Fax: (01873) 890088
⌂5 ⇌1 Open: 1-12; 2 Star Hotel

PRESTEIGNE
Map Ref: Hc2

THE PADDOCK Shobdon, Leominster, Presteigne HR6 9NQ
Tel: (01568) 708176 Fax: (01568) 708829
E-mail: thepaddock@talk21.com ⌂5 ⇌5 Open: 1-12;
Guest House

RHAYADER
Map Ref: Gd2

BRYNAFON COUNTRY HOUSE HOTEL South St, Rhayader
LD6 5BL Tel: (01597) 810735 Fax: (01597) 810111
E-mail: info@brynafon.co.uk Website: www.brynafon.co.uk
⌂16 ⇌16 Open: 1-12; 3 Star Country Hotel

BRYNTEG East St, Rhayader LD6 5EA Tel: (01597) 810052
E-mail: brynteg@hotmail.com ⌂3 ⇌3 Open: 1-12;
3 Star B&B

LIVERPOOL HOUSE East St, Rhayader LD6 5EA
Tel: (01597) 810706 Fax: (01597) 810964
E-mail: ann@liverpoolhouse.net
Website: www.liverpoolhouse.net ⌂8 ⇌7 Open: 1-12;
2 Star Guest House

RIVERSIDE LODGE Elan Valley, nr Rhayader LD6 5HL
Tel: (01597) 810770 Fax: (01597) 810770
E-mail: info@riverside-lodge.com
Website: www.riverside-lodge.com ⌂10 ⇌4 Open: 1-12;
2 Star Guest House

WELSHPOOL
Map Ref: Ec5

HAFREN 38 Salop Rd, Welshpool SY21 7EA
Tel: (01938) 554112 Fax: (01938) 554112 ⌂3 ⇌1 Open:
E-Mail: hafren@tinyworld.co.uk ⌂3 ⇌1 Open:1-12;
2 Star B&B

HEATH COTTAGE Forden, Welshpool SY21 8LX
Tel: (01938) 580453 Fax: (01938) 580453 ⌂4 ⇌4
Open: 4-10; 3 Star Farm

THE HAVEN Winllan Rd, Llansantffiaid SY22 6TR
Tel: (01691) 828101 Fax: (01691) 828101
E-mail: thehaven@ukworld.net
Website: www.ukworld.net/thehaven ⌂3 ⇌1 Open: 3-12;
3 Star B&B

TYNLLWYN FARM Welshpool SY21 9BW
Tel: (01938) 553175 ⌂4 ⇌1 Open: 1-12; 3 Star Farm

Holiday Cottages

BRECON
Map Ref: Ge6

THE HAYLOFT Caecrwn Farmhouse, Battle, Brecon LD3 9RW
Tel: (01874) 625397 Fax: (01874) 625397
E-mail: jill@caecrwn.demon.co.uk
Website: www.caecrwn.co.uk UNITS: 1; SLEEPS: 1-4;
Open: 1-12; 5 Star

TYCERRIG Trallong, nr Brecon LD3 8HP
Tel: (01874) 638848 Fax: (01874) 638848
E-mail: anthbryer@excite.co.uk
Website: www.cottageguide.co.uk/tycerrig Enquiries: Mrs
V.B. Bryer, 'Cae Parc', Trallong, nr Brecon LD3 8HP
UNITS: 1; SLEEPS: 4; Open: 1-12; 5 Star

CRICKHOWELL
Map Ref: Hb7

OAKVIEW Graig Barn Farm, Llangenny Lane, Crickhowell
NP8 1HB Tel: (01873) 810275
E-mail: johng.morris@virgin.net
Website: www.ukworld.net/oakview UNITS: 2; SLEEPS: 1-6;
Open:1-12; 5 Star

PREGGE MILL Pregge Lane, Crickhowell NP8 1SE
Tel: (01873) 811157 Fax: (01873) 811157
E-mail: preggemill@btinternet.com
Website: www.btinternet.com/~preggemill UNITS: 1;
SLEEPS: 2-4; Open: 1-12; 4 Star

LLANDRINDOD WELLS
Map Ref: Ge3

PIPPINS Neuadd Farm, Penybont, Llandrindod Wells
LD1 5SY Tel: (01597) 822571 Fax: (01597) 824295
Website: www.smoothhound.co.uk UNITS: 1; SLEEPS: 4;
Open: 1-12; 5 Star

TRANSEDW COTTAGE Hundred House, Llandrindod Wells
LD1 5RY Tel: (01982) 570362 Fax: (01982) 570362
E-mail: hughrichards@gn.apc.org UNITS: 1; SLEEPS: 6;
Open: 4-10; 3 Star

LLANGORSE
Map Ref: Ha6

OLD VICARAGE COTTAGE The Old Vicarage, Llangorse,
Brecon LD3 7UB Tel: (01874) 658639
UNITS: 1; SLEEPS: 4; Open: 1-12; 4 Star

POWELLS COTTAGE Llangors, nr Brecon LD3 7UE
Tel: (01874) 658672 E-mail: mgjones@lineone.net
Enquiries: Mike or Jill Jones, Oak Cottage, Llangors, Brecon
LD3 7UE UNITS: 1; SLEEPS: 3; Open: 1-12; 4 Star

LLANIDLOES
Map Ref: Gd1

BRELGWYN & TY BYCHAN 12 The Rank, Cwmbelan, nr
Llanidloes SY18 6QA Enquiries: 18 Meadow Rd, Aldridge,
Walsall, West Midlands WS9 0ST Tel: (01922) 452687
UNITS: 2; SLEEPS: 4-5; Open: 3-11; 4 Star

LLANRHAEADR YM MOCHNANT
Map Ref: Eb3

TAN-Y-FRIDD Maengwynedd, Llanrhaeadr ym Mochnant,
Oswestry SY10 0DT Tel: (01691) 791418
Fax: (01691) 791418 Enquiries: Mrs Margaret Hart, Caer
Fach, Llanrhaeadr ym, Oswestry SY10 0DT
E-mail: margarethart@breathemail.net
Website: www.tanat-holidays.co.uk
UNITS: 1; SLEEPS: 6; Open 1-12; 4 Star

LLANWRTYD WELLS
Map Ref: Gc5

CWMIRFON LODGE Llanwrtyd Wells LD5 4TN
Tel: (01591) 610849 Fax: (01591) 610750
E-mail: karin@cwmirfon.co.uk Website: www.cwmirfon.co.uk
UNITS: 3; SLEEPS: 2-6; Open: 1-12; 4 Star

LLANYMYNECH
Map Ref: Ec3

GLEN HELEN COTTAGES Isfryn, Stargarreg Lane, Pant,
Oswestry SY10 9QN Tel: (01691) 830094
Fax: (01691) 830094 E-mail: gaskill@globalnet.co.uk
Website: www.glenhelen.co.uk UNITS: 2; SLEEPS: 3-4;
Open: 1-12; 4 Star

MACHYNLLETH
Map Ref: Dc5

3 IVY COTTAGES Darowen, Machynlleth SY20 8NT
Tel: (01650) 511681 Fax: (01650) 511602
E-mail: morag@perrocarto.co.uk Enquiries: Cysgod y Fron,
Darowen, Machynlleth SY20 8NS UNITS: 1; SLEEPS: 4;
Open: 1-12; 4 Star

BRYNLLWYDYN HALL Uwchygarreg, Machynlleth SY20 8RR
Tel: (01654) 702042 UNITS: 4; SLEEPS: 5-9; Open: 1-12;
3 Star

MIN AFON (RIVERSIDE) Pantperthog, Machynlleth SY20 9AR
Tel: (01654) 702070 Fax: (01654) 702070 Enquiries: Mr &
Mrs A. Britton, 'Pentir', Pantperthog, Machynlleth SY20 9AR
UNITS: 1; SLEEPS: 4; Open: 1-12; 5 Star

MOELFRE COTTAGE Rhosdyrnog, Talywern, Machynlleth
SY20 8NU Tel: (01650) 511288 Fax: (01650) 511288
No. of Units: 1; Sleeps: 4; Open: 1-12; 3 Star

MONTGOMERY
Map Ref: Ec6

ROSE COTTAGE Llandyssil, Montgomery SY15 6LQ
Tel: (01686) 668364 Enquiries: Mrs S. Ralph, Garreg,
Llandyssil, Montgomery SY15 6LQ UNITS: 1; SLEEPS: 4-5;
Open: 1-12; 4 Star

NEW RADNOR
Map Ref: Hb3

HAINES MILL New Radnor, Presteigne LD8 2TN
Tel: (01544) 350327 Fax: (01544) 350327 UNITS: 1;
SLEEPS: 4-5; Open: 1-12; 4 Star

NEWTOWN
Map Ref: Eb6

PORTHOUSE WOOD CABINS Llanllwchaiarn, Newtown
SY16 2DL Tel: (01686) 626856
Enquiries: Myrtle Villa, Llanfair Rd, Newtown SY16 2DL
UNITS: 2; SLEEPS: 4; Open: 1-12; 3 Star

PRESTEIGNE
Map Ref: Hc2

CORNER HOUSE COTTAGE C/o Upper House, Kinnerton,
Presteigne LD8 2PE Tel: (01547) 560207 UNITS: 1;
SLEEPS: 5+2; Open: 1-12; 4 Star

WELSHPOOL
Map Ref: Ec5

DERWEN HOUSE Derwen Garden Centre, Guilsfield
SY21 9PH Tel: (01938) 553015 Fax: (01938) 556170
UNITS: 2; SLEEPS: 6-16; Open: 1-12; 4 Star

VALLEY VIEW & DINGLE COTTAGE Tynllwyn Farm,
Welshpool SY21 9PG Tel: (01938) 553175
Fax: (01938) 555306 E-mail: caroline.emberton@cp.ltd.co.uk
UNITS: 2; SLEEPS: 4-6; Open: 1-12; 5 Star

Abergwesyn Pass above Llanwrtyd Wells

CEREDIGION - CARDIGAN BAY
AREA 6

Hotels, Guest Houses & Farmhouses

ABERYSTWYTH   *Map Ref: Fe1*

BELLE VUE ROYAL HOTEL Marine Terrace, Aberystwyth
SY23 2BA Tel: (01976) 617558 Fax: (01970) 612190
E-mail: reception@bellevueroyalhotel.fsnet.co.uk
Website: www.bellevueroyal.co.uk ⌂34 ⇥34 Open: 1-12;
3 Star Hotel

BRENDAN GUEST HOUSE 19 Marine Terrace, Aberystwyth
SY23 2AZ Tel: (01970) 612252
E-mail: ivor.williams@virgin.net ⌂7 ⇥4 Open: 1-12;
1 Star Guest House

LLETY CEIRO COUNTRY GUEST HOUSE Lôn Ceiro Llandre,
Bow St, Aberystwyth SY24 5AB Tel: (01970) 821900
Fax: (01970) 820966 E-mail: marinehotel@barbox.net
Website: www.marinehotelaberystwyth.com ⌂10 ⇥10
Open: 1-12; 3 Star Guest House

MARINE HOTEL AND RESTAURANT The Promenade,
Aberystwyth SY23 2BX Tel: (01970) 612444
Fax: (01970) 617435
Website: www.marinehotelaberystwyth.com ⌂44 ⇥44
Open: 1-12; 2 Star Hotel

TYCAM FARM Capel Bangor, Aberystwyth SY23 3NA
Tel: (01970) 880662 ⌂2 ⇥2 Open: 4-10; 2 Star Farm

CARDIGAN   *Map Ref: Fa5*

BRYNHYFRYD GUEST HOUSE Gwbert Rd, Cardigan
SA43 1AE Tel: (01239) 612861 Fax: (01239) 612861
E-mail: g.arcus@btinternet.com
⌂7 ⇥3 Open: 1-12; 3 Star Guest House

BRYNOWEN BED AND BREAKFAST Brynowen, Sarnau,
Llandysul, Cardigan SA44 6QT Tel: (01239) 654456
Fax: (01239) 654456 ⌂3 Open: 3-11; 2 Star B&B

DEVIL'S BRIDGE   *Map Ref: Ga1*

HAFOD ARMS HOTEL Devil's Bridge, nr Aberystwyth
SY23 3JL Tel: (01970) 890232 Fax: (01970) 890394
E-mail: enquiries@hafodarms.co.uk
Website: www.hafodarms.co.uk ⌂15 ⇥15 Open: 1-12;
2 Star Hotel

LAMPETER   *Map Ref: Fe5*

BRYNOG MANSION Felinfach, Lampeter SA48 8AQ
Tel: (01570) 470266 ⌂3 ⇥2 Open: 1-12 (not xmas/new
year); 3 Star Farm

HAULFAN 6 Station Terrace, Lampeter SA48 7HH
Tel: (01570) 422718 ⌂3 Open: 1-12; 3 Star Guest House

PANTYCELYN GUEST HOUSE Llanwnnen, Lampeter
SA48 7LW Tel: (01570) 434455 Fax: (01570) 434455
E-mail: huwannj@aol.com Website: www.pantycelyn.co.uk
⌂3 ⇥3 Open: 2-10; 3 Star Guest House

PENLANMEDD Llanfair Rd, Lampeter, Ceredigion SA48 8JZ
Tel: (01570) 493438 Fax: (01570) 493438
E-mail: penlanmedd@coombes-e.freeserve.co.uk
⌂3 ⇥3 Open: 1-12; 3 Star Guest House

LLANON   *Map Ref: Fd3*

FRONDOLAU FARM GUEST HOUSE Heol Llain Prysg,
Llanon SY23 5HZ Tel: (01974) 202354 ⌂3 Open: 1-12;
2 Star B&B

RHYDLEWIS   *Map Ref: Fb5*

NANT Y BRENNI Rhydlewis, Llandysul SA44 5SN
Tel: (01239) 851368 Fax: (01239) 851891
E-mail: sue@philpad.demon.co.uk
Website: www.philpad.demon.co.uk
⌂3 ⇥2 Open: 1-12; 3 Star B&B

TREGARON   *Map Ref: Ga3*

BRYNHEULOG Llanddewi Brefi, Tregaron SY25 6PE
Tel: (01570) 493615 Fax: (01570) 493615
Website: www.brynheulog.com ⌂1 ⇥1 Open: 1-12;
3 Star B&B

THREE HORSESHOE INN Llangeitho, Tregaron SY25 6TW
Tel: (01974) 821244 E-mail: jane.williams6@virgin.net
UNITS : 1; SLEEPS: 3+1; Open: 1-12; 4 Star Inn

Holiday Cottages

ABERPORTH   *Map Ref: Fa5*

GORSLWYD FARM Tan-y-Groes, Cardigan SA43 2HZ
Tel: (01239) 810593 Fax: (01239) 811569 UNITS: 8;
SLEEPS: 6; Open: 3-10

PENFFYNNON PROPERTIES Penffynnon, Aberporth
SA43 2DA Tel: (01239) 810387 Fax: (01239) 811401
E-mail: tt@lineone.net UNITS: 7; SLEEPS: 5-8; Open: 1-12;
4 & 5 Star

ABERYSTWYTH   *Map Ref: Fe1*

ABERLERI FARM COTTAGES Cambrian Coast Park, Borth, nr
Aberystwyth SY24 5JU Enquiries: Freepost Department WB
Tel: (01970) 871233 Fax: (01970) 871124
Website: www.sunbourne.co.uk UNITS: 5; SLEEPS: 2-10
Open: 1-12; 5 Star

ABERCEIRO BUNGALOW Lôn Ceiro, Llandre, Bow St,
Aberystwyth SY24 5AB Freephone: 0800 0190020
UNITS: 1; SLEEPS: 6; Open: 1-12; 4 Star

ABERYSTWYTH HOLIDAY APARTMENTS 9 Northgate St,
Aberystwyth SY23 2JS Tel: (01970) 612878/626004
UNITS: 2; SLEEPS: 2-4; Open: 1-12; 2 Star

GEUALLT COTTAGE Old Goginan, Aberystwyth SY23 3PD
Tel: (01562) 885097 Fax: (01562) 886838
Enquiries: Mrs G. Duffield, 28 Newfield Rd, Hagley,
Stourbridge DY9 0JR UNITS: 1; SLEEPS: 4; Open: 5-10;
4 Star

CARDIGAN
Map Ref: Fa5

APARTMENT 1, GLANAFON COURT Gwbert-on-Sea, Cardigan SA43 1PP Tel: (01239) 612873 Enquiries: Mrs J. Roberts, Awel-y-Nant, Melin-y-Coed, Cardigan SA43 1PQ UNITS: 1; SLEEPS: 4-6; Open: 1-12; 4 Star

LLANYBYDDER
Map Ref: Fd5

FFOSFFALD ISAF/HEN DY PAIR Ffosffald Uchaf, Drefach, Llanybydder SA40 9TA Tel: (01570) 434200 UNITS: 2; SLEEPS: 4-6; Open: 3-12; 4 Star

NEWCASTLE EMLYN
Map Ref: Fb6

THE COTTAGE Llain Brongwyn, Cwm-Cou, Newcastle Emlyn SA38 9PR Tel: (01239) 711024 E-mail: bruce@brongwyn.freeserve.co.uk UNITS: 1; SLEEPS: 4-6; Open: 1-12; 4 Star

DERWIG FARM Drefach, Velindre, Llandysul SA44 5XR Tel: (01557) 371577 E-mail: annebgjones@yahoo.co.uk UNITS: 1; SLEEPS: 2; Open: 1-12; 3 Star

NEW QUAY
Map Ref: Fc4

NO 1 WHITE STREET New Quay SA45 9NH Tel: (029) 2075 8526 Fax: (029) 2075 8526 E-mail: wyngevans@hotmail.com Enquiries: Mr W.G. Evans, 47 Winnipeg Drive, Lakeside, Cardiff CF23 6ET UNITS: 1; SLEEPS: 7; 2 Star

3 BELLE VUE New Rd, New Quay Tel: (01545) 580686 Fax: (01545) 580686 E-mail: hencaliban@hotmail.com Enquiries: Mrs Watson, Blaenddol, Gilfachreda, New Quay SA45 9ST UNITS: 1; SLEEPS: 5; Open: 3-9; 3 Star

YSBYTTY Llwyndafydd, Llandysul, New Quay SA44 6LF Tel: (0116) 2675834 UNITS: 1; SLEEPS: 6-8; Open: 1-12; 4 Star

TREGARON
Map Ref: Ga3

BRYNAMLWG COTTAGE Brynamlwg, Penuwch, Tregaron SY25 6RA Tel: (01974) 821471 Fax: (01974) 821471 E-mail: kdingle@talk21.com

TALFEDW COTTAGE Talfedw, Llangeitho, Tregaron SY25 6QF Tel: (01974) 821444 UNITS: 1; SLEEPS: 6+🛏 Open: 1-12

Caravan & Camping Park

BORTH
Map Ref: Fe1

BRYNRODYN CARAVAN PARK Borth, Aberystwyth SY24 5NR Tel: (01970) 871472 Fax: (01970) 871472 E-mail: brynrodyn@bun.com No. ON PARK 135 🚐 10 🚐 50 ⛺ 50 3 Star Holiday Park

NORTHFIELD HOLIDAY PARK Clarach Rd, Borth SY24 5NR Tel: (01970) 871464 Fax: (01970) 871995 E-mail: ann.moore@which.net Website: www.ukparks.co.uk/northfield No. ON PARK 13 🚐 13 4 Star Holiday Park

PEMBROKESHIRE
AREA 7

Hotels, Guest Houses & Farmhouses

AMROTH
Map Ref: Ka3

BEACHHAVEN GUEST HOUSE Amroth Sea Front, Narberth SA67 8NG Tel: (01834) 813310 🛏3 🍴3 Open: 4-10; 2 Star Guest House

BROAD HAVEN
Map Ref: Jb5

ANCHOR GUEST HOUSE Enfield Rd, Broad Haven Tel: (01437) 781051 Fax: (01437) 781050 E-mail: anch@bdhn.fsnet.co.uk Website: www.anchor-guesthouse.co.uk 🛏8 🍴8 Open: 1-12; 2 Star Guest House

ATLANTIC VIEW Settlands Hill, Broad Haven Tel: (01437) 781589 E-mail: enquiries@atlantic-view.co.uk Website: www.atlantic-view.co.uk 🛏5 🍴5 Open: 1-12; 3 Star B&B

BARLEY VILLA Walwyns Castle, nr Broad Haven Haverfordwest SA62 3EB Tel: (01437) 781254 E-mail: barley-villa@pfh.co.uk 🛏2 🍴2 Open: Easter-11; 3 Star Farm

LION ROCK Broad Haven, Haverfordwest SA62 3JP Tel: (01437) 781645 Fax: (01437) 781203 E-mail: lion.rock@btinternet.com Website: www.jpmarketing.co.uk/lionrock 🛏5 🍴5 Open: 3-10; 3 Star Guest House

CILGERRAN
Map Ref: Fa6

WYNDARRA BED & BREAKFAST Wyndarra, Cilgerran SA43 2RY Tel: (01239) 621243 🛏2 Open: 1-11; 2 Star B&B

CROESGOCH
Map Ref: Jb3

BANK HOUSE FARM Croesgoch, Haverfordwest SA62 5LE Tel: (01348) 831305 🛏2 Open: 3-11; 2 Star Farm

FISHGUARD
Map Ref: Jc2

DOLWERN Feidr Fawr, Dinas Cross, Newport, Fishguard SA42 0UY Tel: (01348) 811266 or 07949 523131 E-mail: annette-keylock@lineone.net 🛏3 🍴3 Open: 1-12; 2 Star B&B

HEATHFIELD MANSION Mathry Road, Letterston, Fishguard SA62 5EG Tel: (01348) 840263 Fax: (01348) 840263 Central Reservations: Tel: (01348) 873484 E-mail: heathfield@p.net.co.uk or angelica.rees@virgin.net Website: www.p.net.co.uk/heathfield 🛏2 🍴2 Open: 3-10; 3 Star Guest House

SEALYHAM FARM GUEST HOUSE Wolfscastle, Haverfordwest SA62 5NE Tel: (01348) 840512 Fax: (01348) 840512 E-mail: lindaroche@uk.packardbell.org Website: www.pembrokeshireholidays.co.uk 🛏2 🍴2 Open: 1-12; 3 Star Farm

GOODWICK Map Ref: Jc2

IVYBRIDGE Drim Mill, Dyffryn, Goodwick SA64 0FT
Tel: (01348) 875366 Fax: (01348) 872338
E-mail: ivybridge@cwcom.net
Website: www.ivybridge.cwc.net
11 11 Open: 1-12; 2 Star Guest House

HAVERFORDWEST Map Ref: Jc5

CUCKOO MILL FARM Pelcomb Bridge, St David's Rd,
Haverfordwest SA62 6EA Tel: (01437) 762139
2 2 Open: 1-12; 3 Star Farm

THE FOLD Cleddau Lodge, Camrose, Haverfordwest
A62 6HY Tel: (01437) 710640 Fax: (01437) 710663
E-mail: cleddau.lodge@btinternet.com 1 1
Open: 3-10; 2 Star B&B

PENRHIWLLAN Well Lane, Prendergast, Haverfordwest
SA61 2PL Tel: (01437) 769049 3 1 Open: 1-12;
3 Star B&B

WOLFSCASTLE COUNTRY HOTEL Wolfscastle,
Haverfordwest SA62 5LZ Tel: (01437) 741688
Fax: (01437) 741383 E-mail: andy741225@aol.com
20 20 Open: 1-12; 3 Star Hotel

LITTLE HAVEN Map Ref: Jb5

THE BOWER FARM Little Haven, Haverfordwest SA62 3TY
Tel: (01437) 781554 Fax: (01437) 781940
E-mail: bowerfarm@lineone.net
Website: www.a1tourism.com/uk/bower.html 4 4
Open: 1-12; 3 Star Farm

WHITEGATES Little Haven, Haverfordwest SA62 3LA
Tel: (01437) 781562 Fax: (01437) 781552 4 4
Open: 1-12; 2 Star Guest House

MANORBIER Map Ref: Jd6

HONEYHILL BED & BREAKFAST Warlows Meadow,
Manorbier SA70 7SX Tel: (01834) 871906
Fax: (01834) 871293 2 2 Open: 1-12; 2 Star B&B

NEWGALE Map Ref: Jb4

WYNDHURST Newgale, Haverfordwest SA62 6AS
Tel: (01437) 720162 3 1 Open: 1-12; 4 Star B&B

NEWPORT Map Ref: Jd2

LLYS DEWI Fishguard Rd, Newport SA42 0UF
Tel: (01239) 820177 3 3 Open: 3-10; 2 Star B&B

SOAR HILL Cilgwyn Rd, Newport SA42 0QG
Tel: (01239) 820506 E-mail: soarhill@hotmail.com
3 2 Open: 1-12; 3 Star B&B

TREE TOPS West St, Newport SA42 0TD
Tel: (01239) 820048 Fax: (01239) 820048
E-mail: bandbtreetops@talk21.com 3 3 Open: 1-12;
4 Star Guest House

PEMBROKE Map Ref: Jc6

THE COACH HOUSE HOTEL 116 Main St, Pembroke
SA71 4HN Tel: (01646) 684602 Fax: (01646) 687456
E-mail: griffin@coachhouse-hotel.co.uk
Website: www.prembrokeshire.co.uk 15 15
Open: 1-12; 3 Star Hotel

HALF-PINT COTTAGE Merrion Village, Pembroke SA71 5HT
Tel: (01646) 661278/07979 535623 3 Open: 1-12;
3 Star B&B

MIDDLEGATE HOTEL 43 Main St, Pembroke SA71 4JS
Tel: (01646) 622442 Fax: (01646) 622442 4 4
Open: 1-12; 1 Star Hotel

POYERSTON FARM Cosheston, Pembroke SA72 4SJ
Tel: (01646) 651347 Fax: (01646) 651347
E-mail: poyerston@pfh.co.uk
Website: www.pfh.co.uk/poyerston 5 5
Open: 1-12; 4 Star Farm

ROSEDENE LICENSED GUEST HOUSE Rosedene, Hodgeston,
nr Freshwater East, Pembroke SA71 5JU
Tel: (01646) 672586 Fax: (01646) 672855
E-mail: eileen@rosedene85.freeserve.co.uk
Website: www.rosedene85.freeserve.co.uk 7 7
Open: 2-11; 3 Star Guest House

SEAHORSES Freshwater East, Pembroke SA71 5LA
Tel: (01646) 672405 2 Open: 5-9; 2 Star B&B

ST DAVIDS MAP REF: JA4

MURMUR-Y-MOR Abereiddy, St Davids, Haverfordwest
SA62 6DS Tel: (01348) 831670 E2 Open: 3-10; 3 Star B&B

PENTIGILI Carnhedryn, nr St Davids, Haverfordwest
SA62 6XI Tel: (01437) 720692 Fax: (01437) 721014
E-mail: Shaun-Rhian@pentigili-bed-and-breakfast.co.uk
Website: www.pentigili-bed-and-breakfast.co.uk 2 2
Open: 4-10; 3 Star B&B

TORBANT FARMHOUSE Croesgoch, Haverfordwest
SA62 5JN Tel: (01348) 831276 Fax: (01348) 831276
E-mail: torbant@pfh.co.uk Website: www.pfh.co.uk/torbant
2 2 Open: 3-10; 2 Star Farm

TWR-Y-FELIN 1 High St, St Davids SA62 6SA
Tel: (01437) 721678 Fax: (01437) 721838
E-mail: stay@tyf.com Website: www.tyf.com 11
Open: 1-12; 1 Star Hotel

WHITESANDS BAY HOTEL St Davids SA62 6PT
Tel: (01437) 720403 Fax: (01437) 720403 12 12
Open: 1-12; 1 Star Hotel

SANDY HAVEN Map Ref: Jb6

SKERRYBACK Sandy Haven, Haverfordwest SA62 3DN
Tel: (01646) 636598 Fax: (01646) 636595
E-mail: skerryback@pfh.co.uk
Website: www.pfh.co.uk/skerryback 2 2 Open: 3-11;
3 Star Farm

SAUNDERSFOOT Map Ref: Je6

BAY VIEW HOTEL Pleasant Valley, Stepaside, Saundersfoot
SA67 8LR Tel: (01834) 813417 11 8 Open: 4-9;
2 Star Hotel

MERLEWOOD HOTEL St Brides Hill, Saundersfoot SA69 9NP
Tel: (01834) 812421 Fax: (01834) 814886
E-mail: merlewood@saundersfoot.freeserve.co.uk
Website: www.merlewood.co.uk 28 28 Open: 4-10;
2 Star Hotel

VALLEY FARMHOUSE Valley Rd, Saundersfoot SA69 9BX
Tel: (01834) 813388 E-mail: gpearson@farmvalley.co.uk
🛏2 🚻1 Open: 4-10; 2 Star B&B

SOLVA
Map Ref: Jb4

LLANDDINOG HOUSE Nr Solva, St Davids, Haverfordwest
SA62 6NA Tel: (01348) 831467 Fax: (01348) 831467
E-mail: llanddinoghouse@solvawales.freeserve.co.uk
Website: www.stdavids.co.uk 🛏3 🚻3 Open: 1-12;
4 Star B&B

TENBY
Map Ref: Je6

ATLANTIC HOTEL The Esplanade, Tenby SA70 7DU
Tel: (01834) 842881 Fax: (01834) 842881 Ext: 256
E-mail: enquiries@atlantic-hotel.uk.com
Website: www.atlantic-hotel.uk.com 🛏42 🚻42
Open: 1-12; 4 Star Hotel

CLARENCE HOUSE HOTEL Esplanade, Tenby SA70 7DU
Tel: (01834) 844371 Fax: (01834) 844372
E-mail: clarencehotel@free.uk.com
Website: www.clarencehotel-tenby.co.uk 🛏68 🚻68
Open: 2-12; 2 Star Hotel

THE DIGGINS Lawrenny SA68 0PW Tel: (01646) 651235
E-mail: alisonlewis@thediggins.freeserve.co.uk
Website: www.ukbnb.net/diggins 🛏2 🚻1 Open: 1-12;
3 Star B&B

FLEMISH COURT St Florence, Tenby SA70 8LS
Tel: (01834) 871413 🛏3 🚻3 Open: 1-12; 3 Star Guest
House

GWYNNE HOUSE Bridge Street, Tenby SA70 7BU
Tel: (01834) 842862 Fax: (01834) 842862
E-mail: gwynnehouse@email.msn.com 🛏4 🚻4
Open: 1-12; 3 Star Guest House

HAMMONDS PARK HOTEL Narberth Rd, Tenby SA70 8HT
Tel: (01834) 842696 🛏13 🚻13 Open: 1-12; 2 Star Hotel

THE KINLOCH COURT HOTEL Queen's Parade, Tenby
SA70 7EG Tel: (01834) 842777 Fax: (01834) 843097
E-mail: kinlochhotel@aol.com 🛏14 🚻14 Open: 1-12;
3 Star Hotel

PEN MAR HOTEL New Hedges, Tenby SA70 8TL
Tel: (01834) 842435 Fax: (01834) 842435
E-mail: penmarhotel@jhurton.freeserve.co.uk
Website: www.s-h-systems.co.uk/a15498.html/
🛏12 🚻6 Open: 1-12; 2 Star Hotel

LAMPHEY COURT HOTEL Lamphey SA71 5NT
Tel: (01646) 672273 Fax: (01646) 672480
E-mail: info@lampheycourt.co.uk
Website: www.lampheycourt.co.uk 🛏37 🚻37
Open: 1-12; 4 Star Hotel

THE ROYAL GATE HOUSE HOTEL North Beach, Tenby
SA70 7ET Tel: (01834) 842255 Fax: (01834) 842441
🛏59 🚻59 Open: 1-12; 1 Star Hotel

ROYAL LION HOTEL North Beach, Tenby SA70 7EX
Tel: (01834) 842127 Fax: (01834) 842441
E-mail: royal-liontenby@hotmail.com 🛏21 🚻21
Open: 1-12; 3 Star Hotel

SEA BREEZES HOTEL 18 The Norton, Tenby SA70 8AA
Tel: (01834) 842753 🛏3 🚻3 Open: 3-11; 2 Star B&B

SUTHERLANDS 3 Picton Rd, Tenby SA70 7DP
Tel: (01834) 842522 🛏3 🚻3 Open: 1-12; 2 Star B&B

TENBY HOUSE HOTEL Tudor Square, Tenby SA70 7AJ
Tel: (01834) 842000 Fax: (01834) 844647 E-mail:
tenbyhouse@virgin.net Website: www.tenbyhousehotel.com
🛏18 🚻18 Open:1-12; 3 Star Hotel

TREFIN
Map Ref: Jb3

THE OLD COURT HOUSE VEGETARIAN GUEST HOUSE
Trefin, nr St Davids, Haverfordwest SA62 5AX
Tel: (01348) 837095
E-mail: oldcourthouse@netscapeonline.co.uk
Website: www.pembrokeshire-online.co.uk/courthouse
🛏3 🚻3 Open: 1-12; 3 Star B&B

Holiday Cottages

BONCATH
Map Ref: Fa6

FRON FAWR Boncath SA37 0HS Tel: (01239) 841285
Fax: 0870 120 9175 E-mail: cottages@fronfawr.co.uk
Website: www.fronfawr.co.uk UNITS: 4; SLEEPS: 2-8;
Open: 1-12; 5 Star

BROAD HAVEN
Map Ref: Jb5

HAVEN COTTAGES Little Haven, Whitegates, Haverfordwest
SA62 3LA Tel: (01437) 781386 Fax: (01437) 781386
E-mail: welshhaven@aol.com UNITS: 2; SLEEPS: 2-8;
Open: 1-12; 3 Star

MILLMOOR COTTAGES & ROCKSDRIFT APARTMENTS
Broad Haven, Haverfordwest SA62 3JH Tel: (0800) 0199930
Fax: (01437) 781002 E-mail: vw@millmoor.co.uk
Website:millmoor.co.uk UNITS: 24; SLEEPS: 2-8;
Open: 1-12; 4 Star

CARDIGAN
Map Ref: Fa5

TRENEWYDD FARM COTTAGES St Dogmaels, Cardigan
SA43 3BJ Tel: (01239) 612370 Fax: (01239) 621040
E-mail: cherylhyde@trenewyddfarm.fsnet.co.uk
Website: www.trenewyddfarm.fsnet.co.uk UNITS: 5;
SLEEPS: 13; Open: 1-12; 5 Star

CLYNDERWEN
Map Ref: Je4

GWARMACWYDD FARM COTTAGES Llanfallteg, Whitland
SA34 0XH Tel: (01437) 563260 Fax: (01437) 563839
E-mail: info@a-farm-holiday.org
Website: www.a-farm-holiday.org UNITS: 5; SLEEPS: 23;
Open: 1-12; 4

CROESGOCH
Map Ref: Jb3

GARN-Y-MÛL Croesgoch, nr St Davids SA62 3JP
Tel: (01959) 562972 Fax: (01959) 565365
Enquiries: Mrs Flynn, Froglets, Brasted Chart, Westerham
TN16 1LY UNITS: 1; SLEEPS: 4-6; Open: 1-12; 3 Star

FISHGUARD
Map Ref: Jc2

PARK VIEW 2 Park View, Ropewalk, Fishguard SA65 9BT
Tel: (01348) 873685 Enquiries: Mrs Beryl Badland, Llain yr
Esgob, Dwrbach, Fishguard SA65 9RR UNITS: 1; SLEEPS: 4;
Open: 1-12; 2 Star

FRESHWATER EAST
Map Ref: Jd6

TREWEN PARK HOLIDAY VILLAGE Freshwater East,
Pembroke SA71 5LP Tel: (01646) 672001
Fax: (01646) 672779 Enquiries: AJEM Holidays,
8 Whiteshott, Basildon SS16 5HF
E-mail: holidays@ajemholidays.co.uk
Website: www.ajemholidays.co.uk UNITS: 10; SLEEPS: 4-6;
Open: 1-12; 2 Star

HAVERFORDWEST
Map Ref: Jc5

CLEDDAU LODGE Camrose, Haverfordwest SA62 6HY
Tel: (01437) 710226/640 Fax: (01437) 710663
E-mail: cleddau.lodge@btinternet.com UNITS: 1; SLEEPS: 7;
Open: 3-10 2 Star

IVY COURT COTTAGES Ivy Court, Llys-y-Fran,
Nr Haverfordwest SA63 4RS Tel: (01437) 532473
Fax: (01437) 532346 E-mail: holidays@ivycourt.co.uk
Website: www.ivycourt.co.uk UNITS: 10; Open: 1-12;
4-5 Star

NEW HOUSE FARM Little Treffgarne, Haverfordwest
SA62 5DD Tel: (01437) 741754 Fax: (01437) 741754
E-mail: newhousefarm@compuserve.com
Website: www.data-wales.co.uk UNITS: 3; SLEEPS: 15;
Open: 1-12

STONELEIGH COTTAGE Ambleston, Haverfordwest SA62
5RD Tel: (01437) 731423 UNITS: 1; SLEEPS: 5+▥;
Open: 1-12; 4 Star

LITTLE HAVEN
Map Ref: Jb5

LITTLE HAVEN COTTAGES Woodlands Farm, Blocketts Lane,
Little Haven, Haverfordwest Tel: (01291) 623337
Fax: (01291) 627631 Enquiries: Mrs Judith Stephens,
Grey Rocks, Woodcroft, Chepstow NP16 7HY
Website: www.littlehavencottages.com UNITS: 9;
SLEEPS: 4-6; Open: 1-12; 4 Star

LYDSTEP
Map Ref: Je6

CELTIC HAVEN VILLAGE Lydstep SA70 7SG
Tel: (01834) 871850 Fax: (01834) 871069
Enquiries: 2 Riverside Quay, Haverfordwest SA61 2LJ
Website: www.celtichaven.co.uk UNITS: 26; SLEEPS: 2-12;
Open: 1-12; 5 Star

MANORBIER
Map Ref:Jd6

LANDWAY FARMHOUSE Manorbier, Nr Tenby.
Enquiries: Park Farm, Manorbier, Tenby SA70 7SU
Tel: (01834) 871264 Fax: (01834) 871264 UNITS: 1;
SLEEPS: 2-8; Open: 5-9; 4 Star

MATHRY
Map Ref: Jb3

BRYNTEG COTTAGE Mathry, Haverfordwest SA62 5HA
Tel: (01225) 311773 Fax: (01225) 311773
Enquiries: Mrs J Charles, 1 St Stephens Villas, St Stephens
Rd, Lansdown, Bath BA1 5PN E-mail: ajcharles@talk21.com
UNITS: 1; SLEEPS: 4; Open: 1-12; 4 Star

NEWGALE
Map Ref: Jb4

BEATTIES COTTAGE No 10 Wood Village, Newgale,
Haverfordwest SA62 6AR Tel: (01244) 300348 & (01437)
710381 Enquiries: Mrs Margaret Moreton, Primrose Cottage,
Green Lane, Picton, Chester CH2 4HG UNITS: 1; SLEEPS: 6;
Open: 1-12

SOLVA
Map Ref: Jb4

LLANDDINOG OLD FARMHOUSE & COTTAGES Llandeloy,
Solva SA62 6NA Tel: (01348) 831224
E-mail: s+pcastl@aol.com
Website: www.pembrokeshireholidays.co.uk UNITS: 3;
SLEEPS: 4-6+▤; Open: 1-12

PRETTY COTTAGE Solva Tel: (01348) 837871
Enquiries: Quality Cottages, Cerbia, Solva, Haverfordwest
SA62 6YE Website: www.qualitycottages.co.uk UNITS: 160;
SLEEPS: 2-14; Open: 1-12

ST DAVIDS
Map Ref: Ja4

CHARACTER COTTAGES ST DAVIDS Llaethdy, Whitesands,
St Davids SA62 6PR Tel/Fax (01437) 721831
E-mail: Peter-Anna@eggconnect.net
Website: www.character-cottages-st-davids.co.uk
COTTAGES: 5; SLEEPS: 4-6+▥; Open: 1-12; 4/5 Star

LOWER MOOR COTTAGES 1 Lower Moor, St Davids
SA62 6RP Tel: (01189) 266094
Enquiries: 140 Church Rd, Earley, Reading RG6 1HR
E-mail: enquiries@lowermoorcottages.co.uk
Website: www.lowermoorcottages.co.uk UNITS: 3;
SLEEPS: 2-16; Open: 1-12; 5 Star

TY GWYN Whitesands, St Davids Tel: (01348) 837871
Fax: (01348) 837876 Enquiries: Quality Cottages,
Cerbid, Solva, Haverfordwest SA62 6YE
Website: www.qualitycottages.co.uk UNITS: 160;
SLEEPS: 2-14; Open: 1-12; 4/5 Star

TY HIR Twr-y-Felin, St Davids SA62 6QS
Tel: (01437) 721678 Fax: (01437) 721838
E-mail: stay@tyf.com Website: www.tyf.com
Enquiries: Tyf, 1 High St, St Davids SA62 6SA UNITS: 1;
SLEEPS: 6; Open: 1-12; 3 Star

WYNCLIFFE COTTAGE Quickwell Hill, St Davids SA62 6PD
Tel: (01437) 720447 UNITS: 1; SLEEPS: 4; Open: 3-11;
4 Star

Y BWTHYN 9 New St, St Davids SA62 6SW
Tel: (01437) 720511 Fax: (01437) 720511
Enquiries: Pam Wilcox, 27 Nun St, St Davids SA62 6NT
UNITS: 1; SLEEPS: 6; Open: 1-12; 4 Star

TENBY
Map Ref: Je6

CARNOCK HOUSE Esplanade, Tenby SA70 7DU
Tel: (01834) 844371 Fax: (01834) 844372
Enquiries: Clarence Hotel, Esplanade, Tenby SA70 7DU
UNITS: 10; SLEEPS: 2/3/4/5; Open: 1-12; 2 Star

NYTH ADERYN FLAT North Cliffe, Tenby SA70 8AT
Tel: (01834) 842842 E-mail: nythaderyntenby@beeb.net
UNITS: 1; SLEEPS: 4-6; Open: 5-9; 3 Star

WALES ⅄ CYMRU

TWO HOURS AND
A MILLION MILES AWAY

The coast between Dinas Head and Fishguard

Caravan & Camping Park

FISHGUARD
Map Ref: Jc2

FISHGUARD BAY CARAVAN & CAMPING PARK Garn Gelli, Fishguard SA65 9ET Tel: (01348) 811415
Fax: (01348) 811425 E-mail: @fishguardbay.com
Website: www.fishguardbay.com No. ON PARK 50 ⏚ 10
⏚ 20 ⏚ 20 ⛺ 30 Open: 3-1; 4 Star Touring & Holiday Park

ST DAVIDS
Map Ref: Ja4

CAERFAI BAY CARAVAN & TENT PARK St Davids SA62 6QT
Tel: (01437) 720274 Fax: (01437) 720274
E-mail: info@caerfaibay.co.uk
Website: www.caerfaibay.co.uk No. ON PARK 33 ⏚ 5 ⏚ 27
⏚ 15 ⛺ 75 Open: 4-10; 3 Star Touring & Camping Park

SAUNDERSFOOT
Map Ref: Je6

SAUNDERSFOOT BAY LEISURE PARK Broadfield,
Saundersfoot SA69 9DG
Tel: (01834) 812284 Fax: (01834) 813387
E-mail: saundersfoot.bay@business.ntl.com
Website: www.saundersfootbay.co.uk No. ON PARK 169
⏚ 55 5 Star Holiday Park

TENBY
Map Ref: Je6

KILN PARK HOLIDAY CENTRE Enquiries: British Holidays,
Normandy Court, 1 Wolsey Rd, Hemel Hempstead HP2 4TU
Tel: (0845) 607 8099 Quote WTB Fax: (01442) 254956
Website: www.british-holidays.co.uk No. ON PARK 620
⏚ 305 Open: 3-10; 3 Star Holiday Park

SALTERN CARAVAN PARK The Green, Tenby SA70 8EP
Tel: (01834) 842157 No. ON PARK 58 ⏚ 58 Open: 4-10;
4 Star Holiday Park

CARMARTHENSHIRE - BEAUTIFUL COAST & COUNTRYSIDE IN WEST WALES
AREA 8

Hotels, Guest Houses & Farmhouses

AMMANFORD
Map Ref: Ke2

BRYNCOCH FARM Llandyfan, Ammanford SA18 2TY
Tel: (01269) 850480 Fax: (01269) 250888
E-mail: bryncoch@tesco.net ⏚3 ⏚3 Open: 1-12;
2 Star B&B

CARMARTHEN
Map Ref: Kc2

GLASFRYN GUEST HOUSE & RESTAURANT Brechfa,
Carmarthen SA32 7QY Tel: (01267) 202306
efax: 0870 1341770 E-mail: joyce.glasfryn@clara.co.uk
Website: www.carmarthenonline.co.uk/glasfryn ⏚3 ⏚3
Open: 1-12; 3 Star Guest House

PLAS FARM Llangynog, Carmarthen SA33 5DB
Tel: (01267) 211492 Fax: (01267) 211492 ⏚3 ⏚3
Open: 1-12; 3 Star Farm

TREBERSED FARM St Peters, Travellers Rest, Carmarthen
SA31 3RR Tel: (01267) 238182 Fax: (01267) 223653
E-mail: trebersed.farm@farmline.com ⏚3 ⏚3
Open:1-12; 3 Star Farm

LLANDEILO
Map Ref: La1

PANT Y BAS Pentrefelin, Llandeilo SA19 6SD
Tel: (01558) 822809 ⏚3 ⏚3 Open: 1-12; 2 Star B&B

PENHILL Trap, Llandeilo SA19 6UB Tel: (01558) 823066
Fax: (01558) 823060 E-mail: simon@thane1.freeserve.co.uk
Website: www.thane1.freeserve.co.uk/penhill.htm ⏚1 ⏚1
Open: 1-12; 2 Star B&B

TŶ CEFN Tregib Ffairfach, Llandeilo SA19 6TD
Tel: (01558) 823942 E-mail: tycefntregib@tinyonline.co.uk
Website: www.bedandbreakfast-llandeilo-wales.co.uk
⏚3 ⏚3 Open: 1-12; 3 Star B&B

WHITE HART INN 36 Carmarthen Rd, Llandeilo SA19 6RS
Tel: (01558) 823419 Fax: (01558) 823089
E-mail: therese@whitehartinn.fsnet.co.uk
Website: www.whitehartinn.fsnet.co.uk ⏚11 ⏚8
Open: 1-12; 2 Star Inn

LLANDOVERY
Map Ref: Gb6

CWM RHUDDAN MANSION Llandovery SA20 0DX Tel:
(01550) 721414 Website: www.visit-
carmarthenshire.co.uk/cwmrhuddan ⏚3 ⏚3 Open: 1-12;
4 Star Country House

CWMGWYN FARM Llangadog Rd, Llandovery SA20 0EQ
Tel: (01550) 720410 Fax: (01550) 720262
E-mail: cwmgwyn@waitrose.com ⏚3 ⏚3 Open: 4-11;
4 Star Farm

LLANERCHINDDA FARM Cynghordy, Llandovery SA20 0NB
Tel: (01550) 750274 Fax: (01550) 750300
E-mail: nick@cambrianway.co
Website: www.cambrianway.com ⇔9 ⇔9 Open: 1-12;
2 Star Guest House

PEMBREY *Map Ref: Kc4*

FOUR SEASONS GUEST HOUSE 62 Gwscwm Rd, Pembrey,
Burry Port SA16 0YU Tel: (01554) 833367
Fax: (01554) 833367 ⇔4 ⇔2 Open: 1-12; 3 Star Guest
House

Holiday Cottages

CARMARTHEN *Map Ref: Kc2*

CWMDWYFRAN FARM COTTAGE Cwmdwyfran Farm,
Cwmdwyfran, Bronwydd Arms, Carmarthen SA33 6JF
Tel: (01267) 281419 E-mail: joan@jbrandick.freeserve.co.uk
UNITS: 1; SLEEPS: 4/5; Open: 3-11

LLANDOVERY *Map Ref: Gb6*

CAE'R BEILI Pen y Fedw, Cil-y-Cwm, Llandovery SA20 0UF
Tel: (01550) 720622 E-mail: tomos@501416a.force9.co.uk
UNITS: 1; SLEEPS: 6+⇔; Open: 1-12; 5 Star

CWM RHUDDAN BACH Cwm Rhuddan Mansion, Llandovery
SA20 0DY Tel: (01550) 721414
Website: www.visit-carmarthenshire.co.uk/cwmrhuddan
UNITS: 1; SLEEPS: 3; Open: 1-12; 4 Star

LLANELLI *Map Ref: Kd4*

BRYNGWENYN FARM Pontyberem SA15 5NG
Tel: (01269) 843990 UNITS: 2; SLEEPS: 5; Open: 1-12

DYTHEL FARM HOLIDAY FLATS Trimsaran Rd, Llanelli
SA15 4RL Tel: (01554)810815 UNITS: 4; SLEEPS: 4/5
(cottage sleeps 10); Open: 3-12; 3 Star

SWANSEA BAY INCLUDING MUMBLES, GOWER, AFAN & VALE OF NEATH
AREA 9

Hotels, Guest Houses & Farmhouses

CYMMER *Map Ref: Lc4*

BRYN TEG HOUSE 9 Craig-y-Fan, Cymmer, Port Talbot
SA13 3LN Tel: (01639) 851820 Fax: (01639) 851820 ⇔3
Open: 1-12; 2 Star B&B

MUMBLES *Map Ref: La4*

ST ANNE'S HOTEL Western Lane, Mumbles, Swansea
SA3 4EY Tel: (01792) 369147 Fax: (01792) 360537
E-mail: pcs.cardiff@btinternet.com ⇔33 ⇔33 Open: 1-12;
3 Star Hotel

SHORELINE HOTEL 648 Mumbles Rd, Mumbles, Swansea
SA3 4QZ Tel: (01792) 366233
Website: www.shorelinehotel.co.uk ⇔12 ⇔12; Open: 1-12;
2 Star Hotel

NEATH *Map Ref: Lb3*

BWTHYN Y SAER Plas Farm, Cilybebyll, Pontardawe,
Swansea SA8 3JQ Tel: (01792) 864611
Fax: (01792) 864611
E-mail: enquiries@welshholidaycottages.com
Website: www.welshholidaycottages.com UNITS: 1;
SLEEPS: 4; Open: 1-12; 4 Star

REYNOLDSTON *Map Ref: Kd5*

GREENWAYS Hills Farm, Reynoldston, Gower, Swansea
SA3 1AE Tel: (01792) 390125 ⇔3 Open: 2-11; 2 Star Farm

STONEY-FORGE GUEST HOUSE Knelston, Reynoldston,
Swansea SA3 1AR Tel: (01792) 390920 ⇔3 ⇔3
Open: 2-11; 4 Star Guest House

SUNNYSIDE Llanddewi Castle Farm, Llanddew, Reynoldston
SA3 1AU Tel: (01792) 390194 ⇔2 Open: 1-11; 1 Star Farm

RHOSSILI *Map Ref: La4*

WORM'S HEAD HOTEL Rhossili, Swansea SA3 1PP
Tel: (01792) 390512 Fax: (01792) 391115 ⇔19 ⇔19
Open: 1-12; 2 Star Hotel

SWANSEA *Map Ref: La4*

BEST WESTERN ABERAVON BEACH HOTEL Neath,
Port Talbot, Swansea Bay SA12 6QP Tel: (01639) 884949
Fax: (01639) 897885 E-mail: sales@aberavonbeach.com
Website: www.aberavonbeach.com ⇔52 ⇔52
Open: 1-12; 3 Star Hotel

THE BEAUMONT HOTEL 72-73 Walter Road, Swansea
SA1 4QA Tel: (01792) 643956 Fax: (01792) 643044
E-mail: info@beaumonthotel.com
Website: www.beaumonthotel.co.uk ⇔16 ⇔16
Open: 1-12; 2 Star Hotel

Seafront gardens, Mumbles

Wales on the Web
www.visitwales.com

Make the most of your visit to Wales by calling into the Wales Tourist Board website. It's your easy route to up-to-date information on attractions and events in Wales, as well as lots of holiday ideas, itineraries and themes to explore.

Book Online! The website is also your gateway to online booking. Just key in your details and we'll come up with options tailored to your needs and budget.

THE GROSVENOR HOUSE Mirador Crescent, Uplands, Swansea SA2 0QX Tel: (01792) 461522 Fax: (01792) 461522 E-mail: grosvenor@ct6.com Website: www.ct6.com/grosvenor ⊨7 ⇥7 Open: 1-12; 3 Star Guest House

HENDREFOELAN HOLIDAY APARTMENTS - UNIVERSITY OF WALES SWANSEA Accommodation Office (HSV), University of Wales Swansea, Singleton Park, Swansea SA2 8PP Tel: (01792) 295101 Fax: (01792) 295327 E-mail: n.s.edmonds@swansea.ac.uk or conferences@swansea.ac.uk Website: www.swan.ac.uk/conferences UNITS: 230; Open: 7-9; 3 Star Campus

THE JARVIS INTERNATIONAL SWANSEA Phoenix Way, The Lakeside Park, Swansea SA7 9EG Tel: (01792) 310330 Fax: (01792) 797535 ⊨120 ⇥120 Open: 1-12; 3 Star Hotel

Holiday Cottages

CASWELL BAY Map Ref: Ke5

CASWELL BAY COURT Caswell Bay, Gower, Swansea SA3 3BP Tel: (01792) 775395 Fax: (01792) 790970 Enquiries: 221 Clasemont Rd, Morriston, Swansea SA6 6BT E-mail:peterjfrost@aol.com UNITS: 1; SLEEPS: 4; Open: 1-12; 5 Star

RHOSSILI Map Ref: Kc5

THE SLOPE Middleton, Rhossili, Swansea SA3 1PJ Tel: (01792) 390500 Enquiries: Mrs B Howe, Old Farmhouse, Middleton, Rhossili, Swansea SA3 1PJ E-mail: berylhowe@aol.com UNITS: 1; SLEEPS: 2; Open: 1-12

SWANSEA Map Ref: La4

BANK FARM HOLIDAY BUNGALOWS Bank Farm, Horton, Swansea SA3 1LL Tel: (01792) 390228 Fax: (01792) 391282 E-mail: bankfarmleisure@cs.com Website: www.bankfarmleisure.co.uk 3 Star

OXWICH LEISURE PARK 35 Oxwich Chalet Leisure Park, Oxwich, Gower, Swansea SA3 1LS Tel: (01792) 527388 Enquiries: Mrs J.M. Scoble, 16 Pockets Wharf, The Marina, Swansea SA1 3XL UNITS: 1; SLEEPS: 4

REDCLIFFE APARTMENTS 6A Redcliffe Apartments, Caswell Bay, Swansea Tel: (01792) 234586 Enquiries: Mrs P. Morgan, 44 Kilfield Rd, Bishopston, Swansea SA3 3DN UNITS: 1; SLEEPS: 4/5

THE VALLEYS OF SOUTH WALES
AREA 10

Hotels, Guest Houses & Farmhouses

ABERDARE Map Ref: Le3

DARE VALLEY COUNTRY PARK Countryside Residential Centre Aberdare CF44 7RG Tel: (01685) 874672 Fax: (01685) 882919 ⊨15 ⇥15 Open: 1-12 (closed Christmas week); 2 Star

BLACKWOOD Map Ref: Mb3

WYRLOED GUEST HOUSE Manmoel, Blackwood NP12 0RW Tel: (01493) 371198 Fax: (01495) 371198 ⊨4 ⇥44 Open: 1-11; 3 Star B&B

CAERPHILLY Map Ref: Ma4

WERN GANOL FARMHOUSE Nelson, Treharris CF46 6PS Tel: (01443) 450413 ⊨6 ⇥6 Open: 1-12; 2 Star Farm

MERTHYR TYDFIL Map Ref: Le2

THE CASTLE HOTEL Castle St, Merthyr Tydfil CF47 8BG Tel: (01685) 386868 Fax: (01685) 383898 E-mail: enquiries@castlehotelwales.com ⊨40 ⇥40 Open: 1-12; 3 Star Hotel

NELSON Map Ref: Ma3

FAIRMEAD GUEST HOUSE 24 Gelligaer Rd, Trelewis, Nelson CF46 6DN Tel: (01443) 411174 Fax: (01443) 411430 E-mail: fairmead@21.com Website: fairmeadhouse.aol.com ⊨3 ⇥3 Open: 1-12; 4 Star Guest House

PONTYPRIDD Map Ref: Le4

HERITAGE PARK HOTEL Coed Cae Rd, Trehafod, Pontypridd CF37 2NP Tel: (01443) 687057 Fax: (01443) 687060 E-mail: heritageparkhotel@talk21.com Website: heritageparkhotel.co.uk ⊨44 ⇥44 Open: 1-12; 3 Star Hotel

TYN-Y-WERN Ynysybwl CF37 3LY Tel: (01443) 790551 Fax: (01443) 790551 ⊨3 ⇥1 Open: 1-12; 3 Star Country Hotel

TREDEGAR Map Ref: Ma2

YE OLDE RED LION 97 Queen Victoria St, Tredegar NP22 3PX Tel: (01495) 724449 Fax: (01495) 711699 ⊨10 ⇥10 Open: 1-12; 1 Star

Holiday Cottages

BLACKWOOD Map Ref: Mb3

GELLIGOEDIOG HOLIDAY COTTAGES Manmoel, Blackwood NP12 0RH Tel: (01495) 371097/246844 UNITS: 2; SLEEPS 6; Open: 1-12; 4 Star

WYRLOED LODGE GUEST HOUSE & HOLIDAY COTTAGES Manmoel, Blackwood Tel: (01495) 371198 Fax: (01495) 371198 UNITS: 2; SLEEPS: 4/5; Open: 1-12; 4 Star

NEWPORT
Map Ref: Mc4

UPPER GRIPPATH FARM Risca, nr Newport NP11 6JB
Tel: (01633) 615000 Fax: (01633) 615000
E-mail: louise.saunders@ic24.net
Website: www.grippath.ic24.net UNITS: 1; SLEEPS: 4;
Open: 1-12; 4 Star

PONTYPOOL
Map Ref: Mc3

JUNCTION COTTAGE Canal Basin, Off Fountain Rd,
Pontymoile, Pontypool NP4 8ER Tel: 0800 5422663
Fax: (01495) 755877 Enquiries: Mrs Appleby, Ty Siân,
27 Top Rd, Garndiffaith, Pontypool
E-mail: junctioncottage@messages.co.uk
Website: www.junctioncottage.co.uk No. UNITS: 1;
SLEEPS: 6; Open: 1-12; 4 Star

Caravan & Camping Park

CROSS KEYS
Map Ref: Mb4

CWMCARN FOREST DRIVE CAMPSITE Cwmcarn,
Cross Keys, Newport NP11 7FA Tel: (01495) 272001
Fax: (01495) 2721001 E-mail: tic@caerphilly.gov.uk
Website: www.caerphilly.gov.uk 🚐 40 🚜 40 ⛺ 40
Open: 1-12; 4 Star Touring & Camping Park

CARDIFF. THE GLAMORGAN HERITAGE COAST & COUNTRYSIDE AREA 11

Hotels, Guest Houses & Farmhouses

BRIDGEND
Map Ld5

COURT COLMAN MANOR Pen-y-Fai, Bridgend CF31 4NG
Tel: (01656) 720212 Fax: (01656) 724544
E-mail: experience@court-colman-manor.com
Website: www.court-colman-manor.com 🛏 34 🍴 34
Open: 1-12; 2 Star Hotel

MAIR'S BED & BREAKFAST 9 Coychurch Rd, Bridgend
CF32 3AR Tel: (01656) 654838 Fax: (01656) 654838
E-mail: mairbb@euphony.net 🛏 6 🍴 3 Open: 1-12; 3 Star
B&B

CARDIFF
Map Ref: Mb5

AUSTINS 11 Coldstream Terrace, City Centre, Cardiff
CF11 6LJ Tel: (029) 2037 7148 Fax: (029) 2037 7158
E-mail: austins@hotelcardiff.com
Website: www.hotelcardiff.com 🛏 11 🍴 4 Open: 1-12;
2 Star Guest House

BEECHES HOTEL 73 Ninian Rd, Roath Park, Cardiff
CF23 5EN Tel: (029) 2049 1803 Fax: (029) 2049 5968
E-mail: paul.sainsbury@virgin.net
Website: www.cardiffcity.net/hotelguesthouses/beeches
🛏 10 🍴 2 Open: 1-12; 1 Star Hotel

THE BIG SLEEP HOTEL Bute Terrace, Cardiff CF10 2FE
Tel: (029) 2063 6363 Fax: (029) 2063 6364
E-mail: bookings.cardiff@thebigsleephotel.com
Website: www.thebigsleephotel.com 🛏 81 🍴 81
Open: 1-12; 2 Star Hotel

CARDIFF UNIVERSITY Southgate House, Bevan Place,
PO Box 533, Cardiff CF14 3XZ Tel: (029) 2087 5508
Fax: (029) 2087 4990 E-mail: groups@cardiff.ac.uk
Website: www.cf.ac.uk 🛏 2500 🍴 2000 Open 18 June/15
Sept 2001; 2-4 Star Campus

EGERTON GREY COUNTRY HOUSE HOTEL Porthkerry, Barry
CF62 3BZ Tel: (01446) 711666 Fax: (01446) 711690
E-mail: info@egertongrey.co.uk
Website: www.egertongrey.co.uk 🛏 10 🍴 10 Open: 1-12;
3 Star

FARTHINGS Lisvane Rd, Lisvane, Cardiff CF14 0SG
Tel: (029) 2075 6404 Fax: (029) 2075 6404 🛏 3
Open: 1-12; 3 Star B&B

THE GREENDOWN INN HOTEL Drope Rd, St Georges-Super-
Ely, nr Cardiff CF5 6EP Tel: (01446) 760310
Fax: (01446) 760937 E-mail: greendownhotel.co.uk
Website: www.greendownhotel.com 🛏 15 Open: 1-12;
3 Star Hotel

HILTON CARDIFF Kingsway, Cardiff CF10 3HH
Tel: (029) 2064 6300 Fax: (029) 2064 6333
E-mail: cwlhitwgm@hilton.com Website: www.hilton.com
🛏 197 🍴 197 Open: 1-12; 5 Star Hotel

PENRHYS HOTEL 127 Cathedral Rd, Cardiff CF11 9UB
Tel: (029) 2023 0548/(029) 2038 7292 Fax: (029) 2066 6344
🛏 18 🍴 18 Open: 1-12; 2 Star Hotel

PLAS-Y-BRYN 93 Fairwater Rd, Llandaff, Cardiff CF5 2LG
Tel: (029) 2056 1717 🛏 3 Open: 1-12; 2 Star B&B

RAMBLER COURT HOTEL 188 Cathedral Rd, Cardiff
CF11 9JE Tel: (029) 2022 1187 Fax: (029) 2022 1187
🛏 9 🍴 4 Open: 1-12; 2 Star Hotel

THE TOWNHOUSE 70 Cathedral Rd, Cardiff CF11 9LL
Tel: (029) 2023 9399 Fax: (029) 2022 3214
E-mail: thetownhouse@msn.com
Website: thetownhousecardiff.co.uk 🛏 9 🍴 9 Open: 1-12;
2 Star Hotel

WESTWINDS 4 Heol-y-Delyn, Lisvane, Cardiff CF14 0SG
Tel: (029) 2068 9228 🛏 2 Open: 1-12; 2 Star

WYNFORD HOTEL Clare St, Cardiff CF11 6BD
Tel: (029) 2037 1983 Fax: (029) 2034 0477 Open: 1-12;
2 Star Hotel

PENMARK
Map Ref: Le6

THE OLD BARN BED & BREAKFAST The Croft, Penmark, nr
Cardiff CF62 3BP Tel: (01446) 711352 Fax: (01446) 711352
E-mail: enquiries@theoldbarnbedandbreakfast.co.uk
Website: www.theoldbarnbedandbreakfast.co.uk 🛏 2 🍴 2
Open: 1-12; 3 Star B&B

PORTHCAWL
Map Ref: Lc5

EDMON HOUSE 33 Esplanade Ave, Porthcawl CF36 3YS
Tel: (01656) 788102 Fax: (01656) 783682
E-mail: edmonhouse@edmonhouse.force9.co.uk
Website: bridgend.gov.uk ⊨3 ⇥3 Open: 1-12; 3 Star
Guest House

ROCKBANK BED & BREAKFAST 15 Debreds Drive,
Porthcawl CF36 3JP Tel: (01656) 785823
Fax: (01656) 785823 E-mail: Jeanlewis@beeb.net
Website: www.jeanlewis.members.beeb.net ⊨2 ⇥2
Open: 1-12; 3 Star B&B

ROSSETT GUEST HOUSE 1 Esplanade Avenue, Porthcawl
CF36 3YS Tel: (01656) 771664 Fax: (01656) 771664
E-mail: rossettgh@netscapeonline.co.uk ⊨3 ⇥2
Open: 1-12; 2 Star Guest House

Holiday Cottages

BRIDGEND
Map Ref: Ld5

TY MAEN FARM Llangynwyd, Maesteg, nr Bridgend
CF34 0EH Tel: (01656) 733505 UNITS: 1; SLEEPS: 6;
Open: 1-12; 4 Star

CARDIFF
Map Ref: Mb5

CARDIFF UNIVERSITY Southgate House, Bevan Place,
PO Box 533, Cardiff CF14 3XZ Tel: (029) 2087 5508
Fax: (029) 2087 4990 E-mail: groups@cardiff.ac.uk
Website: www.cf.ac.uk UNITS: 300; SLEEPS: 4-8;
Open: 18 June to 15 Sept 2001; 2-4 Star Campus

PENTWYN COTTAGE (THE ANNEX) St Mellons Rd, Lisvane,
Cardiff CF14 0SH Tel: (029) 2075 8393
Mobile: 07989 637582 UNITS: 1; Sleeps 2

COWBRIDGE
Map Ref: Le6

TREGUFF FARM COTTAGES Treguff Farm nr Cowbridge
CF71 7LT Tel: (01446) 751342/(01446) 860350 UNITS: 5;
SLEEPS: 2-8; Open: 1-12

PORTHCAWL
Map Ref: Lc5

TY TANGLWYST FARM HOLIDAY COTTAGES Ty Tanglwyst
Farm, Pyle, Bridgend CF33 4SA Tel: (01656) 745635/740224
Fax: (01656) 745635
E-mail: tytanglwystholidaycottages@hotmail.com
UNITS: 2; SLEEPS: 4-5; Open: 1-12; 4 Star

Millennium Stadium, Cardiff

WYE VALLEY & VALE OF USK
AREA 12

Hotels, Guest Houses & Farmhouses

ABERGAVENNY
Map Ref: Mc1

KINGS HEAD HOTEL 59 Cross St, Abergavenny NP7 5EU
Tel: (01873) 853575 Fax: (01873) 853575 ⊨5 ⇥4
Open: 1-12; 2 Star Inn

ROCK & FOUNTAIN HOTEL Clydach North, nr Abergavenny
NP7 0LL Tel: (01873) 830393 Fax: (01873) 830393
E-mail: archer@rockandfountain.fsnet.co.uk
Website: www.rockandfountain.fsnet.co.uk
⊨6 Open: 1-12; 3 Star Inn

LLANSANTFFRAED COURT HOTEL Llanvihangel Gobion,
nr Abergavenny NP7 9BA Tel: (01873) 840678
Fax: (01873) 840674 E-mail: reception@llch.co.uk
Website: www.llch.co.uk ⊨21 ⇥21 Open: 1-12;
3 Star Country Hotel

PENTRE COURT Llanwenarth Citra, Abergavenny NP7 7EW
Tel: (01873) 853545 E-mail: judith@pentrecourt.com
Website: www.pentrecourt.com ⊨3 ⇥4 Open: 1-12;
2 Star B&B

PENTRE HOUSE Brecon Rd, Abergavenny NP7 7EW
Tel: (01873) 853435 Fax: (01873) 851321 ⊨3 Open: 1-12
3 Star B&B

YEW TREE FARM Llanellen, nr Abergavenny NP7 9LB
Tel: (01873) 854307 Fax: (01873) 854307
E-mail: groseandeollanellen@ukonline.co.uk ⊨1 ⇥1
Open: 4-10; 2 Star Farm

CHEPSTOW
Map Ref: Mc4

BRIDGE HOUSE Pwllmeyric, Chepstow NP16 6LF
Tel: (01291) 622567 ⊨2 Open: 1-12; 2 Star B&B

CASTLE VIEW Hotel 16 Bridge St, Chepstow
Tel: (01291) 620349 Fax: (01291) 627397
E-mail: info@hotelschepstow.co.uk
Website: hotelschepstow.co.uk
⊨13 ⇥13 Open: 1-12; 2 Star Hotel

MAGOR
Map Ref: Md4

COMFORT INN Junc 23A, M4 Motorway, Magor NP26 3Y
Tel: (01633) 881515 Fax: (01633) 881896 ⊨43 ⇥43
Open: 1-12; 2 Star Lodge

MONMOUTH
Map Ref: Me1

CASITA ALTA 15 Toynbee Close, Osbaston, Monmouth
NP25 3NU Tel: (01600) 713023 ⊨2 ⇥1 Open: 1-12 (not
Christmas); 2 Star B&B

CHURCH FARM GUEST HOUSE Mitchel Troy, Monmouth
NP25 4HZ Tel: (01600) 712176 ⊨8 ⇥6 Open: 1-12;
2 Star Guest House

THE RIVERSIDE HOTEL Cinderhill St, Monmouth NP25 5EY
Tel: (01600) 715577 Fax: (01600) 712668 ⊨17 ⇥17
Open: 1-12; 2 Star Hotel

NEWPORT
Map Ref: Mc4

CHAPEL GUEST HOUSE Church Rd, St Brides Wentloog, nr Newport NP10 8SN Tel: (01633) 681018 Fax: (01633) 681431 E-mail:chapelguesthouse@hotmail.com
3 3 Open: 1-12; 3 Star Guest House

ELM TREE HOUSE St Brides Wentloog, Newport NP10 8SQ Tel: (01633) 680384 4 Open: 1-12; 2 Star B&B

THE INN AT THE ELM TREE St Brides Wentloog, Newport NP10 8SQ Tel: (01633) 680225 Fax: (01633) 681035 E-mail: inn@the-elm-tree.co.uk Website: www.the-elm-tree.co.uk 10 10 Open: 1-12; 5 Star Inn

KNOLL GUEST HOUSE 145 Stow Hill, Newport NP20 4FZ Tel: (01633) 263557 Fax: (01633) 212168 Website: www.knollguesthouse@activebooking.com
10 8 Open: 1-12; 3 Star Guest House

RAGLAN
Map Ref: Md2

BROOKLANDS FARM Chepstow Rd, Raglan NP15 2EN Tel: (01291) 690782 Fax: (01291) 690782 E-mail: brooklands-farm@raglanf.sbusiness.co.uk
4 1 Open: 1-12; 2 Star Farm

TINTERN
Map Ref: Me3

PARVA FARMHOUSE HOTEL & RESTAURANT Tintern NP16 6SQ Tel: (01291) 689411 Fax: (01291) 689411 Website: www.hoteltintern.co.uk 9 9 Open: 1-12; 2 Star Hotel

Holiday Cottages

ABERGAVENNY
Map Ref: Mc1

SUGAR LOAF COTTAGES Dummar Farm, Pentre Lane, Abergavenny NP7 7LA Tel: (01873) 858675 Fax: (01873) 858675 E-mail: rmhofayz@aol.com UNITS: 5; SLEEPS: 2-5; Open: 3-12

CHEPSTOW
Map Ref: Mc4

THE STUDIO AT THE OLD RECTORY The Old Rectory, Shirenewton, Chepstow NP16 6RQ Tel: (01291) 641503 Fax: 0870 056 8358 E-mail: patricia@milling.demon.co.uk Website: www.cottageguide.co.uk/shirenewton UNITS: 1; SLEEPS: 2; Open: 1-12

MONMOUTH
Map Ref: Me1

STEPPES FARM COTTAGE Rockfield, Monmouth NP25 5SW Tel: (01600) 716273 Fax: (01600) 715257 Website: www.steppesfarmcottages.co.uk UNITS: 6; SLEEPS: 4-6; Open: 1-12

RAGLAN
Map Ref: Md2

BERLLANDERI COACH HOUSE Usk Rd, Raglan NP15 2HR Tel: (01291) 690268 Fax: (01291) 690268 E-mail: coachhouse@berllanderi.freeserve.co.uk Website: www.villarama.com/1495.html UNITS: 1; SLEEPS: 8; Open: 1-12; 5 Star

TINTERN
Map Ref: Me3

CRAIGO BARN Craigo Farm, Botany Bay, Tintern, Chepstow NP16 6SN Tel: (01291) 689757 Fax: (01291) 689365 E-mail: sheron@hassell.com Website: www.tintern.org.uk UNITS: 1; SLEEPS 6; Open: 1-12; 4 Star

THE OLD RECTORY Tintern, nr Chepstow NP16 6SG Tel: (01291) 689519 Fax: (01291) 689939 E-mail: old.rectory@vizzavi.co.uk Website: www.tinternoldrectory.co.uk UNITS: 1; SLEEPS: 3+child/baby; Open: 1-12; 3 Star

TRELLECH
Map Ref: Me2

THE CROFT Trellech, Monmouth NP25 4PA Tel: (01600) 860681/207 UNITS: 1; SLEEPS: 6-7; Open: 1-12; 5 Star

SELF-CATERING AGENCIES

BRECON BEACONS HOLIDAY COTTAGES Brynmore, Talybont-on-Usk, Brecon LD3 7YS Tel: (01874) 676446 Fax: (01874) 676416 E-mail: enquiries@breconcottages.com Website: www.breconcottages.com UNITS: 230; SLEEPS: 2-50; Open: 1-12; 2-5 Star

COASTAL COTTAGES OF PEMBROKESHIRE 2 Riverside Quay, Haverfordwest SA61 2LJ Tel: (01437) 765765 Fax: (01437) 767604 E-mail: info-desk@coastalcottages.co.uk Website: www.coastalcottages.co.uk UNITS: 586; SLEEPS: 2-15; Open: 1-12

NORTH WALES HOLIDAY COTTAGES 39 Station Rd, Deganwy, Conwy LL31 9DF Tel: 08707 559888 Fax: (01492) 572504 E-mail: norwalhols@virgin.net Website: northwalesholidaycottages.co.uk UNITS: 180; SLEEPS: 2-12; Open:1-12; 2-5 Star;

MENAI HOLIDAY COTTAGES 1 Greenfield Terrace, Hill St, Menai Bridge LL59 5AY Tel: (01248) 717135 Fax: (01248) 717051 E-mail: mhc@menaiholidays.co.uk Website: www.menaiholidays.co.uk UNITS: 100+; SLEEPS: 2-20; Open: 1-12; 2-5 Star

QUALITY COTTAGES Cerbid, Solva, Haverfordwest SA62 6YE Tel: (01348) 837871 Fax: (01348) 837876 Website: www.qualitycottges.co.uk UNITS: 160; SLEEPS: 2-14; Open: 1-12; 4/5 Star

Events 2001

Brecon Jazz

*T*here's a lot happening in Wales throughout the year. We start by listing the main events, followed by a selection of the many festivals, shows and local activities taking place. For more details on events call into a Tourist Information Centre when you arrive or look at our website:

www.visitwales.com

Royal Welsh Show

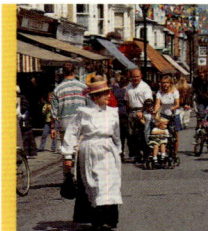

Or send for our free quarterly events leaflet by writing to: Wales Tourist Board (Events Leaflet), PO Box 1, Cardiff CF24 2XN.

Llandrindod Wells Victorian Festival

Where to Stay
Wales

Major Events

All Year
Festival of the Countryside
The UK's largest green tourism festival brings together around 2,000 events and attractions throughout Wales – bird and badger watching, guided walks, canal cruises, craft workshops, farm visits, woodworking courses. Considered by David Bellamy to be one of the best in the world. Free Festival magazine.
Tel (01686) 625384

25 May-3 June
Hay Festival of Literature
Hay-on-Wye, the borderland 'town of books', provides the ideal setting for this literary festival with an international reputation. Attracts leading writers, poets and celebrities. Literature in all its forms, from classical to comedy – and music too.
Tel (01497) 821217

28 May-2 June
Urdd National Eisteddfod
Europe's largest youth arts festival which attracts over 14,000 competitors and more than 100,000 visitors. Enjoy the competitions, entertainment and atmosphere on the lively festival field. Translation facilities available. Like the National Eisteddfod, this event changes location each year. In 2001 it will be held at Cardiff.
Tel (01970) 613110

2-8 July
Llangollen International Musical Eisteddfod
A colourful, cosmopolitan gathering of singers and dancers from all over the world perform in the beautiful little town of Llangollen. A unique festival first held in 1947 to help heal the wounds of war by bringing the peoples of the world together.
Tel (01978) 862000

23-26 July
Royal Welsh Show
Four days of fascination and entertainment at a show that attracts a wide audience to Builth Wells, not just from the farming community but from all walks of life. The biggest crowd-puller of all the major agricultural events in Britain, held in the heart of the country. Covers all aspects of agriculture – and a lot more besides.
Tel (01982) 553683

4-11 August
National Eisteddfod of Wales
Wales's most important cultural gathering, dating back to 1176, and held at a different venue each year. A festival dedicated to Welsh, Britain's oldest living language, with competitions, choirs, concerts, stands and exhibitions. Translation facilities available. This year's event will be held at Denbigh.
Tel (029) 2076 3777

Network Q Rally

10-13 August
Brecon Jazz
The streets of Brecon come alive with the sounds of summer jazz. A great international festival with a wonderful atmosphere which attracts the top names from the world of jazz. 'The most enjoyable of all Britain's festivals,' according to *The Times*.
Tel (01874) 625557

18-26 August
Llandrindod Wells Victorian Festival
The Mid Wales spa town of Llandrindod Wells celebrates its Victorian past. The festival includes street theatre, walks, talks, drama, exhibitions and music – all with a Victorian flavour.
Tel (01597) 823441

Late November
Network Q Rally of Great Britain
Britain's most popular international motorsports event is again based in the Welsh forests, with Cardiff acting as host for the start and finish celebrations. Watch the world's best rally drivers battling it out on classic special stages.

And a Date for Your Diary …

October 2002
International Festival of Musical Theatre, Cardiff
The first event of its kind in the world. A major three-week festival with a wide programme of events.

Llangollen International Musical Eisteddfod

Events for Everyone

1 January

Oakwood New Year's Day Swim, Saundersfoot

5-7 January

Saturnalia, Llanwrtyd Wells

12 January-25 February

Seth Praper Sculptural Ceramics Exhibition, Llantrisant

13 January-31 March

Churchill Exhibition, Wrexham

17 January-4 March

Stretching the Boundaries Embroidered Textiles Exhibition, Llantrisant

3 February

Wales v England – Six Nations Rugby International, Cardiff

10 February

Abergynolwyn Eisteddfod

10 February-2 March

The Marriage of Figaro, Welsh National Opera, Cardiff

19-28 February

La Traviata, Welsh National Opera, Cardiff

24-25 February

Celtic Festival, Trehafod

24 February-4 March

Mumbles St David's Festival

24 February-18 May

Vanities & Virtues – Printmaking in Stuart Britain, National Museum & Gallery, Cardiff

28 February-8 April

Christine Gittins Pottery Exhibition, Llantrisant

1 March

St David's Day Concert, Trecynon

St David's Evening, Trehafod

1-3 March

Beatrice & Benedict, Welsh National Opera, Cardiff

3 March

Festival of Male Voice Praise Rally, Swansea

Wales v Ireland – Six Nations Rugby International, Cardiff

6 March-3 April

Extract (art exhibition), Llantrisant

10 March

Cynon Valley Eisteddfod, Trecynon

10-12 March

Folk & Ale Weekend, Llanwrtyd Wells

26 March

Conwy Seed Fair

31 March

Rhondda Cynon Taff Eisteddfod, Trecynon

16-20 April

Hand-spinning Demonstration, Trefriw

27-28 April

Pembrokeshire Area Final of One-Act Plays, Milford Haven

4-5 May

Celtic Challenge, Aberystwyth

4-7 May

Eisteddfodau Teulu James Pontyfedwen, Pontrhydfendigaid

7-12 May

Llandrindod Wells Drama Festival

10-12 May

Clwyd Area Final of One-Act Plays, Flint

10-13 May

Llantilio Crossenny Festival of Music & Drama

13 May

Rowen Village Gardens Open Day, nr Conwy

18-20 May

Golf – Welsh Open Mid Amateur Championship, Whitchurch

19-26 May

Pontrhydfendigaid Drama Festival

19-30 May

Katya Kabanova, Welsh National Opera, Cardiff

26 May-2 June

St Davids Cathedral Festival

27-28 May

Prestatyn Flower Show & Classic Car Show

29 May-8 June

Tosca, Welsh National Opera, Cardiff

31 May

Rupert Bear Fun Day, Stepaside

2 June

Man v Horse Marathon, Llanwrtyd Wells

2-3 June

Golf – Welsh Open Youths' Championship, Wrexham

7-9 June

The Magic Flute, Welsh National Opera, Cardiff

8-9 June

Wales One-Act Plays Final, Newtown

9-10 June

Smallholder Weekend, Builth Wells

10 June

Golf – Welsh Boys' Stroke Play Championship, Borth

11 June

1930s Reunion of Gold Miners, Llanwrda

12-14 June

Golf – Welsh Seniors' Championship, Aberdyfi

17 & 24 June

Festival of Brass, Rhyl

22-24 June

Golf – Welsh Open Stroke Play Championship, Llandudno

23-24 June

Annual Country Fair, Bodelwyddan

29 June-2 July

Roman Activity Weekend, Llanwrda

30 June-1 July

Adventure Unlimited (weekend of outdoor activity), Builth Wells

30 June-5 July

Barmouth to Fort William Three Peaks Yacht Race, Barmouth

1 July

Royal National Lifeboat Institution Open Day, Tenby

6-8 July

Morris in the Forest, Llanwrtyd Wells

7-8 July

Line Dancing Extravaganza, Rhyl

8-15 July

Summer Celebration in the Park 2001, Brynmenyn, Bridgend

11 July-22 August

American Wrestling, Rhyl

14 July
Pontypridd Carnival

15 July
Country & Western Music Festival, Welshpool

16 July-30 September
Mini Siwr Farm (a look at silkworms), Trefriw

21-22 July
Prestatyn Carnival & Classic Car Show

Young Archaeologists' Weekend, Llanwrda

21-28 July
Fishguard International Music Festival

22 July
Watercolour Painting in the Country Park, Wrexham

23 July-5 August
Cardiff International Festival

25-27 July
Golf – Welsh Boys' Championship, St Mellons

27 July
Celtic Music Evening, Stepaside

27-29 July
The Big Cheese, Caerphilly

28 July
South Wales Shire Horse Show, Abergavenny

31 July-4 August
Golf – Welsh Amateur Championship, Porthcawl

2-5 August
Four Day Mountain Bike Festival, Llanwrtyd Wells

4 August
Talybont & Llanbedr Gala, Talybont

4-5 August
St Asaph Gala Day

4-11 August
Conwy River Festival

5 August
Tenby Summer Spectacular

8 August
St Mellons Agricultural Show, Newport

9-10 August
United Counties Show, Carmarthen

9-12 August
Golf – Welsh Open 2001, Celtic Manor Resort, Newport

11 August
Vintage Machinery Day, Llanwrda

12 August
Chepstow Agricultural Show

12-14 August
Cardigan Bay Regatta, New Quay

14-15 August
Anglesey County Show, Holyhead

14-16 August
Pembrokeshire County Show, Haverfordwest

15 August
Farm Open Day, Llanwrda

16 August
Denbighshire & Flintshire Agricultural Show, Denbigh

18 August
Race the Train, Tywyn

19 August
Tenby Summer Spectacular

22 August
Vale of Glamorgan Agricultural Show, Barry

23 August
Peter Rabbit Fun Day, Stepaside

24-29 August
Presteigne Festival of Music & the Arts

25 August
Prengwyn Sheepdog Trials, nr Llandysul

26-27 August
Line Dancing Festival, Rhyl

27 August
World Bog Snorkelling Championships, Llanwrtyd Wells

29 August
Llangeitho Young Farmers' Agriculture & Horticulture Show

30 August
Monmouthshire Show, Monmouth

1 September
Llandysul Show

2 September
Abergavenny & District Horticultural Show, Abergavenny

8 September
Usk Show

13 September
Conwy Honey Fair

15-16 September
National Heritage Day, Llanwrda

23-29 September
North Wales Music Festival, St Asaph

1-31 October
Tydfil Arts Festival, Merthyr Tydfil

5-20 October
Exhibition by the Carmarthen Embroiders' Guild, Carmarthen

11-13 October
15th Llangollen International Jazz Festival

12-21 October
Llandudno October Festival

16 October
The Welsh Dairy Show, Carmarthen

25 October-25 November
Swansea Festival for Young Musicians

3-4 November
Trelawnyd Male Voice Choir Annual Concert, Trelawnyd, nr Prestatyn

16-25 November
Mid Wales Beer Festival, Llanwrtyd Wells

1 December
Anglesey Winter Show, Holyhead

GWYLIAU CYMRU/FESTIVALS OF WALES

This is the collective voice for over 60 arts festivals held the length and breadth of Wales, ranging from large-scale national events to smaller community celebrations. For more information, please contact:
Festivals of Wales, PO Box 20, Conwy LL32 8ZQ Tel (01492) 573760

Beaches Guide

EXPLAINING EC STANDARDS

The **EC Mandatory Standard**, which all beaches featured here achieve, is the legally prescribed standard test for water cleanliness. But there's even better news for bathers, for many beaches – in particular those with the Blue Flag and Green Coast Award – will have exceeded this by satisfying the higher **Guideline Standard**, which is 20 times more stringent than Mandatory

*H*ere, we introduce you to some of the best of our many beautiful Welsh beaches. Our choice is based on beaches which have been awarded the coveted European Blue Flag, Green Coast Award or Tidy Britain Group Seaside Award. All beaches featured satisfy EC Standards of water quality, so you can enjoy them safe in the knowledge that the water is as appealing as the surroundings.

European Blue Flag

No less than 22 beaches in Wales were awarded this prestigious flag in 2000. In addition, seven locations have received the Marina Blue Flag. Please see the map and list for details.

The Blue Flag, Europe's highest accolade for beaches, is awarded annually. It is based on a total of 26 criteria covering such items as bathing water quality and safety, beach cleanliness, services, wheelchair access, dog control, first aid and so on. Blue Flag beaches must satisfy EC Guideline water quality standards.

Green Sea Partnership and the Green Coast Award

Green Sea is a unique partnership of over 40 public, private and voluntary organisations. The partnership is committed to working together to improve dramatically the quality of the seas and coasts to ensure that Wales's beaches are amongst the best in Europe. Already, much has been achieved – an increase, for example, in Blue Flag beaches from two in 1995 to 22 in 2000.

Another major achievement of the partnership has been the launch of a new beach award, the **Green Coast Award**. This recognises beaches of the highest environmental quality which are without the level of development and intensive management associated with more urban, traditional seaside beaches (typically, these would be more eligible for the Blue Flag). Award-winning beaches must attain EC Guideline water quality standards and have appropriate management to ensure the protection of the natural environment. Twenty-five beaches received this award in 2000. All are identified on the map.

Seaside Award

Seaside Award beaches fly a distinctive blue and yellow flag representing sea and sand. The award identifies well-managed beaches where you can be assured of excellent standards of cleanliness and safety, together with water quality which complies with current European legislation (at least the EC Mandatory Standard, though many will have the higher Guideline Standard). There are two categories of award beach – **Resort** and **Rural**.

A **Seaside Award Resort** beach has facilities for varied recreational opportunities. Award-winning beaches are usually located near a town with access by public transport, and you can normally expect to find a café or restaurant, toilets and public telephones at the beach. Dogs have restricted access. Each beach fulfils 29 criteria which fall into five groups – cleanliness, information, management, safety and water quality.

A **Seaside Award Rural** beach has limited facilities and is visited for its less developed, more natural characteristics. Because of its nature, the beach would not be expected to have the same level of supervision or facilities as a resort. Dogs may be permitted. The beach fulfils 13 criteria which fall into the same five groups as resort beaches.

Where to Stay
Wales

#	Beach	#	Beach	#	Beach
1	Talacre/Gronant	33	Aberffraw, Traeth Mawr	68	Goodwick Sands
2	Prestatyn Central	34	Newborough, Llanddwyn	69	Aber Eiddi
3	Rhyl	35	Y Felinheli/Port Dinorwic Marina	70	St Davids, Whitesand Bay
4	Kinmel Bay	36	Victoria Dock, Caernarfon	71	St Davids, Caerfai Bay
5	Pensarn/Abergele	37	Aberdaron	72	Newgale
6	Old Colwyn	38	Abersoch	73	Nolton Haven
7	Rhos on Sea	39	Pwllheli, Marian y De	74	Broad Haven
8	Llandudno North Shore	40	Pwllheli Yacht Haven	75	Little Haven
9	Llandudno West Shore	41	Criccieth	76	St Bride's Haven
10	Llanfairfechan	42	Harlech	77	Martin's Haven
11	Beaumaris	43	Llandanwg	78	Marloes Sands
12	Penmon	44	Bennar, Morfa Dyffryn	79	Westdale Bay
13	Llanddona	45	Barmouth	80	Dale
14	St David's, Red Wharf Bay	46	Fairbourne, Ffriog	81	Gelliswick, nr Hakin, Milford Haven
15	Benllech	47	Tywyn	82	Neyland Yacht Harbour
16	Moelfre	48	Aberdyfi	83	West Angle Bay
17	Dulas, Traeth Lligwy	49	Borth	84	Broad Haven, Bosherston
18	Cemaes Bay, Traeth Bach	50	Clarach	85	Barafundle Bay
19	Cemaes Bay, Traeth Mawr	51	Aberystwyth North, Traeth y Gogledd	86	Freshwater East
20	Cemlyn	52	Aberystwyth South, Traeth y De	87	Manorbier
21	Rhydwyn, Porth Swtan, Church Bay	53	Llanrhystud	88	Lydstep
22	Llanfaethlu, Porth Trwyn	54	Aberaeron South	89	Tenby South
23	Llanfwrog, Porth Tywyn-mawr	55	New Quay, Traeth yr Harbwr	90	Tenby Castle
24	Trearddur Bay, Porth Dafarch	56	New Quay, Traeth y Dolau	91	Tenby North
25	Trearddur Bay	57	Cwm Tudu	92	Saundersfoot
26	Rhoscolyn, Borth Wen	58	Llangrannog, Cil Borth	93	Saundersfoot, Coppet Hall
27	Rhoscolyn, Silver Bay	59	Llangrannog	94	Saundersfoot, Wiseman's Bridge
28	Rhosneigr, Traeth Crigyll	60	Penbryn	95	Amroth
29	Rhosneigr, Traeth Llydan, Broad Beach	61	Tre-saith	96	Pembrey Country Park, Cefn Sidan
30	Llanfaelog, Porth Ty'n Tywyn	62	Aberporth	97	Rhossili
31	Llanfaelog, Porth Nobla	63	Mwnt	98	Mewslade Bay, nr Rhossili
32	Llanfaelog, Porth Trecastell	64	Poppit Sands	99	Port Eynon
		65	Newport Sands	100	Tor Bay, nr Penmaen
		66	Cwm-yr-eglwys	101	Three Cliffs Bay
		67	Pwll Gwaelod, Cwm-yr-eglwys	102	Pwll-du, nr Bishopston
				103	Caswell Bay
				104	Langland Bay
				105	Limeslade Bay
				106	Bracelet Bay
				107	Knab Rock Marina, The Mumbles
				108	Swansea Marina
				109	Porthcawl, Rest Bay
				110	Penarth Marina

FURTHER INFORMATION

For the most up-to-date information on Wales's cleanest beaches, please see details of the free Beaches leaflet in the 'Publications from the Wales Tourist Board' section. Or visit our website: www.visitwales.com

KEY

- **European Blue Flag Award beach 2000**
  Water quality must be at least EC Guideline Standard (excellent)

- **Green Coast Award beach 2000**
  Water quality must be at least EC Guideline Standard (excellent)

- **Seaside Award Resort beach 2000**
  Water quality must be at least EC Mandatory Standard (good)

- **Seaside Award Rural beach 2000**
  Water quality must be at least EC Mandatory Standard (good)

DOGS

Dogs are welcomed at almost all beaches in Wales, through restrictions may apply. For further information see our website: www.visitwales.com

All featured beaches were monitored during the 1999 bathing season between May and September and met standards equivalent to those used by the UK Government for compliance with the EC Directive Mandatory (I) standard for water quality. The list was compiled with the assistance of Dŵr Cymru/Welsh Water, the Environment Agency, Hyder Laboratories and all the local authorities around the Welsh coastline.

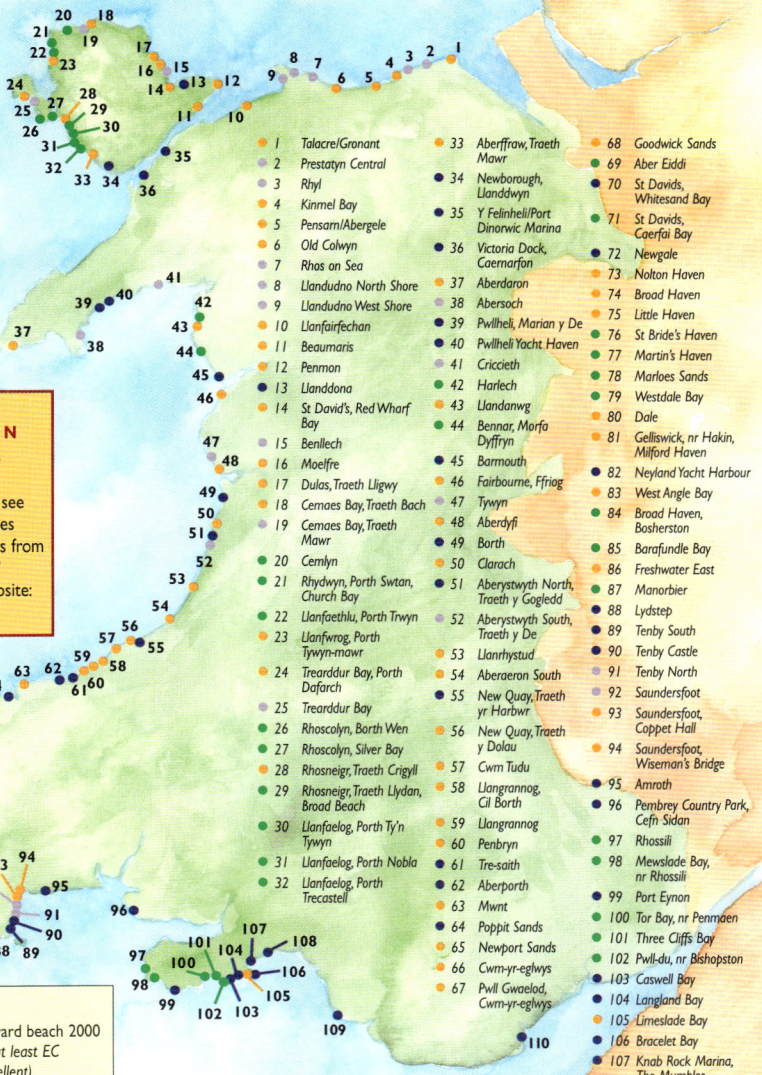

Easy
Going

*O*ne of Wales's big advantages is its ease of access. It's only a few hours by road and rail from most of the UK's main centres. Travel to Wales cuts down on time and cost, so you can enjoy your holiday or short break to the full. And when you arrive, you'll be back in the days when driving was a pleasure on traffic-free highways and byways.

Map of the UK showing road and ferry routes, with major cities and motorways labelled: Inverness, A9, Perth, M90, Glasgow, EDINBURGH, M8, A68, M74, A7, A69, Newcastle, Carlisle, A1(M), M6, A1, A1(M), Leeds, M62, Manchester, M62, Hull, M180, BELFAST, DUBLIN, Dun Laoghaire, Holyhead, Llandudno, Liverpool, Chester, M6, M1, Nottingham, Norwich, A5, A55, A5, A487, A470, Shrewsbury, A5, M54, Birmingham, A11, Rosslare, Aberystwyth, A487, A470, Coventry, Cambridge, M6, M5, M1, M11, Fishguard, Cork, A40, Carmarthen, A470, M50, Ross-on-Wye, M40, Pembroke, M4, A40, Monmouth, M4, M25, Swansea, A470, M48, CARDIFF, M4, Bristol, M3, M25, M20, LONDON, Dover, M5, Southampton, Portsmouth, Folkestone, Exeter, A38, Penzance, Plymouth

MILEAGE CHART

JOURNEY	MILES	JOURNEY TIME BY CAR
Birmingham–Aberystwyth	125	2hrs 50mins
Canterbury–Cardiff	219	4hrs
Coventry–Barmouth	133	2hrs 50mins
Exeter–Swansea	161	2hrs 20mins
Leeds–Llandudno	131	2hrs
London–Cardiff	155	2hrs 40mins
London–Tenby	245	4hrs 10mins
Manchester–Caernarfon	110	2hrs
Nottingham–Swansea	202	3hrs 10mins
Peterborough–Aberystwyth	208	4hrs 30mins
Newcastle-Upon-Tyne–Llandudno	230	4hrs
Reading–Carmarthen	177	2hrs 40mins
York–Welshpool	155	3hrs

BY CAR

Travel to South and West Wales is easy on the M4 and onward dual carriageway systems. With the opening of the Second Severn Crossing, traffic for Cardiff and West Wales follows the revised route of the M4 across the new bridge. For Chepstow and the Wye Valley you'll need the M48 (the old route of the M4) across the original bridge. In North Wales, the A55 coastal 'Expressway' whisks traffic past the old bottlenecks, including Conwy. Mid Wales is easily reached by the M54 which links with the M6/M5/M1.

Driving around Wales is a pleasure, for most highways remain blissfully quiet and uncrowded apart from a few peak summer weekends. Wales is a small yet scenically varied country, so there's no need to rush – take your time and enjoy it to the full.

BY TRAIN

Fast and frequent Great Western InterCity services run between London Paddington and Cardiff (via Reading and Swindon), taking only 2 hours. This hourly service (every half hour at peak times) also runs to Newport, Bridgend, Port Talbot, Neath and Swansea, with onward connections to West Wales. Fast Virgin Trains link London Euston with the North Wales coast, serving both Bangor and Holyhead. Virgin Trains also run a service between the North-East of England and South Wales.

In addition, Wales and West Passenger Trains run Alphaline services direct from London

Waterloo (via Woking and Basingstoke) to Cardiff and other main stations in South and West Wales and the Welsh Marches. There are also convenient and comfortable Alphaline trains direct to Cardiff (some running through to South-West Wales) from:

◆ Manchester/the North-West

◆ Brighton/Portsmouth/ Salisbury/Southampton

◆ The West of England/Bristol

◆ Nottingham/Birmingham/ Gloucester

For Mid Wales there are Alphaline trains to Aberystwyth and other Mid Wales resorts from Birmingham via Shrewsbury. This service connects with Virgin Trains from London Euston at Birmingham New Street Station.

North-West Express train services run direct from Manchester and Birmingham to most resorts on the North Wales coast via Chester.

Exploring Wales by train is a delight. Scenic routes include the beautiful Heart of Wales line from Shrewsbury to Swansea via Llanelli, the Conwy Valley line from Llandudno Junction to Blaenau Ffestiniog and the Cambrian Coaster, which runs along the mountain-backed shoreline from Pwllheli to Machynlleth and Aberystwyth.

Train Information

For enquiries and bookings please telephone **(08457) 484950**, or contact your local travel agent or principal station. Alternatively, you can buy tickets over the internet at **www.thetrainline.com**

BY COACH AND BUS

National Express provides a nationwide network of express coach services, many of which have been upgraded to Rapide specification with on-board washrooms and light refreshments available. Convenient services to Wales operate from London's Victoria Coach Station and from almost all other major towns and cities in England and Scotland.

Towns and resorts throughout Wales are connected by a range of local and regional services. You can travel cross-country by the Traws Cambria service running between Cardiff and Bangor (via Aberystwyth). Details of all bus services in Wales can be obtained from the Passenger Transport Information Cymru helpline on **08706 082608**.

The best way of getting around Snowdonia without a car is on the environmentally friendly Snowdon Sherpa network of buses (including special Park and Ride ▶

services), which operate from June to October (there's also a limited winter service). The network runs into and around the most popular parts of Snowdonia, and also links with main rail and bus services. For details, call into Tourist Information Centres locally or contact Snowdonia National Park, Penrhyndeudraeth LL48 6LF; tel **01766-770274**; website: **www.snowdonia.org.uk**

In South Wales, Beacons Bus operates a similar service in the Brecon Beacons National Park. For details, contact Brecon Tourist Information Centre, tel **01874-622485** (National Park website: **www.breconbeacons.org**). There's also the Puffin Shuttle which operates during summer in the Pembrokeshire Coast National Park – for details, tel **01437-764551, ext 5227**; website: **www.pembrokeshirecoast.org.uk**

Coach Information

Contact your local travel agent or National Express office. For all information and National Express credit/debit card bookings please telephone **(08705) 808080**. For details of your nearest National Express agent please telephone **(08705) 010104** (calls cost a maximum of 8p per minute, less at off-peak times). Website: **www.nationalexpress.co.uk**

NATIONAL TRAVEL HOTLINE
0906 5500 000

One call covers it all. Phone this number for information on all of Britain's train, express coach and rural bus services – and you can also make credit card bookings at the same time. The hotline is open 7am–10pm seven days a week (calls cost £1 per minute).

FLEXI-PASS AND ROVER TRAIN AND BUS TRAVEL

The money-saving **'Freedom of Wales' Flexi-Pass** offers unlimited travel on all mainline rail services in Wales plus most scheduled bus services. For narrow-gauge and steam railway enthusiasts there's the bonus of free travel on the Ffestiniog Railway (Porthmadog) and Rheilffordd Eryri/Welsh Highland Railway (Caernarfon), plus discounts on the Bala Lake, Fairbourne, Gwili, Talyllyn, Vale of Rheidol and Welshpool and Llanfair lines. Eight- and 15-day tickets are available.

Flexi-Pass holders also enjoy reduced admission to properties in Wales under the wing of Cadw-Welsh Historic Monuments, the National Trust and National Museums and Galleries of Wales. Other attractions are joining the scheme for 2001 – please see the website for the latest details.

The **North and Mid Wales Flexi-Rover** and the **Freedom of South Wales Flexi-Rover Tickets** give much the same unlimited travel benefits by train/bus as Flexi-Pass, though on a regional basis. Seven-day tickets are available.

For further Flexi-Pass/Rover details and credit card bookings please contact: **(01766) 512340 or (0870) 9000773**.

Website: **www.travelwales-flexipass.co.uk**

BY AIR

There are direct flights from Amsterdam, Belfast, Brussels, Channel Islands, Dublin, Edinburgh, Glasgow, Isle of Man and Paris to Cardiff International Airport (tel **01446-711111**; website: **www.cial.co.uk**), 12 miles from the city centre. There are many worldwide connections to Cardiff via Amsterdam, Brussels, Dublin and Paris. A rail/air link coach service runs from the airport to Cardiff's central train and bus stations.

Manchester and Birmingham Airports are also convenient gateways for Wales. Car hire is available at Cardiff International, Manchester and Birmingham Airports.

Llanberis Lake Railway

BY SEA

Five services operate across the Irish Sea:

◆ Cork to Swansea

Swansea-Cork Ferries
Tel (01792) 456116
Website: www.swansea-cork.ie

◆ Dublin to Holyhead

Irish Ferries
Tel (08705) 171717
General Enquiries
Tel (08457) 171717
Firm Bookings
Website: www.irishferries.com

◆ Dun Laoghaire/Dublin to Holyhead

Stena Line High-Speed Superferry from Dun Laoghaire or Ferry from Dublin Port direct
Tel (08705) 707070
Website: www.stenaline.co.uk

◆ Rosslare to Fishguard

Stena Line – a choice of two services: Sea Lynx Catamaran and Superferry
Tel (08705) 707070
Website: www.stenaline.co.uk

◆ Rosslare to Pembroke

Irish Ferries
Tel (08705) 171717
General Enquiries
Tel (08457) 171717
Firm Bookings
Website: www.irishferries.com

WALES'S NARROW-GAUGE RAILWAYS

There are nine members of Wales's narrow-gauge 'Great Little Trains':

◆ Bala Lake Railway

◆ Brecon Mountain Railway
(Merthyr Tydfil)

◆ Ffestiniog Railway
(Porthmadog)

◆ Llanberis Lake Railway

◆ Rheilffordd Eryri/Welsh Highland Railway
(Caernarfon)

◆ Talyllyn Railway (Tywyn)

◆ Vale of Rheidol Railway
(Aberystwyth)

◆ Welsh Highland Railway
(Porthmadog)

◆ Welshpool and Llanfair Railway (Llanfair Caereinion)

Details are available from The Great Little Trains of Wales, FREEPOST, The Station, Llanfair Caereinion SY21 0BR. Tel (01938) 810441
Website: www.whr.co.uk/gltw

The railways operating independently of 'Great Little Trains' are:

Fairbourne and Barmouth Steam Railway
Tel (01341) 250362
Website: www.fairbourne-railway.co.uk

Gwili Railway, near Carmarthen
Tel (01267) 230666
Website: www.gwili-railway.co.uk

Llangollen Railway
Tel (01978) 860951
Website: www.langollenrailway.co.uk

Snowdon Mountain Railway, Llanberis
Tel (01286) 870223
Website: www.snowdonrailway.force9.co.uk

Teifi Valley Railway, near Newcastle Emlyn
Tel (01559) 371077
Website: www.teifivr.f9.co.uk

Wales Bus, Rail and Tourist Map and Guide

An essential source of information for those travelling around Wales by public transport. Available free (after Easter 2001) from Wales Tourist Board, PO Box 1, Cardiff CF24 2XN.

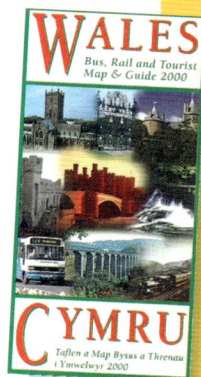

Tourist Information Centres

*M*ake the most of your stay in Wales by contacting one of our Tourist Information Centres for help on all aspects of your holiday. TIC staff will be delighted to assist with:

- *booking your accommodation (see below)*
- *places to visit*
- *places to eat*
- *things to do*
- *routes to take*
- *national and local events*
- *maps, guides and books*

Normal opening times are 10am–5.30pm. These hours may vary to suit local circumstances.

TICs operate a Bed Booking Service which covers their immediate area together with accommodation further afield throughout Wales and the UK.

TICs marked with an asterisk (*) are open seasonally only (April–September).

Accommodating Wheelchair Users

TICs are assessed for access by wheelchair users, based on the following criteria:

Accessible to a wheelchair user travelling independently

Accessible to a wheelchair user travelling with assistance

Accessible to a wheelchair user able to walk a few paces and up a maximum of three steps

Aberaeron
The Quay, SA46 0BT
Tel (01545) 570602
Fax (01970) 626566
E-mail: aberaerontic@ceredigion.gov.uk

Aberdyfi/Aberdovey*
The Wharf Gardens, LL35 0ED
Tel and Fax (01654) 767321

Abergavenny
Swan Meadow, Monmouth Road, NP7 5HH
Tel (01873) 857588
Fax (01873) 850217
E-mail: abergavenny-tic@tsww.com

Aberystwyth
Terrace Road, SY23 2AG
Tel (01970) 612125
Fax (01970) 626566
E-mail: aberystwythtic@ceredigion.gov.uk

Bala*
Penllyn, Pensarn Road, LL23 7SR
Tel and Fax (01678) 521021
E-mail: bala.tic@gwynedd.gov.uk

Bangor*
Town Hall, Deiniol Road, LL57 2RE
Tel (01248) 352786
E-mail: bangor.tic@gwynedd.gov.uk

Barmouth*
The Old Library, Station Road, LL42 1LU
Tel and Fax (01341) 280787
E-mail: barmouth.tic@gwynedd.gov.uk

Barry Island*
The Promenade, The Triangle, CF62 5TQ
Tel (01446) 747171
E-mail: tourism@valeofglamorgan.gov.uk

Beddgelert*
Canolfan Hebog, LL55 4YE
Tel and Fax (01766) 890615
E-mail: ticbeddgelert@hotmail.com

Betws-y-Coed
Royal Oak Stables, LL24 0AH
Tel (01690) 710426
Fax (01690) 710665

Blaenau Ffestiniog
Unit 3, High Street, LL41 3HS
Tel and Fax (01766) 830360

Blaenavon*
Blaenavon Ironworks, Stack Square, NP4 8SJ
Tel (01495) 792615
Fax (01495) 791388
E-mail: blaenavon-tic@tsww.com

Borth* &

Cambrian Terrace, SY24 5HU
Tel (01970) 871174
Fax (01970) 626566
E-mail: borthtic@ceredigion.gov.uk

Brecon &

Cattle Market Car Park,
LD3 9DA
Tel (01874) 622485
Fax (01874) 625256
E-mail: brectic@powys.gov.uk

Bridgend &

McArthur Glen Design Outlet
(Wales), The Derwen, CF32 9SU
Tel (01656) 654906
Fax (01656) 646523
E-mail: bridgend-tic@tsww.com

Builth Wells* &

The Groe Car Park, LD2 3BT
Tel (01982) 553307
Fax (01982) 553841
E-mail: builtic@powys.gov.uk

Caerleon &

5 High Street, NP6 1AE
Tel and Fax (01633) 422656
E-mail: caerleon-tic@tsww.com

Caernarfon &

Oriel Pendeitsh, Castle Street,
LL55 1ES
Tel (01286) 672232
Fax (01286) 678209
E-mail:
caernarfon.tic@gwynedd.gov.uk

Caerphilly &

Lower Twyn Square, CF83 1JL
Tel (029) 2088 0011
Fax (029) 2086 0811
E-mail: tic@caerphilly.gov.uk

Cardiff &

Cardiff Visitor Centre, 16 Wood
Street, CF10 1ES
Tel (029) 2022 7281
Fax (029) 2023 9162
E-mail: enquiries@cardifftic.co.uk

Cardigan &

Theatr Mwldan, Bath House
Road, SA43 2JY
Tel (01239) 613230
Fax (01970) 626566
E-mail:
cardigantic@ceredigion.gov.uk

Carmarthen &

113 Lammas Street, SA31 3AQ
Tel (01267) 231557
Fax (01267) 221901
E-mail: carmarthentic
@carmarthenshire.gov.uk

Chepstow &

Castle Car Park, Bridge Street,
NP16 5EY
Tel (01291) 623772
Fax (01291) 628004
E-mail: chepstow-tic@tsww.com

Colwyn Bay &

Imperial Buildings, Station Square,
LL29 8LF
Tel (01492) 530478
Fax (01492) 534789
E-mail: colwynbay.tic@virgin.net

Conwy &

Conwy Castle Visitor Centre,
LL32 8LD
Tel (01492) 592248
Fax (01492) 573545
E-mail: conwy.tic@virgin.net

Corris* &

Corris Craft Centre, SY20 9SP
Tel and Fax (01654) 761244
E-mail:
corris.tic@gwynedd.gov.uk

Crickhowell* &

Beaufort Chambers, Beaufort
Street, NP8 1AA
Tel (01873) 812105
E-mail: cricktic@powys.gov.uk

Dolgellau &

Ty Meirion, Eldon Square,
LL40 1PU
Tel (01341) 422888
Fax (01341) 422576
E-mail: ticdolgellau@hotmail.com

Fishguard Town &

Town Hall, The Square,
SA65 9HA
Tel (01348) 873484
Fax (01348) 875246

Harlech* &

Gwyddfor House, High Street,
LL46 2YA
Tel and Fax (01766) 780658

Haverfordwest &

Old Bridge, SA61 2EZ
Tel (01437) 763110
Fax (01437) 767738
E-mail:
haverfordwestinformationcentre
@pembrok

Holyhead &

Penrhos Beach Road, LL65 2QB
Tel (01407) 762622
Fax (01407) 761462
E-mail: holyhead.tic@virgin.net

Kilgetty* &

Kingsmoor Common,
SA68 0YA
Tel and Fax (01834) 814161
E-mail: kilgettytic@altavista.net

Knighton &

Offa's Dyke Centre, West Street,
LD7 1EN
Tel (01547) 529424
E-mail:
oda@offasdyke.demon.co.uk

Lake Vyrnwy* &
Unit 2, Vyrnwy Craft
Workshops, SY10 0LY
Tel and Fax (01691) 870346
E-mail: lvtic@powys.gov.uk

Llanberis* &
41b High Street, LL55 4EU
Tel (01286) 870765
Fax (01286) 872141
E-mail:
llanberis.tic@gwynedd.gov.uk

Llandeilo* &
Car Park, Crescent Road,
SA19 6HN
Tel and Fax (01558) 824226
E-mail: carmarthentic
@carmarthenshire.gov.uk

Llandovery &
Heritage Centre, King's Road,
SA20 0AW
Tel and Fax (01550) 720693

Llandrindod Wells &
Old Town Hall, Memorial
Gardens, LD1 5DL
Tel (01597) 822600
Fax (01597) 825905
E-mail: llantic@mail.powys.gov.uk

Llandudno &
1–2 Chapel Street, LL30 2YU
Tel (01492) 876413
Fax (01492) 872722
E-mail: llandudno.tic@virgin.net

Llanelli* &
Public Library, Vaughan Street,
SA15 3AS
Tel (01554) 772020
Fax (01554) 750125

Llanfairpwllgwyngyll &
Station Site, LL61 5UJ
Tel (01248) 713177
Fax (01248) 715711
E-mail: llanfairpwll.tic@virgin.net

Llangollen &
Town Hall, Castle Street,
LL20 5PD
Tel (01978) 860828
Fax (01978) 861563
E-mail: llangollen.tic@virgin.net

Llanidloes &
54 Longbridge Street, SY18 6EF
Tel (01686) 412605
Fax (01686) 413884
E-mail: llantic@powys.gov.uk

Llanwrtyd Wells &
Tŷ Barcud, The Square,
LD5 4RB
Tel and Fax (01591) 610666
E-mail: tic@celt.ruralwales.org

Machynlleth &
Canolfan Owain Glyndŵr,
SY20 8EE
Tel (01654) 702401
Fax (01654) 703675
E-mail: machtic@powys.gov.uk

Magor &
First Services and Lodge,
Jct 23a/M4, NP6 3YL
Tel (01633) 881122
Fax (01633) 881985
E-mail: magor-tic@tsww.com

Merthyr Tydfil &
14a Glebeland Street,
CF47 8AU
Tel (01685) 379884
Fax (01685) 350043
E-mail: merthyr-tic@tsww.com

Milford Haven* &
94 Charles Street, SA73 2HL
Tel (01646) 690866
Fax (01646) 690655

Mold &
Library, Museum and Art Gallery,
CH7 1AP
Tel (01352) 759331
Fax (01352) 754655
E-mail: mold.tic@virgin.net

Monmouth &
Shire Hall, Agincourt Square,
NP5 3DY
Tel (01600) 713899
Fax (01600) 772794
E-mail:
monmouth-tic@tsww.com

Mumbles* ♪
The Portacabin, Oystermouth
Square, SA3 4DQ
Tel (01792) 361302
Fax (01792) 363392

New Quay* &
Church Street, SA45 9NZ
Tel (01545) 560865
Fax (01970) 626566
E-mail:
newquaytic@ceredigion.gov.uk

Newcastle Emlyn* &
Market Hall, SA38 9AE
Tel and Fax (01239) 711333
E-mail: carmarthentic
@carmarthenshire.gov.uk

Newport &
Museum and Art Gallery, John
Frost Square, NP9 1HZ
Tel (01633) 842962
Fax (01633) 222615
E-mail: newport-tic@tsww.com

Newport
(Pembrokeshire)* ♪
2 Bank Cottages, Long Street,
SA42 0TN
Tel and Fax (01239) 820912

Newtown &
The Park, Back Lane, SY16 2PW
Tel (01686) 625580
Fax (01686) 610065
E-mail: newtic@powys.gov.uk

Where to Stay
Wales

Pembroke* &
Visitor Centre, Commons Road,
SA71 4EA
Tel (01646) 622388
Fax (01646) 621396

Pembroke Dock* &
The Guntower, Front Street,
SA72 6JZ
Tel and Fax (01646) 622246

Penarth* ⚐
Penarth Pier, The Esplanade,
CF64 3AU
Tel (029) 2070 8849
E-mail:
tourism@valeofglamorgan.gov.uk

Pont Abraham &
Pont Abraham Services,
Junction 49/M4, SA4 1FP
Tel and Fax (01792) 883838

Pontneddfechan &
Near Glyn Neath, SA11 5NR
Tel (01639) 721795
Fax (01639) 722061
E-mail: pontneddfechan-tic@
tsww.com

Pontypridd &
Historical Centre, The Old
Bridge, CF37 3PE
Tel (01443) 490748
Fax (01443) 490749

Porthcawl* &
Old Police Station, John Street,
CF36 3DT
Tel (01656) 786639
Fax (01656) 782387
E-mail:
porthcawltic@bridgend.gov.uk

Porthmadog &
High Street, LL49 9LD
Tel (01766) 512981
Fax (01766) 515312
E-mail:
porthmadog.tic@gwynedd.gov.uk

Prestatyn* &
Offa's Dyke Centre, Central
Beach, LL19 7EY
Tel (01745) 889092

Presteigne* &
The Judge's Lodgings, Broad
Street, LD8 2AD
Tel (01544) 260650
Fax (01544) 260652

Pwllheli &
Min y Don, Station Square,
LL53 5HG
Tel and Fax (01758) 613000
E-mail:
pwllheli.tic@gwynedd.gov.uk

Rhayader &
The Leisure Centre, North
Street, LD6 5BU
Tel (01597) 810591
E-mail: rhayader.tic@powys.gov.uk

Rhos on Sea* &
The Promenade, LL28 4EP
Tel and Fax (01492) 548778

Rhyl &
Rhyl Children's Village, West
Parade, LL18 1HZ
Tel (01745) 355068
Fax (01745) 342255

Ruthin &
Ruthin Craft Centre, Park Road,
LL15 1BB
Tel (01824) 703992

St Davids &
National Park Visitor Centre,
The Grove, SA62 6NW
Tel and Fax (01437) 720392
E-mail: enquiries@
stdavids.pembrokeshirecoast.org.uk

Saundersfoot* &
The Barbecue, Harbour Car
Park, SA69 9HE
Tel (01834) 813672
Fax (01834) 813673

Swansea &
Plymouth Street, SA1 3QG
Tel (01792) 468321
Fax (01792) 464602
E-mail: swantrsm@cableol.co.uk

Tenby &
The Croft, SA70 8AP
Tel (01834) 842402
Fax (01834) 845439

Tywyn* &
High Street, LL36 9AD
Tel and Fax (01654) 710070
E-mail: tywyn.tic@gwynedd.gov.uk

Welshpool &
Vicarage Garden, Church Street,
SY21 7DD
Tel (01938) 552043
Fax (01938) 554038
E-mail: weltic@powys.gov.uk

Wrexham &
Lambpit Street, LL11 1WN
Tel (01978) 292015
Fax (01978) 292467
E-mail: tic@wrexham.gov.uk

And at Oswestry on the Wales/England border

Oswestry Mile End &
Mile End Services, SY11 4JA
Tel (01691) 662488
Fax (01691) 662883
E-mail:
oswestry.tourism@btconnect.com

Oswestry Town ⚐
The Heritage Centre, 2 Church
Terrace, SY11 2TE
Tel (01691) 662753
Fax (01691) 657811
E-mail:
owbta@micro-plus-web.net

Wales in London's West End

If you're in London and want
information on Wales please call
in at the Wales Desk, Britain
Visitor Centre, 1 Regent Street,
SW1Y 4XT. Tel (020) 7808 3838.

Ferry travellers

There are Information Kiosks at
the Fishguard and Pembroke
Dock ferry terminals. Postal and
general enquiries should be
directed to the main Tourist
Information Centres situated in
these towns.

Further Information

*T*he following organisations and authorities will be pleased to provide any further information you require when planning your holiday to Wales.

Wales's 12 Holiday Areas (see map on pages 2/3)

The Isle of Anglesey
Marketing Section
Economic Development
Isle of Anglesey County Council
Llangefni LL77 7TW
Tel (01248) 752411
Fax (01248) 752192
E-mail: tourism@anglesey.gov.uk

Llandudno, Colwyn Bay, Rhyl and Prestatyn
(FOR LLANDUDNO/COLWYN BAY)
Marketing and Visitor Services
Tourism and Leisure Dept
Civic Offices
Colwyn Bay LL29 8AR
Tel (01492) 575387
Fax (01492) 513664
E-mail: gwen.roberts@conwy.gov.uk
Websites:
www.llandudno-tourism.co.uk
www.colwyn-bay-tourism.co.uk

Llyn Nantlle, Snowdonia

(FOR RHYL/PRESTATYN)
Coastal Tourism Unit
West Promenade
Rhyl LL18 1HZ
Tel (01745) 344515
Fax (01745) 342255
E-mail: rhyl.tic@denbighshire.gov.uk

The North Wales Borderlands
David P. Evans
Tourism Manager
Economic Development and
Tourism Division
Chief Executive's Dept
Flintshire County Council
County Hall
Mold CH7 6NB
Tel (01352) 702468
Fax (01352) 702458
E-mail: david.p.evans@flintshire.gov.uk
Website:
www.tourism-flintshire.org.uk

Snowdonia Mountains and Coast
Business and Marketing Section
Gwynedd Council
Cae Penarlag
Dolgellau LL40 2YB
Tel (01341) 423558 (24 hours)
Fax (01341) 424440
E-mail: tourism@gwynedd.gov.uk
Website: www.gwynedd.gov.uk

Mid Wales Lakes and Mountains
Powys Tourism
Neuadd Maldwyn
Severn Road
Welshpool SY21 7AS
Tel (01938) 551255
E-mail: tourism@powys.gov.uk

Ynys Lochtyn, Cardigan Bay

Ceredigion – Cardigan Bay

Ceredigion Tourism and
Economic Development Unit
Lisburne House
Terrace Road
Aberystwyth SY23 2AG
Tel (01970) 612125
Fax (01970) 626566
E-mail: econ@ceredigion.gov.uk
Website: www.ceredigion.gov.uk

Pembrokeshire

Pembrokeshire Holidays
PO Box 103
Pembroke Dock SA72 6TQ
Tel (01646) 682278
Fax (01646) 682281
E-mail:
tourism@pembrokeshire.gov.uk

Carmarthenshire – Beautiful Coast and Countryside in West Wales

Tourism Unit
Parc Amanwy
New Road
Ammanford SA18 3EP
Tel (01269) 590223
Fax (01269) 590290
E-mail:
tourism@carmarthenshire.gov.uk
Website:
www.carmarthenshire.gov.uk

Swansea Bay including Mumbles, Gower, Afan and the Vale of Neath

Swansea Tourist Information
Centre
Plymouth Street
Swansea SA1 3QG
Tel (01792) 468321
Fax (01792) 464602
E-mail: tourism@swansea.gov.uk

The Valleys of South Wales

Valley Breaks
Tourism South and West Wales
Charter Court
Enterprise Park
Swansea SA7 9DB
Tel (01792) 781212
Fax (01792) 781300
E-mail: valleys@tsww.com
Website:
www.valley-breaks.co.uk

The Glamorgan Heritage Coast and Countryside

Tourism Marketing Officer
Tourism Unit
The Vale of Glamorgan Council
Dock Office
Barry CF63 4RT
Tel (01446) 709328
Fax (01446) 704612
E-mail:
tourism@valeofglamorgan.gov.uk
Website:
www.valeofglamorgan.gov.uk

For information on Cardiff please contact:

Cardiff Visitor Centre
16 Wood Street
Cardiff CF10 1ES
Tel (029) 2022 7281
Fax (029) 2023 9162
E-mail: enquiries@cardifftic.co.uk
Website:
www.cardiffmarketing.co.uk

Wye Valley and Vale of Usk

Tourism Section
Planning and Economic
Development Dept
Monmouthshire County Council
County Hall
Cwmbran NP44 2XH
Tel (01633) 644842
Fax (01633) 644800
E-mail:
tourism@monmouthshire.gov.uk

St Nicholas, Vale of Glamorgan

173

Regional Tourism Companies

North Wales Tourism

77 Conwy Road
Colwyn Bay
LL29 7LN
Tel (01492) 531731
Fax (01492) 530059
E-mail: croeso@nwt.co.uk
Website: www.nwt.co.uk

Mid Wales Tourism

Marketing Dept
The Station
Machynlleth SY20 8TG
Tel Freephone (0800) 273747
Fax (01654) 703235
E-mail:
mwt@mid-wales-tourism.org.uk
info@brilliantbreaks.demon.co.uk

Tourism South and West Wales

Charter Court
Enterprise Park
Swansea
SA7 9DB
Tel (01792) 781212
Fax (01792) 781300
E-mail: marketing@tsww.com

Swansea's Maritime Quarter

Where to Stay
Wales

Wales Tourist Board

Dept VE2
PO Box 1
Cardiff CF24 2XN
Tel (029) 2047 5226
E-mail: info@tourism.wales.gov.uk

BWRDD CROESO CYMRU
WALES TOURIST BOARD

Wales on the Web

Make the most of your visit to Wales by calling into the Wales Tourist Board website. It's your easy route to up-to-date information on accommodation, attractions and events in Wales, as well as lots of ideas for itineraries and themes to explore.

Just key into 'Wales on the Web' at:
www.visitwales.com

Teletext Accommodation Bookings

For the latest information and offers on holidays and short breaks in Wales:

TeLeTeXT

See Teletext Page 251

Look out for the Wales Tourist Board grading on Teletext entries to make sure that the accommodation has been checked out by us.

Historic Conwy

Other Useful Addresses

Brecon Beacons National Park
7 Glamorgan Street
Brecon LD3 7DP
Tel (01874) 624437
Website: www.breconbeacons.org

Cadw: Welsh Historic Monuments
Crown Building
Cathays Park
Cardiff CF10 3NQ
Tel (029) 2050 0200
Website: www.cadw.wales.gov.uk

Environment Agency
(Fisheries and Conservation enquiries)
Rivers House
St Mellons Business Park
St Mellons
Cardiff CF3 0EY
Tel (029) 2077 0088
Website:
environment-agency.wales.gov.uk

Football Association of Wales
3 Westgate Street
Cardiff CF10 1DP
Tel (029) 2037 2325
Website: www.faw.org.uk

Forest Enterprise (Forestry Commission)
Victoria House
Victoria Terrace
Aberystwyth SY23 2DQ
Tel (01970) 612367
Website: www.forestry.gov.uk

National Trust in Wales
Trinity Square
Llandudno LL30 2DE
Tel (01492) 860123
Website: www.nationaltrust.org.uk

Offa's Dyke Association
West Street
Knighton LD7 1EN
Tel (01547) 528753
Website:
www.offa.demon.co.uk/offa.htm

Pembrokeshire Coast National Park
Winch Lane
Haverfordwest SA61 1PY
Tel (01437) 764636
Website:
www.pembrokeshirecoast.org.uk

Ramblers' Association in Wales
Ty'r Cerddwyr
High Street
Gresford
Wrexham LL12 8PT
Tel (01978) 855148
Website: www.ramblers.org.uk

Snowdonia National Park Authority
Penrhyndeudraeth LL48 6LF
Tel (01766) 770274
Website:
www.snowdonia.org.uk (English)
www.eryri.org.uk (Welsh)

Taste of Wales-*Blas ar Gymru*
Food Directorate
Welsh Development Agency
Cardiff Business Technology Centre
Senghennydd Road
Cardiff CF24 4AY
Tel (029) 2082 8984
Website: www.foodwales.com

Wales Craft Council
Henfaes Lane Industrial Estate
Welshpool SY21 7BE
Tel (01938) 555313
Website:
www.walescraftcouncil.co.uk

Welsh Golfing Union
Catsash
Newport NP18 1JQ
Tel (01633) 430830

Welsh Rugby Union
Custom House
Custom House Street
Cardiff CF10 1RF
Tel (029) 2078 1700
Website: www.wru.co.uk

Youth Hostel Association
1 Cathedral Road
Cardiff CF11 9HA
Tel (029) 2039 6766
Website: www.yha.org.uk

Walking in the Dysynni Valley, southern Snowdonia

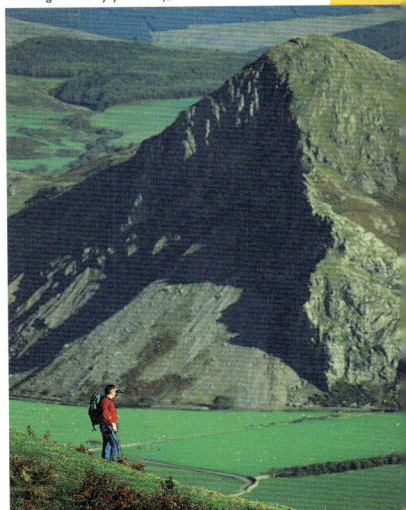

WALES OFFICIAL TOURIST GUIDES ASSOCIATION

Enjoy the diversity of Wales – its history, heritage and beauty – by using WOTGA's expertise to interpret it for you. The training and professionalism of WOTGA, the Blue Badge Guides of Wales, are recognised by the Wales Tourist Board as being of the highest quality. WOTGA guides have specialist knowledge of both the past and present and are experienced in looking after large or small groups or individuals.

Tel (01633) 774796 Fax (01633) 774821

E-mail: enquiries@WalesTourGuides.com

Information for Visitors with Disabilities

Discovering Accessible Wales is an information-packed guide for visitors who may have impaired movement or are confined to a wheelchair. With the help of this free guide they can enjoy holidays with family and friends to the full. Please see 'Publications from the Wales Tourist Board' section for details.

If you are disabled or medically infirm and planning a trip to Wales then contact Holiday Care, an organisation which provides a free specialised information service. Holiday Care can help with travel planning, access, transport and accommodation, and also provides a booking service. For details, please contact:

Holiday Care
2nd Floor
Imperial Buildings
Victoria Road
Horley
Surrey RH6 7PZ
Tel (01293) 774535
Website:
www.holidaycare.org.uk

Other Helpful Organisations

Disability Wales
Llys Ifor
Crescent Road
Caerphilly CF83 1XL
Tel (029) 2088 7325

Wales Council for the Blind
3rd Floor
Shand House
20 Newport Road
Cardiff CF24 0DB
Tel (029) 2047 3954
Website:
www.webnet.freeserve.co.uk

Wales Council for the Deaf
Glenview House
Courthouse Street
Pontypridd CF37 1JY
Tel (01443) 485687
Fax (01443) 408555
Minicom (01443) 485686

TRESPASS – a word of warning

If you're out and about enjoying an activity holiday – walking off established footpaths, mountain biking, or even landing your paraglider – please obtain permission from the landowners. To avoid any problems, it's always best to seek out the appropriate permission beforehand.

Where to Stay
Wales

Welsh Words Explained

*W*elsh place-names can tell us a lot about the town, village, area or mountain in question. Many Welsh placenames are based on local physical or geographic features, such as rivers, hills, bridges, woodlands and so on. *Aber*, for example, means 'mouth of', so *Abersoch* means 'The mouth of the River Soch'.

Here are a few examples of Welsh names you'll come across on your travels:

aber	confluence, rivermouth
afon	river
bach, fach	small
ban, fan	peak, crest
blaen	head, end, source
bryn	hill
bwlch	pass
caer, gaer	fort, stronghold
carreg	stone, rock
castell	castle
cefn	ridge
clawdd	hedge, ditch, dyke
coch, goch	red
craig, graig	rock
crib	crest, summit, ridge
cwm	valley, cirque
cymer	meeting of rivers
dinas	fort, city
du, ddu	black
dyffryn	valley
eglwys	church
ffin	boundary
glyn	glen
gwaun, waen	moor, mountain pasture
hendre	winter dwelling, permanent home
heol	road
llan	church, enclosure
llwyn	grove, bush
llyn	lake
llys	hall, court
maen	stone
mawr, fawr	great, big
merthyr	church, burial place
moel, foel	bare hill
mynydd, fynydd	mountain, moorland
pant	hollow, valley
pen	head, top, end
pentre	village, homestead
plas	hall, mansion
pont, bont	bridge
sarn	causeway, old road
tre, tref	hamlet, home, town
uchaf	upper, higher, highest
ystrad	valley floor

A Few Greetings

bore da	good morning
dydd da	good day
prynhawn da	good afternoon
noswaith dda	good evening
nos da	good night
sut mae?	how are you?
hwyl	cheers
diolch	thanks
diolch yn fawr iawn	thanks very much
croeso	welcome
croeso i Gymru	welcome to Wales
da	good
da iawn	very good
iechyd da!	good health!

British Tourist Authority Overseas Offices

*Y*our enquiries will be welcome at the offices of the British Tourist Authority in the following countries:

Argentina - Buenos Aires
British Tourist Authority, Avenida Córdoba 645, 2nd Floor, 1054 Buenos Aires
Tel: 00 54 (11) 4314 6735
Fax: 00 54 (11) 4315 3161
E-mail: btaarg@comnet.com.ar
(open to public Mon-Thu 1000-1700; Fri 1030-1300)

Australia - Sydney
British Tourist Authority, Level 16, Gateway, 1 Macquarie Place, Sydney, NSW 2000
Tel: 00 61 (2) 9377 4400
Fax: 00 61 (2) 9377 4499
E-mail: visitbritainaus@bta.org.uk
Website: www.visitbritain.com/au

Austria - Vienna
Britain Visitor Centre, The British Council, Schenkestr. 4, A-1010 Vienna
Tel: 0043 (1) 533 26 16 81
Fax: 0043 (1) 533 26 16 85
E-mail: tourist.information@bc-vienna.at

Belgium - Brussels
Visit Britain Centre, Avenue Louise 140, 2nd Floor, 1050 Brussels
Tel: 00 32 (2) 626 35 10
Fax: 00 32 (2) 646 39 86
E-mail: british.be@bta.org.uk
Website: www.visitbritain.com/be

Brazil - Rio de Janeiro
British Tourist Authority,
Rua da Assembleia 10, sala 3707, Rio de Janeiro-RJ 20119-900
Tel: 00 55 (21) 531 1717/0382
Fax: 00 55 (21) 531 0383
E-mail: btabras@vetor.com.br
Website: www.visitbritain.com

Canada - Toronto
British Tourist Authority,
5915 Airport Road, Suite 120, Mississauga, Ontario L4V 1T1
Toll free: 1 888 VISIT UK
Fax: 00 1 (905) 405 1835
E-mail: travelinfo@bta.org.uk
Website: www.visitbritain.com/ca

Denmark - Copenhagen
British Tourist Authority,
Møntergade 3, 1116 Copenhagen K
Tel: (00 45) 70 21 50 11
Fax: (00 45) 33 75 50 08
E-mail: dkweb@bta.org.uk

Finland - Helsinki
British Travel Centre,
Mikonkatu 13A, 00100 Helsinki
Tel: 00 358 (9) 681 2466
Fax: 00 358 (9) 622 1562
E-mail: finlandbtc@bta.org.uk

France - Paris
British Tourist Authority,
Maison de la Grande-Bretagne, 19 rue des Mathurins, 75009 Paris
Tel: 00 33 (1) 4451 5620
Fax: 00 33 (1) 4451 5621
Minitel: 3615 BRITISH
Website: www.grandebretagne.net

Germany - Frankfurt
British Tourist Authority,
Westendstr 16-22, 60325 Frankfurt
Tel: 00 49 (69) 97 1123
Fax: 00 49 (69) 97 112 444
E-mail: gbinfo@bta.org.uk
Website: www.visitbritain.com/de

Hong Kong
British Tourist Authority, Room 1504, Eton Tower, 8 Hysan Avenue, Causeway Bay, Hong Kong
Tel: (00 852) 2882 9967
Fax: (00 852) 577 1443
E-mail: hko@bta.org.uk
Website: www.visitbritain.com/hk

Ireland - Dublin
British Tourist Authority,
18/19 College Green, Dublin 2
Tel: 00 353 (1) 670 8000
Fax: 00 353 (1) 670 8244

Italy - Milan
British Tourist Authority,
Corso Magenta 32, 20123 Milano
Tel: 00 39 (02) 8808 151
Fax: 00 39 (02) 7201 0086

Italy - Rome
British Tourist Authority,
Via Nazionale 230, 00184 Rome
Tel: 00 39 (06) 462 0221
Fax: 00 39 (06) 474 2054

Japan - Tokyo
British Tourist Authority,
Akasaka Twin Tower 1F, 2-17-22 Akasaka, Minato-ku, Tokyo
Tel: 00 81 (3) 5562 2550
Website: www.uknow.co.jp

Netherlands - Amsterdam
British Tourist Authority, Aurora Gebouw (5e), Stadhouderskade 2, 1054 ES Amsterdam
Tel: 00 31 (20) 689 0002
Fax: 00 31 (20) 689 0003
E-mail: BritInfo.NL@bta.org.uk
Website: www.visitbritain.com/nl

New Zealand - Auckland
British Tourist Authority,
17th Floor, NZI House, 151 Queen Street, Auckland 1
Tel: 00 64 (9) 303 1446
Fax: 00 64 (9) 377 6965
E-mail: bta.nz@bta.org.uk
Website: www.visitbritain.uk

Norway - Oslo
British Tourist Authority,
Nedre Slottsgate 21, 4 etg, 0157 Oslo
Tel: (00 47) 22 39 68 39
Fax: (00 47) 22 42 48 74
E-mail: britisketuristkontor@bta.org.uk
Website: www.storbritannia.no

Singapore
British Tourist Authority, 108 Robinson Road, #01-00 GMG Building, Singapore 068900
Tel: (00 65) 227 5400
Fax: (00 65) 227 5411
Website: www.visitbritain.com/sg

South Africa - Johannesburg
British Tourist Authority,
Lancaster Gate, Hyde Park Lane, Hyde Park 2196 (public address)
PO Box 41896, Craighall 2024 (postal address)
Tel: 00 27 (11) 325 0343
Fax: 00 27 (11) 325 0344
E-mail: johannesburg@bta.org.uk
Website: www.visitbritain.com

Spain - Madrid
British Tourist Authority, Calle Santiago de Compostela 100, 2 28035 Madrid (public address)
PO Box 42078 28080 Madrid (postal address)
Tel: 00 902 171 181
Fax: 00 34 (91) 386 10 88
E-mail: turismo.britanico@bta.org.uk
Website: www.visitbritain.com/es

Sweden - Stockholm
British Tourist Authority,
Box 3102, 103 62 Stockholm (postal address)
Klara Norra Kyrkogata 29, S 111 22 Stockholm (public address)
Tel: 00 46 (8) 4401 700
Fax: 00 46 (8) 21 31 29
E-mail: stockholm.internet@bta.org.uk
Website: www.visitbritain.com/sverige

Switzerland - Zurich
British Tourist Authority, Limmatquai 78, CH-8001 Zurich
Tel: 00 41 (1) 266 21 66
Fax: 00 41 (1) 266 21 61
E-mail: ch-info@bta.org.uk

United Arab Emirates - Dubai
British Tourist Authority,
Tariq Bin Zaid Street, Near Rashid Hospital, Al Maktoum Roundabout, PO Box 33342, Dubai
Tel: 00 971 (4) 3350088
Fax: 00 971 (4) 3355335

USA - Chicago
British Tourist Authority, 625 North Michigan Avenue, Suite 1001, Chicago IL 60611
Toll free: 1 800 462 2748
E-mail: travelinfo@bta.org.uk
Website: www.travelbritain.org

USA - New York
British Tourist Authority,
7th Floor, 551 Fifth Avenue, New York, NY 10176-0799
Tel: 00 1 (212) 986 2266
Toll free: 1 800 GO 2 BRITAIN
E-mail: travelinfo@bta.org.uk
Website: www.travelbritain.org

Where to Stay
Wales

178

The beautiful Mawddach Estuary

Publications, Guides and Maps

If you want more information on Wales you'll find it in this extensive range of publications. The SALEABLE books and maps are described on these two pages. Overleaf we feature our comprehensive range of FREE publications.

ALL PRICES INCLUDE POSTAGE AND PACKING

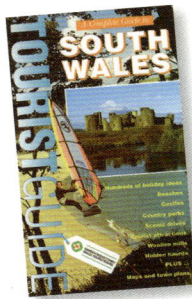

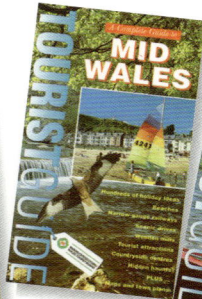

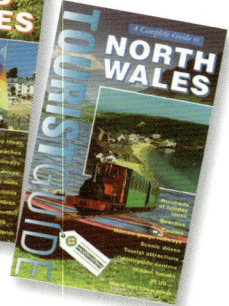

The Complete Guides to South, Mid and North Wales
£5.70 each

A best-selling series, written by Welsh author Roger Thomas. These three books give you the complete picture of Wales's holiday regions. In full colour – and packed with information.

◆ Descriptions of resorts, towns and villages

◆ Where to go and what to see

◆ Hundreds of attractions and places to visit

◆ Scenic drives, castles, crafts, what to do on a rainy day

◆ Detailed maps and town plans

Please complete and send to: **Wales Tourist Board, Production Services, Dept. WTSO1, Brunel House, 2 Fitzalan Road, Cardiff CF24 0UY**

Please enclose the appropriate remittance in the form of a cheque (payable to Wales Tourist Board) or postal/money order in £ sterling. All prices include post and packing.

☐ A Complete Guide to South Wales **£5.70**

☐ A Complete Guide to Mid Wales **£5.70**

☐ A Complete Guide to North Wales **£5.70**

☐ Wales Tourist Map **£2.90**

☐ A Journey Through Wales **£5.10**

☐ Wales – Castles & Historic Places **£7.35**

☐ Travelmaster Guide to South Wales **£8.80**

☐ Ghosts & Legends of Wales **£6.05**

OS Pathfinder Guides:

☐ Brecon Beacons & Glamorgan Walks **£10.80**

☐ Mid Wales & the Marches Walks **£10.80**

☐ North Wales, Snowdonia & Offa's Dyke Walks **£10.80**

☐ Pembrokeshire & Gower Walks **£10.80**

☐ Snowdonia, Anglesey & Llŷn Peninsula Walks **£10.80**

☐ Wye Valley & Forest of Dean Walks **£10.80**

Name *(please print)*: _____

Address *(please print)*: _____

_____

_____ Post Code: _____

Total remittance enclosed:

£ _____

Cheque/PO or Money Order No: _____

Make payable to Wales Tourist Board

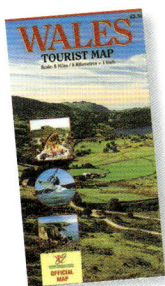

Wales Tourist Map   £2.90

A best-seller – don't travel without it. Detailed 5 miles/inch scale, comprehensive road network, national parks, beaches, forests, attractions all highlighted. Also includes suggested car tours, town plans, information centres.

A Journey Through Wales   £5.10

A magnificent production – 64 big-format pages of the best images in Wales. The 90 photographs take the reader on a tour of Wales's mighty castles, spectacular mountains and coastline, country towns and colourful attractions.

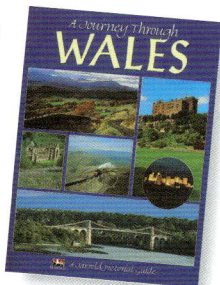

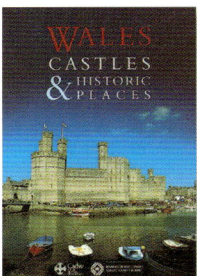

Wales – Castles and Historic Places £7.35

Describes more than 140 sites, including castles, abbeys, country houses, prehistoric and Roman remains – all featured in full colour. An introduction to the history of Wales sets the scene, and detailed maps help visitors plan their routes.

Travelmaster Guide to South Wales   £8.80

A guide in the popular Travelmaster series. This 96-page book, written by Roger Thomas, contains 20 car tours plus information on what to see along the way. Includes the most accurate and up-to-date Ordnance Survey mapping.

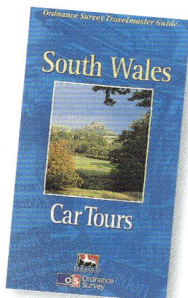

Ghosts and Legends of Wales £6.05

144 pages of fascinating stories, ancient and modern. Some of the happenings recounted may sound incredible, many will leave the reader wondering.

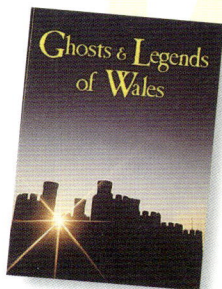

Ordnance Survey Pathfinder Guides £10.80 each

◆ Brecon Beacons and Glamorgan Walks

◆ Mid Wales and the Marches Walks

◆ North Wales, Snowdon and Offa's Dyke Walks

◆ Pembrokeshire and Gower Walks

◆ Snowdonia, Anglesey and the Llŷn Peninsula Walks

◆ Wye Valley and Forest of Dean Walks

80-page books with detailed maps, colour illustrations and descriptions which guide you safely along attractive walking routes.

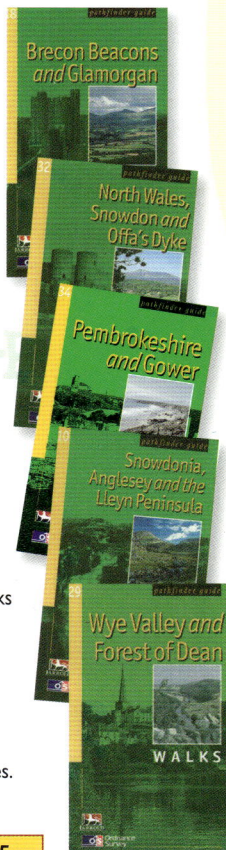

ALL PRICES INCLUDE POSTAGE AND PACKING

FREE PUBLICATIONS

There's an information-packed range of publications available free from the Wales Tourist Board.

Activity Wales

Magazine on all kinds of activities, from abseiling to windsurfing. Lots of information on accredited activity centres and visitor attractions, events, news and articles by well-known personalities.

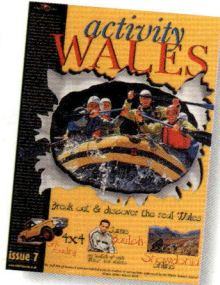

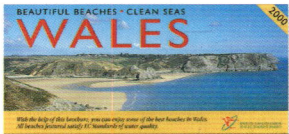

Beaches Guide

This leaflet lists Wales's most appealing beaches. Includes European Blue Flag, Green Coast and Tidy Britain Group Seaside Award beaches. Available spring 2001.

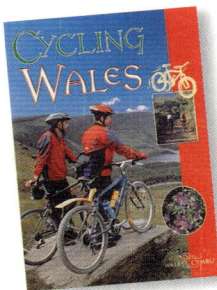

Cycling Wales

Looking for a holiday on two wheels? This brochure covers everything from gentle cycling to adventurous mountain biking. Suggested routes, details of cycle hire and cycling organisations.

Discovering Accessible Wales
(holidays for disabled people)

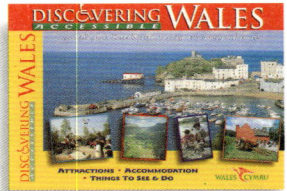

A guide full of ideas and helpful information for people who may have impaired movement or are confined to a wheelchair. Covers everything from accommodation to activities.

Fishing Wales

This brochure, written by well-known anglers, is an essential guide to Wales's superb game and sea fishing. Information on venues, clubs, accommodation and tackle shops.

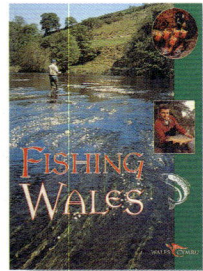

Freedom Holiday Parks Wales

Caravan Holiday Home Park accommodation in Wales is high on standards and value for money – as you'll see from this brochure which only lists parks graded for quality by the Wales Tourist Board.

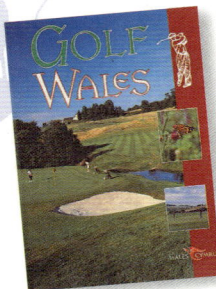

Golfing Wales

Wales's golf courses rank amongst the best in the world. Novices and experts alike will find their ideal course with the help of this brochure, which also includes information on green fees and accommodation.

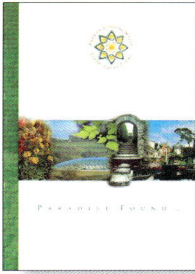

Premier Gardens Wales

The gardens of Wales were, until quite recently, one of Britain's best-kept secrets – but not any more. This publication is your invitation to find out more about these very special places to visit.

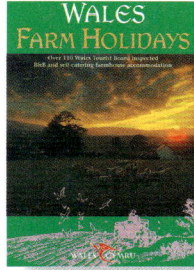

Wales Farm Holidays

Handy publication featuring bed and breakfast and self-catering accommodation at farmhouses throughout Wales.

Riding Wales

Discover why Wales is one of the best parts of Britain for riding and pony trekking. Riding for all abilities, from beginners to experts – and everything from a few hours in the saddle to all-inclusive holidays.

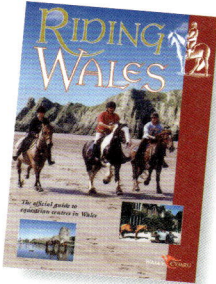

Wales Touring Caravan and Camping

Detailed map of Wales Tourist Board-inspected caravan and camping parks which welcome touring caravans, motor homes and tents.

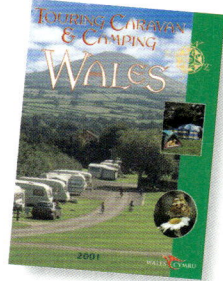

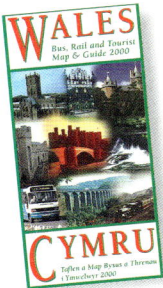

Wales Bus, Rail and Tourist Map and Guide

An essential source of information for those travelling around Wales by public transport. Includes information on rail and bus routes, frequency and journey times. Available Easter 2001.

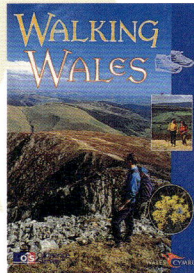

Walking Wales

Brochure on Britain's most popular leisure activity – and the best place in which to enjoy it. Suggested routes, maps, places to stay, carry-ahead and walking tour package information.

Wales Countryside Holidays

Refreshing country breaks at guest houses, farms and small hotels, allied with a choice of activities and special interests, including walking, cycling, fishing, pony trekking and heritage.

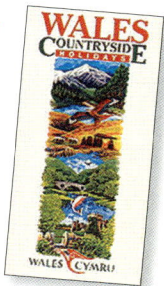

For **FREE** copies of any **TWO** of the above brochures please complete and send to: **Wales Tourist Board, Dept. PP80, PO Box 1, Cardiff CF24 2XN**

- [ ] Activity Wales
- [ ] Beaches Guide (available spring 2001)
- [ ] Cycling Wales
- [ ] Discovering Accessible Wales (holidays for disabled people)
- [ ] Fishing Wales
- [ ] Freedom Holiday Parks Wales
- [ ] Golfing Wales

- [ ] Premier Gardens Wales
- [ ] Riding Wales
- [ ] Wales Bus, Rail & Tourist Map & Guide (available Easter 2001)
- [ ] Wales Countryside Holidays
- [ ] Wales Farm Holidays
- [ ] Wales Touring Caravan & Camping
- [ ] Walking Wales

Name (please print): _____

Address (please print): _____

_____

_____ Post Code: _____

Maps of Wales

The maps which follow divide Wales into 12 sections, each with a slight overlap. The grid overlaying each map will help you find the resort, town or village of your choice. Please refer to the map and grid reference which appears alongside the names of each place listed in the 'Where to Stay' section of the guide.

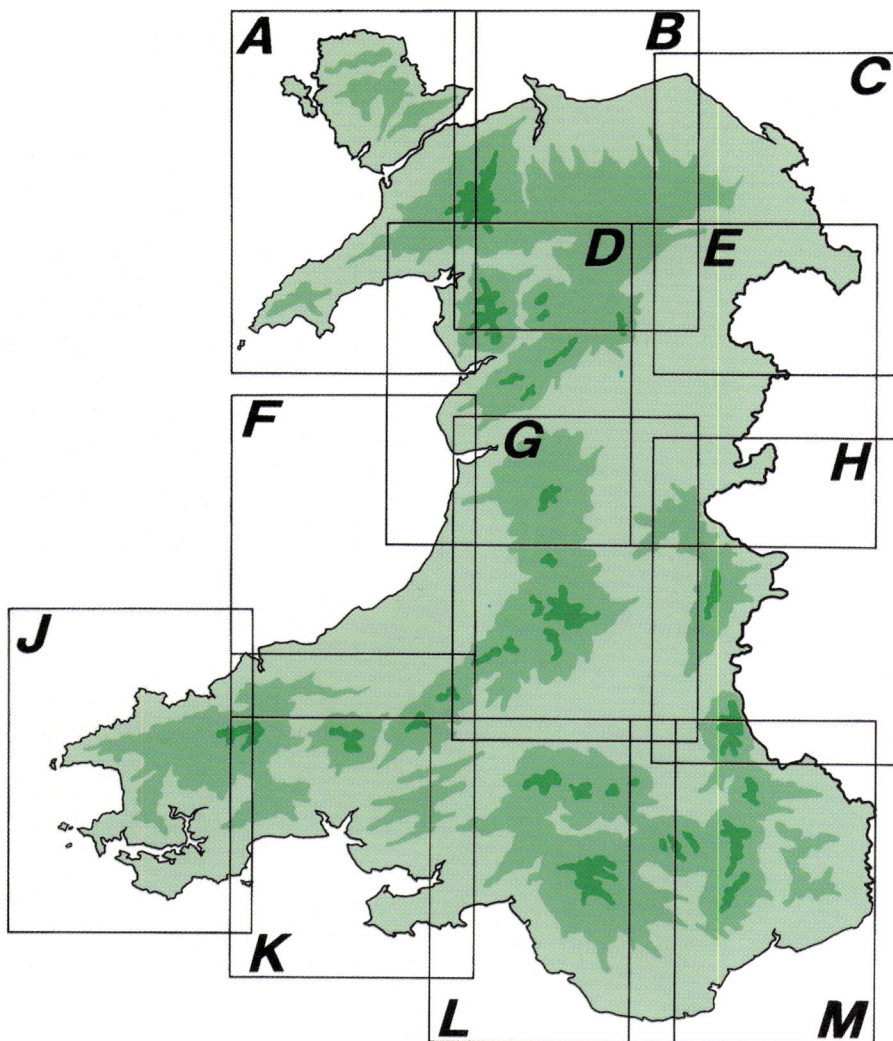

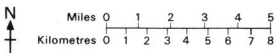

MAP A

MAP B

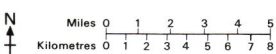

MAP C

N

Miles 0 1 2 3 4 5
Kilometres 0 1 2 3 4 5 6 7 8

a   b   c   d   e

Formby
Skelmersdale
Wi
A49
A565
M58
A49
A580
A570
A570
Liverpool
St. Helen's
le
Bootle
Wallasey
M57
MERSEYSIDE
M62
Hoylake
Wa
Birkenhead
A57
A41
West Kirby
Garston
Widnes
Heswall
Runcorn
Point of Ayr
Talacre
Bebington
LIVERPOOL INTERNATIONAL AIRPORT
A533
DEE ESTUARY
M53
Ellesmere Port
Frodsham
nant wespyr
Ffynnongroyw
A548
Mostyn
Neston
A5117
Hapsford
M56
A56
Llanasa
Trelogan
Whitford BASINGWERK ABBEY
Greenfield
HALL
A5151
Lloc
Gorsedd
HOLYWELL
Bagillt
A541
Carmel
A5026
Saughall
A54
Caerwys
Brynford
Babell
Pentre Halkyn
A548
FLINT
A51
Chester
Kelsall
Tremeirchion
A5112
Lixwm
Flint Mountain
A5119
A55
B5126
Spital
Tarvin
CHESHIRE
Afonwen
Rhosesmor
Northop
CONNAH'S QUAY
A550
Queensferry
Sandycroft
A548
Tarporley
Clwydian
Moel y-parc
Nannerch
Rhydymwyn
Northophall
B5125
HAWARDEN AIRFIELD
Pantymwyn
A541
BUCKLEY
Hawarden
Saltney
Cilcain
A549
Broughton
A51
Moel Llys-y-coed
Gwernaffield
Llong
MOLD
A494
A41
Clwyd
Pen-y-ffordd
A5118
A5104
Nercwys
Maeshafn
Leeswood
Pontblyddyn
A483
Ruthin
RUTHIN
Forest
Pant-y-ffordd
Hope
Rossett
A49
Cryrys
Llanfynydd
Caergwrle
Gresford
Farndon
Clutton
Grainhyd
Cefn-y-bedd
Trevalyn
Llanfair Dyffryn Clwyd
A5104
Rhydtalog
A541
Gwersyllt
Holt
A534
Huomore
Ridley Wood
Graigfechan
Bwlchgwyn
Brymbo
Broughton
Coedpoeth
Minera
WREXHAM
Cefn-coch
A525
Pen-y-stryt
Llandegla
Clywedog
Malpas
No Mans Heath
A41
A49
A542
World's End
Esclusham Mountain
Rhostyllen
ERDDIG
Marchwiel
B5130
Bryn Saith Marchog
A5104
Pentredwr
Rhosllanerchrugog
Johnstown
Worthenbury
Bangor on Dee
Higher Wych
Gwyddelwern
Moel Morfydd
VALLE CRUCIS ABBEY
Pen-y-cae
Acrefair
Ruabon
Eyton
B5426
Tallarn Green
Eglwys Cross
Corwen
A5
Glyndyfrdwy
LLANGOLLEN RAILWAY
Cefn-mawr
A483
Overton
Penley
Bromfield
White

MAP D

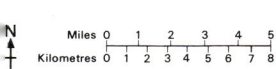

Miles 0 1 2 3 4 5
Kilometres 0 1 2 3 4 5 6 7 8

a   b   c   d   e

Betws Gwerful Goch
A494
Morwynion
Llantysilio Mountain
Moel Fferna 1804ft.
Moel Rhywl Morfydd
1648ft.
Ruabon
Pen-y-cae
Acretair
Worthenbury
Bangor on Dee
Tallarn Green
Maerdy
Tyn-y-cefn
B4378
Carrog
Llantysilio
VALE
CRUCIS
ABBEY CASTELL
DINAS BRAN
A535
Garth
Cefn-mawr
A483
Pentre
Eyton
Overton
A525
Four Crosses
Corwen
A5
Glyndyfrdwy
LLANGOLLEN RAILWAY
LLANGOLLEN
Froncysyllte
Erbistock
Penley
A539
Glan-yr-afon
Cynwyd
Moel Fferna 2071ft.
PLAS NEWYDD
Foel 1713ft.
Knolton
Han
Mynydd Mynyllod
Ceiriog Forest
Pontfadog
CHIRK CASTLE
Chirk
Dee
Cefn-coch
Llandrillo
Pen-plaenau 1775ft.
Glyn Ceiriog
Teirw
Pandy
Dolywern
Llwynmawr
Ellesmere
A495
Cadair Bronwen 2572ft.
Nant-cwm-llawenog
Tregeiriog
B4579
Gobowen
Whittington
A528
Llanarmon D.C.
Mynydd Myfyr
Cadair Berwyn 2830ft.
Garneddwen 1628ft.
Moel Sych 2713ft.
Rhyd-y-croesau
B4580
Baschurch
Pennant Melangell
PISTYLL RHAEADR FALLS
Y Clogydd 1954ft.
Moel Glaswen
Moelfre
Llansilin
Oswestry
A5
A4396
Walford
Harn
Llanrhaeadr ym Mochnant
Pentre'r felin
Trefonen
Llangynog
Penybontfawr
Pen-y-garnedd
Llangedwyn
Pen-y-bont
Llanerch Emrys
Llansantffraid ym Mechain
Hirnant
B4396
Bwlch-y-ddar
Llanymynech
Llanfechain
Llanfyllin
Llanwddyn
Abertridwr
Llanddwyn
Four Crosses
Llandrinio
Crew Green
Severn
A5
Bwlch-y-Cibau
Llanfihangel-yng-Ngwynfa
Allt-y-main 1168ft.
Sarnau
Geuffordd
Crugion 1202ft.
Breidden Hill
Cefn-y-castell 1523ft.
A458
Pont Llogel
Pont Robert
Meifod
A495
Broniarth Hill
A490
Middletown
Cardeston
Dolanog
Groes-lwyd
Pool Quay
Guilsfield
Trewern
A458
Westbury
Llangadfan
Llanerfyl
Maes-mawr
TRALLWNG WELSHPOOL
Buttington
S H
A458
Melin-y-ddol
WELSHPOOL AND LLANFAIR RAILWAY
Sylfaen
A458
Leighton
Minsterley
Pontesbury
Mynydd Cefn y Gribin
Llanllugan
Llanfair Caereinion
Castle Caereinion
POWIS CASTLE
Frop
Kingswood
Llanwyddelan
Adfa
A385
MID WALES AIRPORT
Forden
Chirbury
New Mills
Berriew
Garthmyl
Y Glonc 1513ft.
Tregynon
Betws Cedewain
Montgomery
Corndon Hill 1683ft.
Bwlch-y-ffridd
Gregynog Hall
Highgate
DOLFORWYN
A489
Churchstoke
Hyssington
A488
Clatter
Llanwnog
NEWTOWN DRENEWYDD
A4568
Aberhafesp
Abermule
Cefn y Coed
Snead
A489
Lydham
Caersws
A489
Kerry
Sarn
A4385
Bishop's Castle
Trefeglwys
Mochdre
Llandinam
Dolfor
Ceri Forest
Clun Forest
Lydbury North
A470
Berth-ddu
Pentre
Anchor
B4368
Aston
Crav
Cefn-coed-y-gaer 1183ft.
Y Foel 1423ft.
Llyn-dwr Hill
Black Mountain 1469ft.
Lydham
Wist
Chapel Hill 1398ft.
Rhydd Hywel 1920ft.
Bryn Gydfa 1573ft.
Felindre
Clun
A488
Beguildy
A483
A483

189

MAP F

BAY

Borth
Talybont
Dol-y-bont
Llandre
Wallog
Bow Street
Clarach
Waun-fawr
ABERYSTWYTH
Llanbadarn-fawr
Pen-parcau
Rhyd-y-felin
Llanfarian
Llanilar
Blaenplwyf
Llanddeiniol
Llangwyryfon
Llanrhystud
Trefenter
Llanon
Aeron
Nebo
Pennant
Forest
Aberarth
Cross Inn
Blaenpenal
Bethania
ABERAERON
Penuwch
Cei Bach
Ffos-y-ffin
Llanaeron
Cilcennin
Llangeitho
Llwyncelyn
New Quay
Llanina
Llanerchaeron
Ciliau Aeron
Bwlchllan
Betws Leucu
Cwm Tudu
Llanarth
Gartheli
Cross Inn
Llanfihangel Ystrad
Tal-sarn
Ynys Lochtyn
Llwyndafydd
Dihewid
Temple Bar
Felinfach
Llangybi
Mydroilyn
Llangrannog
Synod Inn
Bettws-Bledrws
Plwmp
Cribyn
LLANBEDR PONT STEFFAN LAMPETER
Mwnt
Traeth Penbryn
Penbryn
Talgarreg
Gors-goch
Aberporth
Samau
Brynhoffnant
Capel Cynon
Cwrt-newydd
Verwig
Blaenannerch
Glyn Arthur
Ffostrasol
Llanwnnen
Ram
Tre-main
Blaenporth
Rhydlewis
Cwm-sychpant
Dre-fach
Allt-y-blaca
Pont-siân
ABERTEIFI CARDIGAN
Beulah
Penrhiw-pâl
Tre-groes
Rhyd Owen
Llanwenog
Pencarreg
Llangoedmor
Brongest
Maes-llyn
Pren-gwyn
Pen Tas-eithin
Cilgerran
Llandygwydd
Aber-banc
Horeb
Capel Dewi
Llanybydder
Cwm-cou
Llandyfriog
Penrhiw-llan
Llanllwni
Maesycrugiau
Rhos-hill
Cenarth
Llandysul
Llanfihangel-ar-arth
Aber Cych
Aberarad
Pont-tyweli
Mynydd Llanybydder
Rhyd-cymerau
Newcastle Emlyn
Henllan
Pentre-cwrt
Llansawel
Newchapel
Felindre
Dre-fach
Banc-y-ffordd
New Inn
Boncath
Pentre-drefelin
Penboyr
Pencader
Edwinsford
Blaenffos
Capel Iwan
Rhos
Gwyddgrug
Bwlch-y-groes
Moelfre
Cwm Morgan
Brechfa Forest
Abergorlech
Star
Mynydd Cynros
Crymych
Tegryn
Cwm-duad
Alltwalis
Mynydd Figyn
Y Glôg
Hermon
Waun-deg
Brechfa
Glandwr
Llanfyrnach
Trelech
Llanllawddog
Llanfynydd
Hebron
Dinas
Cynwyl Elfed
Pont ar Sais
Talog
Pen-y-banc
Llanglydwen
Eglwys Fair a Churig
Coed Deufor
Trelech a'r Betws
Blaen-y-coed
Cwmdwyfran
Rhyd-ar-gaeau
Felingwm Uchaf
Peniel

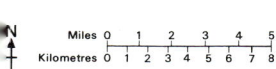

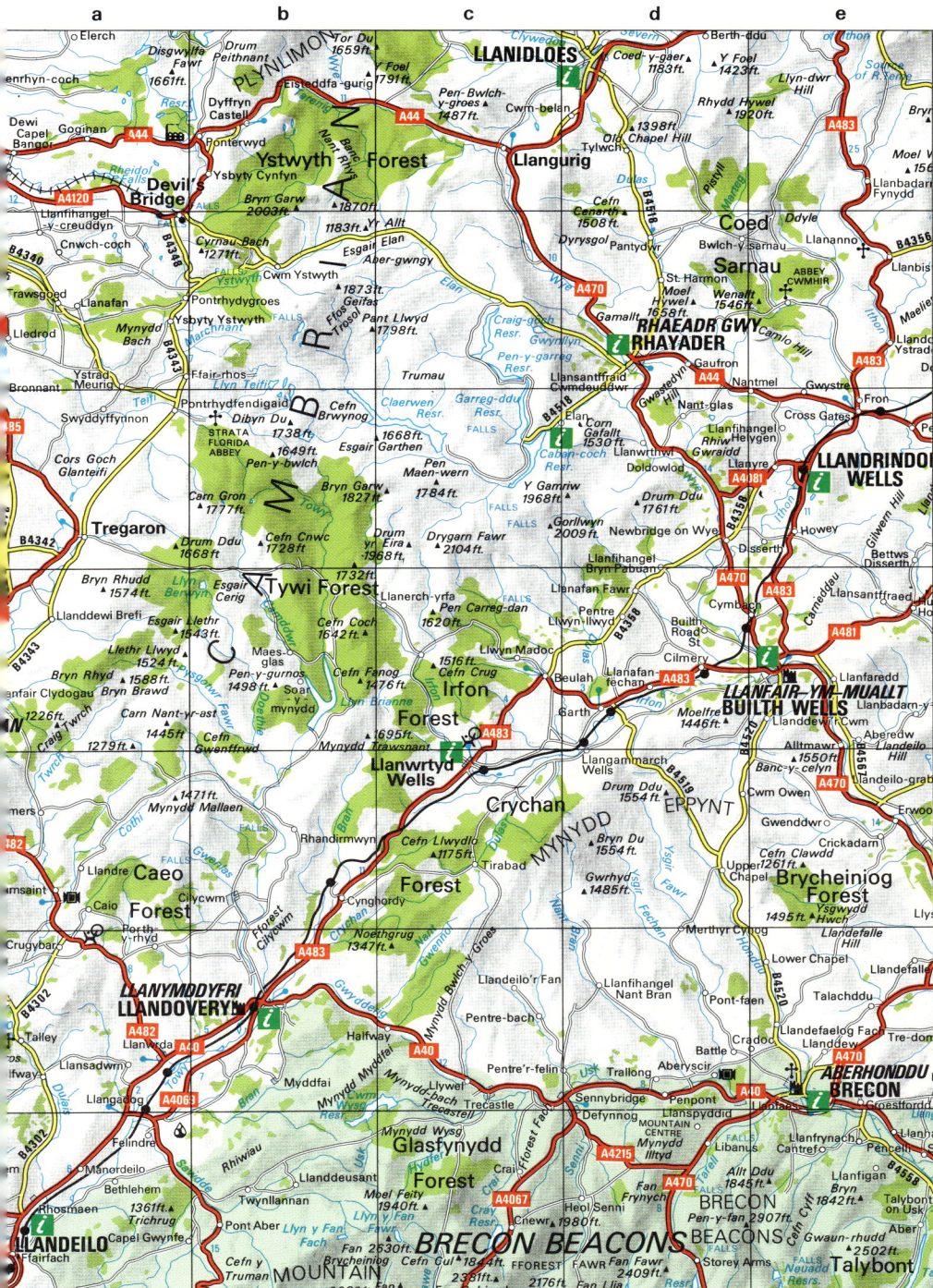

Miles 0 1 2 3 4 5
Kilometres 0 1 2 3 4 5 6 7 8

N

a   b   c   d   e

Elerch
Disgwylfa Fawr 1661ft.
Drum Peithnant
PLYNLIMON
LLANIDLOES
Coed-y-gaer 1183ft.
Berth-ddu
Y Foel 1423ft.
Source of R. Teme
Llyn-dwr Hill

enrhyn-coch
Dyffryn Castell
Eisteddfa-gurig
Y Foel 1791ft.
Tor Du 1659ft.
Pen-Bwlch-y-groes 1487ft.
Cwm-belan
1398ft.
Old Chapel Hill
Rhydd Hywel 1920ft.

Dewi
Capel Bangor
Goginan
A44
Ponterwyd
Ystwyth Forest
Llangurig
Tylwch
A483
Moel
Llanbadarn Fynydd

Rheidol
Devil's Bridge
A4120
Ysbyty Cynfyn
Bryn Garw 2003ft.
1870ft.
Cefn Cenarth 1508ft.
Dyrysgol
Pantydwr
St. Harmon
Coed Sarnau
Bwlch-y-sarnau
ABBEY CWMHIR
B4356

Llanfihangel-y-creuddyn
Cnwch-coch
Cyrnau-Bach 1271ft.
1183ft.
Yr Allt
Esgair Elan
Aber-gwngy
Moel Hywel 1658ft.
Wenallt 1546ft.
Llananno
Llanbis

Trawsgoed
Llanafan
Pontrhydygroes
Ysbyty Ystwyth
Cwm Ystwyth
1873ft.
Ffos Geifas
Pant Llwyd 1798ft.
A470
RHAEADR GWY
RHAYADER
Gamallt
Gwynllyn
B4356
Ystrad

Mynydd Bach
Lledrod
B4343
Ffair-rhos
Pontrhydfendigaid
Trumau
Craig-goch Resr.
Pen-y-garreg Resr.
Gaufron
Gwystre
B4356

Bronnant
Llyn Teifi
Dibyn Digiad
Cefn Brwynog 1738ft.
Claerwen Resr.
Garreg-ddu Resr.
Elan
Corn Gafallt 1530ft.
Nant-glas
Llanfihangel Rhiw Helygen
Cross Gates
Fron

Swyddyffynnon
STRATA FLORIDA ABBEY
1649ft.
Esgair Garthen 1668ft.
FALLS
Caban-coch Resr.
Gwraidd
LLANDRINDOD WELS
A483

Cors Goch Glanteifi
Pen-y-bwlch
Pen Maen-wern 1784ft.
Y Gamriw 1968ft.
Drum Ddu 1761ft.
Newbridge on Wye
Llanwrthwl
Doldowlod
A4081
Howey
Gilwern Hill
Bettws Disserth

Tregaron
Carn Gron 1777ft.
Bryn Garw 1827ft.
Drygarn Fawr 2104ft.
Gorllwyn 2009ft.
Disserth
B4343
Drum Ddu 1668ft.
Cefn Cnwc 1728ft.
Drum yr Eira 1968ft.
A470
A483
Llansantffraed

Bryn Rhudd 1574ft.
Llanddewi Brefi
Esgair Cerig
Tywi Forest
1732ft.
Llanerch-yrfa
Pen Carreg-dan 1620ft.
Llanafan Fawr
Bryn Pabban
CymBach
Llansantffraed

Esgair Llethr 1543ft.
Maes-glas
Cefn Coch 1542ft.
Llwyn Madoc
Pentre Llwyn-llwyd
B4358
Builth Road St.
A470
A481

Llethr Llwyd 1524ft.
Bryn Rhyd 1588ft.
Bryn Brawd
Pen-y-gurnos 1498ft.
Soar y mynydd
Cefn Fanog 1476ft.
Cefn Crug 1516ft.
Beulah
Llanafan-fechan
Cilmery
A483
LLANFAIR-YM-MUALLT
BUILTH WELLS
Llanfaredd

1226ft.
Carn Nant-yr-ast 1445ft.
Cefn Gwenffrwd
Irfon Forest 1695ft.
Mynydd Trawsnant
A483
Garth
Moelfre 1446ft.
Llanddewi'r Cwm
Aberedw
Craig Twrch 1279ft.
Llanwrtyd Wells
Drum Ddu 1554ft.
Banc-y-celyn 1550ft.
Alltmawr
Llandeilo Hill
Llandeilo-grab

1471ft.
Mynydd Mallaen
Rhandirmwyn
Crychan Forest
Tirabad
Llangammarch Wells
Cwm Owen
Erwo
nfair Clydogau

Caeo Forest
Caio
Cilycwm
Cefn Llwydlo 1175ft.
Bryn Du 1554ft.
MYNYDD
EPPYNT
Gwenddwr
Crickadarn
Brycheiniog Forest
Ysgwydd Hwch

Crugybar
Porth-y-rhyd
Cynghordy
Noethgrug 1347ft.
Gwrhyd 1485ft.
Cefn Clawdd
Upper Chapel 1261ft.
1495ft.
Llandefalle Hill
Llandefalle
Lower Chapel

LLANYMDDYFRI
LLANDOVERY
A483
Llanwrda
Myddfai
Llandeilo'r Fan
Llanfihangel Nant Bran
Pont-faen
Battle
Cradoc
Aberyscir
Talachddu
Tre-dom
A470
ABERHONDDU
BRECON

A482
A40
Llansadwrn
Llangadog
A4069
Halfway
A40
Pentre'r-felin
Llywel
Trecastle
Pentre-bach
Sennybridge
Penpont
Trallong
Defynnog
A40
Llanfrynach
Cantref
Llanfigan

LLANDEILO
Trichrug 1361ft.
Capel Gwynfe
Glasfynydd Forest
Moel Feity 1940ft.
Llanddeusant
Twynllanan
Mynydd Wysg
A4215
MOUNTAIN CENTRE
Llanspyddid
Libanus
Allt Ddu 1845ft.
Talybont on Usk

nfairfach
Rhosmaen
Bethlehem
Manordeilo
Felindre
Pont Aber
Rhiwiau
Cefn y Truman
BRECON BEACONS
MOUNTAIN
Brycheiniog 2366ft.
Cefn Cul 1844ft.
A4067
Heol Senni
Fan Frynych
Cray Resr.
Fan Fawr 2409ft.
Storey Arms
Pen-y-fan 2907ft.
BEACONS
Gwaun-rhudd 2502ft.
Talybont
Fan y Big

191

MAP H

MAP J

Miles 0 1 2 3 4 5
Kilometres 0 1 2 3 4 5 6 7 8

a   b   c   d   e

Cardigan Island
Cemaes Hd.
Pen-yr-afr
Mwnt
Gwbert
Poppit Sands
ABER
CAR
ABBEY
St. Dogmael's
Moylegrove
Ceibwr
Glan-rhyd
Bridell
Rhos-h
Nevern
Felindre Farchog
Eglwyswrw

NATIONAL   PARK   COAST

Car Ferry Rosslare-Fishguard

PEMBROKESHIRE

Trwyn y Bwa
Dinas Head
Cwm-yr-eglwys
Pwll Gwaelod
Newport Bay
Parrog
Newport
Carningli Common
Nevern
Ffynnongroes
Brynberian
Crymych

Strumble Head
Wastad Pt.
Carreg
Pen Brush
Pen Caer
Llanwnda
Fishguard Bay
Aber Bach
Goodwick
Dinas
Llanllawer
1008 ft.
1021 ft.
MYNYDD PRESELI
Pentre-galar
Clyn   1209 ft.
Foel Drych

Tref asser
Tremarchog
St. Nicholas
ABERGWAUN
FISHGUARD
Manorowen
Llanychaer
WAUN VALLEY
Pontfaen
Mynydd Melyn
Mynydd Caregog

Aber-bach
Aber-mawr
Pen Morfa
Abercastle
Granston
Mathry
Jordanston
Scleddau
Trec
B4313
Mynydd Cilciffeth
1096 ft.
1535 ft.
Foel Eryr
1760 ft.
Foel Cwm-cerwyn
Mynachlog-ddu
B4329

Pen Clegyr
Porth-gain
Trefin
Llanrhian
Croes-goch
Llanreithan
Castle Morris
Letterston
Little Newcastle
Morfil
Mynydd Castlebythe
Castlebythe
Rosebush
Maenclochog
Llangly

Aber Eiddy
Tretio
Rhodiad
Caerfarchell
Middle Mill
Llandeloy
Newton
Wolf's Castle
Hayscastle Cross
Treffgarne
583 ft.
Woodstock
Ambleston
Llys-y-fran
Pen-ffordd
PENRHOS
Llan-y-cefn
Cilymaenllwyd
Login

St. Davids Head
Whitesand Bay
Ramsey Island
TYDDEWI
ST. DAVIDS
Whitchurch
Caerbwdi
Dinas Fawr
Green Scar
Porthclais
Solva
Brawdy
Dudwell Mt.
Roch
Wolfsdale
Spittal
Walton East
Clarbeston
Bletherston
Egremont
New Moat
Henry's Moat
Tufton
B4313
B4478
Llandissilio
Llanfa

St. BRIDE'S BAY
Newgale
Simpson Cross
Nolton Haven
Nolton
Druidston
Haroldston West
Portfield Gate
Dreenhill
Camrose
Keeston
Pelcomb Br.
Rudbaxton
Scolton
WITHYBUSH AIRFIELD
Clarbeston Road
Wiston
Clynderwen
Castelldwyran
Llawhaden
Clarbeston
Llanddewi Vel
Redstone Bank
Crinow
Narberth

Rickets Head
Reeston Hill
Lambston
Broad Haven
HWLFFORDD
HAVERFORDWEST
A40
Robeston Wathen
Canaston Br.
B4314
Lampeter Velfrey
Princes Gate
Crun

Little Haven
Broadway
Ratford Br.
Freystrop
Hook
The Rhos
Slebech
Minwear
OAKWOOD PARK
Landshipping
Cold Blow
Ludchurch

Talbenny
Rosepool
Walton West
Walwyn's Castle
Johnston
Tiers Cross
Llangwm
Martletwy
Yerbeston
Templeton
A4075
Reynalton
Stepaside

The Nab Head
St. Brides
Musselwick Sands
Hasguard
Marloes
St. Ishmael's
Herbrandston
ABERDAUGLEDDAU
MILFORD HAVEN
Rosemarket
Houghton
Burton
Lawrenny
Jeffreston
Begelly
Kilgetty
Wisen

Garland Stone
Skomer Island
Mew Stone
BROAD SOUND
Skokholm Island
Marloes Sands
Westdale Bay
Dale
Castlebeach
Sandy Haven
Gelliswick
Waterston
Neyland
MILFORD HAVEN WATERWAY
DOC PENFRO
PEMBROKE DOCK
Cosheston
Williamston
Cresswell
W.
Redberth
Cresselly
Broadmoor
New Hedges
Saund

St. Ann's Head
Wick
Mill Bay
Angle
Rhoscrowther
Pwllcrochan
Hundleton
DINBY
TENBY
Saundersfoot
Saunder
PENFRO
PEMBROKE
Milton
Carew Cheriton
Jameston
St. Florence
Gumfreston
Penally
St. Cath

Freshwater West
Castlemartin
Maiden Wells
Orielton
Warren
St. Petrox
Merrion
Kingsfold
Hodgeston
Swanlake Bay
Manorbier
Old Castle Hd.
Giltar Pt.
Caldy Sd.
Caldy
Lydstep
A4139

Sheep Island
Linney Head
Bosherston
Stack Rocks
Saddle Hd.
Stackpole
Barafundle Bay
Broad Haven
St. Govan's Head
Trewent Pt.
Stackpole Bay

PEMBROKESHIRE   COAST   NATIONAL   PARK

193

MAP K

Miles 0 1 2 3 4
Kilometres 0 1 2 3 4 5 6

MAP L

Miles 0 1 2 3 4 5
Kilometres 0 1 2 3 4 5 6 7 8

a   b   c   d   e

Manordeilo
Bethlehem
Llanddeusant
Forest
Crai
Fan
Frynych
Allt Ddu
1845ft.
Llanfigan
Bryn
1842ft.
Talyb
on L
Rhosmaen
Salem
Moel Feity
1940ft.
Llyn y Fan
Fach
Heol Senni
Fan
Cnewr
1980ft.
A4067
A470
Pen-y-fan 2907ft.
BRECON
BEACONS
Gwaun-rhudd
2502ft.
Abe
LLANDEILO
Ffairfach
Capel Gwynfe
1361ft.
Trichrug
Pont Aber
Llyn y Fan
Fawr
Fan 2630ft.
238ft.
Cefn Gul
1844ft.
FFOREST
Fan Fawr
2409ft.
Storey Arms
Neuadd
Resr.
Talybont
Forest
Trapp
CARREG
CENNEN
A4069
Cefn y
Truman
MOUNTAIN
2366ft.
Fan
Hir
Fan Gyhirych
2176ft.
Fan Nedd
Fan Lila
2071ft.
Resr.
Gwaen
Nant-ddu
Pen-twyn
Forest
Derwydd
Foel Fraith
1982ft.
Garreg-goch
1832ft.
NATIONAL PARK
A4059
Nant-ddu
Twyn
Cros
Taf-fechan
Resr.
Gwenlais
BLACK
Garreg-lwyd
2028ft.
DAN-YR-OGOF
SHOW CAVES
Craig-y-nos
Coed Taf
BRECON
MOUNTAIN
RAILWAY
1506ft.
Tair Carn Isaf
A4067
Penycae
Bryn
Bugeiliaid
1254ft.
Ystradfellte
Pontsticill
Vaynor
Glyn-hir
Brynaman
Abercraf
HENRHYD
FALLS
Cader Fawr
592ft.
Bute Tn
Dowlais
A4068
Cwmllynfell
Cwm-gied
Coed y
Rhaiadr
Scwd-yr-eira
Penderyn
Mynydd-
y-glog
Cefn Coed
Cymmer
Garnant
Gwauncaegurwen
Coelbren
Pen-rhos
Onllwyn
MERTHYR
TYDFI
Betws
Mynydd
Betws
Ystradgynlais
A4109
A4221
Seven Sisters
Pontneddfechan
A465
A4059
Hirwaun
Mynydd
Aberdare
Aber-canaid
A474
Ystalyfera
Gurnos
968ft.
Cefn Gwrhyd
Mynydd-y-glyn
Glyn Neath
Aber Pergwm
Pont
Walby
Rhigos
Hirwaun
Common
B4276
Abercynon
Crynant
Forest
Godre'r-graig
Crynant
Rheola
Forest
Blaen-gwrach
Cefn
Resulfen
1257ft.
Cwmdare
A4061
Cwmbach
A4059
Cefn Pennar
1616ft.
A470
Pontardawe
Rhyd-y-fro
Cilybebyll
Allt-wen
Rhos
A4109
B4242
Resolven
A465
Mynydd
Grug
Cefn Tyle
Brych
Rhondda
Forest
ABERDARE
St. Gwynno
Aberaman
Penllergaer
Forest
Craig-cefn-parc
Penscynor
Aberdulais
A474
A4067
Moel-yr-hyrddod
1560ft.
Cefn Mawr
Blaen-Rhondda
Glyncorrwg
ABERDARE
Forest
Treherbert
Maerdy
Penhiwceiber
Felindre
Clydach
Ynystawe
Glais
B4291
A4067
Moel-yr-hyrddod
Cadoxton
Birchgrove
A4068
Blaengwynfi
Cymmer
Treorchy
Pentre
Ystrad
Rhondda
Llanwonno
CASTELL-NEDD
NEATH
Cefn
Morfudd
Forest
Abergwynfi
Cwm-parc
Mynydd Caerau
1828ft.
Clydach
Vale
Tonypandy
Pen-y-graig
Ystrad
Rhondda
Porth
A4058
Landore
Morriston
Tonna
Briton
Ferry
Pont-rhyd-yfen
Duffryn
Caerau
Nantymoel
Blaengarw
Pricetown
Ogmore
Vale
Gilfach
Goch
Treforest
PONTYPRIDD
A483
A4217
Bon-y-maen
Pentrechwyth
A4107
Foel Mynydd
Dyffryn
Nantyffyllon
A4063
A4061
Llangeinor
Sketty
Kilvey Hill 633ft.
A483
B4286
Baglan
Gwmavon
Maesteg
Llangynwyd
A4064
Llantwit Fardre
Church Village
A4118
A4067
ABERTAWE
SWANSEA PORT TALBOT
846ft.
Mynydd Dinas
Aberavon Beach
Margam
Forest
Berw
A4064
A4063
A4061
Glanogwr
A4073
A4119
Blackmill 984ft.
Beddau
Llantrisa
Black-
pill
West Cross
OYSTERMOUTH CASTLE
Taibach
M4
Margam
Moel Ton-mawr
1048ft.
Mynydd-y-gaer
Mynydd
Maendy
Melin Ciwc
Llanharan
A473
Talb
Gree
Groes-f
The Mumbles
Mumbles Hd.
Bracelet Bay
Limeslade Bay
Langland Bay
swell Bay
Margam Sands
ORANGERY
Kenfig
Hill
Abergarw
Tondu
Pencoed
Coed Tre-castell
Pontyclun
Llanharri
Maiken
Margam
Kenfig Pool
Mawdlam
Pyle
B4281
M4
Coity
Llanilid Llanharri
A4222
Nottage
PORTHCAWL
Rest Bay
Kenfig
South
Cornelly
A48
A473
Newton
Down
Laleston
Merthyr
Mawr
Newcastle
BRIDGEND
B4181
Coychurch
St. Mary Hill
Llangan
Pentlyn
Ystradowen
Pendoylan
Llan
A4229
A4106
Newton
Ogmore
Corntown
Treoes
Llysworney
St. Brides
Major
St. Hilary
BEAUPRE
Welsh
St. Donats
Bonvilston
Tusker Rocks
Ogmore-
by-Sea
Pitcot
Llandow
Wick
Nash
Sigingstone
Llandough
St. Mary
Church
Cowbridge
Llanblethian
Llancarfan
Penma
Way
Southerndown
Broughton
Monknash
Marcross
St.
Donat's
STONES
Llanmaes
Llanmihangel
Flemingston
St. Athan
CARDIFF
INTERN'L
AIRPORT
Nash Pt.
Wick
Col-huw
Beach
Llantwit
Major
Boverton
Gileston
Rhoose
Fontygary
The Leys
HERITAGE COAST

TOL CHANNEL